FLORA'S EMPIRE

PENN STUDIES IN LANDSCAPE ARCHITECTURE

John Dixon Hunt, Series Editor

This series is dedicated to the study and promotion of a wide variety of approaches to landscape architecture, with special emphasis on connections between theory and practice. It includes monographs on key topics in history and theory, descriptions of projects by both established and rising designers, translations of major foreign-language texts, anthologies of theoretical and historical writings on classic issues, and critical writing by members of the profession of landscape architecture.

The series was the recipient of the Award of Honor in Communications from the American Society of Landscape Architects, 2006.

FLORA'S EMPIRE
British Gardens in India

⁌ EUGENIA W. HERBERT ⁍

UNIVERSITY OF PENNSYLVANIA PRESS   PHILADELPHIA

Copyright © 2011 University of Pennsylvania Press

All rights reserved. Except for brief quotations used for purposes of review or scholarly citation, none of this book may be reproduced in any form by any means without written permission from the publisher.

Published by
University of Pennsylvania Press
Philadelphia, Pennsylvania 19104-4112
www.upenn.edu/pennpress

Printed in the United States of America on acid-free paper
10 9 8 7 6 5 4 3 2 1

Library of Congress Cataloging-in-Publication Data

Herbert, Eugenia W.
Flora's empire : British gardens in India / Eugenia W. Herbert.
p. cm. (Penn studies in landscape architecture)
Includes bibliographical references and index.
ISBN: 978-0-8122-4326-0 (hardcover : alk. paper)
1. Gardens, British—India. 2. Gardens—India—History. 3. India—Civilization—British influences. I. Series.
SB457.54 .H47 2011
635.0954 22   2011011277

For ELLIE WELD *and* †DAVID APTER

Open your doors and look abroad.

From your blossoming garden gather fragrant memories of the vanished flowers of an hundred years before.

—Rabindranath Tagore,

The Gardener (1913)

CONTENTS

	Preface	xi
	Introduction: *Cowslips and Lotuses*	1

PART I. GARDENERS ABROAD

CHAPTER 1	From Garden House to Bungalow, Nabobs to Heaven-Born	19
CHAPTER 2	Calcutta and the Gardens of Barrackpore	62
CHAPTER 3	Over the Hills and Far Away: *The Hill Stations of India*	97

PART II. GARDENS OF EMPIRE

CHAPTER 4	Eastward in Eden: *Botanical Imperialism and Imperialists*	139
CHAPTER 5	Gardens of Memory	181
CHAPTER 6	The Taj and the Raj: *Restoring the Taj Mahal*	197

CHAPTER 7	Imperial Delhi: *City of Gardens*	227
CHAPTER 8	Imperial New Delhi: *The Garden City*	257
CHAPTER 9	The Legacy	285
	Conclusion: *Garden Imperialism*	303

[COLOR PLATES FOLLOW PAGE 180]

Common Trees, Shrubs, and Plants in India South of the Himalayas	315
Notes	319
Bibliography	353
Index	373
Acknowledgments	387

PREFACE

THE NOVELIST Penelope Lively devotes an entire chapter of her autobiography to her grandmother's gardens over several generations. With their lawns, informal walks, lily ponds, snowdrops, bluebells, and roses, they are virtual palimpsests of English garden history as it is most familiar to us: "Essence of Englishness, you would think, the English garden." But in fact, as Lively points out, there is hardly anything in these gardens except the yew trees and primroses that is native to the British Isles. The garden is rather a "cacophony," filled with plants from all over the world. And when her family moved to Egypt, her mother created a garden there that was unabashedly English in design, even if many of the shrubs and trees were perforce adapted to a warmer climate.[1]

A walk through Kew Gardens reinforces this experience of gardens as a "global reference system." On a May morning Rhododendron Dell is ablaze with the blossoms of these glorious shrubs. But while the dell was laid out by Capability Brown, giant of eighteenth-century English natural landscape design, it had to wait until the next century for the rhododendrons that

Joseph Dalton Hooker brought back from the Sikkim Himalayas. A few years ago I had taken a similar stroll through Haidar Ali's Lal Bagh in Bangalore. Just inside the main gate, I was surprised to come upon a colony of plaster gnomes, statues, and other assorted paraphernalia in a garden initially inspired by Mughal prototypes and later redesigned to accommodate English flowers and flower beds and walkways. At the far end I came to the glasshouse, a miniature Crystal Palace, with the annual Republic Day flower show in full swing. Around the periphery of the Lal Bagh, nurseries clustered, meeting the needs not only of locals but also of patrons from all over India.

It has often been said that the English are a nation of gardeners, with a passion for plants and flowers surpassing that of all other people. "Our England is a garden," wrote Rudyard Kipling.[2] They are also a nation of empire builders, with Kipling in the forefront. Wherever they went, they took with them as part of their cultural baggage their love of gardens and their certainties about what a garden should look like. Nowhere was this more evident than in India. It was one thing to show off tropical exotics in English conservatories or even coax them to grow outside for a season, quite another matter to live in the midst of these exotics in all their terrifying luxuriance. The farther from home one ventured, the more one longed for familiar cowslips and hollyhocks and Michaelmas daisies, for well-trimmed lawns and neat flowerbeds.

Much has been written about architecture and imperialism, little about gardens and imperialism, perhaps because gardens are far more ephemeral and harder to document, perhaps because they seem less serious. And yet almost two decades ago, the garden historian Charles Quest-Ritson pointed out that the history of the gardens of the Raj remained to be written.[3] The present work is intended as a first step in telling the story of the gardens Britons created, or attempted to create, for themselves in India. The gardens are as varied as the characters in the story, from viceroys and their wives to unremembered officials (and their wives) in the remote reaches of the *mofussil* to professional botanists, soldiers, and retirees. The reader will find the text liberally seasoned with quotations from the wealth of memoirs and letters they have left behind in order to let their own voices be heard. To be sure, other imperial powers imposed their gardens on subject lands as well, but it was the British who came to paint most of the world red and whose gardens had the most profound effect. In the end they left a lasting horticultural mark on India, just as India did on them.

INTRODUCTION

Cowslips and Lotuses

WHEN BRITONS arrived in India in the opening years of the seventeenth century, they found the subcontinent awash with flowers. But the flowers were different, their wanton abundance unsettling. Absent were the cowslips and daisies of British meadows and hillsides, in their place strange exotics such as jasmine and lotus. First encounters with alien lands tend to focus on nature, what is reassuringly familiar and what is unfamiliar or even repellent. Nature, however, is rarely left untouched. How it is conceptualized and managed in the form of gardens and man-made landscapes are very much matters of history and culture. The history of gardens in England provides intriguing parallels with the history of British imperialism. The centuries in which the British metamorphosed from traders into imperialists coincided with the period in which they cast off their deference to foreign garden styles and garden designers and gained confidence in their own ability to create new forms or, if they did borrow continental motifs, to do it after their own fashion. At the same time, too, they had to come to terms not only with European traditions but also with those of the East. The result was a delicate balancing act that, for all the picking and choosing, preserved the unquestioned sense of superiority of the British way of doing things, in gardens no less than other spheres of life. British imperialism in India was not static and it was not monolithic. The forms taken by colonial gardens in India encode a complex set of personal responses and cultural beliefs, even political agendas. Examining them closely, we can hope to add to our understanding of the evolving and decidedly nonhomogeneous phenomenon of British imperialism itself.

What would no doubt have struck a visitor in 1600, as it still does, is how profoundly flowers are interwoven into all aspects of Indian culture; they fairly saturate religious observance, social life, art, and politics. In an Indian flower market, tons of marigolds, roses, and jasmine lie in heaps— not cut flowers but heads waiting to be strung into garlands (see Pl. 1). Garlands serve as offerings to the gods in great temples, in domestic rituals, and in public ceremonies of devotion. When Indian television presented the *Ramayana* over the course of a year in 1986, TV sets were frequently garlanded with flowers for each installment, transformed for the moment into sacred objects. And of course flowers are indispensable to weddings and funerals. In mid-nineteenth century Lucknow, the families of the betrothed exchanged gifts of flowers and fruit, often for years until the marriage actually took place. Who can forget the marigold-drenched arches in Mira Nair's film *Monsoon Wedding*? Garlands welcome both friend and stranger. Although Mahatma Gandhi frowned upon the practice, politicians and dignitaries measure their status according to the quantity and kind of garlands bestowed on them.[1]

The custom was seamlessly assimilated to the rituals of empire. Arriving in Bombay in 1876 on a state visit, the Prince of Wales was greeted with "an abundance of sweet-smelling flowers, many of rarity," displayed in pots or arranged in masses near the entrance, while along his progress, Parsee girls in white awaited him with "garlands and baskets of flowers." On his return to Bombay at the end of his tour, Churchgate Station was carpeted and its pillars wreathed in flowers. A decade later, Lady Dufferin, wife of the viceroy, remarked on the charming habit in Benares of offering garlands to guests: "We looked like walking flower gardens when we left." When a district officer and his wife returned to the region of an earlier posting in the Punjab, they were welcomed joyfully by the populace: "Everywhere we went, ... we found the peasants and squires

Fig. 1. Farewell to India, Secunderabad, 1947
[From Charles Allen, *Plain Tales from the Raj*, 1976]

had made gardens round our tents and planted them with flowers, and put up archways of welcome." Reducing the custom to the absurd, the Mahratta servants of Lady Lawrence, wife of a colonial official, seized upon the celebration of the festival of Dussehra to garland everything in sight: horses, bull terriers, bullocks, even the gardeners' tools and watering can.[2] And when at last the British left India in 1947, they left bedecked in flowers (Fig. 1).

Long before the advent of flower markets, each household had its garden to supply garlands and leaves for the family altar, just as every temple maintained a garden where priests directed the gathering of "flowers with which they adorn some idols and embellish others," in the words of a seventeenth-century Venetian adventurer. James Forbes, an Englishman in the employ of the East India Company a century later, remarks that Brahmins always chose lovely spots for their temple gardens, with shade and water. He describes one such garden in Koncan, encircled by groves and fountains, planted with flowers and fruit and "a variety of aromatic shrubs so much esteemed in India." A nearby lake was covered with lotuses. Forbes also witnessed flowery sacrifices offered daily to the divinities of the Nebudda River in Gujarat.[3] At the holy city of Benares vendors with baskets of flowers for sale lined up at dawn in front of the "pagoda" doors: "long rosaries of scarlet, white, or yellow blossoms, seem to be in greatest request, and are purchased by the pious as offerings to their gods; the pavements of the temples are strewed with these floral treasures"—the "only pleasing ceremonial connected with Hindoo worship," in the eyes of Emma Roberts, an intrepid if opinionated English traveler.[4] The Ganges at Benares (now Varanasi) is still a sea of marigold blossoms after the morning and evening *pujas* of the devout. In the high-tech city of Bangalore, some ten kilos of jasmine garlands, supplied by traditional families of florists, still adorn the conical Karaga, a pot carried during an annual ritual celebrating the Mother Goddess.[5]

The irony is that India of the plains, like the British Isles, is actually rather impoverished as far as native wildflowers and herbaceous plants are concerned. Flowers we now associate intimately with the Indian garden—orchids, the *Gloriosa superba* lily, roses, bougainvillea—all came in with the Muslim conquests or later. Even marigolds, "the national flower of Hindoostan," are imports, associated with marriage in Europe long before they arrived in India. Lacking a large repertoire of plants, Indian gardens relied instead on deep-rooted blossoming trees, creepers, and flowering shrubs: mango, *ashoka, champaka, nag-champa, sal* tree, palmyra tree, screw pine, coral tree, and jasmine. With the onset of hot weather in February and March, the bare, leafless boughs burst into glorious bloom, followed by a second explosion with the coming of the rains. Then the rampant verdure threatens to choke out all in its path, and lotus flowers completely hide the surface of ponds.[6]

Every flowering tree is revered in India, but three kinds are indispensable in every garden—mango, *jamun*, and *amlaki*—the leaves and flowers of which are used in worship, in weddings, and at births. Particular blossoms are linked to particular deities: for Ganesh, pink *kanare;* for Hanuman, *akika;* for Krishna, *tulsi;* for Siva, *dhatura.* Other flowers are to be avoided—hibiscus in temples to Krishna, for example, because it has a tongue like that which Kali put out when she stepped on Siva. The *peepal* tree (also known as *bo* or *bodhi*) is universally sacred to Hindus thanks to its association with the triumvirate of Brahma, Vishnu, and Siva. Courts of justice are often held beneath the *peepal* tree, the rustling of whose leaves sounds like falling rain.

For all the variations by locality and particular sect, however, the flower most universally venerated in India is the lotus. Rising from the mud of pool or river to burst into bloom, it symbolizes primordial creation and the transition from darkness to light. "Hail, Lord Creator! The jewel is in the lotus" runs the ancient prayer most sacred to Hindus. The baby Buddha took his first seven steps on lotus flowers. In later iconography he is often depicted emerging from a lotus. Each color of the lotus is sacred to one aspect of the Hindu trinity: the rose-petaled is the flower of sunrise, Brahma's prayer; the blue is sacred to Vishnu, upholder of the blue noontide universe; the white is the flower of evening, the flower of death and resurrection, the emblem of Siva, destroyer and preserver. Lakshmi, the goddess of wealth, sits on a lotus throne with a lotus footstool, holding a lotus flower in her hand. Some claim that Mount Meru itself, home of the gods, is "not shaped as vulgar hills" but bears the elegant form of a lotus. Muslims in turn adopted the lotus as a common symbol of fertility; stylized designs of lotus plants are found, for example, in the scalloped edges of the pools of the Taj Mahal and Mahtab Bagh and sculpted into the pavement of the Rang Mahal in the Red Fort in Delhi. Lotuses figure, too, among the repertoire of flowers in the intarsia decorations of the Taj. The poet Rabindranath Tagore once likened Indian culture itself to a full-grown lotus.[7] Appropriately, the lotus is now emblazoned on the national flag of India and adorns the rumps of innumerable trucks.

The veneration of flowers, leaves, and trees has a long history in the subcontinent. The leaf of a *peepal* decorates a seal and pottery fragments found in excavations of Harappa in the Indus Valley from the third millennium B.C.E.[8] Buddha was born and died in a grove of trees, and he attained enlightenment under the *bo* tree. Gateways on the great *stupa* (dome-shaped shrine) of Sanchi, from the beginning of the present era, depict both the lotus flower and the *bo* tree. At this early stage the Buddha was never portrayed directly.

During his lifetime, indeed, he rejected the use of garlands for himself and his followers in the name of austerity, but over the centuries they became a key part of Buddhist devotion and iconography, and the garden a place of retreat and meditation. The anthropologist Jack Goody has argued that flowers offered a nonviolent stand-in for blood sacrifice for Buddhists and Jains and that eventually their influence affected most strands of Hinduism as well.[9]

Sanskrit literary texts abound in references to more worldly gardens: the great epics of the *Mahabharata* and *Ramayana,* and courtly dramas such as *Sakuntala* and the *Ratnavali.* In Tulsidas's telling of the *Ramayana,* Rama and Sita first meet in a garden "so rich in bud and fruit and flower that in its abundance it put to shame even the trees of paradise."[10] Commonly there is a dualism between the pastoral beauty of an Eden-like wilderness and the lushness of palace gardens. The forests where Rama, Sita, and Lakshman spend the years of exile are idyllic natural landscapes, with shady trees and flower-strewn riverbanks on which they weave garlands to their hearts' delight. In contrast, Ayodhya, from whence Rama has been banished, and Lanka, to which Sita is abducted by the wicked king Ravana, are both described as garden cities. Here the natural is transformed into kingly gardens full of stately trees, orchards, and flowers, with lotus-bedecked ponds and man-made tanks.[11]

The royal garden is above all a place of seduction where flowers speak the language of love. The *Buddhacarita,* a poem of the first century C.E., pictures the young prince before he forsakes the world entering a pleasure garden with its beautiful lotus ponds, flowered pavilions, and lovelorn women. One of the women entreats him to look about him at the trees, flowers, and birds, each of which signifies desire in some way. Buddha resists all enticements, but the story is typical of early medieval Indian courtly culture in exemplifying a view of "courtship as a combat which takes place in a garden." The *Kamasutra* prescribes the type of garden considered essential to the royal household of the Hindu prince. It should have densely shaded bowers, flowering plants, and a swing; above all it should be secluded, protected against prying eyes. Here men and women retire to indulge in amorous adventures. Courtly dramas pick up the theme of the pleasure garden, often with convoluted plots of misunderstanding, disguise, and eavesdropping until the lovers are at last united. Poets frequently describe courtesies between people of rank by means of floral similes—thus the folded hands are like lotus buds, the gestures of the eyes like garlands, and words of praise like offerings of flowers. The human form, too, is similarly analogized: "Like the lotuses and flower buds . . . human limbs in their ideal state were to be smooth and tautly expanded, or blown like the tender and succulent growth of new plants."[12]

Just as Sanskrit texts link the plant world and the erotic, so, too, Persian-influenced literary texts of Muslim India are "redolent of flowers." James Forbes quotes "A Song of Roshan, or Roxana," which details the repertoire of sexually stimulating plants: "The sofa of my beloved is decked with garlands of mogrees, overshadowed by a canopy of jessamin. I have strewed it with the sweet dust of Keurah and perfumed it with ottar [attar] of roses; I am scented with the oils of lahore, and tinged with the blossoms of hinna; haste then, my beloved, to thine handmaid, gladden her heart by thy presence." A deserted woman reproaches her lover: "The gardens and groves, once the fond retreat of thy Selima, afford me no pleasure; the mango and pomegranate tempt me in vain! The fragrance of champahs and odour of spices I no longer enjoy." Sanskrit, Persian, and Deccani poetry as well extolled the sensuality of the garden and its appeal to all the senses: scent above all, but also sound, sight, and even touch.[13]

Islamic gardens did, however, differ from their counterparts in Hindu India. Just how profoundly we do not know, since there are no precise descriptions of the gardens that preceded the series of Islamic invasions that began just decades after the Prophet's death and culminated in the establishment of the Mughal Empire in the sixteenth century. We know what was in these gardens and what took place there (if literary sources are to be believed), but not how they were laid out, nor how their design might have changed over time, independent of foreign influences. Babur, the first Mughal emperor and a passionate gardener, set the tone for future commentators with his dismissal of India as dreary and unpleasant, its gardens without order and without walls. The Muslim tradition, in contrast, is the heir to the Greek in its love of order and logic. "Islamic gardens—like their buildings—are regimented into lines of perfect symmetry; balance and design is all; nothing is left to impulse or chance." They are as alien to the Indian environment, William Dalrymple insists, "as the Brighton Pavilion is to the English south coast, or the Chinese Pagoda to Kew [Gardens]. Outside the garden, all is delightful chaos; inside, reflecting the central concept of Islam, spontaneity is crushed by submission to a higher order."[14]

Fig. 2. Garden, Amber Fort, Rajasthan
[Photograph by author]

Alien or not, Mughal-style gardens gradually took root in India, from Gujarat to Bengal, from the Punjab to the Deccan. They were laid out not only by Muslim monarchs and courtiers but also by Hindu rajahs and, indeed, as we will see, by the British as their last hurrah. Bishop Heber comments on the extensive garden laid out by a Bengali Brahmin with formal parterres of roses, straight walks, fine trees, fountains, and pools and summerhouses.[15] The great palaces of Rajput princes had similar gardens (Fig. 2) as they became thoroughly Indianized. Indeed, they had to; conditions in India simply didn't allow for the literal replication of the type of garden Babur had in mind, the four-part walled garden derived from the Persian *charbagh*. Unlike his beloved Kabul or Kashmir, Hindustan was "flat as a board" and short on water. How could he re-create the cascades of water running down a terraced hillside into myriad fountains, so pleasing for their tinkling sound and cool sprays?

Then, too, the Mughal garden in the hills had been primarily a spring garden, "a pleasaunce of Cherry, Quince, and Apple blossom, with Tulips,

Anemones, Daffodils, Narcissus, Crown Imperials, and Iris scattered in the grass under the great Chenar avenues," on whose heels came peonies, hollyhocks, jasmine, carnations, and roses, with a burst of autumn loveliness after the heat of summer. While the Mughals could acclimate some of the fruit trees and flowers so familiar to them in their Central Asian homeland, they had perforce to rely primarily on Indian flowering trees and shrubs and creepers, all of which "gave a very distinctive character to the garden." Perhaps the moonlight garden was the greatest gift to the conqueror: "Under the influence of Hindu customs," observes Constance Villiers-Stuart, the wife of an early twentieth-century colonial official and pioneer of Indian garden history, "the Mughal garden . . . became essentially a moonlight one." Indian flowering trees are at their best in the heat of summer and in the welcome rains that follow, especially when the cool evening breezes bring out their perfumes to perfection. Until the last century Hindu ladies rarely entered their gardens before nightfall. But after dark it was another world, a place of seclusion, with dark trees, white flowers, illuminations from countless little oil lamps, and the air saturated with heady fragrances.[16]

The Mughal garden was above all a place to gather, whether for affairs of state, for convivial feasting and drinking, or for a combination of the two. Evening entertainments in palace gardens became a staple of social life for visiting dignitaries as well as local elites, both Muslim and Hindu. The illuminated garden of a Punjabi Malik was like nothing so much as "one's ideal of an Oriental love-song." *Nautches*—performances by professional dancing girls—customarily provided the highlight of these entertainments. Depending on one's taste for Indian music and dancing, *nautches* could be magical or "tiresomely monotonous." James Forbes was an enthusiast: "After a recreation in the garden, the nabob [of Surat] accompanied us to the roof of the pavilion, where music and dancing-girls awaited us. Fire-works on the canal illuminated its fragrant borders, and exhibited a curious scene of alternate fountains, playing fire and water, falling among shrubs and flowers. . . . On our taking leave he sprinkled us with ottar [attar] of roses." More censoriously, a nineteenth-century *memsahib* worried about the pernicious attraction *nautch* girls might have for susceptible young Englishmen so far from home. However much Indians enjoyed watching dancing girls, they were scandalized at the notion of dancing themselves at their soirées and even more scandalized by the sight of proper Englishwomen dancing.[17]

A garden created for such pleasures during one's lifetime was often reconfigured after death, the mausoleum taking the place of the pavilion at its center. These gardens consciously invoked the Qur'anic imagery of Paradise, with its four intersecting rivers, as the aspiration for the departed. When Hindu rulers borrowed the concept of the memorial garden and its cenotaphs, as they did, for example, at Orchha and Mandore, it required some theological tweaking. Since Hindus cremated their dead there were no tombs, and since they believed in a cycle of reincarnation there was no promise of Paradise encoded in the garden. What remained was monumental architecture set off in a glade of flower and shade—mausoleums without bodies.

The *zenana* or *purdah* garden was a realm apart. It was probably the first garden to come inside the fort or palace; initially Mughal gardens in India had been freestanding entities, often ranged along a riverbank. Rajput and other Hindu rulers adopted the *zenana* and with it a garden exclusively for the women of the harem, their closest male relatives, and their numerous attendants—a gilded cage where women might pass their entire lives. Fanny Parks, traveling throughout northern India on her own in the 1830s and 1840s, probably knew the *zenana* and its secrets better than any other European. The four walls of the garden, she explains, must be of such a height that no man standing on an elephant can peer over them. There were fine trees and flowers, a fountain with fish swimming in it, and a swing, "the invariable accompaniment of a *zenana* garden." She adds, "The season in which the ladies more particularly delight to swing in the open air is during the rains" (Fig. 3). Larger gardens, such as that of the palace of Lucknow, had tanks for bathing, and sometimes even a "montagne russe" to slide down or meadows for horseback riding.[18]

In the eighteenth and nineteenth centuries the wave of imperial expansion drew ever more Britons to India. They encountered its gardens and flora with only their own landscape traditions as compass. The sweeping greenswards of the eighteenth-century English park, the carpet bedding of the high-Victorian garden, the herbaceous border of the Edwardian homestead must have seemed planets away from the sensuality-drenched, deity-permeated gardens of classic Sanskrit drama, the Buddhist meditation garden, or the geometric intimations of Paradise in the Mughal *charbagh*. Indian gardeners had no interest in topiary and knots, in ruins or grottoes or hermits, no fondness for temples and statuary to heathen gods (except in Lucknow; see

Fig. 3. Women swinging in a Zenana garden, Jodhpur, nineteenth century

[From Leona Anderson, *Vasantotsava*, 1993]

Chapter 5), no particular concern for prospects. They had no need for greenhouses to nurture plants imported from tropical climes. English gardeners might have accepted the identity of trees and divinities as poetic license but drew stricter boundaries between the human and natural world than Hindus, Buddhists, and Jains were wont to do; much as nature might be "worshipped" by eighteenth-century British, it was fully desacralized. Furthermore, English gardeners and their European counterparts looked back to the Garden of Eden or classical Arcadias rather than forward to the heavenly garden awaiting the Muslim faithful.

Nevertheless, the twain of East and West did occasionally meet. The farther back in time one goes, the more one finds points of convergence. The walled garden of the Mughals, with its geometrically laid out parterres, would have been familiar to medieval and Tudor England, although in England flowerbeds were raised to keep the soil from being washed away, rather than sunken to allow for artificial irrigation, reminding us that climate obviously affects garden design. Just so the enclosed English banqueting house was a more climate-appropriate parallel to the open-sided *baradari* or pleasure pavilion. The Mughal delight in terraced hillside gardens had its counterpart in Italian gardens from antiquity onward and in English attempts to replicate them. Similarly, illuminated medieval European manuscripts find echoes in Persian and Mughal miniatures, with their scenes of gardens and foliate margins, different as the stylistic conventions may be. Even the Tudor mount has affinities with the sacred mount at the center of Hindu gardens, later transformed into the hilly slide of the *zenana* garden.

Both East and West looked to plants for their medicinal and symbolic qualities. Almost every plant, wild or cultivated, in medieval England seems to have been prescribed for some ailment. Others had magical properties, to ward off—or cause—evil. The Sanskrit Vedas, while celebrating the unity of man and the natural world, comprise a huge corpus of botanical knowledge, practical as well as esoteric. From them derives the modern practice of Ayurvedic medicine. The "language of flowers," with its many vernaculars, was as widespread in the Occident as in the Orient and India. To medieval and Renaissance England, lilies signified purity, the daisy humility, and the rose with its thorns served as a reminder that pleasure was inseparable from pain. Rosemary, Sir Thomas More tells us, "is the herb sacred to remembrance and to friendship, whence a sprig of it hath a dumb language." It is hardly surprising, too, that this language had long carried over into religion and that flowers figure almost universally in worship. Medieval monks grew flowers to decorate their churches, and priests wore chaplets of blossoms until the Reformation. In the secular sphere as well, the weaving and wearing of garlands was common. Even Chaucer's repulsive Summoner has "a gerland . . . set upon his heed," while the Lover in his translation of *Roman de la Rose* is led into the inner garden of the Rose, a version of the Garden of Eden, by Lady Idleness wearing a garland of roses.[19]

The English pleasure garden no less than the royal gardens of classical India could be a place of amorous dalliance as well as of meditation and repose. What made it particularly seductive was the appeal to the senses: sweet perfumes carried on the zephyrs, birds warbling in the trees, and the sound of running water, all against a backdrop of the brightly colored flowers of daytime or the pale hues of night. "This early evening hour is indeed the best of all," wrote Gertrude Jekyll, the doyenne of late nineteenth-century English garden designers, "the hour of loveliest sight, of sweetest scent, of best earthly refreshment of body and spirit." Compare Forbes's romantic description of the garden of a Mahratta ruler: "After sunset, the atmosphere was filled with fragrance from the orange-trees, tuberoses, champahs and oriental jessamines, wafted by gentle breezes over the lake." There was, however, sharp dissent among many Europeans about what passed for the "sweetest scent." Beautiful as were Indian gardens, a traveler cautioned that "some of them almost overpower the refined nasal susceptibility of the European." Add to this the Indian predilection for anointing the body with attar of roses and pomades and the hair with blossoms of jasmine and mogrey, and the refined nasal susceptibilities were sure to be offended.[20]

Indians for their part found it passing strange that the English used their gardens not simply "as a place for reclining at ease, for quiet enjoyment of music, of conversation and the hukkah, in the cool of the evening," but for exercise and "amusements of an athletic description." Lady Henrietta Clive was quite aware that she was thought "a strange restless animal" because of her passion for walking "upon my own feet at every place where I take up my abode." As one memoirist affirmed, "Nothing surprises the Indians so much as to see Europeans taking pleasure in exercise; they are astounded to see people walking who might sit still."[21] Even odder was the eagerness of some English to roll up their sleeves and pitch into gardening themselves. In the end, they usually yielded to the superior claims of the *mali,* the casted gardener. But it reflected an altogether different attitude toward manual labor.[22] The Crown Prince Frederick and his wife, Augusta, after all, had set an example of hands-on gardening in the mid-eighteenth century (and expected their guests to join them). They could serve as role models for the working classes, for whom gardening was touted as a badge of respectability, a link with the honest yeoman of yore: "Honeysuckle around a cottage door was not just picturesque: it was also a sign of the sobriety, industry and cleanliness of the inhabitants within." Gardening was even proposed as a means to bring down the high rate of illegitimacy in Cumbria in the 1860s.[23]

"English lawns, one of the few things the British are not tiresomely modest about, are without doubt the best in the world." Probably few would dispute this claim, but whence came their obsession with mown grass? Thorstein Veblen looked to the atavistic pastoral heritage of the "dolicho-blond" race: "For the aesthetic purpose the lawn is a cow pasture." He did admit that the lawn has an element of sensuous beauty which, he grudgingly allowed, might appeal as well to "nearly all races and all classes."[24] By Veblen's reasoning India's Aryan and later Mughal invaders, with their pastoral origins in the great plains of Central Asia, should have been just as ardent enthusiasts of the lawn, but of course this was not—and couldn't be—the case in their adopted land. A patch of clover in the Mughal parterre was desirable, but not acres of grass ("imitations of the pasture") interrupted by an occasional copse of trees, a stream, and a bed of flowers. In the end we can only say that the English soil and climate were ideally suited to the apotheosis of the lawn, that the English early learned the techniques of mowing and rolling, that just as early they took to games suited to velvety greens. Still, it is worth remembering that the lawn did not really become the centerpiece of English garden design until the eighteenth century.

Finally, the idea that gardens have a history is itself one of the fundamental differences between Europe and India. How to explain to Indians the restless need for change and novelty, the passion for exotics and experimentation so characteristic of the modern West, the fervor with which English gardeners argued the virtues or vices of bedding-out or topiary, of formal versus informal, of Italian gardens versus French? As Robert Pogue Harrison reminds us, "History without gardens would be a wasteland. A garden severed from history would be superfluous."[25]

The British were not mere transients in India. Over more than three centuries they founded great cities—Madras, Calcutta, Bombay—and vastly altered others, such as Delhi, Lucknow, and Bangalore. They put their stamp on India's great monuments. And everywhere they created gardens, large and small, private and public, that embodied not only aesthetic ideals but also philosophical understandings of the good life, of civilization, and the social and political order. At times they were in direct dialogue with their Mughal predecessors, for whom gardens served just as intimately as models of the world as it should be. The interplay of British and Indian gardens, both Hindu and Muslim, their accompanying ideologies, and what all this may tell us about the nature of imperialism is the subject of our tale.

PART I

Gardeners Abroad

CHAPTER 1

From Garden House to Bungalow, Nabobs to Heaven-Born

Surveying his newly won domains in northern India, Zahirrudin Muhammad Babur was appalled. Descendant of Tamurlane and, more distantly, of Genghis Khan, the victor of Panipat (1526) would have preferred to rule Samarkand; instead he had to settle for the dusty vastnesses of Hindustan. In the few years left to him Babur set about putting the stamp of civilization on the Gangetic plain, creating not palaces and forts and cities but gardens, introducing "marvelously regular and geometric gardens" in "unpleasant and inharmonious India."[1] The Mughal ruler was neither the first nor the last invader to look upon the Indian landscape and find it wanting, and neither the first nor the last to remake it in an image more suited to his own notions of an ordered universe. Just as Mughal gardens were a microcosm of the world as it should be, so British gardens became maps of an ideal world seen through their insular prism.

Babur freely acknowledged that what had lured him to Hindustan was its wealth: it had "lots of gold and money."[2] The same magnet drew the British to India. They came originally not as conquerors but as traders, vying with many other nations for a share of the subcontinent's riches. In 1600 Queen Elizabeth I, a contemporary of Babur's grandson Akbar the Great, chartered the earliest merchant ventures that would evolve into the British East India Company.[3] Their immediate object was to challenge the Portuguese and Dutch in the East Indies and gain a foothold in the lucrative spice trade; India was an unanticipated by-product. William Hawkins, scion of the preeminent Tudor seafaring family, was the first commander of an English vessel to set foot in India, landing at Surat on the northwest coast in 1608. From its modest "factory" or trading station, the Company sent a series of embassies to the court of the "Great Mogul" in hopes of obtaining a *firman* (royal license) that would smooth the path of commerce. Hawkins himself found such favor with Emperor Jahangir that he was presented with "a white mayden out of the palace." Mutual gift-giving was a time-honored lubricant of social, political, and economic relations, and one embassy presented the emperor with paintings, "especially such as discover Venus' and Cupid's actes." In fact European arts, both secular and religious, came to exert a fascination for Mughal rulers and artists.[4]

From Surat British merchants fanned out down the west (Malabar) and up the east (Coromandel) coasts of India, competing with the Portuguese, French, Dutch, and other nationalities. The Portuguese had long dominated the commerce of the Arabian Sea from their outpost in Goa. On the Coromandel Coast, British Madras had to compete with the French Pondicherry, while Calcutta, the latecomer, gradually extended its sway over Bengal, eliminating both European and Indian rivals. Madras, Bombay, and Calcutta became autonomous East India Company "presidencies," each with its fort and godowns (storehouses) and its expanding staff of merchants and "writers" (clerks or junior merchants), as well as garrisons of soldiers. From the beginning the British, like all foreigners, depended on Indian intermediaries and bankers to facilitate trade, especially in the handwoven textiles that formed the bulk of exports before the Industrial Revolution in England reversed the flow. And like all foreigners they relied on good relations with local rulers—or, if not good relations, at least relations of reciprocal self-interest. This became more complex after the death of Emperor Aurangzeb in 1707 and the gradual dismemberment of the Mughal Empire, forcing them to deal with a multiplicity of successor states.

Initially "visions of conquest and dominion . . . seem never to have entered into their minds"—they were hardly necessary—but by the mid-eighteenth century the Company found itself caught up more and more in military confrontations with Indian rulers and with other European powers, often in shifting alliances.[5] At the same time, European mercenaries played an ever-expanding role in Indian armies, their services offered to the highest bidder. Company officials often made policy on the spot, especially in the matter of military adventures, counting on the snail's pace of communication with the directors in London to delay interference until it was too late. Often, too, the three presidencies acted at cross-purposes and were torn by internal dissensions, as indeed were their counterparts in London. Even the formidable Warren Hastings, invested as the first governor-general in Calcutta, found it impossible to control his own council, much less the distant communities of Bombay and Madras and his still more distant employers in Leadenhall Street. Hastings willingly relied on military force to uphold British commercial interests, although he opposed the extension of direct rule in India. Bengal, "this wonderful country which fortune has thrown into Britain's lap while she was asleep," had been ceded to the Company under Robert Clive in 1765, but Hastings's ideal model was derived from the Mughals: an India administered indirectly by Indians in accordance with Indian custom and law, as long as local authorities acknowledged the supremacy of the British governor and council in Calcutta and their right to a portion of landed revenues. Not surprisingly, Calcutta's first newspaper nicknamed him "The Great Moghul."[6]

Within a decade and a half of Hastings's departure from India, however, a sea change had taken place. In 1799 the fourth and last of the wars with Haidar Ali and his son Tipu Sultan and their French allies ended in the total defeat of Tipu, the "Tiger of Mysore," at Srirangapatnam.[7] The victorious general was Arthur Wellesley, later Duke of Wellington. The campaign marked the final transformation from commercial to imperial ambition; empire had duly followed trade. By the time the Company was dissolved in the aftermath of the Uprising of 1857, it had become the shadow master of all India, but its powers had long since been usurped by the British government. It had been "restrained and reformed" by a series of parliamentary acts until it was no longer an independent mercantile entity but a responsible administrative service. The motley collection of "rumbustious and individualistic" traders had metamorphosed into a high-minded team of district collectors, part administrator, part magistrate, part tax collector, and part development officer, "destined to join those many-armed gods in the Hindu pantheon and to become a feature of the Indian landscape." How appropriate that their compatriots referred to them, not always approvingly, as "the heaven-born." Over time they came to form something close to a hereditary caste, as a cluster of fifty to sixty interconnected families supplied the vast majority of the civil servants who governed India for several generations leading up to independence in 1947. The empire, it has been suggested, provided a sort of outdoor relief for the British middle class.[8] Ironically, in the new order of things, the once-glorious merchants (*boxwallahs*) and planters ranked virtually on a par with untouchables.

British India was a curious patchwork, even an accretion. An official during its heyday likened the imperial presence to "one of those large coral islands in the Pacific built up by millions of tiny insects, age after age." Roughly a third of the territory continued to be governed by hereditary princes who exercised considerable autonomy, albeit under the surveillance of representatives of the Indian Political Service. The rest of India was administered directly through the secretary of state in London, responsible to Parliament (when it deigned to take an interest) and the viceroy in Calcutta. Under the viceroy were the governors or lieutenant governors of the individual provinces. While their numbers increased dramatically during the century, the ranks of British civil servants responsible for local administration were ludicrously thin. A thirty-something "collector" might find himself in charge of a population as numerous as that of Elizabethan England, having as his Burghley a magistrate of twenty-eight and his Walsingham a lad who took his degree at Christ Church scarcely fifteen months past.[9] As late as 1921 some 22,000 civilians governed a population of nearly 306 million. Behind them stood a force of about 60,000 British and 150,000 Indian troops. Because both civilian and military expenses had to come entirely out of Indian revenues, poorly paid Indians or mixed-race Eurasians staffed the lower levels of government—police, clerks, and railway workers. Only very slowly did the elite Indian Civil Service admit Indians into its ranks.[10]

How They Lived Then: From Garden House to Bungalow

During the early centuries the Anglo-Indians, as the British came to be known (only later did this term come to designate people of mixed race), had two intertwined goals: to live long enough to bring home a sizeable nest egg, preferably enough to set themselves up as landed gentry, possibly even to buy a seat in Parliament. It was an age

> *When Writers revelled in barbaric gold*
> *When each auspicious smile secured a gem*
> *From Merchant's store or Raja's diadem.*[11]

What could be more tempting for ambitious young men without family fortune than to "shake the pagoda tree" (pagodas were a form of currency) for all it was worth?

And being young men—some as young as sixteen—they no doubt imagined they were immortal. Yet death was omnipresent. In Kipling's words, "Death in my hands, but Gold!"[12]

It has been estimated that about two million Europeans, most of them British, were buried in the subcontinent in the three hundred years before independence. As the proverbial wisdom had it, "Two monsoons are the Age of a Man."[13] Of the nineteen youths who sailed out to India with James Forbes in 1766, seventeen soon died, an eighteenth a little later; only Forbes survived to return home seventeen years after he first landed and to live to a ripe old age.[14] It became a commonplace that one's dinner companion one day might be laid to rest in the churchyard the next—and an often overcrowded churchyard at that, exhibiting "the most frightful features of a charnel-house."[15] As late as 1827 a writer commented, "There is no country in the world where the demise of one of a small circle is regarded with so much apathy as in India. Sickness, death, and sepulture follow upon each other's heels, not infrequently within the four-and-twenty hours."[16] For Emily Eden, sister of a governor-general, there was no such apathy in her reflection that "almost all the people we have known at all intimately have in two years died off. . . . None of them turned fifty." In 1880, by which time a network of railroads crisscrossed the country, the viceroy's chaplain was unnerved to learn that there were coffins stocked in every station along the line as a necessary precaution. Even those who are well, remarked Eden, "look about as fresh as an English *corpse.*"[17] Added to this was the isolation of life in India. The journey from England could take six months or more before the advent of steamships in the mid-nineteenth century and the opening of the Suez Canal in 1869. Communication was achingly slow and unpredictable. Ships were not infrequently lost at sea, with precious cargoes and, for some, even more precious letters, newspapers, and books. "It is really melancholy to think what a time passes between the arrival of each fleet," lamented Lady Henrietta Clive in 1800; one lived with "constant expectation of news and as continual a disappointment."[18]

In the beginning, factors—merchants—were largely confined to Company forts and factories. Here they labored over their account books and dealt as best they could with the steady bombardment of directives from London, usually long out of date by the time they reached India. Not for nothing were the junior factors known as "writers," living "by the ledger and ruled with the quill."[19] As merchants felt more confident, they moved outside the forts, but security was still a concern. A Venetian merchant made several visits to Surat in the mid-seventeenth century when it was still a hub of trade, its port full of ships from Europe, Persia, Arabia, Batavia, Manila, and China. "Upon the sea-shore, on the other side of the river," he writes, "the Europeans have their gardens, to which they can retire should at any time the Mahomedans attempt to attack them. For there, with the assistance of the ships, they would be able to defend themselves."[20] What the gardens looked like we are not told, but they may well have been inspired by those of their Mughal hosts—and sometime enemies—enclosed in walls, with fountains and scented trees and flowers.

Unlike Surat—the principal port of the Mughals—Madras, Bombay, and Calcutta were entirely European creations. Madras was the earliest. Legend had it that its founder, Francis Day, chose the site, a small fishing village, mainly because he was enamored of a lady at the nearby Portuguese fort at San Thomé (supposed site of the martyrdom of the Apostle Thomas of the Indies). Certainly it had no obvious advantages: it was little more than a surf-pounded strand on the Bay of Bengal with no natural harbor or even a navigable river. The irascible Captain Alexander Hamilton pronounced it "the most incommodious place I ever saw," adding that the sea "rolls impetuously on its shore, more here than in any other place on the coast of Coromandel."[21]

For a first-time visitor, landing could be a harrowing introduction to India. Ships had to anchor beyond the bar, unloading their passengers and freight into small native craft (Fig. 4). Passengers climbed down a ladder, jumped into small native boats bobbing in the heavy surf, and were paddled ashore by nearly naked but extraordinarily agile seamen, clad only in a "turban and a

Fig. 4. Surf boats, Fort St. George, Madras. Pencil on paper
[The British Library Board, WD1349]

half-handkerchief," according to Maria Graham, who had married an English naval officer on the voyage out in 1808. Fortunately, their dark skins prevented them from looking "so very uncomfortable as Europeans would in the same *minus* state," as one English lady reassured her readers. The sea could be terrifying—"I don't know why we were not all swamped, as I never saw such frightful waves; and no ordinary boat could have lived in them. I suppose the lightness of the native boats, which are made of bark, sewn together with thick twine, renders them safe. Arrived at the pier a tub was let down, and we were hoisted up in it."[22] This was written in 1867, but little had changed from two centuries earlier except that the boatmen had become Christian and cried out to Santa Maria and Xavier as they battled the surf.

From its founding, Madras was divided into "White Town," the area centered on its "sandcastle fortress," Fort St. George, and "Black Town" along the shore to the north. The three-story governor's house looked out over the Bay of Bengal, with St. Mary's rising within the fort, the first Anglican church east of Suez. Textiles were the making of Madras, and as the trade prospered whole villages of spinners, weavers, dyers, and finishers transplanted themselves from the South Indian countryside to the growing town. They were joined by other artisans, farmers, and a large population of untouchables who did the menial labor; for much of its history Madras remained an amalgam of separate, largely caste- and ethnically based neighborhoods and villages with close ties to the land. "I cannot make out where it begins and ends," wrote Lady Canning in some exasperation in 1856. At what urban core it possessed resided an expanding population of Europeans (civil and military), Muslims, and an influx of North Indians.[23]

With the English came gardens. At first these seem to have been primarily practical—but not entirely. Thus, an account of the 1670s describes English gardens in the heart of the city "where besides Gourds of all sorts for Stews and Potage, Herbs for Sallad, and some few Flowers as Jassamin, for beauty and delight, flourish pleasant Topes [clumps of trees] of Plantains; Cocoes; Guiavas, a kind of Pear; *Jawks* [jackfruit] . . . ; *Mangos,* the delight of India; a Plum, Pomegranets, *Bonanoes* which are a sort of Plantan, though less, yet more grateful, Beetle [betel]." What is interesting in this description is that it includes only native fruits and the quintessential Indian flower, jasmine, and at the same time assumes readers will be unfamiliar with guavas and bananas. But already it singles out mangoes as the Indian treat of treats. A little later Governor Elihu Yale put in a "physick garden," a garden for medicinal plants, within the fort. Although the Company condemned him for this unauthorized expenditure, one sympathizes with his motives.[24] By 1710, however, the Company had built a leisure garden for the governor's refreshment during the hot winds. It contained "a lovely Bowling Green, spacious walks, Teal-pond and Curiosities preserved in several Divisions are worthy to be admired," an enigmatic addendum. Lemons and grapes also grew in the garden but demanded a great deal of water (Fig. 5).[25]

Before long the British were feeling claustrophobic in their tight little enclave. They had taken to picnicking on St. Thomas Mount (San Thomé), a few miles out in the country, where the government maintained a garden and sanatorium "for sickly People to recover their healths." In the second half of the eighteenth century they began building garden houses here and then all over Choultry Plain, closer and more accessible to the center of Madras. "The English boast much of a delightful mount about ten miles distant," wrote. Jemima Kindersley, wife of a colonel in the Bengal Artillery, in 1765, "where the Governor and others have garden houses which, they say, are both cool

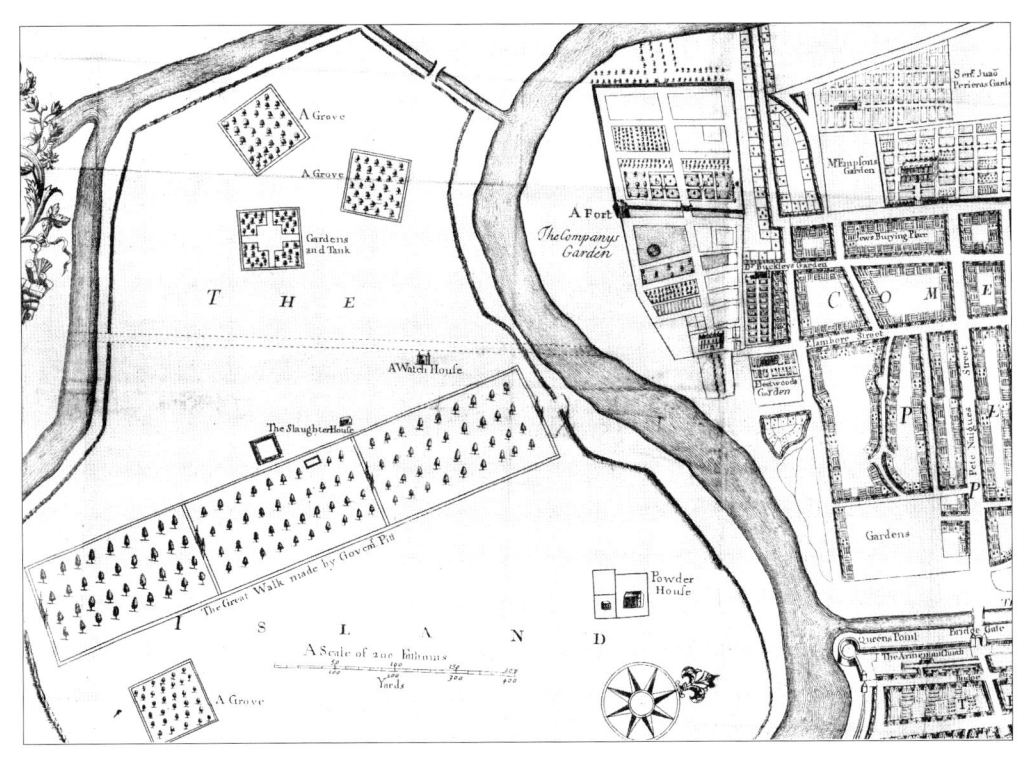

Fig. 5. Fort St. George, Madras: Plan showing Governor Pitt's Great Walk and the Company's Garden on the other side of the river
[From Ray Desmond, *European Discovery of the Indian Flora*, 1992]

and elegant." This was the moment of the "Nabobs," the Jos Smedleys so broadly caricatured in Thackeray's *Vanity Fair* who had shaken the pagoda tree with great success. The move to the suburbs came as a craving for a change of scene, an escape from the sea and sand of their working days in the White Town. "Originally the country house was not a permanent residence for its owner. It was designed for week-ends and holidays, and its great feature was its garden," for fruit and flowers did poorly in the sandy soil and brackish water of the beachfront.[26]

Soon the most prosperous Europeans had settled into these fine houses permanently, commuting into the fort every day in their palanquins or carriages. The air was fresher in the suburbs than in the congested fort area, and here also they could, with some stretch of the imagination, replicate the life of the English gentleman. Houses were "spacious and magnificent," with porticoes open to catch the breeze, surrounded by gardens and trees; some even

Fig. 6. Palladian garden house, Madras, c. 1790. Watercolor
[The British Library Board, Add.Or.740]

boasted ornamental lakes and deer parks (Fig. 6). By 1780 there were two hundred suburban houses in the environs of Madras, with plots ranging in size from a few acres to fifty or more, transforming what had been barren sand into a "beautiful scene of vegetation." *Dubashes,* leading Indian merchants who served as agents to the Europeans, and Muslim officials attached to the court of the Nawab of Arcot shared the taste for suburban living. Their estates on Choultry Plain often outdid the Europeans in size and in the elegance of their European-style mansions and furnishings. By 1800, however, although the number of suburban residences had doubled, land had become scarcer, prices higher, and the average size of holdings smaller in consequence. By this time, too, government regulation of Company employees had begun to curb the excessive fortunes of the earlier period and diminish the role of *dubashes* as intermediaries between the cultures.[27]

In the early twentieth century, Yvonne Fitzroy, secretary to the vicereine Lady Reading, reveled in the surviving eighteenth-century beauty of Madras— "the green, green gardens, the sea ... the smiling faces of the India that escaped invasion and the hand of conquest until the English came." Fitzroy concluded that in contrast to the pretensions of Calcutta and the vulgarity of Bombay, "Madras seems to be less a city than a vast garden where houses happen."[28] She was mistaken in her history, since Madras had been overrun by the French and raided by Haidar Ali on several occasions in the mid-eighteenth century, but correct in emphasizing its sprawling suburban character. As Lord Valentia commented in 1804, there was virtually no proper European town because "the gentlemen of the settlement live entirely in their garden-houses, as they properly call them; for these are all surrounded by gardens, so closely planted, that the neighbouring house is rarely visible."[29] Almost a century later, a visiting journalist looked down from the lighthouse atop its High Court and found Madras "more lost in green than the greenest city further north." On the one side was "the bosom of the turquoise sea, the white line of surf, the leagues of broad, empty, yellow beach; on the other the forest of European Madras, dense, round-polled green rolling away southward and inland till you can hardly see where it passes into the paler green of the fields."[30]

No doubt the avenues of trees lining the main thoroughfares from the fort to European neighborhoods enhanced the greenness that so impressed even early visitors. "The roads," noted Emma Roberts in 1836, "planted on either side with trees, the villas *chunamed* . . . and nestling in gardens, where the richest flush of flowers is tempered by the grateful shade of umbrageous groves, leave nothing to be wished for that can delight the eye or enchant the imagination." She goes on to elaborate the tropical luxuriance: plumelike broadleaf plantain; bamboo, coconut and still taller palms, areca (betel), aloe, "and the majestic banian [banyan], with its dropping branches, the giant arms outspreading from a columnar and strangely convoluted trunk, and precipitating pliant fibrous strings, which plant themselves in the earth below, and add to the splendid canopy above them." The banyan would ever be one of India's arboreal wonders. The *chunam* to which Roberts refers was also a source of awe: a "glittering material" made from burnt seashells, it was used to plaster both government buildings and domestic architecture, giving them a "marble brightness" that may have accentuated still more the deep greens of European Madras. As Eliza Fay had marveled a half-century earlier, the harmony of trees, foliage, and white *chunam* resembled more "the images that float on the imagination after reading fairy tales, or the Arabian Nights entertainment, than any thing in real life."[31] Landing at the city in 1780, seeing it in the brilliant sunshine, a new arrival could not resist the comparison with "a Grecian city in the age of Alexandria."[32] No such flights of Hellenistic fancy for Lady Charlotte Canning, wife of the governor-general. "Madras from the sea," she declared, "looks like a scrap of Brighton, except that the houses are very large." But, then, all that was visible were the endless strip of sand, the fort, and a "few offices and stores," little enough to impress someone coming from Bombay, with its glorious harbor and Malabar Hill rising in the background.[33]

In Madras, as would be the case in British settlements everywhere in the world, Government House epitomized imperial rule and imperial ideology. During the early days, it was tucked safely within Fort St. George, but in the eighteenth century governors, like everyone else, were desperate to escape to the country. The first garden house was destroyed by the French in 1746. It was replaced by a fine new one set in seventy-five acres in the suburb of Triplicane, approached by "an avenue of noble trees" and with a view of the sea and of the fort.[34] We do not know what these early government houses and grounds looked like, but one governor, Lord Pigot, at least had "a very English love of gardens" along with a very English love of hunting. He made the mistake, however, of quarreling violently with his council, who overthrew and took him prisoner (Madras had a habit of deposing its governors). During his captivity he suffered a sunstroke while gardening and died not long afterward.[35]

More fortunate than Pigot, Edward Clive, son of Robert Clive, hero of Plassey, became governor of Madras in 1798 and immediately set about improving Government House and its gardens. He was not a particularly effectual governor ("an amiable mediocrity"), but he and his wife were garden enthusiasts and avid botanists. They also made sure they got their share of the mind-boggling loot that fell to the British with the defeat of Tipu Sultan: ornate weapons, curly-toed slippers, and a jeweled tiger-headed finial from his throne; Tipu's elaborate chintz tent made an ideal marquee for garden parties at Government House. During her travels in southern India in 1800, Henrietta Clive sent not only the spoils of war but also shipment after shipment of plants and trees to her husband in Madras. One of his triumphs was to successfully graft a mango tree that he then sent to Kew Gardens in London. To carry out his ambitious plan of renovating the Triplicane garden house, he brought in the architect-astronomer John Goldingham, who repaired and enlarged the house and laid out a large English park around it. He accentuated aspects of the landscape and added new ones, including artificial mounds and a sunken garden. Most spectacularly, Clive and Goldingham built a sumptuous banqueting hall, detached from the main house and in the form of a Tuscan-Doric temple (Bishop Heber later thought it "in vile taste"). All this expenditure was too much for the court of directors back in London,

Fig. 7. Government House, Madras
[Postcard, author's collection]

especially since it coincided with Lord Wellesley's extravagances in Calcutta and Barrackpore (see Chapter 2), and Clive, like Wellesley, was recalled.[36]

Clive's showpiece fell into neglect after his departure; the house was in ruins and the pleasure grounds a desiccated and dreary dustbowl. When Charles Trevelyan became governor in 1859 he restored both (Fig. 7). It took eleven hundred men just to clear away the undergrowth around the house and in the adjoining park of Chepauk Palace, the proto-Indo-Saracenic pile that had been the pride of the Nawab of Arcot. Ever the civic-minded builder, Trevelyan aimed to open the two as a public park, complete with zoo. With the zeal of a latter-day Capability Brown, he envisioned a "picturesque wilderness laid out according to the most approved principles of landscape gardening," with ornamental lakes like those in St. James's Park and a palmetum displaying "all kinds of rare flowering trees, graceful bamboos and creepers along the waterside."[37]

The main reason for the neglect of the governor's house in Triplicane was the addition of still another official country retreat in Guindy Forest, some six miles farther out of the city. The property had passed back and forth between Company and private hands, both Indian and European, until at last it was purchased for official use by Governor Sir Thomas Munro in 1824. Munro argued that the governor needed a quiet place "where he could transact public business uninterruptedly," insisting that Clive's country house was no longer in the country, thanks to encroaching urbanism, while the residence in the fort was being taken over by the secretariat.[38] His adored wife loved flowers, and his little son Campbell (Kamen) loved to play in the gardens at Guindy. When the child became ill and his mother had to take him back to England, Munro's visits to Guindy became almost unbearably sad. Just before leaving for a long tour of southern India, he spent a last weekend there, and he wrote to her: "I took as usual a long walk on Sunday morning; there had been so much rain [it was July], that the garden looked more fresh and beautiful than I ever saw it; but I found nobody there. . . . It was a great change from the time when I was always sure of finding you and Kamen there. It is melancholy to think that you are never again to be in a place in which you took so much pleasure." He knew she would want to hear how luxuriantly the *hinah* and *baboal* hedges were doing and the geraniums in pots, which looked to his untutored eye like wild potatoes, but, alas, the place "has the air of some enchanted deserted mansion in romance."[39]

As so often happened in India, wife and child survived, husband/father did not: Sir Thomas, one of India's most enlightened governors, succumbed to cholera while on tour. Guindy, however, remained the official country residence, added to and improved by later governors. It was much admired by Lady Dufferin (1886), who found the "gardens glowing with the most lovely and brilliant crotons." On another occasion the house was illuminated as a backdrop while she and her party "sauntered for a little" in the pretty garden.[40] In late 1929 Viceroy Lord Irwin pronounced Guindy "the most delicious place I have seen in India," adding, "It stands in the middle of a delightful garden, exactly like a big English garden. . . . It really is the most English place I have seen."[41] By then it was clearly no longer Lady Munro's garden, but more likely a testimony to the English gardener whom Lady Beatrix Stanley, wife of the governor of Madras, had brought with her (Fig. 8).

The Hyderabad Residency told an even more romantic tale. It was built by James Achilles Kirkpatrick—he who married Khair in-Nissa, the greatniece of the Nizam—at just the time Clive created his showpiece in Madras. It was also contemporary with the U.S. White House, which it resembles in its domed semicircular bay on one front and colonnaded portico on the

Fig. 8. Government House, Guindy
[Photograph by author]

other (Fig. 9). This extravagant Palladian villa, "one of the most perfect buildings ever erected by the East India Company," was set in the midst of a vast if decayed stretch of much older Mughal pleasure gardens that lined the River Musi. In the center of the garden was a *baradari,* the open pavilion typical of Mughal gardens, adapted by the British for dining and entertaining. An avenue of mature cypresses formed an axis from which ran channels of water, fountains, pools, and beds of flowers; palm trees towered over luxuriant shrubbery. And tucked away in its own walled-off garden was the *zenana* built for his beloved wife (and pulled down sixty years later by a Victorian Resident, uncomfortable with reminders of the freer ways of an earlier time). Kirkpatrick kept his Mughal garden pretty much as he found it, but added fruit orchards and vegetables, looking for a "good English gardener" or one from China to assist him. When a treaty in 1800 conveniently expanded his estate, he conceived the more ambitious plan of a "natural" parkland in the style of William Kent and Capability Brown, now increasingly passé in England but a novelty in the Mughalesque garden culture of Hyderabad. He stocked it with deer, and then, because the deer needed company, elk from Bombay, and a

Fig. 9. The British Residency at Hyderabad, 1813. Aquatint, colored
[The British Library Board, X400[19]]

herd of Abyssinian sheep. To prevent everything from withering away in the intense heat of Deccan summers, he sent to Bombay for fire engines to water the shade trees and pleasure grounds. Like so much of Kirkpatrick's lifestyle, the Residency and its gardens were an amalgam of Indian and European, or, as a less charitable visitor put it, "Major Kirkpatrick's grounds are laid out partly in the taste of Islington & partly in that of Hindostan."[42]

Bombay and Calcutta were also maritime emporia built around forts. Here, too, wealthy Europeans segregated themselves in garden houses and governors outdid themselves in the magnificence of their residences. In contrast to Madras, however, Bombay and Calcutta developed as urban entities rather than simply clusters of suburban villages. And as British power moved inland to embrace the entire subcontinent and the political center of gravity moved northward, Madras was eclipsed by its sister presidencies and the burgeoning outposts of the Gangetic plain. The city that, in Kipling's words had been "crowned above Queens" became "a withered beldame . . . Brooding on ancient fame," left behind in the new age of imperial India.[43]

While the British worked day in and day out with Indians and filled their homes with Indian servants, they contrived to separate themselves increasingly from Indian life. William Dalrymple may overstate the case for the easy intermingling of races and nationalities in the earlier period, but it seems clear that the trend toward self-segregation intensified during the nineteenth century, accelerated by the agonizing events of 1857. Already in the 1790s the Company had tried to discourage the "orientalizing" proclivities of some of its employees and the common European practice of taking Indian mistresses or even wives. Some have pointed the finger at the mushrooming numbers of memsahibs flocking to India who set themselves up as "guardians of English domesticity and gentility."[44] But this is only a partial explanation and needs to be factored in with the rising tide of European theories of racial purity over the course of the century. Furthermore, there were differences in place as well as time. Maria Graham noted that there was much greater social distance between Europeans and Indians in Calcutta than in Bombay in 1810. In Bombay she had been able to meet Indian families and stop by their houses, something that was not possible in Calcutta. She does not try to explain the differences in social relations between the two cities, but it may have had something to do with the ferocious patriotism of the English in Calcutta, where society might be more refined than elsewhere but every Briton "prides himself on being outrageously a John Bull."[45]

To be sure, intercourse between Europeans and Hindus was more complicated than that with Muslims or Parsees, thanks to rigorous caste and food taboos. When Hindus did entertain Europeans, they often served them separately or did not dine with them. Dwarkanath Tagore, for example, maintained a sumptuous residence primarily to receive the social elite of Calcutta, and although he served all meats save beef to Europeans and sat with his guests as they dined, he did not touch the food. Even this was too much for his female relatives, who banished him from the family house.[46] Several decades later, Lady Dufferin was struck by the fact that at a large official dinner given by the outgoing viceroy, "Some native gentlemen who cannot eat with us sat in another room till dinner was over."[47]

Whatever their effect on social interactions, the memsahibs played a preeminent role in the garden history of British India in the nineteenth and twentieth centuries. With a house full of servants, husbands on tour or shut up in their offices, and children sent home to attend school from an appallingly early age, time and loneliness often hung heavy upon them. "Nearly unmitigated ennui is the lot of the majority of luckless women in India," lamented Emma Roberts.[48] Gardening offered some diversion for those able to brave the heat. We have already seen the hand of Lady Munro in the gardens at Guindy in the 1820s. A sisterhood of gardeners followed in her wake, and many left memoirs and letters that detail this role. Most were motivated by a desire to replicate home as much as possible, and often this meant replicating English gardens and growing, or trying to grow, English flowers. To an extent, indeed, one can divide them and their consorts roughly into two groups: those determined to make their gardens a little corner of England (in particular, "their" corner of England) and those more open to the tropical flora around them.

Among the latter, myriad variations were possible. Some combined English design with indigenous plantings. Mrs. Sherwood, writing in 1805, referred to Dr. Anderson's house in Madras as built in "a garden, beautifully laid out in the English fashion"; it abounded, however, "with trees and shrubs and flowers, such as are not known in Europe except in conservatories and hot-houses."[49] James Forbes suggests something similar in the description of the garden he laid out at Baroche, in Gujarat: "I formed it as much as possible after the English taste, and spared no pains to procure plants and flowers from different parts of India and China: it contained several large mango, tamarind, and burr trees, which formed a delightful shade; besides a variety of smaller fruit trees and flowering shrubs. . . . Shade and water were my grand objects; without them there can be no enjoyment of an Indian garden."[50] Maria Graham, too, was quite delighted with her hybrid garden in Bombay, with its walks made of ground-up seashells rather than gravel. There were *chunam* seats under spreading trees and "flower-beds filled with jasmine, roses, and tuberoses, while the plumbago rosea, the red and white ixoras, with the scarlet wild mulberry, and the oleander, mingle their gay colours with the delicate white of the moon-flower and the mogree."[51]

Then there were the "white Mughals," relics of an earlier age who had married Indian women and adopted Indian lifestyles and Indian gardens to varying degrees: the Kirkpatricks, Palmers, Ochterlonys, Metcalfes, Frasers, and Gardners, among others. To Colonel William Linnaeus Gardner, an American

Loyalist, India was more "home" than England; he had married a Muslim princess and after an active military career settled down on his estate at Khasganj in northern India. Gardner came by his middle name as the godchild of the great botanist and, as Fanny Parks notes, was himself "an excellent botanist and pursues the study with much ardour." The garden at Khasganj was "very extensive and a most delightful one, full of fine trees and rare plants, beautiful flowers and shrubs, with fruit in abundance and perfection; no expense is spared to embellish the garden." Since the Begum, his wife, and other women in his family observed *purdah,* there was also a walled *zenana* garden exclusively for their use, a "pretty garden" with a summerhouse in the center and fountains. The women and girls were fond of spending time out of doors, delighting especially in swinging under the large trees during the rains.[52]

Hybridity was common in British gardens during much of the Company period: "a pleasing hybridity," mingling "Eastern exoticism with European familiarity."[53] Garden houses looked to English parks, with their emphasis on trees and water and expansive grounds, for inspiration, but the trees and shrubs were of necessity tamarinds and palms and mangoes rather than oaks and elms and ash, and the lakes closer to tanks. In areas of the north, Mughal influences appealed, offering quiet seclusion and a sense of order as at Khasganj. Even the walled gardens of Peshawar in the shadow of the Hindu Kush had an "unmistakably English air about them" to the eyes of Montstuart Elphinstone, thanks to familiar plants and flowering fruit trees.[54] As the garden house yielded to the bungalow, however, gardens came to reflect both the altered character of the British population and changing horticultural fashions at home, with the greater emphasis on flowers and, where possible, English flowers.

The bungalow was itself a quintessential architectural hybrid. Both name and structure were of Indian origin, but Europeans put their own distinctive stamp on them. The Bengali prototype was a simple village hut, single-story, rectangular in plan and with a raised floor. The roof was thatched or tiled and generally extended over the verandah, supported on rough-hewn posts. The classically inspired mansions with their Palladian facades that had so entranced visitors to Madras and Calcutta were not really well suited to Indian climates, no matter how beautifully polished their chunam-coated exteriors. In the nineteenth and twentieth centuries, these were superseded by brick bungalows, varying in size and elaboration but based on a similar module.[55]

Throughout British India—and, indeed, across the empire—bungalows served as the building blocks of European life, both civil and military.[56] The typical station would be set well away from its native counterpart, with streets laid out in straight lines and bordered with freestanding bungalows flanked by gardens in the middle of walled or hedged-in compounds. This contrasted with Indian houses that tended to be built around an interior courtyard garden— it was as if Indian houses were turned inside out. The size of the compound and elegance of the bungalow depended on the rank of its occupant; higher ranking officials enjoyed spacious enclosures of three to ten acres of lawn and garden (Fig. 10). A gravel path led up to a colonnaded porte-cochere—ideally high enough for an elephant to pass under—extending out from the deep verandah that encircled the house on all sides but the south and provided protection against both sun and rain. Path, verandah, and portico were lined with flowering shrubs, masses of potted plants, and climbers on elaborate trellises. The invaluable film footage in the BBC documentary series *The Lost World of the Raj* shows row upon row of potted plants on verandahs and along drives during the last colonial generation, as do countless photographs of bungalows

Fig. 10. Croquet on the Lawn
[Courtesy of the National Army Museum, London]

Fig. 11. Vizianagram, 1889

[From Charles Allen]

spanning the century before independence (Fig. 11). Iris Portal's dominant memory of the Delhi of her youth as daughter of the governor of the Central Provinces was the ranks of little red pots filled with chrysanthemums. Exiled to boarding school in England like so many colonial children, she missed India terribly; she remembers the joy of returning to Delhi at last and seeing the mums in their pots and thinking, "Ah! I'm back!"[57]

The verandah was also the rare space where Indian and European met: here tailor, vendor, and craftsman displayed their wares or plied their trades. Larger towns were sure to have a club—European members only, with garden, tennis courts, and croquet lawns—as well as a church and a few European shops, stocked with tinned meats and preserves and chintzes. Indian bazaars, colorful as they might be, stayed in the native town. In small stations in the *mofussil,* the back of beyond, where Europeans were few, the bungalows might be very simple, but they were still removed from Indian settlements and they still had their gardens, however struggling.

Military cantonments, having long since outgrown the original forts, adjoined the larger colonial enclaves; in some cases they were the main raison d'être for a British presence. In these camps British troops lived separately from the larger contingents of Indian levies, but both were commanded by British officers. The officers were housed in bungalows similar to those of civilians, while British Other Ranks (BOR) lived in barracks and Indians in rows of tents, usually concentrated in the no-man's-land between the native city and the Europeans. In time, cantonments added messrooms, officers' clubs, racecourses, polo fields, wide green *maidans* (parade grounds), garrison churches, and prisons. If the bungalow was a "stationery tent," the cantonment, adapted from the peripatetic government of Mughal rulers, was a "petrified military camp."[58] And yet the cantonment near Baroda reminded Bishop Heber of nothing so much as "one of the villages near London," with its small brick houses, adorned with sloping tiled roofs, trellises, and wooden verandahs, "each surrounded by a garden with a high green hedge of the milkbush." Gay and pretty as was the effect, the practical bishop wondered if the thatched roofs and deep enveloping verandahs of "up-country" bungalows might not be more appropriate to the climate. Edward Lear also found the cantonment of Monghyr on the Ganges decidedly English in layout: long streets, broad and well kept and traced at right angles, named Queen Street, Victoria Street, Albert Street, Church Street, and the like. Houses stood detached in "nice gardens in which are no end of all possible kind of vegetables, and often delightful flowers."[59]

Ironically, in view of later history, some of the finest cantonment gardens were in Cawnpore (Kanpur). Cawnpore was, to Emma Roberts's surprise, "an oasis reclaimed from the desert." Its bungalows, their verandahs supported by Ionic columns, were situated picturesquely on high banks overlooking the Ganges, as Lady Amherst had noted, with extensive gardens of fruit trees overshadowing "a rich carpet of flowers which charms the senses by the magnificence of its colours, and the fragrance of its perfumes." Military men were clearly no less keen gardeners than civilians, perhaps bearing out Winston Churchill's dictum that war and gardening are the normal occupations of man. Furthermore, gardens were embraced as wholesome distractions for the Other Ranks, urged on an often bored and lonely white soldiery as an alternative to drink: "The men are given seeds, and encouraged to grow vegetables and flowers, as the life of a garrison gunner in an Indian fort is a very dull one."[60]

Nevertheless, the garden was usually woman's domain. Mostly she relied on the services of a *mali* to supervise the actual work (Fig. 12),

MAHLI.

Fig. 12. Mali, c. 1840
[From Leopold von Orlich, *Travels in India*, 1845]

although Maud Diver, outspoken chronicler of the Raj, maintained that if Englishwomen had a "knowledge of the ways and needs of plants" and got out in the garden "under an Indian sun," it would prove a "certain passport to the respect and admiration of the *mali,* and an excellent safeguard against his simple wiles"—and avoid the embarrassment of cabbages being planted near the front drive.[61] *Malis* were part of every household staff, frequently drawn from the ranks of poorer Brahmins. In Assam, however, Naga *malis* shocked the wife of a Resident by gardening in the nude. She gave them each a pair of bathing trunks "in an effort to inculcate decency," but abandoned the idea when she found them using the garments as turbans. The *mali* as head gardener was assisted by a large staff that might include convicts. As late as the early 1940s the political agent at Udaipur lived in a palace with a splendid garden in which "50 prisoners in fetters weeded the lawns and the five grass tennis courts."[62] Mostly, though, labor was so cheap that one didn't really need convicts—a scene in *The Lost World of the Raj* shows groups of Indian women cutting grass by hand. For grand events such as imperial *durbars* (ceremonial occasions) that needed instant greenswards, grass would also be planted by hand, blade by blade.

Every morning the *mali* was expected to rise early and bring in a bouquet of cut flowers and a basket of fruits and vegetables for the memsahib's table. It was a standing joke that one could get along perfectly well without a garden, with all its mud and snakes and insects, as long as one had a good *mali*. As Lady Dufferin put it, "The proper and healthy thing to do is to have a gardener but no garden—his duty being to provide you with flowers at your neighbours' expense, so that you always have as many as you possibly can want, and are spared the disagreeables incident to growing them for yourself." She adds, "I did not invent the system."[63] Whatever the "disagreeables" attendant on gardens in India, however, most expatriates were determined to forge ahead.

How Does Your Garden Grow?

Fortunately the Victorians were an instructive lot. Garden books, journals, and nurseries mushroomed in the nineteenth century to feed an ever-growing appetite for guidance. At times gardening took on attributes of a bloodsport, so fierce were the debates between partisans of different styles. The rage for bedding-out—starting tender plants in greenhouses and then setting them out in neat beds in patterns that resembled carpets—dominated the mid-century. This provoked a vehement reaction in the name of "naturalism," spearheaded by William Robinson and Gertrude Jekyll. They favored hardy perennials or semiannuals set out in herbaceous borders, along with rock and water gardens drawing on the many exotics that could adapt to the English climate without coddling. At the same time, some garden gurus promoted a return to the formalism of Italian gardens with their statuary, terraces, and topiary. Manuals devoted to gardening in India remained largely apart from these squabbles, only distantly reflecting the changing fashions. One, dating from 1872, approved the rather garish color schemes typical of carpet bedding, but of course in India the plants had no need to be started in hothouses. A later manual recommended William Robinson's *English Flower Garden* "as a reward once one has mastered the abc's" of gardening, declaring, "it is the most instructive book in the world in English." Agnes Harler, author of *The Garden in the Plains* (first published in 1901), had also clearly absorbed her Robinson and Jekyll, offering chapters on rockeries and water gardens. She suggested that a formal garden was best suited for very small compounds without room for wide lawns or spreading trees; however, she cautioned against herbaceous borders, noting that they are ill-suited to India's lower elevations, where only a few perennials do well and even these refuse to bloom all at the same time to produce the desired color effects.[64]

The most popular manuals on gardening in India went through many editions and covered the whole gamut of topics.[65] They provided detailed chapters on soils, temperatures, manure, watering, drainage, tools, growing from seed, grafting, pruning, transplanting, potting, kitchen gardens (best kept out of sight), noxious insects, lawns, and conservatories, along with designs for flowerbeds adapted from England and the continent. They advised how to create a spacious feeling even in a modest compound (mass shrubs and strongly colored flowers farther from the house; keep the garden simple and uncrowded) and stressed the importance of making sure that the view from the spare bedroom wasn't onto "decaying cabbage stalks or servants hanging out the wash"—plant a little lawn under the windows with a bed of cannas or a flowering shrub or two, or a screen of climbers "to hide backyard activities." One of the most popular offered plans for larger or smaller spreads that were simply English plans adapted only slightly to Indian conditions (Fig. 13).

Manuals were also full of advice about how to grow English garden plants. Northern India, where the bulk of Europeans were stationed, presented particular problems because of heat and aridity: gardens had to be watered during many months of the year from a well, the "life-source" of the garden. "Morning and evening the great cream-coloured humped bullocks labour up and down an inclined plane," wrote Edith Cuthell, wife of an official in Lucknow, "drawing up the water in a kind of square bag made of the skin of one of their deceased relatives," which was emptied into the runnels

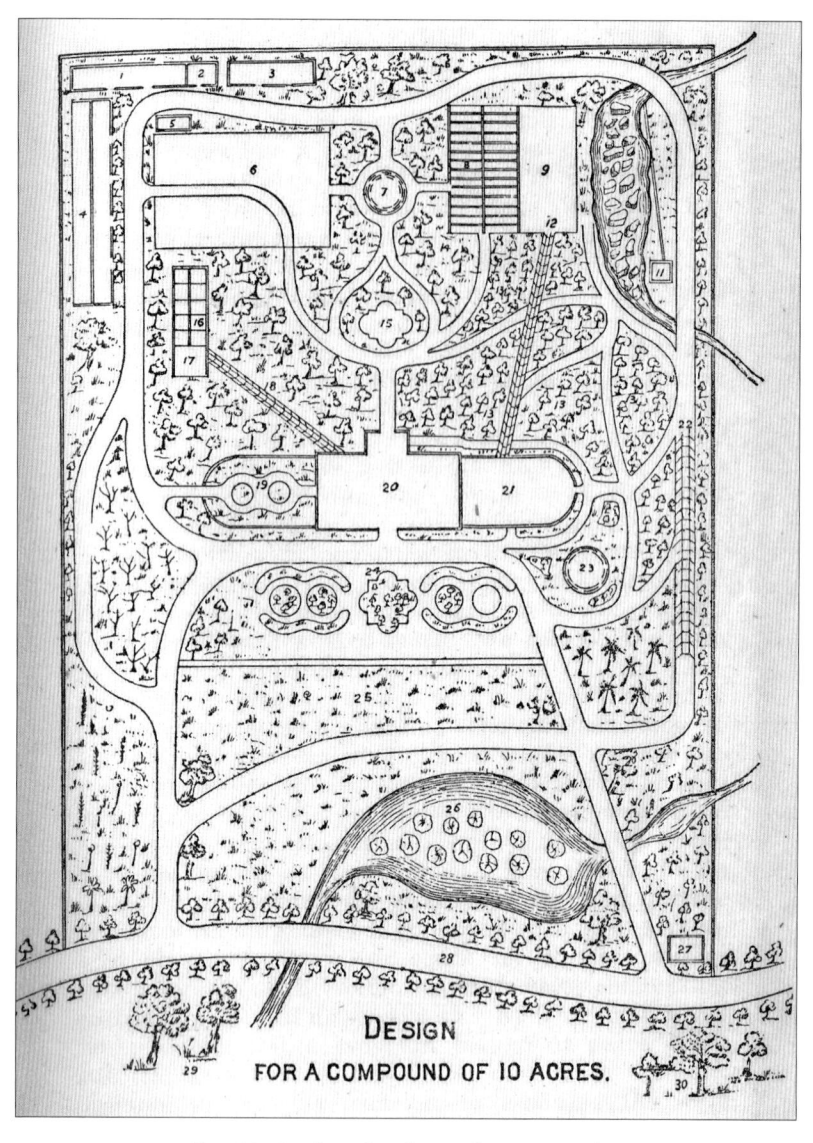

Fig. 13. Garden plan for gardeners in India
[From G. Marshall Woodrow, *Gardening in India*, 5th ed., 1889]

irrigating flowers and vegetables.[66] In the driest of times, the bullocks plodded back and forth all day (Fig. 14). During the monsoons the problem was reversed: gardens were turned into the bogs that Lady Dufferin so abhorred. Manuals proposed raising beds two inches above the grass to avoid flooding, but standing water in gardens was a perpetual breeding place for mosquitoes. When Constance Villiers-Stuart tried to impose an English plan of flat paths with raised herbaceous borders on her garden, she was overruled, quite rightly, by her *mali,* who pointed out the obvious fact that in an irrigated garden, the walks must be raised for water to run under them, just as the Mughals had done.[67]

One of the most encyclopedic manuals for the memsahib was *The Complete Indian Housekeeper and Cook* by Flora Annie Steel and Grace Gardiner. The book is written in the no-nonsense voice of an English games-mistress. It is dedicated "to the English Girls to Whom Fate may assign the task of being house-mothers in our eastern Empire." Chapter XI, on gardening, follows a brief one on dogs. The authors take a dim view of "native gardeners," who have no real sympathy, they claim, for flowers and must be trained to obey orders "and nothing more." While one horticultural writer maintained that "there is no branch of gardening in India that is more overdone in the plains than pot plants" and that there is "scarcely a house or compound that is not belittered with far too many poorly kept and untidily arranged flower pots" taking up altogether too much of *mali*'s time,[68] Steel and Gardiner were all for pots and hanging baskets. "Nothing makes an Indian house look so home-like and cheerful as a verandah full of blossoming plants, and hung with baskets of

Fig. 14. J. L. Kipling, *The Persian Well*
[From *Beast and Man in India*, 1891]

ferns," they declared, adding, "Silent as flowers may be in complaint, they are eloquent in their gratitude, and their blossoming service of praise will make your home a pleasant resting place for tired eyes. And *how* tired eyes can be of dull, dusty 'unflowerful ways,' only those can really know who have spent long years in the monotonous plains of Northern India. There, it seems, the garden is not merely a convenience or a pleasure, it is a duty." To back up their exhortations, they insisted that with proper manure and leaf mold almost anything could be grown.[69]

But could it? That was the problem for those for whom the symbol of home was an English garden. Emily Eden spent more than five years (1846–52) in India as hostess for her bachelor brother, Governor-General Lord Auckland, and kept a journal of a long official tour. It begins and ends with nostalgia for the gardens and lawns of home, for Greenwich and Kensington Gore.[70] As Eden herself discovered, it *was* possible to grow many English flowers in India; it all depended on geography and season. In Sholapur, in the Deccan, George Roche remembers his mother's garden: "[She] planted English seeds—sweet peas, petunias, phlox, balsam and clarkias, which, by Christmas time were in full flower. . . . The display of blooms could not have been bettered in any English garden." Sholapur stood a thousand feet above sea level, but even at that altitude her success was unusual and made her the envy of the other ladies of the station; her son attributed it to manure from their own stables.[71] The North-West Frontier Province, isolated though it might be, was far better suited to English preferences, thanks to both latitude and altitude. Posted to the garrison town of Rawalpindi, an official couple lived in a "charming house, surrounded by a garden where roses climb up trees and hang from their branches and mignonette and sweet violets pervade the air with their perfume."[72] Peshawar offered a similar climate: "Here we are, right on the Frontier," exclaimed Lady Reading, wife of the viceroy, in 1922, "and it is the first place, strange to say, that has reminded me of England since I landed in India. Such green grass and tall trees. . . . The garden here [at the Residency] is heavenly with rows of orange trees in full bloom, beds of pansies and a rose-garden with such Maréchal Niel!"[73]

Even lowland India does, in fact, have a winter. As Emma Roberts noted in 1836, "The climate all over India, even in Bengal, is delightful from October until March . . . ; summer gardens glow with myriads of flowers, native and exotic. . . . This is the gay season." Even if a true herbaceous border was not possible at low elevations, a border of mixed annual flowers made a good substitute. Most cold-season flowers sown in late September or early October would bloom in the winter months, and planning such a garden was "one of the joys of an Indian year."[74] The author Rumer Godden's mother would have heartily agreed. As soon as the rains were over, she began to plan her garden in Bengal. The packets of seed of "precious English flowers" were sown in shallow earthenware pans set in little bamboo houses on stilts. Every evening their mat roofs were rolled back so that the little seedlings could enjoy the cool air and morning dew. When the sun grew too strong, the mats were put back again. The *mali* watered the tiny plants by dipping a leaf in water and shaking it over the pans, explaining that even the finest nozzle on a watering can would give too strong a jet of water. When they grew big enough, the pansies, dianthus, stocks, sweet peas, and sweet sultans would be transplanted into the flowerbeds or into the big pots set along the verandahs.[75]

Lady Beatrix Stanley made something of a study of what flowers would grow in India "to remind one of home." In the south annuals were limited mainly to large-flowered zinnias, coreopsis, gaillardias, phlox, and petunias, all of which could be planted in the open, or, if space was lacking, in pots. Salvias, cosmos, and various sunflowers also did well, although "roses are of no use in Madras"—in contrast to New Delhi, where they could hold their own with the best of England.[76] At Agra, Baron von Orlich, a Prussian officer fighting the Sikhs alongside the British, observed that only after the monsoon did flowers reach their full perfection. Then the air was filled with the balsamic perfume of roses, violets, and myrtles. An early December morning in Dinapur seemed to Edward Lear "exactly like of a lovely autumn or even June, morning in England; zinnias, balsams, and roses included." In the plains, annuals such as phlox and nasturtiums, pansies and corn-bottles, sunflowers and daisies did indeed grow wonderfully fast—"In India the gardener has very little waiting to do."[77] Among the tea planters in Assam there were also many passionate gardeners. One of them has left a moving memoir of her twenty years as the often frustrated and alienated wife of a planter. She describes how the hot weather lessened in early October: "There was a new smell and we walked out into a thick white mist and knew the cold weather had begun; golden days when the compound filled with English flowers mixed in with mimosa and poinsettias and the vegetable garden gave us salads and pineapples." Evenings were at last cool enough for fires and buttered toast in front of them. At the club, gardeners competed to see who could bring in the first sweet peas or cauliflowers.[78]

For Edith Cuthell, too, the world came back to life in October. "For us, Westerns, the Indian year has, as it were, begun. Life is once more endurable; the rains and the hot winds have ceased." Her *My Garden in the City of Gardens,* first published anonymously in 1905, is one of the most complete garden chronicles, following the seasons in Lucknow. Needless to say, the bulk of it is devoted to the cold weather and her efforts to grow annuals from seed, first in pots on the verandah, then in beds: pansies, sweet peas, stocks, nasturtiums, balsams, verbenas, heartsease—the whole repertoire. The garden reaches a climax in January and February; by April the English flowers and vegetables have been "scorched by the brand of the blinding heat" and by June she is off to the hills. But, oh, the joys of those winter months! Her rapturous paean to the violets she coaxed into blooming is quoted in almost every work on British life in India: "My violets are in bloom! You cannot think how one treasures out here the quiet little 'home' flower, buried in greenery.... Dear little English flower!" They demanded more care than all the "lurid tropical flowers" put together, kept always in their pots out of the direct rays even of the winter sun and watered by the *mali* carefully trickling the stream through his fingers: "for are they not the *memsahib*'s most cherished plants?" She was almost as ecstatic over her bed of watercress, "a pearl of great price," which with much care could be kept going all through the cold weather, along with expatriate vegetables and fruits: cauliflowers, turnips, carrots, asparagus, tomatoes, strawberries. Then there were the roses. Roses might be the "real flower of the East," but they cannot stand the tropical sun and in the plains bloomed only in the cold weather.[79]

It was widely believed that the most reliable seeds came from England, ordered from catalogs or brought by friends. Even then, it was a case of "Darwinian survival"—many of Cuthell's seeds sent out weeks earlier in tins arrived "mildewy and spoilt." European plants required a constant succession of fresh seeds, "for, unless the cultivators of distant places exchange their seeds with each other, foreign productions soon dwindle and die away."[80] Firms in Calcutta or Poona and botanical gardens sought to fill the growing demand for such plants. Emma Roberts gives a long account of Deegah, a remarkably extensive farm and nursery near Patna on the Ganges where a Mr. Havell raised for sale all manner of livestock (including English breeds), plants, and fruit trees, and offered warehouses full of dry goods, provisions, furniture—all that a well-heeled clientele might want. The gardens "contain an immense profusion of European flowers," carefully tended by native "mallees" under the supervision of Dutch and Chinese gardeners. Visitors were invited to walk in the gardens, as Roberts did, observing that "its English flower-beds [show] how bright a paradise an Indian garden may be made by practiced hands." Inevitably, Havell's prices were high in spite of government subsidies, but even so Roberts doubted Deegah would outlast Havell's death.[81] And even Havell's gardeners, "men of science and practical knowledge" though they might be, would not have been able to grow spring bulbs in the Gangetic plain. Raleigh Trevelyan's parents brought with them to Gilgit daffodil bulbs specially sent out from England: At 3,000 feet Gilgit was high enough and far enough north for bulbs to flourish, just as some varieties did fairly well in the Nilgiri Hills in the south, although they rarely flowered after the first year since the weather was simply not cold enough for the dormancy all bulbs require.[82]

The lawn, that sine qua non of any proper English garden, presented the greatest challenge of all. Without a lawn, the "centre of social life," how could one hold garden parties? Or play croquet or badminton or cricket? It was a particularly precious thing in hot countries, as Lady Dufferin observed. Grindal's *Everyday Gardening in India* declared that the lawn should be "the principal general feature of the garden," adding, "The more wide and unbroken the lawns, the more beautiful and restful the effect. A beautiful lawn well may be compared to a beautiful carpet, without which any scheme of furnishing is ruined"—an interesting analogy in view of the close relationship of Mughal gardens and Persian carpets. Another guide proclaimed the lawn "the heart of the garden and the happiest thing that is in it." It was the setting for flowering shrubs and dwarf flowering trees as well as a few formal beds of annuals, although not too many. A heading in Mrs. Temple-Wright's highly popular *Flowers and Gardens in India: A Manual for Beginners* reads "A Lawn, an absolute necessity." Even if you can't manage a garden, she insists, "make only a lawn, or grass-plot, and this, with cleanly kept soorkee [brick dust] paths, and a few plants in pots, will be sufficient to keep up the degree of harmony you intend to maintain between the outside and inside appearance of your abode."[83]

HOW THEN TO ACHIEVE this oasis of greenery? In 1836 Lord Brougham had arranged to have English turf brought out by boat for his chateau at Cannes, "stupéfiant les Cannois en créant d'immenses pelouses toujours vertes" [amazing the people of Cannes by creating immense lawns forever green], but this was hardly feasible in India. Stationed in Gujarat and the Koncan in the second half of the eighteenth century, Forbes had bemoaned the fact that the "great desideratum" of a "verdant lawn" seemed an impossibility: "A tropical sun would not admit of it in the fair season, and during the rainy months the rank luxuriant grass more resembles reeds and rushes than the soft carpet bordered by an English shrubbery."[84] Seasoned gardener though she was, Edith Cuthell didn't even bother with a lawn in Lucknow, considering it far too expensive a luxury for any but high functionaries "who dwell more permanently than ourselves in Government Houses and the like."[85] Nonetheless, she was an exception. All the garden books provided detailed recipes for preparing the soil and tending the grass, sowing not the finely textured English varieties but the coarser, wiry Indian *doob*. Adapting the English formula of alternately rolling and mowing, Temple-Wright exhorts the reader that "the more like velvet you wish your lawn to appear, the more you must Mow, Sweep, Roll, Water"[86] For Steel and Gardiner the advice was simpler and sterner: "*Make the grass grow.*"[87]

The *maidan*, at the heart of most British towns and cantonments, was the lawn writ large. The East India Company trader William Finch described the *maidan* in Surat early in the seventeenth century as "a pleasant greene in the midst whereof is a maypole."[88] It had its origins in the parade ground but served also as a public park and playing field. In the course of the nineteenth century British authorities added more public parks: Elphinstone Gardens, Horniman Circle, and Victoria Gardens in Bombay (see Pl. 2); Eden Gardens in Calcutta, and the "club-strewn" Lawrence Gardens in the heart of British Lahore.[89] In Lahore, too, they undertook the restoration of the lovely Shalimar Garden that had been laid out by Shah Jahan in 1642 but largely destroyed under Sikh rule. As was so often the case with their "restorations," the result was more British than Mughal: they cut down the beautiful cypresses and mango trees that were the central feature of the lowest level and transformed the terrace into flowerbeds.[90]

The success or failure of lawns depended on season and place. The monsoon itself could turn the landscape green: "The whole face of the country is covered with a lovely carpet of grass just like the meadows at Richmond," wrote a Mrs. Terry from Bombay in the mid-1840s. Unlike Richmond, hyenas still came out at night and killed her ducks, alas.[91] Assiduous gardeners could achieve some success, creating "a lawn quite English-looking," as Augusta King, an official's wife, noted in Morabadad. And when she heard the sound of a mowing machine, she wrote, "I could almost fancy we were in England"[92] (Fig. 15). Such machines were expensive in India, however, and hardly necessary in a country where labor was so cheap. In Poona, "children rolled and crawled and played on the lawn that was of almost English thickness," and in Peshawar Elphinstone found fields covered with a thick, elastic sod, that perhaps was never equaled but in England." Returning home from the misery of school in England to their father's plantation in Bengal, Jon and Rumer Godden were ecstatic as they rumbled through the great wooden gates arched with a canopy of bridal creeper and caught the first glimpse of what they, in fact, considered their real home: "Lawns spread away on either side, lawns of unbelievable magnitude after the strip of London garden we had grown used to."[93] This was December—"the balmy noon of a December day"—when lawns and gardens everywhere were at their dazzling peak. With

Fig. 15. Olivia Fraser, *Lawn Mowing*
[From William Dalrymple, *City of Djinns*, 1993]

the first blasts of summer, lawns turned brown and English flowers wilted and died. "They struggle so gallantly to pretend that they are happy, to persuade you that this is not so very far from England; and they fail so piteously. They will flower in abundant but straggling blossoms; but the fierce sun withers the first before the next have more than budded.... It is a loving fraud, but a hollow one."[94]

Other obstacles plagued the gardener. In Karachi, apart from the scorching temperatures, the soil was almost pure sand; if one dug deep, a "saltish damp oozed up, destroying all plant roots. All you could hope for was a few palms, casuarinas and oleanders."[95] The holy city of Benares swarmed with sacred bulls, who laid waste to English gardens. The only effective remedy was to yoke them and put them to hard labor for a day or two, "which so utterly disgusts them with the place that they never return to it."[96] Lord Valentia probably exaggerated when he claimed that one couldn't have trees in the English quarter of Benares "unless you choose to be devoured by mosquitoes."[97] Dacca, in East Bengal, was considered a punitive military posting, not least because of its haunted houses and gardens.[98] More generally, white ants were the scourge of India, "the vilest little animals on the face of the earth." They ate their way through walls, through wooden beams, through furniture, through carpets, mats, and chintz. When they attacked the roots of trees and plants, they killed them in a day or two. In the garden the solution Fanny Parks recommended was a solution of assafoetida, but the ubiquitous pots also offered protection.[99] Then there were the snakes—it was a good idea to lay a carpet on the lawn before guests moved out to the garden after dinner, since snakes like to lounge on the warm ground after sunset.[100]

All these inconveniences paled before the impermanence of expatriate life. As soon as one was settled in one station and began literally to sink roots, one faced transfer to another outpost, sometimes in a very different part of the country. This meant that garden design counted for less than just getting beloved flowers to grow. The Steels moved fifteen times in sixteen years. Since they spent three years in one station and two in another, the rest of the postings were very brief indeed. "We are but birds of passage in India," lamented Anne Wilson, another civilian wife, "and have to build our nests of what material we can find." They might cultivate gardens with plants they would never see open. Some were too discouraged to exert themselves or to settle for more than a few halfhearted shrubs at the doorstep. Nonetheless, even the birds of passage were reminded that they could still spruce things up a bit before they moved on: cut the grass, trim the shrubs, repot the plants, and maybe even sow some annuals.[101] All those potted plants had the virtue of being portable and were often transported from post to post or on the annual transmigration to the hills (see Chapter 3).

If gardening in India was in the end an "act of faith,"[102] the most successful gardeners learned to temper their longing for English flowers with a leavening—one might almost say a *masala*—of indigenous plants. In some cases it was by necessity, in others by preference. Steel's husband discovered in his planting of roadside gardens in the Punjab that only indigenous plants would keep on growing, while European ones tended to peter out after a few years. The contrast was marked in her own garden on a summer's day: "The English flowers meet the sun's morning kiss bright and sweet as ever, but by noon are weary and worn by his caresses. Yet there were heaps and heaps of Oriental beauties ready for it."[103] Beatrix Stanley advised "all who care for gardening and who try it in India, to grow as many of the native plants, shrubs and creepers as possible, for although they do not always remind one of home, yet unless a few of these are grown one misses many lovely and interesting plants." Her view was evidently shared by Rumer and Jon Godden's mother, who added to her "precious English flowers" and pots of budding chrysanthemums abundant plantings of hibiscus and oleanders, bougainvilleas, plumbago, and a hedge of poinsettia. Just so, Edith Cuthell's garden grew "flowers of home" alongside tropical flowers, shrubs, fruits, and trees, "lurid" though they might be.[104]

Manuals sensibly suggested combining the best of both worlds wherever possible: masses of annuals along with "flaming tropical flowers" in the hot months.[105] There were also instructions for creating a moonlight garden, the quintessential Indian form. It would feature pale yellow or white flowers which don't close up at night, "and since there is a theatrical quality about moonlight in the tropics, these flowers should be given as 'stagey' a setting as possible"—grouped around a tank or at the end of a stretch of grass. Climbers look "more ethereal" if attached to a wire mesh support or a pergola behind the flowerbed.[106]

Practicality aside, some reveled in tropical flora, while others detested them. Forbes might talk of laying out a *Jardin à l'Angloise,* a garden laid more or less "in the European taste," but he stocked it with the Indian flowers and creeping vines he adored.[107] Emma Roberts was more a Romantic than an Orientalist, but she shared Forbes's sensual appreciation of Indian nature. One of her most memorable experiences was a stay in the house of the Collector at the small civil station of Arrah, in Bihar, not far from Patna. The "spacious mansion," the cages filled with "brilliantly-plumed birds," the immense chameleon, the exquisite view from the balcony over "bright parterres of flowers," a small lake with its "calm and silvery waters," against a glorious background of forest trees, "bearing the richest luxuriance of foliage"—all calculated to inspire bursts of enthusiasm in the weary traveler. She conjured up images of enchanted castles, of "youthful visions of the splendid retreat of the White Cat, the solitary palace of the King of the Black Islands, or the domicile of that most gracious of beasts, the interesting Azor." Walking at dusk in the garden, which blended both Indian and European flowers, she came to a large tank in the middle of which was an island covered with lustrous flowering shrubs with innumerable small white herons daring in and out of the foliage. A *ghat* or flight of steps led down to the tank and opposite it a "superb tree," a "monarch of the forest . . . held in great reverence by the Hindoo population" (a *peepal* tree, perhaps?), gave shade to the graceful forms of natives filling up their water-pots. The "crimson splendours of a setting sun . . . lit up the whole scene with hues divine." Imagine her bafflement when she later met with many persons, presumably compatriots, who were familiar with this "glorious landscape" but spoke of it with indifference, when to her, even in weak health and much fatigued, it appeared "one of the loveliest spots of earth on which my eyes had ever rested."[108]

Roberts's contemporary Fanny Parks offers a glowing and only slightly more down-to-earth description of her own extensive garden at Allahabad, illumined for the Hindu festival of Dewali. Like Forbes, she had her own bower, a favorite retreat on the banks of the Yamuna, "which is quite as beautiful as the 'bower of roses by Bendameer's stream.'" The garden was full of luxuriant creepers and climbers forming a canopy over her bower, exuding delicate fragrances, attracting hummingbirds and butterflies. Blossoms hung from surrounding trees and nymphaea floated on the water. Among her favorite plants were two species of *sag* [spinach], the koonch [?], several brilliant hibiscus, and a salvia. The salvia was tended with particular care in view of the well-known adage, "Cur moriatur homo, cui salvia crescit in horto?" (Why should a man die who has salvia growing in his garden?). She writes about her flowers with "a tremulously lyrical ecstasy," evoking Thomas Moore's Oriental romance, *Lalla Rookh,* with her "plaintive apostrophe" to the "sorrowful nyctanthes" (*Nyctanthes arbor-tristis*), the night-flowering jasmine: "Gay and beautiful climber, whence your name of arbor tristis? Is it because you blossom but to die? With the first beams of the rising sun your night flowers are shed upon the earth to wither and decay." She does not mention a single English flower, noting that in the bouquet presented to her every morning by her *mali* "many were novelties to an European." Parks had taken to India like a duck to water, and yet nostalgia could steal upon her unbidden: cooped up in her stifling house during the heat of the rains, there were moments when even she longed to walk among the wildflowers of home: "Here we have no wild flowers; from the gardens you procure the most superb nosegays; but the lovely wild flowers of the green lanes are wanting."[109]

As keen students of botany, William Jones, Lady Amherst, and Lady Canning (all of whom will reappear in subsequent chapters) also took a particular pleasure in Indian flora. Lady Amherst found it a little foolish of the missionary Dr. William Carey to insist on growing plants from England in his garden upriver from Calcutta in a "climate nature never intended them for." Conversely, as Lady Canning was wont to remind her friends and family back home, many of the exotics in her garden had become familiar in England as hothouse plants.[110] Neither Jones nor Canning lived to return home, but a few of those who did sought to re-create something of India in England. James Forbes brought back more than two hundred seeds from Gujarat for his garden at Stanmore Hall, in the midst of which he placed an octagonal temple filled with Hindu sculpture. In his glass conservatory he succeeded in growing many of the flowers celebrated by Indian poets: the crimson ipomea, the "lovely Mhadavi-creeper, . . . the changeable rose (hibiscus mutabilis), the fragrant mogree, attracting alhinna, and sacred tulsee." At Daylesford Warren Hastings, too, tried to propagate the plants he had most appreciated in India. Drawing on meteorological data he had collected in Calcutta, he designed a stove house intended to provide the right environment for his lychees and custard apples. His attempts to cross Indian animals, such as the shawl goat from the Himalayas, with English breeds were less successful. In other respects, to be sure, Hastings's estate was more typical of the parks of his neighbors, with extensive lawns of carefully manicured grass, beds of flowers, carefully arranged clumps of trees, and a grotto.[111]

Nabobs returning from India drew not only on their own experience but also on the hugely influential work of the artists William Hodges and Thomas and William Daniell, whose engravings of Indian monuments and landscapes had caught the imagination of the English public. Sir John Osborne displayed his disgust over Hastings's impeachment trial by erecting a Hindu temple designed by Thomas Daniell in his park in Wiltshire. It pointedly featured a stone bust of Hastings rising from a lotus flower as an incarnation of the Hindu deity Vishnu, "who, according to the belief of the Brahmans, has from time to time appeared under various material forms for the support of religion and virtue and the reformation of mankind." The most ambitious, if less sacrilegious, orientalizing project was that of Sir Charles Cockerell at Sezincote in the Cotswolds. On his retirement from India about 1805, Cockerell decided to build a house in the Indian style, choosing his younger brother as architect, Humphry Repton as garden designer, and Thomas Daniell as advisor to both. Daniell's painting of the house in 1817 shows it to be a mélange of Hindu and Mughal elements: a central blue-green onion dome, multifoil arches, *chhatris* (small open pavilions positioned at corners on the roof), and *chujjas* (deep-set cornices). Daniell himself designed a little Hindu temple to the sun-god Surya, a bridge over a ribbon of pools embellished with statues of Nandi, the sacred bull associated with the god Siva, and a fountain in the shape of a Siva *lingam*. Repton's actual contribution to the garden is unclear—echoes of a Mughal *charbagh* are later additions—but he was so taken with his introduction to Indian architecture at Sezincote that the plans he submitted for the Prince Regent's Brighton Pavilion are infused with "Indian forms." In the end, the plans proved too expensive; when it was finally built by John Nash, the architect of Bath, the pavilion distilled a far more fanciful potpourri of domes, minarets, and colonnades gleaned from Daniell's *Oriental Scenery*.[112]

Perhaps what separated those who loved Indian flora from those who did not was the matter of scent, the "amber scent of odorous perfume" that floats over Indian gardens. As Forbes noted, Indian flowers and odoriferous plants were "much esteemed by Asiatic ladies, but generally too powerful for Europeans." Many of the flowers in Parks's garden were indeed notable for their strong "odour," but the only ones she singles out as yielding "the most overpowering fragrance" are those of the male screw-tree, commenting, like Forbes, that the fragrance is "esteemed very highly by the native." Julia Maitland, a Company official's wife in the 1830s, found herself still trying to rid her hands and arms of the scent of a garland of flowers bestowed upon her by a well-to-do Madrasi the day before. Like its brilliant colors, the "heavy perfumes" of India could be an acquired taste.[113] The garden maven Agnes Harler *did* advise putting the scented plants of the moonlight garden at a distance.

"The Land of Regrets"

In her novel of the 1857 uprising, *On the Face of the Waters,* Flora Annie Steel personified in the Erltons and the Gissings the contrasting attitudes toward what made a proper garden. For Kate Erlton the cult of home is a religion; her house and garden in Lucknow are "English in every twist and turn of foreign flowers and furniture." She grows—or tries to grow—heartsease and sweet peas and pansies, "for she loved her poor clumps of English annuals more than all the scented and blossoming shrubs which . . . turned the garden into a wilderness of strange perfumed beauty." The Gissings' house, too, stands in a large garden, but although it is "wreathed with creepers, and set with flowers after the manner of flowerful Lucknow, there was no cult of pansies or such like English treasures here. It was gay with that acclimatized tangle of poppies and larkspur, marigold, mignonette, and corn cockles which Indian gardeners love to sow broadcast in their cartwheel mud-beds." For Steel, the explanation was quite simple: the Gissings prefer India, where they were received into society, to England, where they were not, while the Erltons have no such insecurities.[114]

Steel's claim that class counted for less in British India than in the homeland may raise a few eyebrows, and certainly gardening tastes did not always follow social status. Nevertheless, her contrast alerts us to the fact that gardens signify more than meets the eye. The garden served as a sort of synecdoche, the part standing for the whole of one's response to an alien culture and to the life that exile imposed, especially on women. And there could be many responses, just as there could be many approaches to gardening. There is of course the stereotype of the expatriate Englishman—and woman—traveling like a tortoise with his or her own shell to keep the outside world at bay. Early in the nineteenth century Maria Graham, returning from India via the Cape of Good Hope, had remarked that "the English people at the Cape live like the English everywhere, as much in the manner they would do at home as circumstances would permit." Julia Maitland found the same in Madras where it seemed that everyone was trying to make the city as English as possible ("like England in a perspiration"), "though without much success, except doing away with everything curious." Subsequent writers have taken up the refrain, reinforced latterly by rosy memories of elderly colonials, such as the aged sisters who had spent their entire lives in India and insisted that India "before" (i.e., before independence) "was . . . just like England." Whether it was the flowered chintz curtains on the windows, the tinned meats, or the attempts to grow herbaceous borders in their gardens, Brits did what they could to create "some sad verisimilitude of home." At Christmas Edith Cuthell festooned the pillars on her verandah with marigolds, taking them down on Twelfth Night and reminding herself that they were English every bit as much as Indian, admired in Tudor times as "one of the plants of the sunne." Iris Macfarlane's grandmother created "the life of Eastbourne and Drayton Gardens" with her bungalow and acres of gardens in Burma. More often, every letter from England brought a wave of nostalgia, conveying one "to the verdant lawns and flower-enamelled meadows of his native country." Anglo-Indians loved to write verses touched with melancholy longing for the "green fields, simple flowers, and soft rain of England." As one of the last colonial wives lamented in hindsight, "We could have had the most marvelous gardens with orchids and all sorts of things, but, no, they must be English flowers."[115]

Maintaining a garden—a proper English garden—was, as Anthony King argues, one of the ways a person could establish and constantly reinforce his identity as a member of a group distinct from indigenous society. Manicured gardens with neat lawns and flowerbeds were a means of distancing oneself from the smells and dirt of India. Conversely, departure from the norms of group behavior raised the specter of "going native."[116] The garden, the club, the segregated military and civil lines all served the dual purpose of reinforcing English mores and setting an example of "civilized" life for the "natives." Add to these the public park, the regular streets, and the well-planted roundabouts (Fig. 16) and the model is complete. And yet, like any neat model, this is replete with exceptions and qualifications in the matter of gardens and probably of much else. First, a static model cannot account for the evolution of British gardens in India. The bungalow with its gravel paths, shrubs, flowerbeds, and attempts at lawn is a nineteenth-century creation, replicating, however imperfectly, the middle-class Victorian aesthetic of house and garden. Earlier garden houses took as their ideal the country estate with its sweeping

Fig. 16. View from the town hall of Elphinstone Circle and Gardens, Bombay, c. 1880
[From Miriam Dossal, *Imperial Designs and Indian Realities*, 1991]

park, copses of trees, and water. Even in the nineteenth century, bungalow gardens varied in size and layout but tried only halfheartedly to keep up with the changing modes of the motherland.

Nor can such a model admit the idiosyncratic responses of individuals; it was, after all, a "various universe." In all periods there were some who embraced the almost terrifying luxuriance of Indian nature wholeheartedly, others only timidly or not at all, still others somewhere in between. Elizabeth Fenton's early months in India (before her Army husband died suddenly) are filled with rapturous descriptions of the rich vegetation of the country. "I feel still as if I should never weary of the aspect of nature in her tropical garb," she wrote in her journal as she sailed up the Ganges in her *budgerow*, a distinctly Indian type of barge that is usually towed, marveling at the "prodigious banyans," the "elegant bamboo and palmira trees." Similarly, Captain Skinner found everything bathed in an "air of romance," redolent of picturesque sights and aromatic odours of herbs and plants. While one thinks of this openness as more characteristic of the earlier period of contact, before the British became more numerous and their attitudes more rigid, this is not entirely the case. Edward Lear was not unique in the sheer ecstasy of his first encounter with the glories of Bombay in 1873. The drive to Breach Kandy "left me nearly mad from sheer beauty and wonder of foliage! O new palms! O flowers!" True, Lear was a traveler, not an expatriate sahib, but his enthusiasms were echoed by Henry Sharp, who was a sahib. Like Lear, he was dazzled by the "wonder" of his first sight of the Orient, the human and the natural landscape: "blossom-laden trees, poinsettias flaunting brilliance of green and red, croton and caladium of incredible dimensions"—all this matched by the kaleidoscopically costumed array of women, peddlers, soothsayers, and snake-charmers, "the strange medley of the East." The wonder did not fade after almost thirty years of service as a district officer. When in the early 1920s "for the last time I saw the Colaba light fade . . . I felt I was leaving a land whose glories I had not fully savoured, whose secrets I had not half fathomed."[117] Possibly memoirs are biased toward those who found India "interesting"—what would there have been to write about if one saw nothing behind or ahead but endless days of boredom in an alien land?

Notions of the picturesque and subsequently of the romantic, however contested their meanings, held sway in Great Britain for several generations from the later eighteenth century onward. Inevitably they colored one's vision of India and its landscapes and how eagerly one embraced or rejected it. Fanny Parks's journal was titled *Wanderings of a Pilgrim in Search of the Picturesque During Four-and-twenty Years in the East,* reflecting her openness, indeed enthusiasm for the sights, sounds, and even scents of India. Lear might have given his journals a similar title, although they cover a much shorter span. For him "picturesque" was the highest accolade he could bestow and it was reserved above all for what he found truly to be truly Indian, with the "Anglo-Saxonisms happily out of sight." What delighted him was the "impossible picturesqueness" of the Indian landscape: one hour of Benares or Brindaban, he declared, "is worth a month of thy [Delhi's] Britishized beauties which, whatever they once were, please this child very little now." The glories of Kanchenjunga at sunrise or sunset and the lushness of the foliage on the descent to the plains more than made up for the "vicious" cold of Darjeeling or the inconveniences of travel.[118]

Emily Eden, on the other hand, might view India through the lens of the picturesque but this did not lessen her melancholy and impatience to return home. For her as for so many Britons, Babur's dusty Hindustan would remain a "land of regret"; even its most splendid landscapes could not vie with the land of their birth. With more self-awareness than many, Emma Roberts noted that "persons who have never quitted their native land, cannot imagine the passionate regrets experienced by the exile, who in the midst of the most gorgeous scenes pines after the humblest objects surrounding that home to which he dares not hope to return." Perverse it may be, but understandable as well that he will "contrast the Ganges with some obscure rivulet, the magnolia with the daisy, to the disparagement of the mighty river and the monarch of flowers." With every mile that separated them, the landscapes they had left behind became not only dearer but lovelier. As the Reverend William Arthur insisted, "Those who have wandered in the woods of Bolton-Abbey, by the banks of the Dart, the Avon, or the Wye, have stood on Croagh-Patrick, or Richmond-Hill, or sailed on the waters of Lough-Erne or Lough-Gill, need not sigh for the region of cloudless suns, nor envy 'the green of its shores, or the blues of its skies.'" There were no doubt legions who would echo Kipling's lament, "I am sick of endless sunshine, sick of blossom-burdened bough." And just as it was for Babur, the solace of the exiles would be to create what was most familiar to them, the gardens of home—or as close to home as a climate and topography allowed, "homely cottages of comfort" with "smiling" flowers and shrubbery hedges.[119]

But even colonials most intent on surrounding their bungalows with English gardens as a cordon sanitaire to keep India at bay usually acknowledged in the end that, realistically, they must include tropical plantings. Like the mulligatawnies and curries that were not quite Indian and not quite English, colonial gardens, too, often ended up as creoles, their mix of familiar and exotic flowers growing under the shade of mangoes and palms and *peepals* in lieu of the stately elms and oaks of home.

CHAPTER 2

Calcutta and the Gardens of Barrackpore

BARRACKPORE, IN former times the country retreat of the governor-general of India, lies some fifteen miles upriver from Calcutta. A short distance, one would think, but enough to guarantee a respite from the sweltering heat that descended on the capital of British India for much of the year. Its gigantic trees, luxuriant shrubbery, and gentle lawn sloping down to the river's edge held the promise of shade and fresh breezes, even a hint of home in a distant land. Like the name of the place itself (referring to the nearby cantonment of soldiers), the garden was a hybrid, both Indian and English. As it evolved, it mirrored not only the individual tastes of the inhabitants of the house but also the exigencies of the country itself. At the moment when India was reeling from the unexpected ferocity of the Uprising of 1857, the gardens of Barrackpore reached their apogee under the gentle hand of Lady Charlotte Canning.[1]

From *Urbs Inter Paludes* to City of Palaces

By the late eighteenth century, Calcutta was renowned for its fine mansions and elegant public buildings. It boasted theaters, an orchestra, and even a choir that performed Handel's *Messiah* for homesick Britons.[2] Few would have foretold this flowering of culture, however, when Job Charnock founded the settlement on August 24, 1690, as a trading factory for the East India Company. Legendary for having snatched his future wife from the suttee pyre, Charnock was, in the laconic words of his epitaph, a "wanderer." He was also mean-spirited, cantankerous, and eccentric, but above all he had an iron constitution that enabled him to survive some thirty years in the pestilential remotenesses of the Bay of Bengal. Supposedly he chose the site of the future metropolis because of the pleasure he took in sitting and smoking a "meditative hookah under the shade of a spreading peepal tree" as he conducted business.[3] His superiors in Madras protested against the choice of a deserted fishing village of no obvious advantages, but history proved him right: a century later, Calcutta was the second city of the British Empire in spite of its insalubrious and often violent climate and the treacherous 125-mile passage up the Hughli, a branch of the Ganges, from the Bay of Bengal. While British India consisted of three autonomous presidencies, Calcutta was *primus inter pares,* the seat of the governor-general. When the Company was disbanded in 1858 and Queen Victoria became Queen of India, the governor-general assumed the august title of viceroy.

Nevertheless, the first few decades of the city's history were hardly promising. When Charnock died in 1693, there was as yet no factory; most of the merchants still lived in the stifling cabins of their boats or in mat hovels on the shore. The town took shape with no apparent plan, company agents enclosing land, digging tanks, and building more permanent houses where and as they pleased. Captain Alexander Hamilton, "an eighteenth-century Sinbad" who traded all over Asia and was often at odds with the East India Company, was not impressed with what he found twenty years after Charnock had marked out the site: "[Charnock] had the Liberty to settle an Emporium in any part of the River's Side below *Hughly* [an earlier post], and for the sake of a large shaddy [*sic*] Tree chose that Place, tho' he could not have chosen a more unhealthy Place on all the River; for three Miles to the North-eastward is a Salt-water Lake that overflows in *September* and *October,* and then prodigious numbers of fish resort thither, but in *November* and *December,* when the Floods are dissipated, those Fishes are left dry, and with their Putrefaction affect the Air with thick stinking Vapours, which the North-east Winds bring with them to Fort *William,* that they cause a yearly Mortality."[4] The "fever-haunted swamps" beyond the river also exacted a terrible toll. Hamilton estimated that of the 1,200 English resident in Calcutta in 1710, no fewer than 460 died between August and the following January.[5] Adding to these tribulations were French rivals upriver at Chandernagore and conflicts with local rulers, culminating in the temporary occupation of the fort and city by Siraj-ud-daula and the infamous episode of the Black Hole (1756).

At last, with English victories in 1757, the fortunes of the East India Company in general and Calcutta in particular rebounded, notwithstanding periodic setbacks from epidemics, famines, and cyclones. Calcutta soon eclipsed Surat, a continent away on the northwest coast, as the great emporium of India. With commercial success came almost legendary wealth, mirrored in both public and domestic architecture. A "Georgian city" rose from the malarial swamps.[6] Count Grandpré, visiting the city in 1789, declared it "the finest colony in the world," adding, "The magnificence of the edifices, the luxury which has covered the banks of the river into delightful gardens, and the costliness and elegance of their decorations, all denote the opulence and power of the conquerors of India and the masters of the Ganges."[7]

At the heart of the original settlement was Fort William, flanking the river on its eastern shore. It was subsequently rebuilt and shifted a little downriver. In its new incarnation it was considered impregnable "in case of invasion from abroad or rebellion at home," with "provisions and stores to withstand a siege as long as that of Troy."[8] Unlike the old Fort William, it was never put to the test. To the north of the fort was the Writers' Building, a long three-story building painted by the Daniells in 1786. Here lowly clerks and wealthy nabobs transacted the business of the East India Company, commonly known as "John Company." In time it was joined by the High Court, the Custom House, an array of churches and burial grounds, and the palatial Government House, built at the turn of the century by Lord Wellesley. Government House proved so costly that the Company recalled Wellesley before he could extend his extravagances to the weekend retreat of Barrackpore.

The lungs of the city were provided by the grassy—or dusty, depending on the season—*maidan,* the vast parade ground that would be replicated in cities throughout British India. Originally a "tiger-haunted jungle which cut off the village of Chowringhee from the river,"[9] it was cleared bit by bit. This, together with the filling in of the creek to the south, opened up the village of Chowringhee to European settlement. By the 1760s the Esplanade and Chowringhee were conspicuous for the fine Palladian houses of the wealthy: "Mansions with classical facades . . . set in smooth lawns with shrubberies and shade-giving trees."[10] At the northern end of the *maidan,* the Esplanade was a favorite promenade for "elegant walking parties" on moonlit evenings, although it was a long time before other parts of the *maidan* were finally rid of the "rascally characters" who had succeeded the tigers and would rob servants returning home at night.[11]

Anyone who could afford to also built a garden house along the river to escape the heat, filth, and plagues of the city. Before reaching the busy *ghats* and godowns of Calcutta itself, a visitor tacking up the Hughli in the 1780s would have come upon Garden Reach as a welcome surprise. After being tossed about "in small and confined quarters for anything from three months to a year, with few sights of land and rare stops to lighten the monotony of the voyage," he (it was usually *he* in the early years) would make the tedious journey upriver in an oar-propelled and mosquito-infested budgerow, arriving, in Percival Spear's memorable phrase, "in a very chastened frame of mind."[12] Then, marvelous to behold, Garden Reach came into view, "rising like a fairy isle . . . and offering to the view a succession of beautiful villas, surrounded by lofty trees."[13] In 1780 Eliza Fay described the garden houses as "elegant mansions, surrounded with groves and lawns which descend to the water's edge, and present[ing] a constant succession of whatever can delight the eye, or bespeak wealth and elegance in the owners."[14]

Sir William Jones, justice of the High Court, Orientalist, and founder of the Asiatic Society, had a house at Garden Reach to which he retreated each night, dating his letters as from "Gardens on the Ganges." Governor-General Warren Hastings, on the other hand, built a country retreat at Alipur, just upriver from Garden Reach, as well as a house and park, later known as Belvedere, south of the *maidan* in the city. Hastings was never happier than when pottering about his garden in shabby clothes, experimenting with "curious and valuable exotics from all quarters." At the same time, he also had honeysuckle and sweetbriar seeds sent out from England, instructing that they be packed for the voyage "in small bottles with ground-glass stoppers."[15] Hastings's nemesis, Philip Francis, also had both a mansion in the city and a villa in Alipur. "Here I live," he boasted to a friend in the 1770s, "master of the finest house in Bengal, with a hundred servants, a country house, and spacious gardens, horses and carriages."[16] Well might the East India Company inveigh against the sumptuous habits of its employees, listing gardens along with cook rooms and horses as unnecessary expenses, but London was far away and men on the spot could do pretty much as they pleased unless their excesses were on the scale of Wellesley's.[17]

Lest one paint too rosy a picture of the houses and gardens of Calcutta and its environs, it is well to remember that the city always had its detractors; Hamilton was the first but hardly the last. In 1767 a visitor to the city wrote that "after Madras, it does not appear much worthy describing [*sic*], for although it is large, with a great many good houses in it, it is as awkward a place as can be conceived; and so irregular that it looks as if all the houses had been thrown up in the air, and fallen down again by accident as they now stand." To make matters worse, "the appearance of the best houses is spoiled by the little straw huts . . . which are built up by the servants for themselves to sleep in: so that all the English part of the town . . . is a confusion of very superb and very shabby houses, dead walls straw huts, warehouses and I know not what."[18] In contrast to the palaces of Chowringhee, the huts of "Black Town" were mostly of mud and thatched, "perfectly resembling the cabins of the poorest class in Ireland."[19] Sir George Trevelyan declared Calcutta to be "so bad by nature that human efforts could do little to make it worse: but that little has been done faithfully and assiduously."[20] Rudyard Kipling is responsible for the enduring image of Calcutta as the "city of the dreadful night'" (the title of a book of essays, later recycled to apply to Lahore as well).[21]

What did the early gardens of Calcutta look like? They are often mentioned but rarely described. Many were undoubtedly utilitarian, growing fruit and vegetables. In 1712 John Burnell found the garden adjoining the Company's factory "abounding in sallading and sweet herbs, beans, pease and turnips." But it was not "wanting in flowers, of which it hath variety" and had "a fine shady walk, and a noble large fish-pond." A visitor in 1748 was impressed with the "elegant, airy and spacious" town houses of the British, "with Gardens producing, Fruits, Vegetables and Flowers of the Torrid and many of those peculiar to the temperate Climes."[22]

The garden houses that came into their own later in the century, however, had greater pretensions. An account of 1792 refers to them as "surrounded by verdant grounds laid out in the English style,"[23] meaning that they probably attempted to translate the landscapes in vogue in late eighteenth-century England, the "natural" style of Capability Brown and his followers, with an emphasis not on flowers but on trees and lawns and ornamental structures, on the creation of picturesque perspectives—thus Fay's groves and lawns descending to the water's edge. This seems still to have been typical of Garden Reach in the late 1820s, when Elizabeth Fenton enthused about a "beautiful house . . . on the bank of the river, in an extensive lawn sprinkled with cedar, teak, and mango trees." There were even a few goats and cows taking shelter from the heat in the shade of banyan thickets. A series of plans and illustrations of Hastings's Belvedere estate, on the other hand, show an evolution over the century following his departure from India that mirrors changing styles at home but with a significant time lag. The earliest, drawn in 1794, shows the grounds laid out in a simple, geometric pattern in front and behind the house. A plan from 1828 indicates a shift away from formal straight lines and rectangles to groupings of trees along the boundary and surrounding walks. Not long after, the main garden area to the south of the house was transformed into a large lawn leading to a tank and with a path shaded by mature trees winding around it, proper for walking. Finally, shrubs and beds bordered the building itself.[24]

Phebe Gibbes's description of Park St. Cemetery, the oldest in the city, may suggest the patterns of other gardens and parks: "Obelisks, pagodas, &c. are erected at great expence; and the whole spot is surrounded by as well-turned a walk as those you traverse in Kensington Gardens, ornamented with a double row of aromatic trees, which afford a solemn and beautiful shade: in a word, not old Windsor churchyard, with all its cypress and yews, is in the smallest degree comparable to them." Predictably, her description follows reflections on the omnipresence of death in Calcutta and the brevity of life in its clime: "Born just to bloom and fade."[25]

The invocation of British parallels would be a staple of all such commentaries on gardens and parks in India for the next century and a half. The first glimpse of Calcutta's gleaming white houses in 1824 inspired Bishop Heber to compare the effect to that of "Connaught-place . . . as seen from a distance across Hyde Park."[26] In 1836 Emily Eden described a house and garden in

Garden Reach as "much like any of the Fulham villas, only the rooms are much larger; but the lawn is quite as green and rivers are rivers everywhere."[27] The botanist Joseph Hooker was so impressed with the riverfront gardens of a chief justice that he dubbed them the "Chatsworth of India," a reference to the great estate of the Duke of Devonshire and his pioneering gardener, Joseph Paxton.[28] Later visitors scaled down their praises, referring, for example, to the "cockney-looking villas" along the riverbank, or invoked their counterparts at Richmond.[29] Edward Lear, too, couldn't resist branding the Eden Gardens, laid out about 1840 by Emily and Fanny Eden and considered the pride of Calcutta, as "a sort of Cockney-Calcutta Kensington Gardens."[30] In due time the Gardens would sport a cricket pitch, a sports stadium, and a racecourse.[31] The *maidan* itself struck a visiting journalist at the turn of the century as "magnificently English, Clapham Common, Hyde Park & Sandown Park all in one."[32] Of course the clubs that became so integral a part of British Calcutta replicated life back home even down to the trim lawns and rustic chairs ("Bombay fornicators") beneath the shade trees; here expatriates could "perhaps imagine themselves on an uncommonly stifling day at home in or on a visit to the suburban woodlands of England."[33]

During the nineteenth century, flowers came to play a much larger part in gardens in England, prompting heated debates about how best to display them. An expanding bourgeoisie could choose from a cornucopia of exotics from all around the world as well as hybrids newly created by horticulturists and nurserymen at home. In India, however, there was already enough that was exotic, and many gardeners yearned for those gardens that seemed to them quintessentially English, even if more and more old-fashioned. Lawns and shade trees were the irreducible minimum; the rest was problematic. Much as Bishop Heber admired the stately houses of Calcutta, "ornamented with Grecian pillars," he found that they were surrounded "for the most part . . . by a little apology for a garden."[34]

Nevertheless, the wife of a chief judge managed to grow violets and sweetbriar in her Garden Reach estate and therefore, Emily Eden allowed, "probably has many other good qualities."[35] But Eden lamented in her diary: "We cannot achieve a cowslip and nobody has ever seen a daisy, but the yucca . . . with its thousands of white bells, grows along the sides of every road, and lovely it looks. Then there are roses all the year round; that is some compensation."[36] Still, the "Sahib" who published an article in the *Calcutta*

Review in 1849 insisted that "although the general opinion is exactly the opposite . . . there is no place in the world, where the flower-garden affords a more pleasing amusement" nor any city in the world with such facilities for gardening as in Calcutta. Whereas in England one has to wait for months to decide if something will grow, and then the verdict is usually negative, in Calcutta results are almost instantaneous. Even as he wrote he claimed to be looking out on a garden "which we venture to say contains as many fine flowers as could be found in any garden in England"—and at much less cost. With a nod to Roberts's complaint, he acknowledged that one could not enjoy a walk in the garden during the heat of midday, but "where in the wide world is there a greater proportion of really enjoyable mornings and evenings than in this maligned climate of Bengal?" He cited a number of beauties, such as the poinsettia introduced by Lord Auckland (brother of Emily and Fanny Eden), bougainvillea, and other flowering shrubs. Poinsettias, indeed, were a reliable standby, along with mangoes, jackfruit, and other oriental trees, but these were hardly the flowers of home.[37]

To feed the nostalgia for English flowers and vegetables, Calcutta importers offered a wide assortment of seeds. One advertisement announced that recently arrived stock was "warranted, having been tried in a garden near Calcutta, and all have succeeded." It included the familiar staples of the English cottage garden: stock, carnation, marigold, larkspur, mignonette, honeysuckle, polyanthus, poppy, and Sweet William. Several decades later another firm advertised eleven sorts of European fruit trees and several thousand European annuals and perennials. While British officials were encouraged to collect Indian specimens for the mother country, the Horticultural Society of London and private nurseries contributed plants they deemed best suited to India in a reciprocal exchange.[38]

Europeans in Calcutta had no monopoly on gardens. Amid the squalor and jumble of the Indian quarters of the city, some of the rajahs and wealthy merchants had homes every bit as grand (and as Grecian) as their British counterparts. Of the quarter inhabited by Armenians, Parsees, and Bengalis, Emma Roberts wrote that "the avenues which lead to these mansions are exceedingly narrow, but the premises themselves are often very extensive, the principal apartments looking out upon pretty gardens, decorated with that profusion of flowers which renders every part of Calcutta so blooming."[39] Among the earliest and richest was the wily Punjabi Sikh Omichand, who amassed a fortune as middleman "between Country and Company" during the tenure of the equally wily Robert Clive.[40] The Chitpore *nawab,* Mahomed Reza Khan, the representative of the Great Mughal during the second half of the eighteenth century, boasted an estate whose buildings were sumptuously furnished and whose gardens were laid out in English style. "They not only cover a wide extent of ground but are furnished with all the beauties and perfumes of the vegetable kingdom."[41] Mughal influence was more evident in the garden of Babu Hurree Mohun Thakur, described by Bishop Heber as "laid out in formal parterres of roses intersected by straight walks, with some fine trees, and a chain of tanks, fountains and summer-houses."[42]

A later "pleasure mansion" belonged to the scion of the Tagore family, Babu Dwarkanath Tagore, the wealthy merchant prince whom we met in the last chapter. Tagore aggressively bestrode the Indian and English worlds of his time, the role that had caused his banishment from the family home because of ritual "impurity." Undaunted, he created a lavish country villa at Jorasanko. In its heyday in the 1830s and early 1840s, Belgatchia was viewed as a second Government House, the grandest of the *bhadralok* palaces—the houses of the westernizing elite of Bengal. Tagore redesigned what had formerly been the country house of Lord Auckland with the aid of an English architect, "the gardens and pleasure-grounds being laid out in a style correspondent with the interior." This meant a spacious lawn "adorned with a mosaic of flower beds, enlivened and refreshed by a beautiful sheet of water" that was spanned by four rustic bridges, with a fountain in the center, and, beyond this, an artificial lake. Sprinkled throughout the grounds were classical statues, Japanese temples, Chinese pagodas, and pillars topped with flames. Here Tagore received "entirely after the European fashion," even serving meat (except for beef), although a Hindu. Renowned for his hospitality, he held lavish garden parties, complete with elephants on the lawn and boats on the tank, and generously lent the mansion to European brides and grooms as a honeymoon retreat. Emily Eden, a hard guest to please (especially where Indians were concerned), declared that Tagore was "the only man in the country who gives pleasant parties." After his death in England in 1845, the family was forced to auction much of the estate to pay off debts, leaving the surrounding gardens sadly diminished.[43]

Family tastes changed, too. Dwarkanath's grandson, the Nobel Prize–

winning poet Rabindranath Tagore, has left a charming description of the very different, very disheveled garden of his Calcutta childhood in the 1870s:

> To call our inner garden a garden is to say a deal too much. Its properties consisted of a citron tree, a couple of plum trees of different varieties, and a row of cocoanut trees, In the centre was a paved circle the cracks of which various grasses and weeds had invaded and planted in them their victorious standards. Only those flowering plants which refused to die of neglect continued uncomplainingly to perform their respective duties without casting any aspersions on the gardener. . . . None the less I suspect that Adam's garden of Eden could hardly have been better adorned than this one of ours; for he and his paradise were alike naked; they needed not to be furnished with material things.[44]

No pretense of an English garden here (Fig. 17).[45]

Perhaps the most unusual "occidentalist" creation of all was the Marble Palace, built in North Calcutta in 1835 by Rajendro Mullick, a wealthy Bengali merchant. A massive Palladian mansion complete with Greek columns and architrave, stuffed full of western paintings, statuary, and curios, it is set in the midst of a vast garden adorned with "a fountain . . . that would not be out of place in the Piazza Navona" and home to "pelicans and peacocks, mallard and teal." On the surface the palace would seem to be an homage to all things European, but in its private apartments and religious observances it determinedly asserted Mullick's devout attachment to the Hinduism of his forebears.[46] Remarkably, the Marble Palace still survives (and is lived in) in a quarter of Calcutta once known as the "thieves' garden."

The easygoing relations between Europeans and Indians in the eighteenth century gave way to greater social distance in the nineteenth. European visitors continued to extol the "enchanting beauty of European houses and gardens in Garden Reach" during the first half of the century. In 1857, however, the deposed king of Awadh (Oudh) and "his swarm of followers" (estimated, no doubt with some exaggeration, at 40,000) acquired the beautiful house and grounds of a former chief justice and re-created a microcosm of *nawabi* culture complete with a menagerie boasting tigers, venomous snakes, and a hookah-smoking chimpanzee. Many Europeans declared the suburb irreparably

Fig. 17. "The inner garden was my paradise"
[Rabindranath Tagore, *My Reminiscences*, 1917]

tarnished and fled to the colonnaded mansions of Chowringhee. Now out of vogue, Garden Reach was gradually overrun with railroad offices, agencies handling foreign coolie emigration, docks, mills, and the like.[47]

There were other changes as well. By midcentury the railroad was putting its stamp on Calcutta as on all of India. A company town was created ex nihilo outside of the city, devoted solely to the needs of the East Indian Railway and inhabited by its servants. "Its general aspect," according to Kipling, "is that of an English village, such a thing as enterprising stage-managers put on the theatres at home." Laid out "with military precision" in the 1850s or early 1860s, Jamalpur's houses were all of a single design: one- or two-story bungalows loyally situated along Prince's Road, Queen's Road, Victoria Road, Albert Road, and Steam Road. Each house had its "just share of garden," a pounded brick path, and its "neat little wicket gate." The gardens of the town were shaded with crotons, palms, mangoes, mellingtonias, teak, and bamboos, while brilliant color was supplied by poinsettias, bougainvillea, the so-called railway creeper (morning glory), and *Bignonia venusta*.[48]

The *Maidan*

The glory of Calcutta was the *maidan*. A word of Persian origin, it referred to a large open space, in this case a sort of oversized—two miles by one mile— village common. Sir Edwin Arnold pronounced it "about the finest piece of open ground possessed by any capital."[49] Earlier, Bishop Heber described it as a "vast square . . . grassed over, and divided by broad roads of 'pucka' or pounded brick with avenues of tall trees stocked with immense flights of crows."[50] An 1860 watercolor painting of the southern corner of the *maidan* probably exaggerates its bucolic as well as its multicultural aspects, with a pair of cows reposing in the shade in the foreground next to a small Hindu temple, several native women with loads on their heads in the middle ground, and the spire of St. Paul's Cathedral in the background (see Pl. 3). A view from the Esplanade at the other end of the *maidan* a decade earlier is equally romantic: it shows a procession dominated by an elephant with howdah, a camel, and a bullock cart, also enclosed with a domed canopy. Only Indians are depicted, save for two British soldiers leaning against a fence, but Government House and the architecture of imperial Britain loom across the entire background of the print.

In spite of these Orientalist depictions, however, the *maidan* was quintessentially British space, "a necessity of English life," as the journalist G. W. Steevens put it.[51] Here small English children would ride out for exercise on beautifully bedecked ponies, accompanied by a retinue of *ayahs*, coachmen, umbrella bearers, watchmen, syces and other attendants for man and beast.[52] Calcuttans were also constantly reminded of its military purpose as a parade ground: On New Year's Day, for example, the entire garrison turned out for the Proclamation Parade.[53] With the fort and the river on one edge, the *maidan* was surrounded on the other three sides with majestic neoclassical buildings, "a line of shining white houses, elaborately porticoed and colonnaded."⁵⁴ They formed both a barrier and a contrast to the Black Town that lay beyond to the east. It was all too English, however, to suit Lady Canning: "There is nothing Eastern or picturesque here. It is like the Regents Park—large and good houses, and . . . not a particle of Indian architecture." The view from her quarters at Government House was "covered with short *green* turf, and quantities of small cattle, like the ugly part of Hyde Park."⁵⁵

As the century progressed many of these stately mansions were replaced by stores, hotels, and boardinghouses in the ubiquitous red brick, a change that Steevens attributed to the fact that the British no longer settled for a lifetime in India but had become temporary sojourners, staying for five or ten years and then returning home for good, all this made possible by speedier means of transportation.⁵⁶ They had little incentive to match the extravagant but lovingly created garden houses of an earlier era. Steevens might also have added that the civil servants of a later period no longer had the same opportunity to amass huge fortunes as the nabobs of the East India Company.

Lord Dalhousie supervised the planting of trees on the *maidan*, but many of these were blown down in the great cyclone of 1864.⁵⁷ A photograph of the northern end from the 1870s shows only a scatter of trees, but many were subsequently replanted. Sir Evan Cotton, historian of Calcutta at the height of the Raj, declared that "there are few sights which can challenge comparison with the *maidan* when it is ablaze with the scarlet splendour of the blossoming gold mohur trees."⁵⁸ While the tanks scattered around the *maidan*, from which much of the populace drew its water, were fringed with cool green foliage, there were no flower gardens on the *maidan*. These were left for the Eden Gardens at its northwestern corner: a large "green sward," winding paths, a winding artificial lake with an arched stone bridge, "realistic artificial rocks cropping out of the grass . . . a genuine Burmese pagoda," and "a profusion of flowering trees and shrubs."⁵⁹ A photograph in Arnold's account shows the tank surrounded by an abundance of vegetation, not easily identifiable except for the palm trees,⁶⁰ but it did sport the horticultural symbol of empire, a *Victoria amazonica* water lily.⁶¹ "A pleasanter place for a morning or evening stroll," Cotton concluded with justifiable pride, "cannot be found."⁶² With the "unending file of carriages" passing up and down to watch the sunset and the band playing in the bandstand, it is small wonder that Steevens felt that everything an Englishman could wish for was at hand. And just for reassurance, the *maidan* was crowned with statues of Hardinge, Lawrence, Mayo, Outram, Dufferin, and Roberts, proconsuls all.[63]

Nevertheless, when Lord Curzon arrived in Calcutta as viceroy in 1899, he found the city sorely in need of uplift and set out with his customary energy, indeed single-mindedness, to remedy the situation. Roads and footpaths were improved and extended; lighting was installed in the business quarter. He was distressed that the *maidan* was so bare—"unbroken," he later claimed, "by a single enclosure or even by a single tree."[64] He had flowerbeds laid out at its northern end, still known as Curzon Gardens.[65] Dalhousie Square and its tank were renovated and replanted as well: "I laid out the ground afresh, squared the famous Lal Dighi, or Red Tank, surrounded it with a pillared balustrade and a beautiful garden, swept away the unsightly sheds and public conveniences, and converted it into an open-air resort for the public and a Valhalla for the Bengal Government." Hither, too, he transferred a number of statues of imperial "forefathers." As a last gesture, he tidied up the debris-ridden area from Esplanade Row to the Ochterlony Monument, filling in the Dharamtolla Tank and converting the entire area into an "exquisite garden." Some years later he noted sadly that "the site has not indeed relapsed into a wilderness, but my garden planning lost a good deal of the symmetry and completeness which I designed."[66]

Government House

All these projects Curzon saw as enhancing the majesty of Government House itself, the viceroy's abode, and "rendering seemly its immediate surroundings and approaches (to which nobody in recent years seemed to have devoted even a passing thought), and thus enabling Calcutta, a city that aroused my warmest affection, to vindicate the proud title which destiny at that time seemed to have placed within her grasp, of Queen of the Eastern Seas."[67] It was a curious coincidence that a century earlier Wellesley had adapted the design of Government House from plans of Curzon's own family seat, Kedleston Hall in Derbyshire. Curzon himself was an architect/landscape designer manqué. Or perhaps not really manqué since he was, as we will see, a compulsive renovator of gardens as well as buildings in India and in England.

Job Charnock had had to make do with a thatched hut. In subsequent years, as John Company's fortunes improved, it housed its governors-general in more opulent quarters, although no more opulent than those of other wealthy merchants. This did not suit Richard Wellesley. Flush with the defeat of Tipu Sultan in 1799, he set about creating a palace to match his sense of his own importance and that of the empire he was determined to extend. In so doing he displayed the same "sublime indifference" to his London overlords as he did in his military adventures; taking advantage of the fact that communications from London required the better part of a year to make their way to Calcutta, he simply ignored cautions and rebukes from the Council of Directors.[68]

His friend Lord Valentia, who attended the inaugural ceremonies of the new mansion in 1803, defended it against charges of "Asiatic pomp":[69]

> India is a country of splendor, of extravagance, and of outward appearances: that the Head of a mighty Empire ought to conform himself to the prejudices of the country over which he rules; and that the British, in particular, ought to emulate the splendid work of the Princes of the House of Timour [i.e., the Mughals], lest it be supposed that we merit the reproach which our great rivals, the French, have ever cast upon us, of being altogether influenced by a sordid, mercantile spirit. In short, I wish India to be governed from a palace, not from a counting house; with the ideas of a Prince, not with those of a retail dealer in muslins and indigo.[70]

Bishop Heber's judgment was more succinct. "Government House," he declared, "is, to say the least of it, a more showy palace than London has to produce."[71] Grand it might be, and yet Government House had its awkward aspects. At midcentury, there were still no WCs in all of Calcutta, including Government House.[72]

There was so little accommodation for guests in the mansion that at Christmastime, when they arrived in great numbers, they had to stay in tents on the lawn. Lord Lytton complained that it was full of cockroaches the size of elephants. Then there was the matter of the kitchen: it was "somewhere in Calcutta," Lady Dufferin commented, "but not in this house."[73] In fact it was some two hundred yards distant, in the squalid streets to the north, so that every dish had to be carried in green wooden boxes, rather like a sedan chair, with "no means of keeping the soufflés from collapsing on the way."[74] This was not remedied until the early twentieth century.

But what is most striking about early views of the new Government House is how barren it looks (see Pl. 4). An engraving accompanying Maria Graham's *Journal of a Residence in India* of 1809–11 confirms this: No trees, no gardens, no leafy paths in the twenty-six acres of grounds.[75] Were they afraid the tigers, newly removed from the *maidan*, might again take up residence if the foliage were too inviting? For several decades the only decoration seems to have been provided by guns commemorating notable imperial campaigns, beginning with the victory over Tipu Sultan at Srirangapatnam. Twenty years later Lord Hastings imported "fine sparkling gravel" all the way from Bayswater to mark the walks of the house. But the building itself was so exposed—"like a huge wedding cake on a bare table cloth"—that a viewer on the *maidan* could see clearly every window and doorway in the southern facade.[76] During the years of the great uprising, 1857 and 1858, it was said that the lonely figure of Lord Canning might be seen through the balustrade, pacing the (Bayswater) gravel paths, the only exercise he allowed himself during those troubled months.[77] The openness of the grounds did lend themselves to croquet. Sir John Lawrence, viceroy in the mid-1860s, was so fond of the game that he would often continue to play by lamplight after the short Indian twilight, to the delight of spectators massed in the street beyond the paling.[78]

There were sporadic attempts at a garden before midcentury. Lady Amherst made a start in the 1820s, creating a "magnificent garden round the house."[79] Her daughter Sarah Elizabeth described it in a letter to her brother. On the west side was a flower garden, one part of which "resembles the parterre before the conservatory at Oakly Park [the family home in England]. This is on Mama's side [the governor and his wife inhabited opposite wings of Government House] and the beds are full of beautiful shrubs and flowers and creepers raised on bamboo baskets. On Papa's side there are larger flowering shrubs dotted about on the grass, and in front [on the north side of the building] large clumps. . . . On the south side of the house, the circle only is planted and the large field of grass left untouched, and beyond it we look over a fine plain of grass [the *maidan*] enlivened with numerous flocks of cattle." An artist of some skill, Sarah made several drawings of the house. One shows the circle of flowers set rather starkly in the open space in front of the south

Fig. 18. Lady Sarah Elizabeth Amherst,
the south front of Government House, Calcutta. Pen and ink
[The British Library Board, WD 3904]

portico (Fig. 18). This, Sarah explained, was the "private side of the house," open only to the privileged few. In the center was a beautiful marble basin. It had been brought hither from Shah Jahan's imperial bath in Agra in 1825 with the intention of making a fountain, but the water of the Hughli proved too muddy and the problems of raising it from the river too intractable; instead the Amhersts had "two arches of iron made to spring from the angles and meet at the top and with creepers planted at the foot it has a very pretty effect." Another drawing shows the majestic staircase on the north side used for formal arrivals and departures, and indicates the "clumps" referred to in the letter as well as a regular pattern of circular flowerbeds.[80]

Unfortunately, Lady Bentinck, who succeeded Lady Amherst as chatelaine of Government House, considered flowers "very unwholesome" and saw to it that everything was immediately uprooted. Emily Eden in her turn embarked on a restoration, setting out a garden "close by the house," in an area where there were no flowers.[81] As depicted in a lithograph made in 1847, a few years after Eden left Calcutta, these gardens consisted of an ornate hourglass pattern of flowers or shrubs, with a central walk leading into a rectangular garden (Fig. 19). Unfortunately, Eden does not say what she planted, and the garden seems to have disappeared by the time Charlotte Canning arrived in 1856. Nevertheless, Lady Canning was enraptured to find a little gem of a garden right under her window at Government House. An accomplished botanist and artist in her own right, she described it in some detail in a letter home: "By this enormous house it looks small and like a London square. The flowers, however, are most beautiful, and there is no smoke to spoil them. Imagine Cape jessamine as high as shrubbery laurels and covered with flowers, scarlet ixoras the same. The roses are very lovely and of a kind I never saw before—very sweet for a short time, and in clusters of six or seven on a branch. Then there are scarlet euphorbias, pancratiums, white bedechium, and scarlet amaryllis, many sorts of Jessamine and palms, oleanders, double hibiscus, &c."[82]

An engraving made to accompany the published volume of her letters and journals shows the south facade of the house with an extensive lawn, bordered with some of the plants she lists along a path (presumably the one her

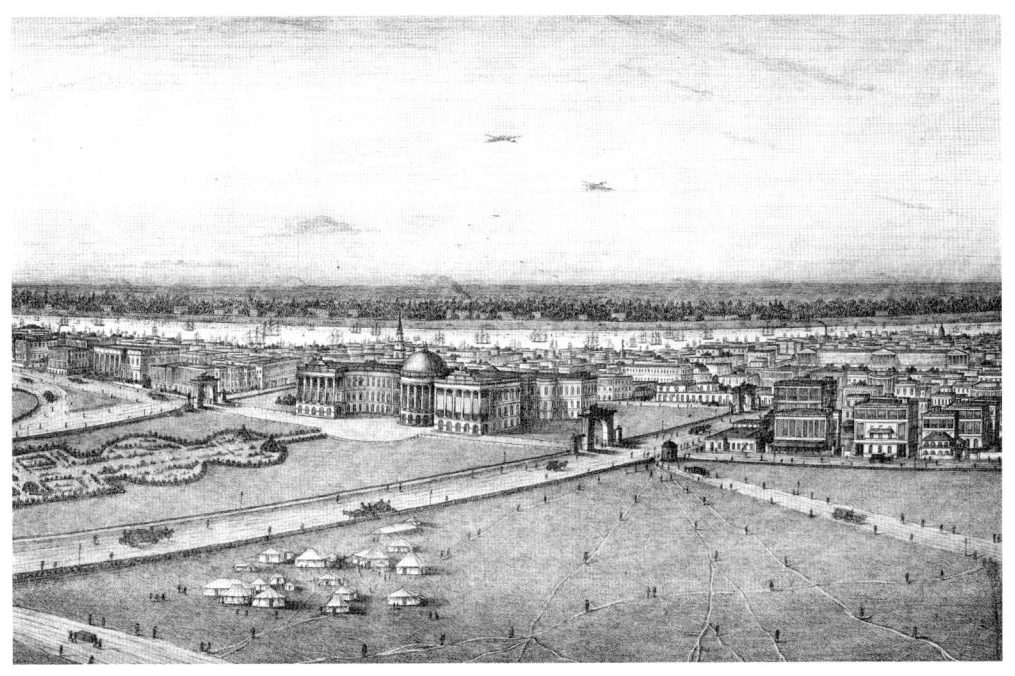

Fig. 19. Frederick Fiebig, Government House, *View of Calcutta*, 1847
[The British Library Board, APAC P65-70]

Fig. 20. Government House, Calcutta

[From Augustus J. C. Hare, *The Story of Two Noble Lives*, 1893]

husband was to pace a year later), but still few trees except for palms (Fig. 20). Eventually two of these were planted on either side of the majestic staircase on the north side of the building, with ivy circling their trunks—"England and India intertwining."[83] The staircase was used only for ceremonial occasions (*durbars*); since the palms furnished no shade at all, the "nobles of Hindostan [who] come in all their barbaric pomp to pay their respects at the Viceregal Court" were still left to wilt as they toiled up the "noble flights of steps" in the blazing heat of Calcutta, just as they were in Emma Roberts's day.[84]

The garden was seriously expanded in the 1870s and 1880s under the "fostering care" of vicereines Lady Mayo and Lady Lytton.[85] By the turn of the century Government House was completely screened off from the *maidan*; only the dome and the parapet were visible through the "umbrageous garden." The foliage became so rapacious that it had to be cut away, lest it swallow up the sculpted lions surmounting the gateways. Visitors remarked on the "splendid clusters of trees" and "flowery parterres." There were great lawns of *doob* grass, intersected by "leafy walks and winding ponds." The garden itself was enclosed by a dense belt of bamboos, palms, and other tropical flora, so dense, in fact, that for a time it was home to a colony of thirty to forty *malis* (gardeners) living in mat huts and entirely hidden from view.[86]

Once a year the grounds were thrown open for the State Garden Party, to which some fifteen hundred to two thousand of the cream of Calcutta society were invited, both European and Indian. The tea party was not only an English institution, it was also, as Percival Spear has explained, the rare occasion that neatly circumvented the dietary obstacles to social interaction between Hindus, Muslims, and Christians.[87] To add to the beauty of the scene, clouds of green parakeets erupted from the trees and roosted on the cornices of the mansion. Still, Curzon admitted that it was, "like all garden parties, a somewhat depressing function." When it was moved to the evening, it was more exciting: "At that hour great flying foxes or bats used to lurch from tree to tree . . . ; toward midnight jackals emerged from the drains and howled in the shrubbery, and stinking civet cats would clamber up the pillars or pipes to the roof of Government House. There they liked to linger, sometimes descending at night and even entering the bedrooms on the Southern side, in surreptitious search of food or drink."[88] The greater seclusion of the garden guaranteed greater privacy for the human inhabitants of Government House as well, who could wander or play croquet now free from the gaze of strangers.

Enthralled by the rich history of Calcutta, Curzon could not resist buying Hastings House on behalf of the Indian government. Warren Hastings built it about the time of his marriage to Marian Imhoff in 1777, giving up Belvedere, his earlier estate in Alipur. With its huge shady jackfruit tree and receding parkland, it forms the idyllic background for Johann Zoffany's "conversation piece" painting of the governor-general and his wife (Fig. 21). This was the house that Hastings tried to replicate on the banks of the Thames at Daylesford, where he "laid out the grounds after the fashion of an Indian country seat," extravagantly planting mangoes from Bengal along with Lombardy poplars, acacia, tamarisk, and tulip trees. Whether the estate was in the end more Indian or more English seems to have depended on the eye of the beholder.[89]

By the time of Curzon's arrival Hastings House was "bedraggled and unkempt" but "alive with memories," at least to one of his romantic sensibilities. The excuse for the purchase was that a proper venue was sorely needed to entertain visiting Indian princes when they came to the capital. While the princes received touring viceroys "with truly regal splendour," when they returned the visit, they were "compelled to put up in mediocre hotels where they were mer-

Fig. 21. Johann Zoffany, *Warren Hastings and Mrs. Hastings, c. 1784–86*
[Victoria Memorial Hall, Calcutta]

cilessly fleeced." Hastings House proved the ideal remedy to this humiliating situation. It also provided Curzon with ample opportunity to indulge his architectural and landscaping passions: "I took an immense amount of trouble about the place, laying out and planting the gardens, weeding and mowing the lawns, cleaning the tank, and entirely refurnishing the house. I converted one wing into a fine durbar room for the exchange of the obligatory visits with the Princes, I provided a billiard room for those who had modern tastes (a not inconsiderable number), and I arranged the bedrooms and bathrooms in suitable manner upstairs." Above the portico he affixed a tablet:

THIS HOUSE KNOWN AS HASTINGS HOUSE
ORIGINALLY THE COUNTRY SEAT OF
WARREN HASTINGS
FIRST GOVERNOR GENERAL OF FORT WILLIAM IN BENGAL (1774–1785)
WAS BOUGHT AS A GUESTHOUSE FOR GOVERNMENT BY
LORD CURZON
VICEROY AND GOVERNOR GENERAL OF INDIA IN 1901

The house functioned perfectly, hosting a roster of maharajas and other worthies until "in an evil hour" the government of India was moved to Delhi in 1912.[90]

Barrackpore

Curzon himself pointed out the irony embedded in the splendor of Calcutta's Government House. It has always been, he noted, "a sort of nomad camp, albeit invested with the dignity and stability of a permanent habitation. For at least seven and frequently eight months of each year it remained . . . unoccupied and closed. . . . Then suddenly in the month of December it leaped into life, and a feverish activity converted it into the place of residence and daily work of hundreds of human beings," to say nothing of the scene of gala entertainments and official pomp.[91] The seven or eight months when it remained unoccupied were those in which the heat and stench of Calcutta were unbearable, and the government moved upriver to Barrackpore and, soon after midcentury, to Simla. Calcutta's gentry followed suit, shifting their own retreats from the older suburbs to Barrackpore and its environs.

East India Company correspondence refers to a series of "garden houses" providing an escape from the "pestilential smells and abominable unhealthiness" of an already congested Calcutta before Lord Wellesley settled on the site upriver from Calcutta, farther from the city than Garden Reach or Alipur and with fresher air and clearer water. Barrackpore had begun as a British cantonment in 1775. Gradually it acquired bungalows and more elaborate buildings to house senior officers. In 1801 Wellesley appropriated the residence hitherto reserved for the commander-in-chief of the forces. His intention was to tear it down and replace it with a splendid palace in a beautifully landscaped park, a rural twin for his newly erected Government House in the city. Demolition was complete and rebuilding under way when he was recalled by his irate employers; these extravagances were the final straw. Wellesley's successors were thus faced with an empty shell and a pile of construction materials.[92]

Even the shell had its admirers, thanks to the bosky, riverain setting. Stepping ashore on a moonlit night in 1810, Maria Graham was seized by an excess of Romantic enthusiasm: "Its unfinished arches showed by the moonlight like an ancient ruin, and completed the beauty of the scenery." Something about the scenery brought to mind the banks of the Thames—"the same verdure, the same rich foliage, the same majestic body of water." Grandly trampling on Alexander Pope's injunction to "consult the Genius of the Place in all," Wellesley had attacked the flat muddy jungle of the riverbank and transformed it into a park that any English nobleman would have envied. Marshes were drained, earth mounded up to form hillocks—"*mountains* . . . 15 or 20 feet above the valleys"—and undulating lawns, tanks dug and rimmed with ornaments, bridges and roadways laid out, all the while preserving the magnificent shade trees of the site. The governor-general was pleasantly surprised to find that as convict labor became more and more skilled, it could replace day laborers, a rare nod to economy. Fortunately for those who came after, the park was largely finished before he was recalled. "The grounds around this retreat," wrote a contemporary of Graham, "are laid out with infinite taste in imitation of our parks in England, and produce a splendid effect on the eye." To be sure, the trees "through whose branches the moon threw her flickering beams on the river" were not the stately oaks and elms, larches and beeches of an English country home but tamarinds, *peepals*, mangoes, acacias, and coconut palms.[93]

Eventually Wellesley's half-built palace was pulled down and a new one constructed. Although slightly elevated so that it commanded a view more than six miles down the river, it was rather modest by the standards of the day, scarcely able to accommodate the governor-general and his family. This suited Emily Eden very well, since it meant that guests were not underfoot but were housed in thatched bungalows arranged within the park.[94] Gradually, however, the house was expanded and other attractions added to the grounds: an artificial lake at the north front, graced by an Arcadian bridge (see Pl. 5), an aviary and menagerie, and an elephant stud; a Temple of Fame and Gothic ruin (belated nods to English landscape fashion); and later tennis courts and a golf course. For more than a century the estate was the retreat where the governor-general "could throw off some of the restraints, if few of the cares of State, and where his wife or himself could find in the delights of the garden or in the amusements of the menagerie, the elephant, and the links, some relief from the ceaseless persecution of official routine." True, the dispatch boxes followed him, and for many months of the year Barrackpore was the seat of government itself. Nevertheless, as Lord Minto so pithily put it: "Barrackpore takes the sting out of India."[95]

But the chief glory of Barrackpore was the park (Fig. 22). It covered some

Fig. 22. Park at Barrackpoor
[From Bishop Reginald Heber, *Narrative of a Journey through the Upper Provinces of India*, 1828]

three hundred acres, with a circumference of about three miles. Visitors and officials alike were unanimous in their praise of its "enchanted glades." Although almost everything about it was artificial, most concurred with Lady Amherst that it was so well done as to appear "perfectly natural."[96] Capability Brown would have approved. Among the many descriptions from the first half of the nineteenth century, Emma Robert's is the most complete. Since she counted the trip to Barrackpore from Calcutta "enchanting for those who delight in forest-scenery," let us join her on her way from the capital.

The journey could be made by boat, but then one was at the mercy of the tides. Roberts therefore came by land, taking advantage of the road staked out by Wellesley himself, "one of the finest roads in the world, very broad, kept in excellent repair, and shaded, to the great delight and comfort of the various traversers, by an avenue of trees." Was Wellesley thinking of his Hindu and Mughal predecessors who lined the thoroughfares of their empire with ranks of shade trees? The road was always busy, with "*coolies* and *hurkaras* [messengers] of every description journeying to and fro at all hours of the day," although the English tended to avoid the midday sun (*pace* Noel Coward). "A dense jungle appears to close in on either side. Native huts, of the wildest and simplest construction, meet the eye in the most picturesque situations, many with scarcely any roof excepting that afforded by the overhanging branches of trees, which never lose their leafy mantles."

CALCUTTA AND THE GARDENS OF BARRACKPORE

Once arrived at Barrackpore, only the house of the governor-general was immediately visible, thanks to its "commanding situation." The other buildings were

> embosomed in trees . . . and only peep out between the branches of luxuriant groves. The country all round is wooded to excess, affording a most agreeable shade, and offering specimens of floral magnificence not to be surpassed in any part of the world. The magnolia attains to a gigantic size, and fills the air with perfume from its silvery vases; other forest-trees bear blossoms of equal beauty; the richly-wreathed pink acacia, and numerous tribes, adorned with garlands of deep crimson and bright yellow abound; and although, with the exception of the park, which has been raised into sweeping undulations by artificial means, the cantonments and their vicinity present a flat surface, the combinations of wood, water, and green sward, in numberless vistas, nooks, and small open spaces, yield scenes of tranquil beauty, which eyes however cold can scarcely contemplate unmoved.

However much Wellesley's extravagance may have alarmed his superiors, the park he created, Roberts declared, "is justly considered one of the finest specimens of dressed and ornamented nature which taste has ever produced . . . and the gardens attached to [the mansion] are unrivalled both in beauty and stateliness, combining the grandeur of Asiatic proportions with the picturesqueness of European design."

Roberts goes on to describe the graveled paths wide enough for carriages that wind through the brilliant flowerbeds and shrubberies, "sometimes skirting along high walls of creeping plants trained against lofty trees, at others overlooking large tanks so completely covered with pink blossoms of the lotus, as to conceal the element in which this splendid aquatic plant delights." Of course she was enraptured with the elephants seen "pacing along the flowery labyrinths, to European eyes strange guests in a private garden." She does not remark on the menagerie for the simple reason that it had been dismantled by the economy-minded Lord Bentinck, but she does note the abundance of "bright-winged" parrots, which, alas, were often the targets of parrot-shooting, a sport to which some of the great men of the presidency were addicted.[97]

To the beauty of Barrackpore was added the view across the river to the

Danish settlement of Serampore. Lord Wellesley had endowed its church with a steeple, even though it represented an alien creed (Baptist), because, he is supposed to have explained, "nothing was wanting to Barrackpore Park but the distant view of a steeple."[98] The Baptist missionary, William Carey, created a garden in Serampore that was the envy of many visitors, thanks to his botanical connections. Ever eager for English plants, he was forever wheedling friends at home, suggesting that they pay young boys a trifling amount to gather seeds of "cowslips, violets, daisies, crowfoots, etc." and send them along with "a few snowdrops, crocuses, etc., and other trifles." Even common weeds, and nettles and thistles, would be welcome, he added wistfully, as long as they were English.[99]

Serampore was much more open than Barrackpore, with a broad esplanade running along the river, so that the mansions lining it—"Serampore's proud palaces" in Roberts's rhapsodic prose—were "mirrored on the glassy surface of the stream." For all its handsome architecture (she considered it "the best-built and best-kept European settlement in India") and tidy streets, cleaned and weeded by convict labor, the English viewed the town with some condescension: it was a sanctuary both for those fleeing Calcutta creditors and for others (possibly the same people) contracting clandestine marriages or seeking quickie divorces ("the Gretna Green of Bengal," according to Roberts). Somewhat paradoxically, Roberts considered it a pretty dull place, its missionary and merchant inhabitants "indispose[d] to gaiety," with only their daily promenades for amusement.[100]

Every governor-general—or more often his wife or sisters—added to or subtracted from the park and gardens of Barrackpore. In a misguided effort to nurture plants from home in a hostile clime, Lady Hastings, wife of Wellesley's immediate successor, had a large greenhouse constructed on the site of his erstwhile palace. Intended to shut out the heat, it no doubt had the opposite effect.[101] As might be expected from her comments apropos of William Carey's misguided passion for English flowers quoted in the preceding chapter, Lady Amherst reveled in the plethora of exotic plants at Barrackpore. Her delight was to stroll through the garden with Nathaniel Wallich, head of the Calcutta Botanical Garden, as her guide: "I find new flowers, the names, properties, and culture of which I know nothing till Dr. Wallich inform'd me upon all these points. His knowledge of Botany and Horticulture is only to be equall'd by his extraordinary retentive memory."[102]

Where Lord Bentinck did away with the menagerie, Lord Auckland and his sisters, Fanny and Emily Eden, restored it and added an aviary. They took great pleasure in their almost daily elephant rides about the grounds: "There is something dreamy and odd in these rides when the evening grows dark. There is a mosque and a ghaut [ghat: stone steps leading to the water] at the end of our park where they were burning a body tonight; and there were bats, as big as crows, flying over our heads." More a gardener than a botanist (unlike Lady Amherst), Emily planted a secluded flower garden for the familiar English flowers that reminded her of home, but she also enriched Barrackpore with quantities of plants provided by Wallich.[103] With her brother and sister, she converted one of the thatched bungalows to a plant and seed house. Lord Auckland, however, could be something of an ogre. Harriet Tytler, whose father was stationed at the cantonment, remembers taking walks in the park with him when she was a child: "With my passion for flowers . . . I could never resist gathering one or two. Lord Auckland, the governor-general in those days, was a very disagreeable, austere old bachelor. The servants used to terrify me by saying, 'There comes the Lord Sahib, if he knows you have been gathering his flowers, he will assuredly put you into prison.'" She also remembers that the first strawberry plants to be grown in India were to be found in the Barrackpore gardens about 1836: "My father and mother . . . went to see these wonders, and I was allowed to accompany them"—apparently the berries were reserved for Lord Auckland's consumption, but Harriet bravely sneaked a couple when no one was looking. Nasturtiums were another novelty in the India of the 1830s.[104]

Lady Canning's "Jungle"

If Government House reached its self-conscious apogee under Lord Curzon, Barrackpore bloomed most splendidly under the tender ministrations of Lady Canning almost a half-century earlier. Charlotte Canning was married, not too happily, to the governor-general (later viceroy) who had the misfortune of serving during the time of the Uprising of 1857. Before her marriage she had been lady-in-waiting to Queen Victoria. Surviving are many letters and journals destined for her beloved family as well as letters to the queen, along with a treasure trove of drawings, watercolors, and photographs (she was one of the earliest photographers in India). To the royal children she sent a steady stream of natural history specimens, while the queen, enamored of India and Indians (but too fearful of snakes and insects to travel hither), pressed her for details of the life around her.

Lady Canning's first visit to Barrackpore a few weeks after her arrival in Calcutta in 1856 was disappointing. The beautiful trees that bordered the road—the trees that had so delighted Emma Roberts—struck her as "poisonously green," offering "a notion of unwholesome damp." At last the party turned off "into the most English well-kept green park, of good rounded trees, I ever saw." But instead of pleasing her, it had the opposite effect. Just as she had compared the *maidan* in Calcutta to Regent's Park, so the grounds at Barrackpore were "too English for me to appreciate properly, being quite a matter-of-course-looking place like Sion [Syon, the Duke of Northumberland's estate across the Thames from Kew], or any villa or park anywhere, short grass well-mown and smelling of hay, and not a cocoa-nut in sight." Bishop Heber had fancied himself on the banks of the Thames instead of the Ganges, save for the fact that he was exploring Barrackpore on the back of an elephant, but this was hardly what Canning wanted from India. Then there was Barrackpore House. Like her predecessors, she was appalled by the shabbiness of its furnishings, so appalled that she had to resort to French to describe the "*délabré* villa,*" "this exceedingly ill *monté* house; the dinner, with its cotton tablecloth and Bohemian glass and candlesticks, looks exactly like a *table-d'hôte*." There were even snakes in the servants' rooms below stairs. For her the elephants at least offered some solace: "Not quite a pleasure, but I was glad to try the experiment." Riding on these docile behemoths she found she could look deep into the trees, right on "a level with their flowers."[105]

Canning immediately set out to remedy the deficiencies of both house and park. She had several models in mind. One was Parel, the residence of the governor-general of Bombay Presidency, Lord Elphinstone, which had so charmed her on first setting foot in India with the "beauty of the tropical vegetation" (see Pl. 6). Parel had been a Jesuit seminary during the brief period the Portuguese occupied the islands that became Bombay. When the territory passed into English hands as part of the dowry of Catherine of Braganza, the seminary was converted into a lovely villa. Admirably adapted to the climate, it had verandahs running around all the rooms. From her window, Charlotte could look out on "groves and groves of cocoa and palm overtopping round-headed trees; then burnt-up ground [it was the dry season]; mango-trees in flower exactly like Spanish chestnuts; tamarinds in the style of acacias, but much thicker; peepal-trees, higher a good deal than the rest, with trembling leaves—very green, and pinkish stems, like white poplar; a teak tree, with large leaves and sort of bunches of berries." She added, "The flowers are lovely—bougainvillia, oleander, jessamine, poinsettia, and there are old cypresses entirely covered with flame-coloured bignonia." On the table were strange fruits and strange flowers. After Parel, Barrackpore was a letdown but at the same time a challenge: "All my efforts," she wrote to a friend, "are to try and reach the model of 'Elphy's' establishment, but I hardly hope to succeed." Some months later, 450 yards of chintz, pictures on the walls, an array of armchairs and small tables, and "flower-pots in numbers" had so improved the house that it could now hold its own with Parel, and she was ready to invite Elphy himself.[106]

Her plans for the garden and park were more ambitious and took much longer to realize. It was fortunate, she acknowledged, that the work was well underway before the troubles broke out: "Had it not been ordered in our peaceful prosperous days, it would not have a chance now." Thanks to her sketches and paintings and the accounts in her letters, we can conjure up the Eden she created on the banks of the Hughli. Her original inspiration may have been Highcliffe, her family home overlooking Christchurch Bay atop a bluff on the Hampshire coast. The castle was built in the 1830s in the "Romantic and Picturesque style of architecture"—and with a romantic and picturesque view out over its landscaped gardens to the Needles and the Isle of Wight in the English Channel. What Barrackpore lacked in dramatic location, she made up for with her own artistic eye, beginning with the terrace overlooking the river. The terrace walk along the riverbank needed to be relandscaped both to position it more properly in relation to the house and to provide an airy seat at the water's edge—"a stone bench where I can go and sit and breathe fresh air in the evening." By early September 1858, she could report that the new terrace "is now of an excellent shape, exactly the right line, and it fully satisfies me as to giving a straightening effect to the crooked view, much as the Highcliffe terrace has down," adding, "Only the foundation and piers of the balustrade are finished, but it looks beautiful" (see Pl. 7).[107]

The water itself offered an ever-changing vista. High tides covered the low ground between the walk and the river, an area about fifty yards wide. "When the river is over this, the view is beautiful. It is a sort of lake and covered with picturesque native boats."[108] Sometimes, indeed, the drama of life and death played out along the river was almost more than she could bear: the religious festivals with their often fearsome deities and the piles of wood stacked along the *ghat,* ready to be weighed and sold for burning the bodies of the dead— hardly the scenes on view in Christchurch Bay.

Gradually other improvements took shape. She opened up an enormous banyan tree that was hidden by shrubs and it became a favorite retreat: "I can sit out nearly all day under the great Banyan and its creepers" (see Pl. 8). Her overall plan was to simplify patterns and widen walks in the garden. A new raised road led to the boat landing, and "a great many groups of plants with brilliant flowers" were set out near the ponds and tanks. A clipped evergreen hedge four feet high contrasted with a bamboo fence covered with convolvus—"when in flower, it will be like a blue wall." The soil was so improved that "the starved look of many plants is at an end." There were roses in abundance and "great sweet pancratiums."[109]

While she cleared excess trees and shrubs to open up new vistas and made new walks about the park, Lady Canning had come to love Barrackpore in all its tropical glory—the "labyrinth of jungly lanes—so beautiful and green." Indeed, "jungly" becomes a refrain in her letters home: referring to the "jungly groves," she writes, "I can never describe the beauty of these—like Portlaw Wood, only of mango, bamboo, cocoanut, plantains, arums, &c., paths branching off in all directions, little huts, now and then small temples, ruined gardens; great sameness perhaps, but such beauty, and great variety of trees and creepers, tanks and ponds everywhere amongst all sorts of gardens and groves." In another letter she is in awe of "the beauty of the Bougainvillias, wreaths of lilac as brilliant as a lilac flame, a colour that seems full of lights, and that no paint or dye could imitate." The park was at its greenest during the monsoons, when she could fill the rooms with a "*luxe* of flowers," something few visitors seemed to appreciate but which she acknowledged to be "a craze of mine." Other flowers reached their peak in the cold season from November to February: heliotropes, mignonette, and "what are called English flowers."[110] The pools were covered with water lilies, smaller than their English cousins. In fact large masses of flowers—camelias, peonies, and roses—were less common than in England. But, as Charlotte reminded her correspondents, many of the plants she described they would know only from the Palm House at Kew or from hothouses. What English gardeners strove to replicate in the "stovehouses" that had become such status symbols in the first half of the nineteenth century, Lady Canning had all about her, and it delighted her more and more with each visit to Barrackpore.

Alas, these visits were few and far between. Lord Canning was a driven man and for months on end found the pressures of work too heavy to allow an escape to Barrackpore, close as it was. He hardly fit Curzon's description of the governor-general who spent seven or eight months of the hot season there, to say nothing of long weekends at other seasons. With the outbreak of mutiny in the spring of 1857, the pressures increased a hundredfold. Charlotte, herself a very astute reporter of events as they unfolded, felt obligated to stay with him, for not only was he faced with unending decisions and anxieties, he was also under incessant attack in India and in England, at first for being too lenient—"Clemency" Canning—and then for being too harsh. Fortunately for both Cannings, they enjoyed the unswerving support of the queen. Finally in April 1859, after peace had finally been restored, Lord Canning returned to Barrackpore. It was his first visit in more than two years, Charlotte noted, but at least he could see all that she had accomplished: "my beautiful terrace, which is now finished and full of flowers, and the most wonderful improvement to the place."[111] Even the end of the uprising did not bring much leisure. Lord Canning undertook an ambitious round of tours to reestablish confidence in the government and reaffirm the loyalty of local rulers to the man who was now viceroy of India.

Charlotte accompanied her husband on some of these tours, as well as making several long trips on her own. They provided an opportunity to see more of the country, but also to pursue her natural history interests. At Barrackpore she would often gather plants on her morning and evening rides about the park and bring them in to sketch or paint, and she did the same on her travels. Her cousin Minnie joined her on a trip through southern India that included the Nilgiri Hills, a botanist's paradise. "Char's genuine love of plants and flowers makes every step in this country of interest to her."[112] As she scrambled up and down the steep hills, Minnie at first tried to keep up with her but soon gave up the effort. "After a rainy middle of the day," Charlotte wrote in her journal,

> we went out, carrying a great tin box, to search for ferns. A slippery path took us down a woody glen, where we gathered eight varieties,

and went on & on & down & down by zigzags into another glen, to a beautiful walk I had never seen before. The larger stream was fuller of water and of great beauty. By the side I saw the Hedychium growing wild, but rather of a creamy white variety, and a pretty Begonia on a great rock, for once within reach. . . . I never saw more gorgeous foliage, and a tangle of creepers, sometimes like curtains of great green leaves looped up with coils of ropes, finding the trees together, unlike anything in Europe. A few great black monkeys, jumping from branch to branch, relieve these spots delightfully. The stems of the trees are nearly all white, and a great many have bright pink or red young shoots or leaves.[113]

To this day one of her favorite spots for sketching, on the edge of a steep bluff overlooking a gorge cutting through the escarpment, is known as "Lady Canning's Seat."

She sent the ferns home to her mother, along with portfolios of sketches of flowers from time to time. When one box arrived, her mother was ecstatic: "*C'était à se mettre à genoux devant!* The glorious flowers surpass any we have yet beheld, and the sketches took us to the Hills, and along the Ganges."[114] Fortunately these had escaped the fire that broke out in camp near Meerut when she was touring with the viceregal entourage and that damaged or destroyed some of her journals. Perhaps out of politesse, perhaps out of genuine enthusiasm, John Ruskin admired her flower paintings, praising especially the subtle use of color in her depictions of trumpet flowers, bougainvillea, and poinsettia.[115]

Since her arrival in India, Charlotte had yearned to visit the Himalayas, a fascination that only intensified after her meetings with Dr. Thomas Thomson, superintendent of the Calcutta Botanical Garden from 1855 to 1861. Thomson had spent more than a decade botanizing in the western and eastern portions of the range. With him she could share her passion for plants and flowers. He happily obliged with information and with plants for her gardens. As the long-postponed return to England approached, she determined to make the trek to Darjeeling. She had cared little for the hill station of Simla; why, she thought, should Europeans not prefer Darjeeling, which was so much closer to Calcutta? By rights this ought to be the "Sanatorium of Calcutta," a bitterly ironic comment, as it turned out.[116]

On her last visit to Barrackpore before departing, she sorted and labeled her scrapbooks. "I have been very busy," she wrote her aunt, "and it is all rather tidily done now—two volumes and a portfolio, a few more flowers, and a great bundle of journal of the last march." She sent a gardener on ahead "to help me bring back all sorts of treasures in the way of orchids and seeds, &c.," and predicted, "It will in all ways be a great holiday, and very wholesome." Some of these plants she looked forward to bringing to her new home in England, fancying that she might rival her friend Viscount Sydney "in garden and flowers."[117]

Darjeeling may have been far closer to Calcutta than Simla—350 miles rather than a thousand-plus—but it was still a "tedious journey," as she wrote Queen Victoria. "After crossing the Ganges and above 200 miles of railway there is still at least 3 nights traveling in the most disagreeable of all conveyances—a palanquin!" Nevertheless, she was looking forward to the trip and to being in a "spot with the highest mountains in the world immediately before one in full view." In fact, she was able to ride up the last stretch of the mountain on her white pony. Darjeeling did not disappoint. From time to time she was rewarded with glimpses of the sun's rays striking the loftiest peaks, and her excursions through the wooded hills were sheer delight: "The forests never cease & give me an idea of damp as I never saw, but then it is such wonderful luxuriance—quite unlike all else tho' perhaps I saw forests as fine before, yet never anything like this extent of them."[118]

Her letters to her husband are an antiphony, alternating pleasure in the beauty of Darjeeling with excited anticipation of home and plans for the new house and garden offered them by a grateful queen. From her earliest days in Calcutta, Charlotte had heard about the pestilential jungle at the foot of the hills, the *terai,* which later gave its name to a felt sunhat stocked by colonial outfitters. Having survived more than five stress-filled years in India, however, she no doubt thought she would surmount this last peril and had the palanquin set down so that she could make one last sketch of the mountains. Whether it was an illness acquired while still in the Himalayas or fever picked up in the jungle, she was very sick when she reached Calcutta and died not long after. "India," Mary Curzon would observe, "slowly but surely murders women."[119] She may have had Lady Canning in mind; she surely had herself.

Charlotte Canning was buried, fittingly, in a corner of Barrackpore that she had always thought of as her garden. "It is a beautiful spot," Lord Canning wrote Queen Victoria, "looking upon that reach of the grand river which she was so fond of drawing, shaded from the glare of the sun by high trees, and amongst the bright shrubs and flowers in which she had so much pleasure."[120] Leaving Barrackpore's gardens, she had confessed, would be her only regret on parting from India; now she would never leave it. Lord Canning returned to England, a broken man. He died a few months later. The monument, "in the sweetest nook of the vice-regal gardens," continued to be strewn with flowers for years afterward.[121]

After Lady Canning, succeeding residents of Barrackpore enjoyed the giant banyan tree as an exotic place to pass the time, but they and their visitors chose to see the park once again through English-tinted glasses. Lady Lytton loved Barrackpore precisely because "the park is like England and the river like the Thames at Mortlake."[122] For Lady Dufferin it conjured up Cliveden. Nevertheless, it was she who most shared Charlotte Canning's love of the park and its gardens. "We fell in love with Barrackpore on the spot," she wrote after her first visit in 1884. She found the gardens "quite perfect," marveling at the "roses in greatest profusion . . . some of them quite enormous; the large blue convolvus climbs all over along a low wall, which surrounds a little garden full of heliotrope and other sweet flowers, and where a little fountain plays in a marble basin; there are bushes of red and purple blossom and a lovely orange creeper covers the balcony near which I write."[123] The Dufferins' special treat was breakfast under Charlotte's banyan tree.

At the turn of the century Lady Curzon also took pleasure in sitting peacefully under the banyan, still festooned as in Lady Canning's day with orchids and creepers.[124] Her husband, however, compulsive "improver" that he was, undertook various projects. The course of the river had wandered from its earlier course, leaving a "broad belt of foreshore" some hundred yards wide between the upper and lower landings. This had been used as a polo ground, but Curzon felt it was now time to turn it into another garden. He drew up plans for a "great stretch of sward with broad graveled walks and patterned flower-beds, and a pool and fountain in the center"—a wonderfully English touch, which his successor was forced to abandon when it turned out not to be so far above the flood line as Curzon had imagined. More successful was his "draining and turfing" of Moti Jheel, a long tank north of Barrackpore House, and the expansion of the rose garden to encompass the entire area that had been devoted earlier to vegetables. The nursery thrived so spectacularly,

Curzon boasted, that it could at any time supply the three thousand blooms that were required for the state ball at Government House in Calcutta. One suggestion he rejected was the proposal to create a water park, evidently a sort of Disneyland *avant la lettre,* nearby; Barrackpore Park had long been open to the public, but this would be going too far.[125]

Steaming up the Hughli about the same time, the journalist George Steevens described the potpourri of ships and "country boats and bathing natives," the low banks of the river "punctuated with red and grey temples, bordered with an unbroken fringe of trees, out of which palms lift their heads daintily." An oriental scene until at last the grass parts; one pulls up to the landing and proceeds through a tunnel of green to "an English garden and park translated into India." While broad drives might cleave through undulating lawns, in India's long dusty dry season, the grass was gray and ill-assorted, with the "trees swayed by the wind into bows, trees shooting bolt upright or drooping to earth, symmetrical or gadding into feathery tumult."[126]

In truth Barrackpore had lost its main raison d'être. With the consecration of Simla as the summer capital of India beginning in the mid-1860s, Barrackpore was demoted to something closer to Chequers or Camp David—a weekend retreat rather than a seasonal seat of government. This became all the more feasible with the railroad connection to Calcutta or the small steam launch that brought Curzon upriver "in the twilight of a Saturday evening" and downriver "in the dewy radiance of a Monday morning."[127] Once Delhi became the capital of imperial India, Barrackpore lost even its status as a destination for visiting viceroys: it was given to the government of Bengal and used for occasional visits by the governor.[128]

CHAPTER 3

Over the Hills and Far Away

The Hill Stations of India

INDIA WAS not for the fainthearted. Those who arrived in the cool season were agreeably surprised by the sunshine and pleasant temperatures, such a contrast to the Stygian gloom of British winters. But all three presidency towns—Madras, Calcutta, and Bombay—were low, swampy, and pestilential. For much of the year the heat was well-nigh unbearable; even the monsoons did little to moderate it, adding only an enervating humidity and rampant mold. Flowers and people alike wilted after the first freshness of dawn, and life was lived from sunrise to sunset in the semidarkness of shuttered rooms. For the first centuries of East India Company presence, there was little escape except to garden houses in the suburbs—airier but scarcely cooler—or, all too often, to the peace of the churchyard. "Sing a song of sixpence," went the ditty,

> *Purchased with our lives,*
> *Decent English gentlemen*
> *Roasting with their wives,*

In the plains of India,
Where like flies they die.[1]

Over time the British adapted their architecture, adding verandahs to shade their houses from the relentless sun. The surrounding garden, however, was too hot to venture into during the daylight hours of summer. For whatever reason, Europeans never imitated the plan of the Indian *haveli* which François Bernier had found so deliciously cool, "with its courtyard, gardens, trees, basins of water, small jets d'eau," and terraces where the whole family might sleep at night.[2] A few of the more Indianized Delhi officials did adopt the Mughal *tehkhana,* an underground room or set of rooms in which one could repose until the late afternoon made them too hot and stuffy. More commonly they borrowed the use of screens of fragrant grass on outer doors, constantly soaked in scented water to catch what breezes there might be. In addition, *punkahs* hung from the ceilings. These were simply fans writ large: rectangular pieces of cloth, pulled to and fro by servants, typically via a string attached to the big toe. A visitor summed up life in the burning plains through the long summer months: "The fair fresh Western faces become paler, and more pale, as they lie gasping under the monotonous swing of the punkah, dreading heat-apoplexy, should the weary 'punkah-wallah' fall asleep (as he is only too likely to do)."[3]

A more ambitious contrivance was the thermantidote, first invented about 1830. "Awful to behold," the thermantidote was an enormous machine made of wood and standing some seven feet high, four or five feet across, and nine or ten in length, with small wheels to make it more maneuverable. When set up on the verandah, it forced air into the window of a house through a funnel by means of four large metal fans attached to an iron axle and turned constantly by two men. On its way into the house the air passed through *tattis,* mats of woven grass. These in turn required relays of coolies handing up water in earthen pots to other coolies on top of the machine seeing to it that the *tattis* were kept dripping wet. "By this means all the air that passes into the body of the machine through the wetted *khas-khas* [grass] is rendered cool and fit to be forced into the house by action of the fans in their circular course." "You have no idea," Fanny Parks adds approvingly, "how fragrant, delicious and refreshing is the scent of the fresh *khas-khas.*"[4]

Unique to Bombay was the custom of building temporary residences on the Esplanade facing the sea during the hot season: rows of bungalows made of bamboo and plaster, lined with "strained dungaree" (a "coarse kind of unbleached cloth" dyed a pale straw color) and shaded by flowering creepers and luxuriant shrubs from the midday sun. Offices were placed near the bungalows and the whole enclosed in a "pretty compound, filled with fine plants, arranged in tubs, round the trellised verandahs." In the tubs the shrubs flourished in spite of the sea air, "usually considered too inimical to the labours of the horticulturists." This was hardly camping out. As Marianne Postans, an upcountry official's wife, commented with satisfaction, "Elegance combines with comfort, in making these pretty abodes truly pleasant; and a fine-toned piano, and a good billiard table, are the usual addition to varied articles of luxury and convenience." With the "sweet perfume" of the flowers and the fresh sea breezes of evening, what more could one wish for? Alas, as the rains approached these structures had to be pulled down and stored, sending their inhabitants reluctantly back to the confines of the fort as the Esplanade disappeared under a sheet of water.[5]

But things were changing. Fanny Parks was of the first generation that could flee the heat and dust of the plains to the hills where, as Kim's *Lama* put it, "the air and water are fresh and cool."[6] The East India Company's more aggressive expansion toward the end of the eighteenth century had several major consequences. First of all, it opened up for exploration and exploitation new regions of which the British had been only dimly aware. Second, it required a much greater military and civilian presence, with attendant concerns about how they were to survive in the hostile climate of the tropics. In the early decades of the nineteenth century these conquests coincided with a burst of scientific interest in epidemiology and the health-restoring benefits of higher altitudes. Just when disease-ridden soldiers and enervated officials most needed them, the higher altitudes were providentially at hand, from the Himalayas in the north to the Nilgiris in the south. To go to the hills was, as one subaltern put it, like "passing through the Valley of Death to Paradise."[7] Here a very different India beckoned, an India where familiar flowers bloomed, where nights were cool and sallow complexions regained a rosy glow. One could almost imagine one was at home.

All told there were some eighty hill stations in India, ranging in altitude between 2,500 and 8,000 feet. The best known were those in the foothills of the Himalayas (Simla, Naini Tal, Mussoorie-Landour, Dalhousie, Muree, Darjeeling) and in the Nilgiris (Ootacamund, Coonor), but there were also

Matheran and Mahabaleshwar in the Western Ghats, inland from Bombay; Mount Abu in the Aravalli Mountains of southern Rajasthan; Shillong in Assam; and others sprinkled in the Deccan and southeast. The lower ones offered fresher air, cooler temperatures, and more pleasing prospects than the plains, but they were still within the malaria belt, which extended to 4,500–5,000 feet.

As more upland regions came under British control through conquest and treaty, Company officials were charged with finding suitable locations for sanatoria, especially for the British military, whose morbidity and mortality rates were alarming. The devastating epidemic of cholera that swept across the continent in from 1817 to 1821 added to the urgency of the quest. Lacking an understanding of the etiology of tropical diseases, medical opinion at first simply designated heat as the cause, so that the obvious remedy was removal to cooler climates. Theories became more nuanced when experience showed that not all diseases responded to a spell in the hills—indeed, overcrowding and poor sanitation in time spawned outbreaks of cholera, dysentery, and typhoid in the hill stations themselves—but in general it became accepted wisdom that almost everyone benefited from the tonic effect of an escape from the "burning plains."

If this was true for soldiers and bureaucrats, missionaries, and planters, it was equally so for women, who began to arrive in India in increasing numbers once the East India Company lost its power to restrict immigration in 1833.[8] After her first night in Mahabaleshwar, the hill station for Bombay, Lady Falkland, wife of the governor, enthused: "You think you have received a new set of bones: you get up refreshed and your feet seem to run away with you."[9] Fanny Parks was just as ecstatic as she journeyed to Landour through forests of rhododendron, her attendants filling her lap with wildflowers along the way: "The delicious air, so pure, so bracing, so unlike any air I had breathed for fifteen years—with what delight I inhaled it! It seemed to promise health and strength and spirits. . . . I felt a buoyancy of spirit, like that enjoyed by a child."[10] Her father, Major Edward Archer, had felt the same delight when he first ventured into the hills, declaring that those flocking to the hills in search of health "fully believe Hygeia herself has taken up her abode among them."[11] The effect on children was, if anything, more salutary. "It is incredible," Sir Joseph Hooker observed, "what a few weeks of that mountain air does for the Indian-born children of European parents: they are taken there sickly, pallid or yellow, soft and flabby, to become transformed into models of rude health and activity."[12] To Fanny Parks the children in Mussoorie looked "as well and as strong as any children in England"; indeed, she went so far as to declare the climate in the hills to be "far superior to that of England."[13]

Most of the hill stations were founded in the 1820s and 1830s by military or civilian employees of the East India Company. By the second half of the nineteenth century Europeans retreated to the hills for a sizeable portion of the year and continued to do so until the eve of the Second World War. Inevitably stations soon arranged themselves in a pecking order: the highest altitudes were the preserve of the social and official elite, while the *boxwallahs* recuperated at lower levels, along with the soldiery in adjacent cantonments. Dominating all was Simla, the summer capital of the Raj. Others hosted provincial governments: Ootacamund, Madras; Naini Tal, the United Provinces; Mahabaleshwar, Bombay; Murree, Rawalpindi; Darjeeling, the lieutenant-governor of Calcutta and his staff. Low down on the totem pole was Yercaud in the Shevari Hills of the Eastern Ghats. For all its lovely views and equable climate, to say nothing of its proximity to Madras and Salem, it became all too exclusively identified with the coffee planters of the region.[14] Within the British population of each station there was also a keen awareness of who was who, the Order of Precedence serving as Holy Writ for social relations. "Like oil and water, Simla's social classes did not mix."[15] Altitude reflected social status: thus the viceroy and commander-in-chief inhabited the peaks of Simla. The same was true of most other stations. Kodaikanal, founded in the mid-1840s by American missionaries in Madurai, was the sole exception, with its more egalitarian society. Appropriately, too, the roof of its first church was made entirely of flattened Huntley and Palmer biscuit tins, in contrast to the stately Anglican spires in other stations.[16]

Stations of the Himalayas

Gods have always been partial to mountains; witness Sinai and Olympus. Long before the British first set foot in them, the Himalayas were revered as the dwelling place of the greatest of the Hindu deities; it was *Devbhumi*, the Land of the Gods, claimed "by a host of divine characters from the mythic past."[17] At Mount Kailash, Siva lived with his consort, Parvati, daughter of Himalaya, king of the mountains. At Gangotsi Glacier in Garhwal, the goddess Ganga was brought to earth as a result of the pious austerities performed by the sage Bhagirath. Lord Siva received the full force of the river in his matted locks so that Ganga would not fall directly on the earth and destroy it.[18] For Indians, the mountains are still linked to the heavenly hosts: "This is the hill where Shiva danced," or "This lake was made by Arjuna's arrow."[19] Sacred sites such as Hardwar attract millions of pilgrims all year round to bathe in the Ganges where it emerges from the Himalayas. In the same manner, pilgrims flock to the Amarnath Cave in Kashmir every summer to worship at the giant ice *lingam* of Siva. "Who goes to the Hills," runs a Hindu proverb, "goes to his mother."[20]

But if the Indians of the plains dotted the mountains with temples, they had no desire to live there, leaving the craggy fastnesses and deep valleys to indigenous "tribals." The Mughals, on the other hand, found the heat of the plains as unbearable as the British did. The answer to their prayers was Kashmir, first visited by Emperor Akbar in 1589. Akbar made of Kashmir what he once called his private garden. He and his successors delighted in its natural beauty but at the same time embellished it with matchless gardens: Shalimar, Achibal, Verinag. They laid out gardens along the route to Srinagar to camp in during the long journey, and then all about the shores of Dal Lake, glorying in the cascading streams from the melting snows of spring and summer, the verdant meadows, the infinite possibilities for terracing that abounded, "their water-courses dropping from level to level down rippled concrete falls"—so unlike the flat vastnesses of the Gangetic plain (see Pl. 9). Akbar's son Jahangir adored Kashmir beyond all other places on earth, proclaiming that "he would rather lose all his empire than Kachmire." In his memoirs, he referred to Kashmir as "a perennial garden," noting that "red roses, violets, and narcissi grow wild; there are fields after fields of all kinds of flowers."[21] Indeed, his passion for plants and flowers recalled that of his great-grandfather, Babur; he gladly left the governing of his realm to his beloved wife, Nur Mahal, so that he could devote himself to the study of nature and the planning of gardens. A count taken during his reign showed more than seven hundred in Kashmir alone.[22]

"Who has not heard of the Vale of Cashmere, / With its roses the brightest that earth ever gave, / Its temples, and grottoes, and fountains as clear / As the love-lighted eyes that hang over the wave?"[23] The romance of Kashmir had stirred the imagination of the British through Thomas Moore's *Lalla Rookh* not long before they began to look seriously at hill stations. The poem purports to tell the story of a Mughal princess who falls in love with a Persian poet while journeying to meet her betrothed. "If woman can make the worst wilderness dear," wrote Moore, "Think! Think! what a Heaven she can make of Kashmir."[24] With or without woman, Kashmir has continued to represent Paradise on earth. While generations of Anglo-Indians made their individual pilgrimages to Kashmir, they could not appropriate it as they did land elsewhere in the Himalayas, for the simple reason that they did not control it. The province had been ceded to the British after the First Sikh War in 1843, but they immediately sold it to Gulab Singh, the Raja of Jammu, for £750,000. The move was criticized on strategic grounds but had other repercussions as well. The ruler and his successors refused to allow the British full legal title to land, so that although they might flock to Gulmarg, Srinagar, and Sonamurg ("surely the most beautiful place in the world"), they did not invest the same resources in Kashmir as in other stations. They managed, however, to circumvent the ban on owning land by taking to its lakes in houseboats, serviceable but "evidently derived . . . from Oxford college barges, or the boats of City livery companies."[25]

For the Mughals, the lure of Kashmir was its mountain valleys and lakes and meadows for their garden retreats. In contrast, the British chose to settle on the ridges and hilltops themselves. Simla, Lord Dufferin acknowledged, was "an absurd place situated on the narrow saddle of one of a hundred mountainous ridges that rise around us in labyrinthine complexity like the waves of a confused and troubled sea."[26] No doubt, higher was deemed better in terms of health, but Europeans were also responding to an aesthetic revolution, the emotional appeal of the Sublime. And nothing inspired emotions of sublimity—the combination of terror and beauty—more than mountains.[27] Ascending from the plains to Simla, Lady Amherst allowed that "one must become accustom'd to look down precipices—without terror or giddiness—before admiration can be join'd to *perfect ease*."[28] Describing the scenery between Landour and Mussoorie, Fanny Parks notes that while the setting of the former on the southern side of the hill "is of a tamer cast," reminiscent of the "back of the Isle of Wight," travel to the northern side is another matter altogether:

> A wildness and grandeur, unknown on the southern side, is all around you; the valleys fearfully deep, the pathway narrow, and is some parts so bad, only one foot in breadth is left for a pony. At first I felt a cold

shudder pass over me as I rode in such places. . . . A pathway three feet in width at its utmost breadth is a handsome road in the Hills; a perpendicular rock on one side, and a precipice, perhaps three or four hundred feet deep, may be on the other. . . . If looking over a precipice makes you giddy, shut your eyes and give your *gūnth* [mountain pony] the rein, and you will be sure to find yourself safe on the other side. . . . I was delighted with the wildness of the scenery—it equalled my expectations.[29]

Not so many years earlier the poet Thomas Gray had declared that "Mont Cenis . . . carries the permission mountains have of being frightful rather too far,"[30] but by the early decades of the nineteenth century travel in the Alps had become quite safe, depriving the Sublime of its delicious frissons of terror. This was not yet the case in the Himalayas. Many were the tales of both man and beast falling to their deaths from the narrow paths Parks describes or crushed by avalanches of crumbling rocks. The mountain tracks her father followed in the mountains beyond Simla were vertiginous in the extreme. The reward, however, was scenery of the most sublime sort imaginable. But when Archer turned to his "Mahomedan" servant at one particularly enthralling sight, asking if the view was not grander than anything he had ever seen, the servant (who had evidently been to England) replied, "Oh no! Vauxhall beats it hollow, as did the illumination in London, when the English took Buonaparte!" Chastened, the major allowed that "this sounded so strange as to make me come down a peg from the height to which my enthusiasm had elevated me."[31] Beauty is indeed in the eye of the beholder.

The drawback was that hill stations were a very long way from the cities of the plains—Simla, for example, was over a thousand miles from Calcutta—and demanded an arduous and uncomfortable journey. Before the age of railroads, travelers might ride part of the way on horses, camels, or elephants; but once in the mountains, these animals were not very surefooted, and one had to rely on mountain ponies or be tortured in conveyances such as palanquins, *jampans,* or *doolies,* all variants of covered litters carried by relays of coolies.

"Hill station" may seem too benign a term to apply to settlements perched on narrow ridges seven or eight thousand feet high. Fanny Parks, however, made a distinction between "Hills" and "Snowy Ranges." "In any other country," she conceded, "these hills would be called mountains; but, being near the foot of the Himalaya that in the distance tower over them, they have obtained the title of the 'Hills.'" The term "Hills" in contradistinction to "Plains" seems to have been in common use even earlier: Lady Amherst refers to "the Hills" in her journal even as she was making her way thither in 1827, one of the first to do so. A half century later Lady Dufferin also separated the "brown rippling hills near at hand" from the "rolling sea of mountains" that lay some fifty miles beyond. Nor could Edward Lear resist a punning distinction between the "*Low* Malaya" and the "true *High* Malaya." Dane Kennedy is not convinced. He argues that "mountain" conjured up altogether too "sublime," too unsettling an image for repose and recuperation. Labeling the Himalayan settlements "hill stations" was a way to domesticate them, an agenda that was eventually furthered by appropriating and Anglicizing the environment.[32] Perhaps. But when Emily Eden remarks after a few days in Simla, "altogether the Himalayas are sweet pretty little hills," one feels she is making the same distinction as Amherst, Parks, and Dufferin (and Lear). Indeed, a day or two later she reports in tones of almost Jane Austen–like irony that it has snowed and then hailed, "and is now thundering, in a cracking, sharp way that would be awful, only its sublimity is destroyed by the working of the carpenters and blacksmiths, who are shaping curtain rods and rings all round the house."[33] She was quite capable of coping with the Sublime.

In 1827, only three years after the first house had been built in Simla, Lord Amherst trekked to what would become the de facto (and later de jure) summer capital of India. It was here that the governor-general uttered his unforgettable words, "The Emperor of China and I govern half the human race and yet we find time for breakfast."[34] Governing his portion of the human race from a Calcutta that was unbearably hot for six months of the year was a trial, however, and Amherst's almost fortuitous retreat to Simla after a long tour of the plains set in motion what was to become an annual ritual of removal that was finally made official in 1864. The irony was that, as Lord Lytton remarked, Simla was not actually British territory: "The whole Government of India is the tenant of its smallest feudatories."[35] And as this government expanded, the migration involved increasing numbers of civilians and military. Where it had taken seventeen hundred coolies to drag the baggage for Lord Amherst's suite of six hundred up the steep mountain track (not counting the accompanying regiment and bodyguard), just over a decade later the procession had swelled prodigiously when Lord Auckland

and his sisters, Emily and Fanny Eden, made the journey, with an entourage of over ten thousand, along with 850 baggage camels, several hundred horses and bullocks, and 140 elephants—"ten miles of beasts of burden" to meet the needs of nine Europeans, as Emily put it.[36]

Indeed, her account of their quasi-royal progress is not so different from that of François Bernier, a French physician at the Mughal court, who accompanied Aurangzeb from Lahore to Kashmir in 1665. The Mughal emperor moved with two camps, one always a day in advance of the other; if Bernier is to be believed, each required sixty elephants, two hundred camels, a hundred mules, and a hundred human porters for the ruler, his seraglio, and courtiers. In addition he was attended by 35,000 cavalry and more than 10,000 infantry and artillery men.[37] Europeans for their part quickly learned to settle into Simla with equal comfort, albeit without seraglios. Above the elephant and camel line, locally "recruited" coolies toiled miserably up the vertiginous paths, bearing on their sweating backs not only tons of dispatch boxes and files—the paraphernalia of empire—but also musical instruments (Lady Lytton brought her new Broadwood piano out from England), trunks full of theatrical costumes for amateur theatricals, crates of provisions, crockery, rugs, and curtains, baskets of linens, favorite armchairs, chandeliers, aspidistras, and faithful spaniels in traveling boxes, along with their mistresses in *jampans*. It was all, commented one official, "romantic but rather horrifying."[38]

By the 1840s cart roads were being built, followed by a burst of railroad construction soon after midcentury. Nevertheless, narrow-gauge passenger trains did not make their way to Darjeeling until 1881, to Simla until 1903. The ascent of the 5,000 feet from Kalka to Simla involved 103 tunnels, a succession of tight curves, and two miles of dizzying viaducts.[39] Emily Eden had anticipated the railroad's arrival when she published her memoir in 1866 and was not happy with the prospect. Already nostalgic for the "barbaric gold and pearl" of the past, she lamented that thanks to the "curse of railroads" the "splendour of a Governor General's progress is at an end" and that "these contrasts of public grandeur and private discomfort will probably be seen no more, on a scale of such magnitude." Henceforth the governor-general will be just another "first-class passenger with a carpet bag."[40] Not quite. "Splendour" could also ride the rails in British India.

The object of these long treks was not only to breathe the fresh air of the hills—the "Terrestrial Paradise"—but also to create "little islands of

Englishness" where colonials could feel at home as they never could submerged in the sea of India below.[41] Ascending from the plains, "all Nature seemed changed."[42] Suddenly familiar plants and trees evoked wave after wave of delicious nostalgia. Charles Metcalfe, "King of Delhi," recorded the ecstasy of his encounter with Kasauli and its surroundings in 1827: "Nature is here in luxurious fecundity—the hills are covered with trees and shrubs and flowers—what delights us Indians most is to see the earliest acquaintances of our Infancy, on which we have not before set eyes since we quitted England—daisies, buttercups, nettles, dandelions, etc. strawberries, raspberries, roses, growing wild, with larkspur, columbine, violets etc. and the oak too, the leaf different from ours, but the acorn the same." To Metcalfe it seemed a sin to pluck them, to "shorten the period of their brief existence." And he added, "There is a sentiment in Persian Poetry which has always struck me as beautiful, 'The Stone and the Plant which you imagine silent, have voices which reach to the Ear of Heaven.'"[43] A contemporary wrote of the "emotions at once gratifying and regretful" awakened by the sight of European shrubs and trees, by wild cherry and pear and modest violets rearing their heads: "such humble instruments as simple wild flowers—these make the heart yearn with tenfold eagerness to retrace the distance between it and the objects of its earliest and best remembrance."[44]

Later visitors to the Himalayas might have lacked the Orientalist culture of Metcalfe's generation of "Indians" but echoed his refrain, reveling in the flora of the hills, at once familiar and yet more glorious than at home. There were violets, dog-roses, lily of the valley, even English holly; primroses, cowslips three feet high, "an exquisitely blue miniature species [of polyanthus], whose blossoms sparkle like sapphires on the turf"; there were gentians beginning to unfold "their deep azure bells, aconites to rear their tall blue spikes, and fritillaries and Meconopsis burst into flower." Botanizing in the foothills of the Himalayas en route to Darjeeling, Joseph Hooker came upon brambles, violets, wild strawberries, and geranium, "flowers . . . so notoriously the harbingers of a European spring that their presence carries one home at once."[45] When the fog lifted over Simla, Emily Eden found the hills "all blue and green and covered with flowers," and she wrote, "I have felt nothing like it, I mean nothing so English, since I was on the terrace at Eastcombe."[46]

New arrivals recognized with equal pleasure flowers growing wild, such as begonias and cannas, that they had known only as hothouse flowers at home.[47] Most of all they were struck by the profusion and size of rhododendrons.

"Such beautiful rhodedendrons [sic]," Fanny Parks exclaimed. "They are forest trees, not shrubs as you have them in England." Indeed, she was surprised to find that they were commonly referred to as "flower wood" and burned as fuel.[48] In April, when they were at their height, the hills were blanketed with scarlet blossoms, "shaded with deep crimson." Framing them in their dark foliage were the snowy peaks of the higher mountains and the brilliant blue of the sky—"anything more dazzling . . . you cannot imagine." Sadly, their glory was short-lived. By May the blossoms were beginning to "fall like a shower of fire, and alight on the richest carpet of maiden-hair fern, and blue dog-violets, which everywhere clothe these hanging woods, so that you can scarcely set your foot on the earth without crushing a tuft of such treasures as would enchant the heart of an English gardener."[49]

Lady Canning, much more of an adventurer than most of her sister Englishwomen, traveled far beyond Simla to the border of Tibet by Lord Dalhousie's "road"—a narrow defile carved out of steep mountainsides that rose to 15,480 feet with terrifying drops below—and could report on the different rhododendrons growing at different altitudes. The scarlet variety was universal between 6,500 and 10,000 feet; higher up, she came upon "very fine large spotted pink" ones and, later, beautiful large lilac and white trees. The Alpine rhododendron, she noted, was bright yellow, not pink, in these mountains. Edward Lear, fortunate to be in Simla as the rhododendrons reached their peak, was "bewilder[ed]" by the beauty of hill after hill aflame with crimson blossom, a "mass of ineffable colour . . . like nothing one ever saw or imagined." And everywhere: splendid deodars, identical to the cedars of Lebanon, and ilex woods.[50] There were also wild roses, encircling thirty-foot pines "in robes of the whitest blossoms," inspiring one military man to liken them to "so many maidens of the forest in their bridal garments." It was, as he declared, Europe, not Asia.[51]

If getting English flowers to grow in the plains required the patience of Job, it was almost child's play in the hills. Every bungalow had its garden, however minute, as part of the effort to re-create the life of home. "We pass our lives in gardening," wrote Emily Eden in 1838. Since virtually all of the spring plants of the Simla area were similar to those in Europe, one did not have to go far for bulbs.[52] "We ride down into the valleys and make the syces dig up wild tulips and lilies, and they are grown so eager about it that they dash up the hill the instant they see a promising looking plant and dig it up."

The strawberries were as fine as any in England. In early June she declared that she "never saw anything so pretty as the shrubs are just now," with "both pink and white roses in large masses." Indeed, her garden almost reconciled her to being in India, although there were setbacks, such as the time that a "mighty storm" brought devastation to all she had created—and worst of all to her double dahlia in colors of "rhubarb and magnesia"—the only double dahlia in India, she boasted.[53] A half-century later, gathering wild ferns and replanting them in rockeries below their windows became for Lady Dufferin and the entire viceregal family a "new mania" as they discovered the unwonted pleasures of getting dirt under their fingernails and shooing off servants all too eager to help.[54]

The problem with Himalayan hill stations, however, was that they teetered precariously on ridges with scarcely any level ground. One writer has characterized Simla as a "mixture of Surrey and Tibet," the "knot where half a dozen ridges of high ground meet, a starfish or an octopus of narrow ridges."[55] On her first visit, Lady Curzon was struck by the sight of "houses slipping off the hills and clinging like barnacles to the hill-tops."[56] Bungalows were set on little shelves hewn out of the hillside along steep, narrow paths. They might gamely carry names redolent of olde England—Victoria Lodge, Ladyhill, Richmond Villa, Primrose Cottage, Strawberry Hill—and aspire to a rustic half-timbering-cum-Gothic architecture, but the terrain was altogether different. Houses were mostly cramped, with small rooms, dark, dank and leaky during the rainy season. This made it all the more important to orient the living areas and garden so as to maximize sunlight. In Simla, Sir Edward Buck advised an east-northeast aspect since it "suits English plants better than any other, and seems to be equally good for English men and women and especially for children."[57]

Hill gardeners, then, had to deal with their often minute portion of the shelf plus the *khud,* the precipice that dropped off from it. The writer M. M. Kaye remembers that many houses had room for at most a front drive barely wide enough for a rickshaw, with a small lawn to one side with a single flowerbed, supplemented by flower pots hanging from the verandah.[58] A garden in Landour was a very tiny one, and yet "our estate is a large one, for it goes down the khud on both sides for a long way, and is only spoilt for our use by lying at an inconvenient angle of 70°." The *khud* sported its own flora, in this case daylilies and blue iris as spring blossoms, with dahlias to follow in the autumn, along with a host of ferns and other plants unfamiliar to the English eye.[59] Sara Duncan declared that her *khud* had its own "demon and can't be tamed." Even the rhododendron, ablaze on its incline in the spring, was unwelcome because in this clime it overshadowed everything else.[60]

Duncan was lucky, however, in having more level space than most for her garden. While she may be arch on occasion, with references to her colonial official husband as Tiglath-Pileser and friends as Thalia and Thisbe, her book offers an invaluable season-by-season account, "a novel of manners," she calls it, whose characters are ants and earwigs and above all flowers, "an artificial little community . . . eight thousand feet out of the world." She begins in April, the time of the annual migration from the plains, and runs until November, when things are packed away for the descent. To be sure, it is her *mali* who actually tends the garden, but she is very much in charge (and snips off wilted blossoms). What cannot be found native to Simla and environs, she obtains from Mr. Johnson, whom everyone goes to for seeds and bulbs as well as advice. One of the few flowers that are not available—one that has been "left at home . . . in the general emigration of English flowers"—is the peony, somewhat to her regret. For it is indeed an English garden that Duncan sets out to replicate in her bit of "shelf," although she admits to importing goldenrod from Canada.

In April, May, and June, pansies reign in her garden and everywhere in town ("they seem to like the official atmosphere"). There are also daffodils and thick borders of blue forget-me-nots along the drive, sweet peas, honeysuckle, wisteria, hollyhocks, petunias, and coreopsis. As the pansies begin to peter out, stocks come into bloom; snapdragons, tall field daisies, and mignonette thrive. Then, as the dry season reaches its height, the roses burst into bloom, climbing all over the house and spreading into the borders: "I don't believe there is another shelf in Simla that holds so many." Once the roses are out, all other flowers pale in comparison, and Duncan does not even try to tone down her paeans to their glory.

The monsoon rains begin about mid-June and last until September. They are not at all like "the gentle thing" that falls in England but "untamed, torrential." They wash the soil away and it must be replaced, basketful by basketful. Most people sit out the rainy season, leaving their gardens to the slugs, but Duncan this year has ventured on a "rains garden." There is an uncomfortable fortnight when the dry-weather plants turn leggy; then the rain-loving plants come into their own: "The verandah is odorous with lilies," both Japanese and day; tall stalks of tuberoses shoot up among the rose bushes; clumps of cannas "lord it at chosen corners on each side of the drive"; lobelia, salvia, fuchsias, sunflowers, nasturtiums, and even Michaelmas daisies among the (imported) goldenrod. She prefers flowers in the ground, rather than in the pots and hanging baskets beloved of many expatriate gardeners, so they can "move [their] feet and stir about at night, and take [their] share in the joys of the community." Nevertheless, she makes an exception for the hydrangea: "Put him in the ground and at once he grows woody and branchy and leafy, imagining perhaps," she adds somewhat surprisingly, "that he is intended to become a shrub." Dahlias crop up everywhere (Emily Eden's double dahlias are no longer exceptional) in the garden and on the *khud*-sides all over town. The dahlia took possession of Simla the same year as the government of India did (1830), she announces, and "mixes itself up with finance and foreign relations," growing promiscuously about the various government offices and along the roadways, painting "our little mountain town with the colours of fantasy and of freedom."[61]

Even Duncan, however, finds the unbridled promiscuity of the rainy season unnerving. "The jungle triumphs . . . , it overwhelms the place. Even on the shelf it is hard enough to cope with, creeping up, licking and lipping the garden through the paling, but out upon the public khud-sides it is unchecked and insatiable. We hate the jungle." Newcomers may rhapsodize about the "glorious freedom of the wilderness," but veterans see it as an intimation of Bacchus running amok on the hillside, seducing English flowers from the "paths of propriety" to the temptations of "unregulated living."[62] Perhaps it was a metaphor for India itself, pursuing the British even to their mountain retreats.

The Viceregal Lodge: Heyday of the Raj

Over the years, the wildflowers that had so delighted early visitors to the hills became scarcer and scarcer; gone were the days when Emily Eden could create a garden overnight simply by transplanting from the wild. By the turn of the century, "hardly a wild flower can be found in the vicinity of the station woods, chiefly owing to the fact that for many years past *jampanis* [the litter bearers] have constantly stripped the hill sides to decorate Simla dining tables."[63] As Simla grew from the tiny station of the 1830s to the seat of the government of India for half the year or more, the population swelled. Emily Eden had put the European summer population of Simla at 150 in 1838; a half-century later, the summer census counted 3,400 Europeans.[64] Within the limits imposed by topography, estates became grander and often vied with one another for the elegance of their architecture and of their gardens.

Barnes Court set the tone. More like an old English country house than any other in Simla, with its "nostalgic Half-timbering," it was built on a spur so that it had fine views in three directions. Unlike many Simla houses, it had a level stretch of lawn and terraced gardens and pretty walks "in the English style, its trees cunningly disposed."[65] Over time, it received its share of distinguished guests, including governors-general and commanders-in-chief; eventually it became the residence of the lieutenant-governor of the Punjab and later the state guest house, Even more ambitious was Rothney Castle, acquired in 1867 by Allan Octavian Hume, officially Secretary for Agriculture to the Government of India and unofficially ornithologist, Theosophist, and founder of the Indian National Congress. Once Hume took up Theosophy, with its insistence on the sanctity of all life, he had to instruct those supplying him with bird specimens that they could no longer shoot them. The religion did not enjoin its adepts to asceticism, however, and Hume was free to realize his ambition of turning Rothney into a showplace. He spent some two *lakhs* (200,000) of rupees of his personal fortune to convert the house into a "veritable palace" where he hosted large dinner parties and balls. Madame Blavatsky, the high priestess of Theosophy, was a frequent guest, happy to escape the broiling heat of Madras and bask in the adulation of her followers. To create a garden worthy of the house, Hume brought out a European gardener and added a conservatory. The result was a "perpetual horticultural exhibition," gardens so magnificent that visitors were more than willing to brave the laborious climb to the castle.[66]

Local gossip had it that Hume poured enormous sums of money into Rothney Castle, fully expecting to sell it to the government to serve as official residence for the viceroy, but apparently the ascent was too torturous for all but the stoutest of heart. Although governors-general and, later, viceroys had been summering in Simla off and on for decades, they had no permanent quarters and had to settle for what was on offer. In the early days this was less of a problem. Once they improvised curtains, put down the carpets, chandeliers, and wall shades they had brought from Calcutta, and installed their French chef, Lord Auckland and his sisters were content with what Emily described as "very like a cheerful middle-sized English country-house." To be sure they had to hastily construct huts for their 120 servants, watch the beaten earth roof for leaks during the monsoon season, and contend with the plague of fleas ushered in by the rains. But all in all she pronounced the seven months they spent in Simla in 1838 a time "as good as it is possible to pass in India—no trouble, no heat, and if the Himalayas were only a continuation of Primrose Hill or Penge Common, I should have no objection to pass the rest of my life on them."[67]

When the annual exodus to Simla was officially—if reluctantly—sanctioned by the home government, the problem of appropriate housing became more acute. By the 1870s the viceroy's entourage had swollen and the number of servants doubled; balls and dinners had to accommodate many more than the cozy—all too cozy—society of Lord Auckland's day. *Faute de mieux,* they fell back on Peterhof, a hilltop pile rented from the Raja of Sirmur, which served as the viceregal residence from the 1860s until 1888. It was rumored to have been on the site of an old cemetery and inspired little affection. Indeed, it seemed to embody the odd mixture of opulence and tawdriness peculiar to the Raj. The roof leaked, plaster fell from the ceiling in the monsoons, and the lack of plumbing condemned inhabitants to the much-detested "thunderbox." Lord Lytton dismissed Peterhof as "a hideous little bungalow, horribly out of repair and wretchedly uncomfortable," in fact, "a cow stable." More charitably, his wife likened it to "a large rectory," while Lord Ripon's private chaplain referred to it as a "shooting box." Eventually there were suspicions that the hill upon which it sat might slip away. Still, many a gala was held under the festive *shamiana,* a flat-roofed tent on the lawn outside the mansion.[68]

Viceroys came and went every few years, and much as they might grumble and plead for a house to match their imperial state, they did little about it until Lord and Lady Dufferin arrived in 1884. Lady Dufferin dismissed Peterhof as little more than a cottage, quite suitable for a family leading a domestic life but "very unfit for a Viceregal establishment," so small were its drawing rooms and apartments and so cramped its grounds. "Altogether," she added, "it is the funniest place! At the back of the house you have about a yard to spare before you tumble down a precipice, and in front there is just room for one tennis court before you go over another. The A.-D.-C.s are all

Fig. 23. Viceregal Lodge, Simla
[Postcard, author's collection]

slipping off the hill in various little bungalows, and go through most perilous adventures to come to dinner."[69] Her husband had long fantasized about building a dream castle somewhere—in his native Ireland, in his previous postings to Canada, Russia, and Turkey—but had always been frustrated by a lack of resources, either personal or public. Now, with the blessing of Lord Randolph Churchill, the secretary of state, he built his enchanted palace atop Observatory Hill, a few hundred yards from Peterhof and appropriately the highest point in Simla (Fig. 23). Appropriately, too, this symbol of empire stood astride the great subcontinental divide: a glass of water thrown out on one side of the house would end up in the Bay of Bengal and on the other in the Indian Ocean.[70]

Like the later Lord Curzon, Dufferin was very much a hands-on potentate, determined to oversee every aspect of his Elizabethan "stronghold." It was designed by the architect Henry Irwin with a nod to the historicism of the later nineteenth century but without any of the orientalizing tendencies of the Indo-Saracenic style so prevalent in contemporary India. There was much to oversee. First of all, the crest of Observatory Hill had to be sheared off to provide a level plateau; next, large amounts of concrete poured over the crushed shale to provide a secure footing. The stone originally chosen for the walls proved too porous, so that quarries farther down had to be requisitioned for the tons of material carried up by trains of bullock carts; stone cutters balked at the demands made on them over the cold winter. During the season, Lord Dufferin liked nothing better than to offer guided tours of the work site. His wife describes one such inspection, clambering over scaffolding and teetering over "yawning chasms." She marveled at the employment of young Indian women "in necklaces, bracelets, earrings, tight cotton trousers, turbans with long veils handing down their backs, and a large earthenware basin of mortar on their heads." They walk, she noted, "with the carriage of empresses, and seem as much at ease on top of the roof as on the ground floor."[71]

When the Dufferins arrived for their last season in Simla, they were dismayed at "how unpromising" it all looked, and yet by late July they were able to move in. But this was the middle of the monsoon season, which sorely tested the house: "The rain falls in the most vicious manner, with the plain intent of entering our new house and of discovering every weak place in it." It also washed away the carriage roads leading to Observatory Hill and obscured the lovely views that were the glory of the Viceregal Lodge.[72] Nevertheless, the Dufferins delighted in showing off the wonders of the building, with its stately entrance hall, its ballroom that could hold eight hundred, and—*mirabile visu*—electric lights powered by a generator that had been dragged up the hill. It was the first house in Simla to boast electricity, but when the first ball was held many ladies found to their dismay that their gowns, "so bewitching by lamp- and candle-light, now appeared distinctly shabby."[73] Unusual, too, was the large, white-tiled kitchen in the basement (not a distant cookhouse as in Calcutta) and the facilities for the *dhobis* or laundrymen. Now, instead of squatting "on the brink of a cold stream there to flog and batter our wretched garments against the hard stones until they think them clean," they "will be condemned to warm water and soap, to mangles and ironing and drying rooms."[74]

Not everyone shared the Dufferins' enthusiasm for the Viceregal Lodge. The India Office, under new management, was staggered by the cost—over a hundred thousand pounds to build and a huge budget for annual upkeep as well (a satirist declared it "a joy and an expense forever").[75] Critics compared it uncharitably to a Scotch hydro, to Pentonville Prison, to St. Pancras Station. One early twentieth-century visitor remarked: "The hall had an almost loveable naïve ugliness as, I think had the whole of Vice-Regal Lodge, apart from the outside which glories in a spa-like monstrosity. Those who built it had no doubts about the suitability of an enlarged English country-house ... being set down in India."[76] Future viceroys and their consorts also found much fault with it. "A Minneapolis millionaire would revel in it," commented Lady Curzon, who knew whereof she spoke since she was herself the daughter of a Chicago millionaire. Only Edward Buck seems to have noticed that the builders of the Lodge neglected to orient the dwelling rooms east-northeast as local knowledge dictated, but there wasn't much that could be done about that.

Still, the Lodge *did* capture the magnificent views of the distant mountains. It was set, as the editor of the *Civil and Military Gazette* declared, "amid a panorama of beauty which almost takes the breath away."[77] The views were complemented by gardens of a spaciousness never possible at Peterhof. And, rare for precipitous Simla, it had real lawns (although not nearly as extensive as those of Naini Tal's Government House—officials tended to be competitive on the subject of lawns).[78] Lord Lansdowne, who followed close on the heels of the Dufferins, brought in an English gardener to landscape the grounds, planting appropriate trees and shrubs and laying out flowerbeds and terraces, all quite suitable for Lady Lansdowne's garden parties and afternoon teas. In Lord Curzon's view, the grounds were the only thing that made the Lodge bearable. He extended the lawns, and added an avenue of limes and a rose pergola, the latter a typical feature of late Victorian estates.[79] Lady Minto was credited with the rose garden and herbaceous borders. *Thacker's New Guide to Simla* (1925) noted approvingly that the grounds were beautifully laid out. "To the west are terraces well turfed, prettily planted with ornamental shrubs and flower beds around the margin of beautifully kept lawns."[80] After the rains the borders were resplendent with hollyhocks, cornflowers, dahlias, salvias, buddleias galore. "I have a gardener," Lady Reading noted with satisfaction, "who does not object to cutting, so my sitting-room looks a picture with masses of Madonna lilies and huge bunches of every other shade of blossom." Needless to say, her gardener was assisted by an army of *malis* to "plant, hoe, and water a patch of hillside into an English-looking garden"—with ten or more at any one time to keep the monkeys from vandalizing the herbaceous borders.[81]

If the rulers of India retreated to Simla to escape from the plains, they found in time that they also needed a retreat from Simla and its endless round of official duties, garden parties, balls and dinners, charity functions, gymkhanas at Annandale, and so on—just browsing through Lady Dufferin's diary leaves one vicariously exhausted, and she was only the viceroy's wife! For those who could afford it, Mashobra, some six miles from Simla, was the ideal weekend destination. It lay on a ridge stretching away to Mahasu on the slopes above Simla. Boasting some of the finest woodlands in the region, Mashobra escaped the heat and dusty roads of Simla during May and June before the rains settled in; in late September and October, the climate was "superb." Lord Elgin acquired the "Retreat" at Mashobra in 1896 and other viceroys followed suit, appreciating the more "earthy" character of the house, which, although hardly a simple cottage, was built in the local vernacular of wooden beams packed with stone and a mortar of clay or baked lime (Fig. 24). Even during the monsoon, Lady Reading took pleasure in the "undergrowth of maiden-hair fern, fresh green ferns and masses of wild flowers, wild lily of the valley, baby orchids, etc." The return to Simla on a Monday morning was no less a "delight, the rickshaw ride down-hill all the way, the wonderful views over the hills and mountains a continual joy."[82]

Fig. 24. The Retreat at Mashobra, near Simla. Samuel Bourne, 1860
[The British Library Board, Photo 15/1(53)]

Mashobra was also a favored haunt of Lord Curzon's nemesis, General Kitchener, commander-in-chief of the Indian Army. While Curzon was perforce contenting himself with minor improvements to the Viceregal Lodge—removing the heavy embossed wall coverings, installing in the dining room a replica of the carved screen from the imperial throne in the Forbidden City, and expanding the gardens—Kitchener was remodeling Snowdon, his half-timbered mansion on the far side of Jakko Hill, far more dramatically. "Lord Kitchener has carried his genius for organization into Snowdon, which is transformed beyond recognition," gushed Lady Wilson. New hall, new dining room, new library, all filled with objets d'art; a music room adorned with trophies of war and of the chase; a fine collection of rare old china and a "specially beautiful Japanese picture painted on silk, calculated to make any one break the tenth commandment"; and a lovely garden with terraces and rose gardens and fruit trees. Local gossip had it that he could be seen pottering about the roses early in the morning, clad in bright blue pyjamas.[83]

But it was at Wildflower Hall in Mashobra that Kitchener most fully indulged his passion for gardening. At an elevation of 8,000 feet, the estate commanded magnificent views of the snowy ranges beyond Simla. Earlier, the hero of Omdurman had created Eden on an island in the Nile facing one of the cataracts; later he won prizes for his orchids at the Calcutta flower show. Now it was the turn of the mountains. He had the tops shaved off two hills to open up the views. After church on Sundays he would station himself in the garden, directing the workmen planting trees, flowers, and herbaceous borders. His efforts were chronicled by the *Englishman,* a Calcutta newspaper: "It is an open secret that the Commander-in-Chief is an enthusiastic gardener: indeed, it is said that he is never happier than when improving the grounds at Mahasu [site of Wildflower Hall]. . . . The only fault apparently that Lord K. has to find is that shrubs and flowers do not grow quickly enough."[84]

Not eager to rub elbows with Kitchener at leisure as well as at work, Lord Curzon escaped in the opposite direction, to Naldera. Simla had never been to his liking and became all the more distasteful for having to be shared not only with the commander-in-chief, with whom he was engaged in a power struggle over the role of the military, but also with the lieutenant-governor of the Punjab, living in baronial splendor at Barnes Court, with whom he had also quarreled. A beautiful glade tucked among the deodars with stretches of grass "like English downs," Naldera overlooked the Sutlej River. It was the only place in the hills Curzon truly loved—so much so that he gave the name to one of his daughters. Here he had a nine-hole golf course laid out, but he also often carried out his administrative duties for days on end from a huge tent pitched nearby, which he much preferred to the Viceregal Lodge. He was able to communicate between the two, it was said, by means of heliographs sending signals in Morse code between the two points by means of flashes of sunlight.[85]

Simla took itself very seriously, but other Himalayan stations could rival it for climate, natural and cultivated beauty, and Englishness. By rights, Darjeeling probably should have been chosen as the imperial summer capital. Charlotte Canning certainly thought so. Not only was it far closer to Calcutta, but it also offered spectacular views of some of the world's highest mountains. By the late 1850s, more than half the journey from Calcutta could be made by rail. But Darjeeling had two main defects: Simla had gotten off to a head start and snared the elite of officialdom, leaving Darjeeling primarily to—horror of horrors—*boxwallahs* and tea-planters. Moreover, to reach Darjeeling, as we have seen, travelers had to cross the *terai,* characterized all too accurately by Lady Canning as "a jungle, pestilential at some seasons."[86]

Dehra Dun also had its partisans. It lay in the beautiful Doon Valley, encircled by the Ganges to the east, the Yamuna to the west, and mountains to the north and south. Easier of access than Simla, it had a pleasant climate most of the year. It stands in the middle of the plain, "like a lovely English village, each house surrounded with rose hedges, and bowery, billowy greenness." There was scarcely a house without a cluster of tall bamboo; collectively these formed a long avenue through the town, swaying in the breeze "like gigantic clusters of ostrich feathers." And, growing in clusters around the little church in the middle of the village, the *hibiscus mutabilis,* a rose that changed color over the morning from pure white to deep crimson.[87] Lady Reading, too, was enraptured by one of Dehra's gardens: "a riot of sweetpeas, verbena, cornflowers, hollyhocks," with, somewhat incongruously, a band of Gorkhas playing on the lawn.[88] Small wonder that it was Lord Hardinge's favorite spot in India or that many Britons, unable to face the thought of returning to their homeland, chose to retire there.[89]

For the few months when Dehra Dun was uncomfortably hot, residents could climb the twenty-six miles up to Mussoorie-Landour, four thousand feet higher. Although Edward Lear found Mussoorie too much like an English watering place for his taste, the views out over the Doon valley, he wrote, "are lovely, and recall Italy and Claude's pictures." The winding Yamuna River in the distance reminded him of the Thames at Richmond, the vegetation, however, a mixture of Indian and European.[90] Fanny Parks had found old friends in Mussoorie—oaks in bud, raspberries, clematis, woodbine delighting her "with its fragrance, and the remembrance of days of old." Later in the season the yellow broom was in full flower, putting her "in mind of the country by the seaside at Christchurch, Hampshire, where the broom is in such luxuriance."[91]

At the height of the Raj, Mussoorie was smaller than Simla, and decidedly less claustrophobic, physically and socially. As Lady Dufferin noted, it had the great advantage of lying on an outside spur of the Himalayas, at the edge of the mountains, so that it did not feel cut off from the world: "You can't imagine what a delightful sense of freedom this gives, because you don't know what it is to be encaged in the very heart of the Himalayas for the greater part of the year."[92] Further, while viceroys might drop in occasionally, there was no official presence, making for an infinitely less stuffy atmosphere. While all the hill stations were gossipy places, Mussoorie acquired in time the raciest reputation of all as a place for assignations, still more enticing when the railroad made it a possible weekend destination from Delhi. Coincidentally or not, it also was alleged to have even more—thoroughly English—ghosts than other hill stations.[93]

Ootacamund: "The Sweet Half-English Neilgherry Air"

There were difficulties in replicating idyllic English villages atop narrow Himalayan ridges, with houses confined to whatever bits of level ground could be carved out and gardens dropping away to nothingness. Colonel Waddell might insist that "many of the walks [around Darjeeling] are very pleasant and resemble English lanes,"[94] but for most it was a stretch to project scenes of the English or even the Scottish countryside onto the Himalayas. Lady Dufferin was perhaps closer to the mark when she first set eyes on Simla: "The only place that I have ever imagined at all like this spot is Mount Ararat with the Ark balanced on the top of it, and I am sure that when the rains come I shall feel still more like Mrs. Noah."[95] As indeed she did during the unusually wet spring and summer of 1885.

The effort was far more convincing in the open, grass-covered Nilgiri Hills of southern India. Here one could find landscapes to feed the most voracious nostalgia. Ootacamund, known as Ooty by the "abbreviating Saxon," was most commonly likened to the South Downs of Sussex.[96] Many were the other candidates, however: "Hertfordshire lanes, Devonshire Downs, Westmoreland lakes, Scotch trout streams and Lusitanian views" (Lord Lytton); "the vegetation of Windsor Forest or Blenheim spread over the mountains of Cumberland" (Macaulay). During the rainy season the points of comparison were equally British, albeit not always favorable. Richard Burton, on sick leave from the army in 1847, found the combination of monsoon weather and dull society nearly intolerable: "What a detestable place this Ootacamund is during the rains! From morning to night, and from night to morning, gigantic piles of heavy wet clouds, which look as if the aerial sprites were amusing themselves by heaping misty black Pelions upon thundering purple Ossas.... When there is no drizzle there is a Scotch mist: when the mist clears away, it is succeeded by a London fog."[97] Lord Lytton, on the other hand, found the rain reinforced his view of Ooty as "a paradise": "The afternoon was rainy and the road muddy, but such beautiful *English* rain, such delicious *English* mud."[98]

Ooty was the most important of several stations in the Nilgiris or "Blue Mountains." The name was attributed by some to the blue haze that often blankets them, by others to a shrubby blue wildflower, *Strobilanthes callosa*, which blooms only every few years. Sir Thomas Munro, governor of Madras, had the good fortune to arrive at such a moment: "[It] makes them look," he wrote, "as if they were covered with heath [heather]"—possibly a case of wishful thinking, since the bloom is paler than the purple of true heather. Ooty itself lay on a rolling plateau whose highest peaks were over 8,000 feet, near the line of demarcation of the two monsoons from east and west.[99] The founding father of the settlement was the Collector of Coimbatore, John Sullivan. Quickly following up on the glowing report of two of his scouts, he made a tour of the region in 1819, accompanied by a French naturalist. The naturalist, who had felt himself "aux portes du tombeau" down in the plains, underwent a miraculous cure in the mountains, which seemed to confirm everyone's view that this would be an ideal place to recover one's health. Dr. Baikie, medical resident at the station in the early 1830s, pronounced its climate "the most perfectly European of any point in the hills," generally less affected by the vicissitudes of the monsoons, than any other. If proof were needed that the climate of the Nilgiris were ideally adapted to "our constitution," Baikie declared, "it would be sufficient to look at the European children, whose rosy chubby cheeks, sparkling eyes, and buoyant spirits, form a pleasant contrast with the pale, languid, irritable-looking little wretches one is so often doomed to see dying by inches in the low country." Burton acknowledged the truth of such observations but couldn't resist observing St. Stephen's churchyard: "so extensive, so well stocked, that it makes one shudder to look at it."[100]

Within a year or two of first reconnoitering the hills, Sullivan settled himself and his family in Ooty, spending more time speculating in real estate than on his official duties, much to the annoyance of his superiors. Under his supervision, the station took off more rapidly than Simla. It was nearer both Madras and Bombay (although refugees from the two presidencies made a point of not mixing), and once Sullivan had put local convicts to work cutting a road (he felt certain there was no place in the wilderness they would want to escape to), it was relatively accessible: from Madras, depending on the route chosen, it was between 332 and 393 miles; from Bombay, one sailed down the coast to Calicut (the sea voyage itself being recommended for invalids) and then traveled inland some 150 miles. The most agreeable route from Madras ran through Vellore, Bangalore, and Mysore, but one was warned not to pass the night in the broad belt of jungle along the way. Unless officials were already on tour in the south, it was too long a trip for comfort from Calcutta, since it involved a long passage at sea down the length of the east coast and doubling stormy Cape Comorin, but Governor-General Lord Dalhousie made it nevertheless. "Broken by the death of his wife, overwork and ill-health," Dalhousie came to the Nilgiris for a prolonged stay in 1855, favoring Rota Hall, with its beautiful views of the Blue Mountains and gardens fragrant with *Datura brugmantia*.[101]

It was not by chance that Ooty came to look so English. In this landscape of open, grass-covered downs, Brits were able to "complete the curious illusion of England-in-India"[102] far more easily than in the Himalayas (see Pl. 10). Sullivan himself set the tone. The estates he and his associates carved out in the hills were called Grasmere Lodge, Kenilworth, Woodcock Hall, Apple Cottage; what passed for the town center was grandly named Charing Cross; and the "loch" created by damming a rivulet had an extension christened

Windermere. A great lover of gardening, Sullivan laid out a garden wherever he built a house. At his own expense he imported a gardener from England who brought the first seeds for apples, peaches, strawberries, raspberries, and hollyhocks. Others imported a range of English and Scottish flowers, and oaks and firs, and experimented with them at different altitudes and different exposures in the hills. An account of 1832 refers to a garden at Ooty where the "fragrance of roses, heliotrope, mignonette, geraniums and violets . . . filled the air." Roses, too, were soon a staple, with newer varieties constantly replacing the older stock. Poppies were originally grown for opium by Badaga villagers lower down the slopes, but after this was prohibited in 1854, they were found only in European gardens.[103]

Sullivan was also eager to promote the cultivation of European vegetables in Ooty and its environs: potatoes, turnips, radishes, tomatoes, string beans, artichokes, lettuce, Brussels sprouts. Within a year or two of settling there, he had applied for and won government permission to appropriate more than nineteen hundred acres, ostensibly for agricultural experimentation; in fact, it seems to have been mainly a way to take up the land for his own uses. Nevertheless, various plans for agricultural development were mooted in the following years. In the 1840s the botanist Robert Wight was sent out by the Madras government to study crops appropriate to the temperate climate of the hills, especially the possibilities for growing European produce: "Despite the joys of Indian fruit and veg (mangoes and okra) it seems that expatriates still pined for strawberries and lettuce."[104]

A scheme had been floated in the 1830s to import small farmers and mechanics from England to cultivate the land, and two European gardeners were charged with ordering quantities of seed and fruit trees from England and Persia. The directors of the East India Company vetoed the settlement idea and cancelled most of the order. More realistic was a plan to offer land to British officers who wished to retire to India and devote themselves to farming according to "the British system of husbandry." In fact, the Nilgiris did become such a favorite retirement spot that by the turn of the century it seemed to resemble nothing so much as Guy de Maupassant's description of an Algerian village inhabited solely by generals. For officers who had spent a lifetime in the subcontinent and lost all touch with the homeland, it was far preferable to Cheltenham or Tunbridge Wells—both England and India. They left it to others, however, to turn the grassy meadows into potato fields and tea plantations, choosing instead to cultivate roses and sweet peas and begonias in anticipation of the annual flower show in the Botanical Garden.[105]

Not surprisingly, English flowers thrived spectacularly in the Nilgiris (as did dandelions, docks, and thistles, which had stowed away with imported seeds). Baikie reported a heliotrope bush ten feet high and thirty feet in circumference, while Charlotte Canning marveled at specimens twenty feet in diameter. Geraniums grew as hedges. A Mr. Rhode sowed gorse bushes broadcast on the downs. His house, The Cedars, built about 1860, was considered the "most English-looking" house in Ooty, both inside and out, and surrounded by beautifully planted grounds. When Macaulay, no lover of things Indian—or of nature, for that matter—visited the station, he found himself smitten with the place: it had "very much the look of a rising English watering place," with his cottage "buried in laburnums, or something very like them, and geraniums which grow in the open air." In 1848 a public botanical garden was created, laid out and supervised by a gardener who had trained under Joseph Paxton at Chatsworth. Visiting a decade later, Lady Canning was impressed with what he had accomplished on a small budget. She especially admired new varieties of fuchsias, heliotropes, and verbena eleven feet high—"as large as the largest shrub of lauristinus." Several decades later, when a permanent summer residence for the governor of Madras was at last built after years of renting one house or another, its primary virtue was a location just above these gardens, together with grassy lawns, terraced beds, and rose nursery. The building itself, so lovingly modeled by the Duke of Buckingham after his own ancestral pile at Stowe, "may, without libeling it," Price allowed, "be called distinctly ugly."[106]

Lady Canning preferred Coonoor, the hill station on the southern escarpment of the Nilgiris, for its dramatic views. Here, she wrote Queen Victoria, "I have a view across the valley of hills, with woods of evergreen and rocky precipices," and beyond, "a glimpse of the burning plain, just enough to remind me of what I have left." To her, the country was like the "Highlands on a gigantic scale." But although she welcomed the familiar sights, the rose-covered cottages with their beautiful gardens, and appreciated the unwonted joy of wearing warm clothes, she was drawn especially to "the gorgeous foliage and tangle of creepers, sometimes like curtains of great green leaves looped up with coils of ropes." She loved to drive down several thousand feet "into damp regions full of beautiful plants." The one cottage in Ooty that met with her approval was Woodcot, built on a ridge by Colonel Cotton of the Madras Engineers. Mrs. Cotton, she noted, "is very English & came late to India & knows how to appreciate the things new to her instead of wanting what is not to be had, & her garden & collection of orchids show this." The comment reveals as much about Charlotte Canning as about Mrs. Cotton.[107]

Had there been more Mrs. Cottons and Lady Cannings, Edward Lear would have been a great deal happier. Between Canning's visit to the Nilgiris in 1858 and his own more than fifteen years later, the population had mushroomed. This trend was accentuated when the Presidency of Madras's summer exodus was regularized in 1870 and the whole government took to the hills. What with cricket grounds, gymkhanas, libraries, hunt clubs ("If you wish to enjoy deer-stalking in perfection, and without restraint, go to the Neilgherry Hills"),[108] and garden parties at the governor's residence, the ambiance became suffocatingly English (see Pl. 11). Lear found Coonoor, with its croquet ground and all too British houses, "totally undrawable as Indian scenery—it is not unlike Bournemouth here and there, but with different foliage." Ooty was no better. While the walk around the lake might be beautiful, it was bordered by English furze, and roses abounded everywhere. Only the view from the rock known as Lady Canning's Seat inspired enthusiasm. Other than this, the "impossible picturesqueness"—the exotic, the unfamiliar, the colorful—that he sought was not to be found in the hill stations of India.[109] Had Lear come a decade or two later, his sharp eye might have detected that from the terrace of Government House in Ooty, the slope of Mount Dodabetta bore an "astonishing and uncanny" likeness to the English Prime Minister, Lord Salisbury.[110] Not picturesque, hardly exotic, but interesting.

Ironically, however, Ootacamund was being Australianized as fast as it was being Anglicized. Lear had noted in his journal that there were "trees everywhere, which is not what I was led to expect." What he did not realize was that the once open hills were now overrun with invasive eucalyptus, melanoxylon (blackwood), and wattle, the kudzu of the Nilgiris. In 1826 Sir Thomas Munro had described the ride from Kotaghery to Ooty as "beyond comparison, the most romantic I ever made." Before reaching John Sullivan's house the party halted on the highest ridge and marveled at the scene below: "The face of the country is covered with the finest verdure, and is undulated in every form. It is composed of numberless green knolls of every shape and size, from an artificial mound to a hill or mountain. They are as smooth as the lawns in an English park, and there is hardly one of them which has not, on one side or other, a mass of dark wood, terminating suddenly as if it had been planted."[111]

In succeeding years, however, the "masses of dark wood," or *sholas* (forests of stunted evergreens), were felled for firewood. They were replaced by imported species from Tasmania and Australia, an unhappy example of arboreal globalization. By the end of the century one was hard put to it to find vestiges of pristine beauty, so completely had the invaders colonized lake shore and hillside. On page after page, Frederick Price, historian laureate of Ooty, rails against their disfiguring presence: "The green grassy slopes and pretty sholas of the valley have . . . disappeared. The former are now nearly everywhere covered with the dark and dreary gum tree [eucalyptus], and the equally depressing melanoxylon [blackwood]—in many cases so thickly that the houses erected on them are hidden." The wattle, an acacia, has grown so densely that it forms a thick scrub. Some of this planting was sponsored by the government itself; in other cases, large tracts of land were turned over to speculators for commercial plantations.[112] To add insult to injury, Sullivan's lake had become polluted early on. Burton mocked those who compared it to Lake Como or to the original Windermere: its waters were even then (in 1847) muddy, on its northern bank was a "dirty, irregular bazaar," and it was cut up by three embankments (later a railroad embankment further reduced its size).[113]

Shangri-La

What a bittersweet pleasure it was to "throw yourself upon the soft turf bank, and [pluck] the first daisy . . . you ever saw out of England."[114] Even the splenetic Burton was disarmed by simple reminders of the flora of home. When the swaggering, pig-sticking soldier from Sind looked beyond the muddy lake and filthy bazaar to the glories of the Nilgiri Hills, mockery gives way to poetic ecstasy. He describes the "beauties of the view: "On both sides of the water, turfy peaks and woody eminences, here sinking into shallow valleys, there falling into steep ravines, the whole covered with a tapestry of brilliant green, delight your eye. . . . The back-ground of distant hill and mountain, borrowing from the intervening atmosphere the blue and hazy tint for which these regions are celebrated, contrasts well with the emerald hue around."[115]

Burton's account does not ignore, as so many did, the two contrasting realities of the hill stations. Much as the British tried to insulate themselves from India, to create "landscapes of memory,"[116] the "native" bazaar was as much a part of hill life as the Mall. Life in the hills was just as dependent on Indians as it was in the plains, both the "tribals" native to these regions and the servants brought with them, often miserable in the cold. It has been estimated that, all things considered, it required ten Indians to support one European in the life to which he or she had become accustomed.[117] At the other end of the social scale, elite Indians followed the British to the hills in increasing numbers. In comparatively egalitarian Kodaikanal, they built bungalows, planted lovely gardens, played tennis, and joined in the season's activities. The Maharaja of Mysore settled into Fernhill in Ooty, while several Indian princes had residences in Mussoorie. Wealthy Parsees were especially prominent in the hill stations near Bombay and, being meat eaters and wine drinkers, found ready acceptance among the otherwise self-segregating British.[118]

Burton makes all too clear how claustrophobic the little society of the hill stations could be—not for nothing would Ootacamund become known as "snooty Ooty." An official wife compared life in the smaller stations to "being on a long voyage on a ship, with little news from the outer world."[119] In a station such as Simla at the apex of the political pyramid, it was not only the endless round of social events with the same people but also the jockeying for position and influence in the status-bound world of the "little tin gods." Even in the matter of planning dinners and garden parties, Lady Lawrence complained, "it is impossible to hear yourself speak because of the grinding of axes and gnashing of teeth."[120]

To many, it was preposterous even to think of governing India from remote hilltops for seven or eight months of the year—Gandhi referred to it as "government working from the 500th floor," while an American seconded to the British during World War I declared that officials were "as inaccessible as Mahadeva on Mount Kailash."[121] And yet it happened, informally or formally, for more than a century. Emily Eden could be as aloof as the best of them, but in a letter of May 1839 she offers a remarkably astute commentary on Simla:

Twenty years ago no European had ever been here, and there we were, with the band playing the "Puritani" and "Masaniello." and eating salmon from Scotland, and sardines from the Mediterranean, and observing that St. Cloup's [their French chef] potage à la Julienne was perhaps better than his other soups, and that some of the ladies' sleeves were too tight according to the overland fashions for March, &c; and all this in the face of those high hills, some of which have remained untrodden since creation, and we, 105 Europeans, being surrounded by at least 3,000 mountaineers, who, wrapped in their hill blankets, look on at what we call our polite amusements and bowed to the ground if a European came near them. I sometimes wonder they do not cut all our heads off, and say nothing more about it.[122]

One is bound to share Eden's wonder that the Raj was able to pull this off. And in the end, it was not British heads that rolled. . . .

While not all could dine on imported delicacies prepared by a French chef, with a band playing in the background, even more lowly Brits could aspire to something like the comforts of home in the hills. Just as the Romans replicated an alien way of life in England with their villas and baths and gardens, the British, too, built cottages with homey names and homey gardens. Indeed, the Mughals provide a closer analogy than the Romans, with their palaces and gardens in the verdant valleys of Kashmir, with its terraced hills full of fragrant flowers and fruits and sunlit water cascading to the lakes below. Was the annual exodus to the hills of the viceroy, council, commander-in-chief, and supporting bureaucrats more preposterous than that of the entire Mughal court with army in tow to distant Kashmir?

The British for their part were intent on re-creating the "England of our dreams" to an extent impossible in the lowlands.[123] But it was an exaggerated Englishness, an Englishness with "Cheltenham trappings," with "shooting sticks and riding whips in the shop windows; in the net-curtained bungalows named 'Pine Breezes' and 'Fairview'; in the crumbles and custards on the boarding-house menus." And it was all "counterfeit," in William Dalrymple's judgment: "Simla was and always has been an idealized picture-postcard memory of England, all teashops, village churches and cottage gardens—the romanticized creation of addled exiles driven half-mad by the Delhi heat. It looked as if it had been built from paintings on the tops of tins of shortbread. You kept asking yourself: what on earth was this strange half-timbered English village doing here in the middle of the Himalayas?"[124] To the novelist Mukul Kesevan, it was not really so strange; it existed as "not-India," not the "flat, hot, dusty, brown, diseased and overcrowded" India to which "the sahib gave his life in heroic service."[125] Why would he not feel entitled to an escape to the familiar?

But not everything about the hill stations was counterfeit, nor was the eagerness to see the landscape through England-colored glasses pure self-delusion. One should not make light of the joy with which the exile comes unexpectedly upon flowers of home growing in the wild. "I shall never forget this day," wrote Sir William Lloyd, one of the earliest travelers to the Simla hills (1821), when he came upon "the fir, the oak, the apricot, the pear, the cherry, together with wild roses, raspberries, thistles, dandelions, nettles, daisies, and many others," for they reminded him "of home, the days of my boyhood, my mother, and the happiest of varied recollections." Lloyd makes clear that it "was not, however, the effect of the prospects, for they were unlike those amongst the Welsh hills, but it was because I recognized a great number of trees and flowers common there."[126] It was not a matter of mistaking the Himalayas for the Welsh hills; the scenery was different but the vegetation similar. In a sense the flora had a metonymic effect, a part inspiring thoughts of the whole, a single flower or tree conjuring the totality of home. Sometimes the evocations are totally unexpected, as when Sara Duncan remarks of the "refreshment to exile [of] the cold, sharp fragrance of chrysanthemums" of her fall garden: "It brings back, straight back, the glistening pavement of Kensington High Street on a wet November night, and the dear, dense smell of London and a sense of the delight that can be bought for sixpence there."[127]

Cultivated gardens were also different in the hills. Where it was a constant battle to get English flowers to grow in the wilting heat of the plains, one could revel in all the familiar blossoms and scents, even if it was sometimes hard to find level ground or keep the *khud* at bay in steeper stations such as Simla. One thinks of Mabel Layton's garden in Pankot. Rose cottage, the garden, and Mabel form almost a single entity. "Her days are spent in celebration of the natural cycle of seed, growth, flower, decay, seed." The roses were of English stock, but flourished in her care.[128] Mabel and Pankot are fictional, but Paul Scott knew his English gardeners well. Babur and Jahangir, too, would have recognized in her a kindred spirit.

Bangalore: The Pensioners' Paradise

There was for some, however, an alternative to the bifurcated existence between plains in the winter, hills in the summer. Situated at an altitude of almost 3,000 feet in the midst of the Mysore tableland, Bangalore offered such a salubrious climate that it soon became the most important cantonment in peninsular India, with a corresponding expansion of the civil presence and all the support population that this implied. For nine months of the year, it was a "spot of England in India," or, as another writer puts it, "India without its scorching sun and Europe without its snow." Here, as one official gloated, one could play cricket on the parade ground for eight months of the year without ill effects.[129] Even in the summer months, one could pull on a shawl of a cool evening and enjoy lovely walks in the garden. With possibly a modicum of exaggeration, a French historian had pronounced "the plains of Mysore . . . the most beautiful habitation that nature has to offer to mankind upon earth." Once the British took these plains in hand and made Bangalore a capital in their own image, nature was, if anything, improved upon. Approaching the city of an evening in 1839, the Reverend William Arthur exclaimed over "hedgerows skirting the broad, regular roads, English-looking gates, lights shining from between clumps of trees, the white fronts of houses glistening in the brilliant moonlight, and the stir of buggies hurrying hither and thither."[130]

The city had fallen into British hands with the final defeat of Tipu Sultan in 1799. It had begun life in 1537 as the fortress city of Kempe Gowda, a local military chief tributary to the Vijayanagar Empire of South India. In time it was conquered by Haidar Ali and supplied the "sinews of war"—cannons, guns, and swords—for the armies of Mysore. It had also developed into a center of agricultural commerce and silk production under Haidar and his son Tipu. Soon after the conquest Francis Buchanan made an extensive survey of the territories newly won and found them exceedingly promising.[131] Bangalore, he noted, drew commerce from far and wide. Within a few years, too, the British realized that it was a far healthier place for a military camp than the old fort at Srirangapatnam, a pestilential island in the Cauvery River near Mysore where soldiers were dying like flies, and shifted their forces accordingly. It was, Henrietta Clive declared, a "country . . . well worth the pains of taking it." Settled into Tipu's palace, with its lovely garden full of "sweet roses," a year

Fig. 25. Bungalow, Bangalore
[From Janet Pott, *Old Bungalows in Bangalore*, 1977]

after the British victory, she had every reason for patriotic self-congratulation (and every reason to be glad she was not one of Tipu's poor wives when she learned how miserably they had been treated).[132]

Because the colonial city took shape only in the nineteenth century, well after the heyday of the Company nabobs, Bangalore skipped the garden house phase, passing directly into bungalow-imperial. Indeed, Bangalore's bungalows became celebrated throughout India for their whimsical ornamentation, cultivating forms of the Picturesque long after it had gone out of style in England. Classical and Gothic details "combined in wonderful flights of imaginative fancy": crenellated gables and towers, fretwork canopies known as "monkey-tops," and carved bargeboards over doors and windows. As the city grew, land became scarcer and the size of compounds smaller, adding pressure to expand upward from the one-story ur-model (Fig. 25). This allowed for even greater flights of fancy in the matter of crested roofs and embellished turrets. Edward Lear's entire Indian trip was a quest for the Picturesque, but even he found Bangalore's "queer houses . . . odd indeed." Still, for us they have something of the same charm in microcosm as Bombay's Victoria Terminus in macrocosm. And when cascades of brilliant bougainvillea bedecked the trelliswork, the result was a "fairy-tale atmosphere, a Gothick Arcadia."[133]

A floral Arcadia, too—a "garden paradise," as one visitor put it—thanks to the relatively temperate climate. Coming to Bangalore in 1839 after several lethargic years in Madras, Julia Maitland felt like Sleeping Beauty waking at last. "The early mornings especially are as pleasant as anything I can imagine," she declared. "They have all the sweetness and freshness of an English summer. The air smells of hay and flowers, instead of ditches, dust, fried oil, curry, and onions, which are the *best* of the Madras smells. There are superb dahlias growing in the gardens, and to-day I saw a real staring full-blown hollyhock, which was like meeting an old friend from England, instead of the tuberoses, pomegranates, &c., I have been accustomed to see for the last two years. We have apples, pears, and peaches. . . . The English children are quite fat and rosy, and wear shoes and stockings."[134]

Whatever his feelings about Bangalore's architecture, Lear, too, found its flowers delightful. Here, as in the hills, English flowers thrived, although one did have to be on guard against the pernicious ague that lurked in damp recesses at certain seasons. The elegant bungalow facades opened onto spacious lawns, with leafy shrubs and flowers blooming throughout the year— and, inevitably, ranks of potted plants edging the house and marching up onto the verandah. As a young cavalry officer stationed in Bangalore early in the twentieth century, Winston Churchill and two chums took a palatial bungalow "wreathed in purple bougainvillia. It stood in a compound of some two acres with a garden of "about a hundred and fifty splendid standard roses: Maréchal Niel, La France, Gloire de Dijon, etc.," set out, no doubt by someone who knew his roses. Churchill, incidentally, is still conspicuously visible on the blacklist at the Bangalore Club for nonpayment of dues.[135]

And not just English flowers, but English vegetables. The success of private gardeners growing European fruits and vegetables hitherto unknown in India stimulated a boom in market gardens supplying not only the local British population but also eager consumers as far away as Madras and Pondicherry. In fact, a hereditary community of gardeners long settled in Bangalore, the Vahnikula Kshatriya, showed a remarkable ability to adapt to the demands of cantonment and civil station. Ironically, much of the land and tanks appropriated for the expanding city had once belonged to them. They continued to grow flowers as well as fruits, vegetables, and spices in their plantations on the margins of the city, even exporting seeds and plants to England. The same community was instrumental in landscaping the city's many gardens and parks.[136]

It was their land, too, that was probably the source of Cubbon Park, named for Sir Mark Cubbon, who presided over Bangalore's coming of age from 1834 to 1861. The most extensive of Bangalore's numerous parks, it was "a lush grassy expanse with flower beds, shady bowers and flowering trees," covering some 320 acres and linking the cantonment and city—or separating the two. In due time it acquired a bandstand, statues of Queen Victoria, King Edward VII, and Jaya Chamarajendra Wodeyar, Maharajah of Mysore, and a Children's Park. Strolling across the lawns of a Sunday, listening to the military band, embraced by the reassuring presence of the queen, one might for a moment imagine oneself back home in summertime—that is, until one looked at the trees and acknowledged there was not a single English species in the lot: *champaks, gulmohurs,* jacaranda, frangipani, *neem,* sandal, and *ashoka,* African tulip, beautiful trees from all over the world except the northern climes.[137]

Near the western or city end of the park stood the Residency, a majestic white Palladian structure set in the midst of a "vast, undulating, and imperial garden" of ninety-two acres and lovingly tended by a succession of commissioners from Cubbon onward. Until its acreage was gnawed away for a number of public buildings, it rivaled the Lal Bagh in its splendid plantings, many of them in fact borrowings from the botanical garden. At its peak it even claimed a collection of 3,400 potted plants. As originally laid out, a central path marked by rows of royal palms led to the front portico, flanked on either side by green lawns, rose gardens, and arches covered with creepers. The path encircled a round pool with a central fountain spraying up into a fan palm. On the periphery of the formal garden there was an orchard of fruit trees and a kitchen garden. At some point a replica of an Ashoka Pillar was positioned at the entrance to the Residency and an artificial waterfall created to suggest the terraced watercourses of the Shalimar Gardens of the Mughals, both intended, perhaps, to reclaim its Indian heritage.[138]

For many of Bangalore's garden enthusiasts, however, the Lal Bagh was the real Mecca, especially since the Residency was off-limits to ordinary citizens. Combining a wealth of indigenous and exotic trees and plants, it was renowned for its annual flower shows (see chapter 4). The Reverend Norman

Macleod left a rapturous account of such a show around 1870, reminding us that vegetables can evoke as intense emotions of nostalgia as flowers:

> Our home feeling was greatly intensified by attending a flower show.... The most remarkable and interesting spectacles to me were the splendid vegetables of every kind, including potatoes which would have delighted an Irishmen; leeks and onions worthy of being remembered like those of Egypt; cabbages, turnips, cauliflowers, peas, beans, such as England could hardly equal; splendid fruit—apples, peaches, oranges, figs, and pomegranates, the display culminating in a magnificent array of flowers, none of which pleased me more than the beautiful roses, so redolent of home! Such were the sights of a winter's day in Bangalore.[139]

The area around the Lal Bagh became an important center of the nursery trade, drawing serious gardeners from all over India.[140]

English flowers, English vegetables, English church spires, English parks, non-English weather—is it any wonder that Bangalore was a plum posting for British military and civilian personnel alike? "Going into Bangalore from the districts is looked upon in the light of a trip to Paris, or a run up to town in England," wrote Commissioner Bowring.[141] No wonder, too, that the city became a paradise for Anglo-Indian pensioners from all over India. Not everyone could face "living out old age at Cheltenham or in the Asia Minor of South Kensington," in a homeland that became more alien with every year away. At home they were highly unlikely to have enormous houses, fine carriages, and a regiment of uniformed servants not only for themselves but even for their horses and dogs. And the climate: on coming ashore in Plymouth in mid-May after seventeen years in India, Fanny Parks was stung by the bitter sleet beating on her face. Everything looked "so wretchedly mean," the ladies' fashions so ugly and dull, the British Museum's collection of Hindu "idols" so pitiful—"and as for Ganesh, they never beheld such an one as mine, even in a dream." Parks might well have lamented with the Urdu poet the loss of "the garden and my nest." All that redeemed England in her eyes was the wonder of the new steam trains and the Devon hedgerows in their mantel of primroses, heatherbells, and wild hyacinths. Emily Eden encountered a woman who had been living in India for fifty years save for a year in England four years earlier: "She thought it a horrid country, and came out again. She is now 84, and is now going home, 'to give England another chance.'"[142]

There were more of those disinclined to give England a second chance than one might have imagined. Such was the canal engineer George Faulkner, a "man of a type perhaps little known in England, but far from uncommon in India, the Englishman to whom India has become a second mother-country, and who," claimed a fellow official, "would be unhappy and totally misunderstood and out of place in England." And yet Faulkner was so English in manners and feelings that although he had been in India for forty years, he spoke barely a dozen words of any Indian language, "grew the most beautiful flowers, planned and laid out the most lovely gardens"—in what style his chronicler does not say but we can guess—and was quite content to pursue his vocation and indulge his inventive genius in India. What was more, all of his seven children had been sent to England (and Paris, in the case of his daughters) for their education and all had returned to the picturesque seaside town of Cuttack in Orissa, where their hard-drinking, Ruskin-loving, "old Viking" of a father ran his hydraulic workshop like an oriental despot, to the despair of the Public Works Department.[143]

Men like Faulkner often chose to spend the evening of their lives in Bangalore, where a number of new suburbs beckoned. After a lifetime in the employ of the telegraph, the post office, and the Great Indian Peninsular Railway, John Hawkins, for example, retired to the city in 1909. For him it was the "salubrity and cheapness" that drew him, but for his wife it was the chance to indulge her three hobbies: poultry, cattle (i.e., buffalo), and flowers. Twenty years later he described their garden to his grandson as including fourteen large mango trees, much attacked by servants, squirrels, and crows. But it was the flower garden that was "a great source of pleasure to us," he wrote. "It is grandma's realm entirely. We have lovely dahlias in bloom now [August], also goldenrod, chrysanthemums, geraniums and hibiscus." He elaborated on the various species of the hibiscus family. Photographs of the multigabled brick house show a profusion of shrubs and flowers and, of course, a fine lawn.[144] As the old bungalows passed more and more into Indian hands, the new owners often carried on Bangalore's love affair with gardens until they, too, were overtaken by the ceaseless remaking of the city into its present incarnation as the Silicon Valley of India.[145]

Fig. 26. Carpet bedding in the Lal Bagh, Bangalore.
Curzon Collection, photographer unknown
[The British Library Board, Photo 430/4(7)]

The history of Bangalore has a stolidly British, middle-class continuity to it. After the excitement of Haidar and Tipu that preceded its anglicization, Bangalore evolved peacefully, almost uneventfully throughout the nineteenth and early twentieth centuries; even the tumultuous events of 1857–58 created scarcely a ripple in its Deccan calm. It was the epitome of a British colonial enclave, a city of parks and gardens, domestic, public, and market. The parks commemorated founding fathers such as Sir Mark Cubbon while the gardens proclaimed a sense of order and ease, replicating English tastes and English nostalgia, even for those pensioners who had no intention of returning to the chilly mists of their native country and even when they incorporated plants that were foreign to it (Fig. 26). As with the hill stations, Bangalore represented one end of the spectrum: the happy congruence of geography and climate that enabled the British to re-create their England as a garden in India. So successful were they, so much was it an improvement on the original, that frequently they never wanted to leave.

PART II

Gardens of Empire

CHAPTER 4

Eastward in Eden

Botanical Imperialism and Imperialists

In 1760 Haidar Ali, soldier of fortune and de facto ruler of Mysore, ordered the creation of a botanical garden in Bangalore, the first in India. He gave it the common name of Lal Bagh, or "red garden," for its abundance of roses and other red flowers. Inspired by the French gardens in Pondicherry and even more by the Mughal garden in newly conquered Sira, he wanted a similar retreat of his own. Like its Mughal models, it consisted of a series of square parterres intersected by paths lined with fruit trees. Cypresses framed rose bushes and flowerbeds. A small tank at the south end provided water. Haidar augmented the local flora with exotic plants from other regions of India. Flowers were one of his few indulgences in a Spartan life of almost constant warfare. A Portuguese soldier serving in one of his regiments recounted how Haidar would walk in his garden of an evening with his concubines, each holding a nosegay of flowers. Those from whom he plucked a bouquet would be his companions for the night.[1]

Haidar's son Tipu Sultan extended the gardens. "They please me very much," commented James Achilles Fitzpatrick, British Resident at the court of Hyderabad, "and are laid out with taste and design, [and] the numerous cypress trees that form the principal avenues are the tallest and most beautiful I ever saw."[2] Tipu shared his father's love of flowers and was in the habit of presenting a garland of jasmine to guests as a mark of particular favor. Frescoes of the battle of Polilur, his greatest triumph against the British, painted for the summer palace, depict him on horseback, incongruously smelling a bouquet of flowers amid the carnage all about him.[3] But Tipu was far more educated and cosmopolitan than his father, possessing a "large and curious library."[4] Like his Enlightenment contemporaries in Europe, he was an "improver," eager to embrace the latest technology and to experiment with new varieties of crops and plants, some from as far away as Afghanistan, Persia, and Turkey. He promoted agriculture in his dominions, introducing higher-yielding strains of rice. More significantly, he set up twenty-one stations for silkworm cultivation, with adjoining mulberry plantations, laying the foundations for the later preeminence of Mysore's silk industry.

In the summer of 1788 Tipu sent a stunningly ill-timed embassy to the French king, Louis XVI, in hopes of creating a grand alliance against the East India Company, with which Mysore (and France) had been sporadically at war for several decades. The ambassadors had a thoroughly good time and caused an Orientalist furor in the French capital. "They were," writes Joseph Michaud, "the subject of all conversations, on them all eyes were fixed, and the name of Tippoo Saheb became, for a moment, famous among the lighthearted people who were more struck by the originality of Asiatic costumes than by the importance of their possessions in India."[5] Having soon run through their funds, the envoys reluctantly returned, deeply in debt, bringing with them seeds and bulbs from the Jardin du Roi, along with gardeners, engineers, a clockmaker, and a disappointingly small military contingent. A decade later Tipu, ever hopeful of raising armies against the British, sent another embassy to the French colony of Mauritius in the Indian Ocean. This, too, was more successful botanically than militarily: the envoys brought back twenty chests of plants and seeds, along with clove and nutmeg trees that required eighty men to carry them over the Western Ghats from the port of Mangalore.[6]

After Tipu's death in 1799 at the battle of Srirangapatnam (where he also had an exquisite garden that reminded Lady Clive of Chantilly), the Lal Bagh passed into the possession of the victorious British army, presided over by a

British officer who amused himself stocking it with European and Chinese plants until he was transferred elsewhere and handed the garden over to the Madras Presidency. After several decades of intermittent neglect, William New, a Kew-trained gardener, was put in charge. New energetically resuscitated the garden and made it a botanical showplace, adding plantings from China, South Africa, the Indian Ocean, and Kew, as well as walks and avenues of fast-growing *Grevillea robusta*. Under New and his successors, it became a center of scientific research and oversaw the development of plants of ornamental and economic value.

As Ray Desmond would later write of Kew itself, Haidar's Lal Bagh is a palimpsest of garden styles and functions.[7] Like Kew, it evolved from a royal pleasure garden into a botanical garden; like Kew, it endured periods of neglect, shifting administrations, and debates about its very nature. What was it to be—the handmaiden of commerce and agriculture or a beacon of science? Or should it be above all a "green place," with, in Edward Lear's words, "something very rural quiet" where ordinary people could escape the hurly-burly of urban life?[8]

"Imperial Kew"

The botanic garden had its roots in the royal garden on the one hand and the physic garden on the other. Private gardens with their follies and temples, knots and pagodas had long been the preserve of princes and nobles, vying with each other for the elegance of their estates and the services of the most noted garden designers, who often crossed national borders, spreading styles and creating vogues. Italian craftsmen were especially in demand, for example, at Hampton Court during the sixteenth century. The first physic garden, too, was Italian. Established in Padua in 1545, it was attached to the medical school. Other physic gardens followed across Europe: Oxford in 1621, Chelsea in 1673. Practical rather than ornamental, these gardens served apothecaries with an array of medicinal plants whose history stretched back to antiquity.[9]

The influx of plants in the wake of the period of European exploration known as the Discoveries and consequent imperial expansion enriched both types of gardens. In the medieval period, the Arabs had been the principle agents of diffusion from east to west, bringing rice, citrus fruits, melons, mulberry trees, cotton, and sugar. At the same time they expanded the spice trade from Southeast Asia and India, whetting insatiable appetites for pepper, nutmeg, cinnamon, cloves, ginger, and more. The opening up of sea routes to Africa, Asia, and the Americas not only took Europeans to the sources of these spices, cutting out Arab and other intermediaries, it also unleashed on the continent a flood of new and exotic plants. For a moment, eager collectors fantasized that it might at last be possible to reconstruct the Garden of Eden with an ingathering of every known species, a sort of floral Noah's Ark. Soon, however, they were overwhelmed by a tsunami of new plants.

The problem was how to order them. Up until now botanists had relied on systems of classification dating from classical times, but these proved hopelessly inadequate to the task. Gradually the idea caught on of classifying plants according to family relationships, using binomial nomenclature to indicate genera and species. In a pioneering work of twelve volumes (1623), Gaspard Bauhin managed to describe some six thousand species accordingly before this system, too, succumbed to the flood of new plants, especially those supplied by Dutch enterprise in the East and West Indies. It was left to the Swedish botanist Carolus Linnaeus to bring order out of rising chaos, declaring, it was said, "Deus creavit: Linnaeus posuit." In other words, God had preordained him to reveal the order that lay behind the original creation of nature. Linnaeus proposed an entirely new basis for classifying plants, one that he readily acknowledged to be "artificial" (the natural relationships of the divine plan not yet having been revealed to mankind). Since plants reproduced sexually, they should be classified by a single feature, namely the numbers and arrangements of male stamens and female pistils each possessed. He came up with twenty-four classes, subdivided into orders, families, and finally into Bauhin's genera and species. Almost from the start, however, Linnaeus, too, found himself under attack from fellow botanists who considered his system an arbitrary one and, more to the point, incapable of absorbing many plants from distant corners of the globe, since counting stamens and pistils alone meant that many unrelated plants ended up quite literally as bedfellows—Linnaeus's terminology was heavy on marital metaphors.[10]

Initially botanists were most interested in pursuing the medicinal promise of new exotics. In time, however, large European trading companies such as the British East India Company and its Dutch and French counterparts realized the huge commercial potential of a wider range of plants and avidly sponsored the search for new species, less out of scientific curiosity than in hopes of enriching themselves and their nations. The Dutch had taken the lead in experimenting with potentially lucrative exotics with their gardens in Cape Town (1694), followed by the French, who established Pamplemousses on Mauritius (1735), both of which eventually ended up in British hands. The British also laid out a pioneering botanical garden on the island of St. Vincent in the West Indies in 1764. When Queen Victoria ascended the throne in 1837, there were about ten active British botanical gardens; at her death in 1901, the empire boasted 126.[11]

At the nerve center of this network was the Royal Botanic Gardens at Kew, the British counterpart of the French Jardin du Roi. The guiding forces behind the ascendancy of Kew were two remarkable amateur botanists, Lord Bute and Sir Joseph Banks. Bute joined with the Dowager Princess Augusta and George III to create one of the finest Georgian gardens in the land. He secured government funding of hitherto unimagined munificence, brought in a number of gifted architects and landscape designers, and augmented its stock of rare plants. By 1767 he boasted that "the Exotick Garden at Kew is by far the richest in Europe[,] . . . getting plants and seeds from every Corner of the Habitable world."[12]

When Bute fell from favor and Princess Augusta died, the vacuum at Kew was filled by Banks. The son of a wealthy Lincolnshire landowner, he had been captivated by natural history as a schoolboy. Still in his twenties, he circumnavigated the globe with Captain Cook, having paid his own way and that of a small entourage of transnational scientists and illustrators. The *Endeavour* returned to port in 1771 with a collection of some 3,600 dried plant species, of which more than a third were new to science, along with a wealth of seed and pickled specimens of animal and marine life, a portfolio of drawings, and assorted oddities from the Antipodes. Although the voyage had taken the lives of thirty-eight of the ship's crew and five of his scientist companions, Banks was immediately lionized by society and received by King George III at St James Palace.[13]

Banks went on to an illustrious career as president of the Royal Society for over thirty years (1788–1820) and the dominant power at Kew for even longer. He seemed to know and correspond with everyone, from the king on down. His interests spanned the globe. As overseer of the Gardens he excelled less as a scientist in his own right than as botanical entrepreneur and facilitator. He encouraged collecting by diplomats, merchants, military officers, and missionaries—in short anyone who might be traveling to distant shores. Just as importantly, Kew-trained gardeners now fanned out all over the world to collect and to supervise local establishments. The result was a steady influx of plants and seeds to Kew as well as a reciprocal outflow to the West Indies, India, and Australia.[14]

If Erasmus Darwin could sing of "Imperial Kew by Thames's glittering side,"[15] this was largely due to Banks. He had determined to make the garden "a great botanical exchange house for the empire." In an age that stressed not only the exotic and the beautiful but above all the useful—Louis XVI wore a boutonnière of potato flowers offered by Parmentier—Banks detailed the potential agricultural benefits of botanic exploration, for both the motherland and her colonies. Botany became the symbol, as Richard Drayton has written, of an "improving plantocracy."[16] Kew itself reflected this perspective: while botanical activities garnered much of the public attention, they occupied only a small corner of the garden; the bulk of its acreage was devoted to providing fruit and vegetables for the palace tables, raising cattle and pheasants, and growing grain. And flowers: during the reign of George III, there were also hothouses and flowerbeds reserved solely for the sovereign's nosegays and floral arrangements.[17]

Banks died in 1820, the same year as his supportive but long-incapacitated sovereign. His death coincided with a declining interest in botany after the glory years of the eighteenth century, when it could well claim to be the queen of the sciences. With a severe cut in official support as part of the retrenchment that followed the Napoleonic Wars, the Botanic Gardens entered a period of neglect and uncertainty. Already during Banks's tenure, private gardeners and nurserymen had been clamoring for a share of Kew's exotics. Rare plants were much in demand and commanded lucrative prices. Smuggling was an ongoing problem, no doubt abetted by some of the garden staff. The royal household was less and less inclined to fund the gardens with their earlier lavishness, so that overstuffed hothouses fell into disrepair, the lake silted up into a muddy pond, and buildings grew shabbier and shabbier. The *Gardener's Gazette* declared in 1837, "The state of the place is slovenly and discreditable, and that of the plants disgracefully dirty."[18]

As Kew's fortunes declined, other institutions rose to challenge it. Under attack from all sides, Kew faced an identity crisis. Should it be useful or ornamental, royal or public? What was to be the role of science? Above all, where would the funding come from? It had become a battleground, fought over with a surprising—or perhaps not so surprising—degree of vitriol and old-style politicking.[19] It was pulled back from the precipice by the skillful intervention of several champions, and just in time. In 1840 the Royal Botanic Gardens was transferred from the monarch to Her Majesty's Government and Sir William Hooker, professor of botany at the University of Glasgow, put in charge. His appointment represented a victory for the partisans of botany over horticultural entrepreneurs who favored subordinating science to ornamental gardening. The price exacted was the opening up of the garden for public recreational use. Nevertheless, Sir William and the dynastic succession of son Sir Joseph Hooker and son-in-law Sir William Thiselton-Dyer cemented their control over Kew until the early years of the twentieth century. By the late 1870s they had achieved their goal of making it the world's foremost center of botany and botanical research, with ties to gardens, planters, and administrators on every continent.

Kew's directors became adept at the art of tying botany to the imperial enterprise. Not only would it be the repository of the world's flora—"a garden in which a vast assemblage of plants from every accessible part of the earth's surface is systematically cultivated"—it would increasingly assert its right as final arbiter in naming new plants, superseding Linnaeus as imperial Adam. At the same time, it actively promoted the economic exploitation of major agricultural commodities such as cinchona and rubber from South America, tea from China, indigo, sisal, and spices. The Colonial Office itself, with mushrooming African dependencies under its wing, depended on Kew's expertise in its endeavors to make colonies profitable, or, if not profitable, at least self-supporting.[20]

"The Most Perfect Thing of Its Kind": Calcutta's Botanic Garden

John Lindley's report to the Royal Gardens Committee in 1838 amounted to a "mission statement" for Kew as a "National Botanic Garden," the nexus of a global network.[21] It would be the sun around which the satellite imperial gardens revolved, bestowing their beneficial rays on British commerce, agriculture, medicine, horticulture, and manufactures. And so it came to pass, thanks in large measure to the skillful leadership of the Hookers. At the head of Lindley's list of botanic gardens were those of India: Calcutta, Bombay, Saharanpur. To these he might also have added Madras, whose founder discovered that a type of prickly pear was effective against scurvy, the bane of sailors.[22] With the exception of Saharanpur, a former Mughal garden, these were colonial creations in the capitals of the three presidencies. In time more would be added, from the Himalayas in the north to the Nilgiris in the south, but Calcutta remained to Indian gardens what Kew was to the empire as a whole.

In 1786 Colonel Robert Kyd proposed to the Court of Directors of the East India Company the creation of a "Botanical Garden" in Calcutta. A military man who was also an amateur botanist, Kyd argued that such a garden should be founded "not for the purpose of collecting rare plants as things of curiosity or furnishing articles for the gratification of luxury, but for establishing a stock for disseminating such articles as may prove beneficial to the inhabitants as well as the natives of Great Britain, and which ultimately may tend to the extension of the national commerce and riches." In official correspondence, he of course had to emphasize the commercial benefits to be expected from the garden, while privately he was just as concerned with importing drought-resistant crops, such as sago palms from the Malay Peninsula and date palms from Persia, that could be distributed to peasants in drought-prone areas of India. Britain, he believed, had a responsibility for protecting the citizens of newly acquired Bengal from the devastation of recurrent famine.[23]

The Company, on the other hand, was far more interested in Kyd's suggestion that Dacca cotton could be widely cultivated in India. In the 1780s India was draining precious bullion from British coffers and Indian cottons were competing with those of the nascent British textile industry. If India could be turned into a supplier of raw materials—not only cotton, but also spices, indigo, tea, coffee, tobacco, sandalwood, teak, hemp—and a market for British manufactures, the balance of trade might be reversed.[24] The idea of "economic botany" was very much in the air. The Company had already been encouraging the search for useful plants and the introduction of exotic crops into India on a modest scale, and was therefore in a receptive mood for Kyd's proposals.

The Calcutta Botanic Garden opened in 1787 on a site next to Kyd's own garden at Shalimar, on the west bank of the Hughli at Sibpor. As its first superintendent, he launched an ambitious but ultimately unsuccessful program of introducing spice-yielding trees and vines: nutmeg, cloves, cinnamon, pepper. He was more successful in other areas, establishing some three hundred species in the garden and participating in an active exchange of plants and seeds with both other Company gardens and Kew. Kyd died in 1793. He had hoped to be buried in his beloved Shalimar, but his wishes were disregarded on the grounds that so distinguished a servant of the Company should not be buried in unhallowed ground but rather in the South Park Street cemetery.[25]

Kyd's work was carried on for the next half century by two remarkably able botanists, both of whom shared his eagerness to develop plants that would benefit the native population as well as the Company's balance sheet. A surgeon in the East India Company's navy, later a botanist stationed in Madras, William Roxburgh became known as "the Indian Linnaeus," "the father of Indian botany." Over the twenty years of his stewardship, he transformed the Calcutta garden into the largest and most scientifically organized in Asia, adding some 22,000 species of plants and more than 800 trees. His successor, Nathaniel Wallich, had originally come to India as surgeon at the Danish settlement of Serampore, upriver from Calcutta. When Serampore was captured by the British in 1813, he was taken prisoner, but once his botanical abilities were recognized, they were quickly exploited. It was Wallich's infinite knowledge of plants that had so delighted Lady Amherst. Indeed, if less scientifically gifted than his predecessor, he was the consummate field botanist, collecting specimens in Nepal, Singapore, Penang, and Burma, as well as much of India. Together, Roxburgh and Wallich made Calcutta a center of experimentation with living plants from all over the subcontinent and the world as well as with dried specimens stored in the herbarium for study, classification, and illustration. Ships outward bound from Calcutta were prevailed upon, however reluctantly, to stow plants and seeds from the Botanic Garden (which took up space and were often a nuisance to keep alive on long voyages); in return came treasures from the Indies and the Cape of Good Hope.[26]

Lord Valentia visited Roxburgh's garden in 1803. "It affords," he wrote, "a wonderful display of the vegetable world, infinitely surpassing any thing I have ever before beheld. It is laid out in a very good style, and its vast extent renders the confinement of beds totally unnecessary." Nevertheless, he regretted that so little space was allotted to "a scientific arrangement." It was, to be sure, hardly surprising that "utility seems to have been more attended to than science." Still, he noted that Calcutta was the center "where productions of every climate are assembled, to be distributed to every spot where they have a chance of being beneficial." Already the garden had disseminated thousands of teaks, loquots, grafted mangoes, and other trees valuable for fruit and timber throughout Britain's "Oriental territories." Lovely nymphaeas bloomed in the pond, but the prize specimen was a "noble" *Ficus bengalensis,* swathed in epidendrons—the great banyan tree that is still the garden's main attraction, covering an area nearly 1,300 feet in circumference in spite of having its central trunk eviscerated in 1925 because of fungus damage (see Pl. 12).[27] It was, incidentally, under the spreading arms of a *Ficus* that Adam and Eve took refuge after the Fall:

> *... Not that tree for fruit renown'd,*
> *But such, and at this day to Indians known*
> *In Malabar or Deccan spreads her arms,*
> *Branching so broad and long, that in the ground*
> *The bended twigs take root, and daughters grow*
> *About the mother tree....*

And with its leaves they gird their waists "to hide thir gilt and dreaded shame."[28]

Bishop Heber had happier thoughts. Touring the garden with Lady Amherst, he was minded less of the expulsion from Eden than of Paradise. The scene, he wrote, "more perfectly answers Milton's idea of Paradise, except that it is on a dead flat instead of a hill, than any thing I ever saw." Lady Amherst herself characterized the garden as "this superb establishment," declaring that it "is the most perfect thing of its kind existing certainly in the East—the vast collection of plants from all parts of the world in the finest state of luxuriant growth." Her only lament: trees imported from England failed to thrive. A giant baobab from Senegambia, however, was doing splendidly. Heber found that this "elephant of the vegetable creation," about which he had heard so much, bore more resemblance to "that disease of the leg which bears the elephant's name, than tallies with his majestic and well-proportioned, though somewhat unwieldy stature"—part of a long-winded explanation of why he did not find the tree particularly attractive. Heber also noted with satisfaction that public establishments such as the Botanic Garden were no longer cultivated by "convicts in chains" but by peasants hired by the day or week, a change that was cheap "as well as otherwise advantageous and agreeable." The only problem was summoning them to work on time, a problem solved by the installation of a very large brass bell, specially cast in Canton.[29]

Wallich subsequently immortalized Lady Amherst with *Amherstia nobilis,* otherwise known as the Pride of Burma or Orchid Tree because of its spectacular hanging flowers with their crimson tips. Legend had it that the tree was so beautiful it was offered as a sacrifice to Buddha (Wallich found it in a ruined monastery). Gardeners all over the world vied in their attempts to acclimate it; it defeated them all until Louisa Lawrence brought it to bloom in her villa garden at Ealing Park. By the end of the century Calcutta could boast a magnificent *Amherstia* forty feet tall, its pendulous boughs resplendent with blossoms of scarlet and gold.[30] Naming rights were, incidentally, one of the few favors botanists dispensed, and some used them as judiciously as any politician.

A few plants were too delicate even for Bengal's mild winter. Still, the nutmeg, "a pretty tree, something like a myrtle, with a beautiful peach-like blossom," was finally coaxed to grow by matting it carefully and putting it in the most sheltered spot.[31] Eventually, like Kew, the Botanic Garden added conservatories for plants not indigenous to India of the plains, especially for orchids. Like Kew, too, Calcutta had its Palm House, "an enormous octagonal structure, with a central dome" and framed in iron; unlike Kew, however, the sides and roof were covered with wire netting, on top of which there was a thin thatch of grass. Inside, the palms were planted in the ground rather than in pots, conveying a more natural effect. But nothing could protect the garden from the periodic cyclones that devastated Bengal.[32]

There were, alas, serpents in Calcutta's Eden. Some were mundane, like the perennial tussle with the Company and later the Government of India over funds. Others were ideological differences about the true calling of a botanical garden, echoes of those waged in Great Britain itself. At its inception, Banks had not been happy with Kyd's suggestion that the Calcutta garden be open to the public as "a not inelegant retreat for such of the members of administrations whose indisposition may preclude [them] from the duties of their station"—in other words, a refuge from the city's insalubrious climate. More generally, Calcutta, like botanic gardens the world over, could not resist pressures to take on more and more of the attributes of a public park.[33]

Lord Valentia had also called attention to the conflict between utility and science, a conflict not easily resolved. If the pendulum seemed at first to swing in the direction of utility, this was not always the case. During one of Wallich's extended sick leaves, William Griffith was put in charge of the garden. A brilliant and courageous collector who amassed some nine thousand specimens of natural history from Afghanistan to Malacca, he was a disaster as curator. In a few short years he managed to wreak greater havoc than the cyclone of 1842, all in the name of science. Considering the existing plan something of a hodgepodge, he reordered it into a circular garden intended to reflect Jussieu's and de Candolle's classification of plants; complementing this was a separate display of medicinal and useful plants native to lower Bengal. When Joseph Hooker first visited the garden in 1848, "nothing was to be seen of its former beauty and grandeur, but a few noble trees or graceful palms rearing their heads over a low ragged jungle, or spreading their broad leaves or naked limbs over the forlorn hope of a botanical garden, that consisted of open clay beds, disposed in concentric circles, and baking into brick under the fervid heat of a Bengal sun." An "unsparing hand" had swept away the avenue of Cycas palms "unmatched in any tropical garden" and destroyed the groves of "teak, mahogany, clove, nutmeg, and cinnamon." The great *Amherstia* had nearly succumbed to injudicious treatment and the baking of the soil over its roots, and even the celebrated banyan tree almost ceased sending out descending limbs thanks to neglect in providing the wet clay and moss it required. In Ray Desmond's words, Griffith was "completely insensitive to any aesthetic considerations"; for him the garden was "no more than an open-air laboratory." With phenomenal but misguided energy and vision, he pursued his blinkered agenda. "Where is the stately, matchless garden that I left in 1842?" wrote Wallich in despair to William Hooker at Kew on his return two years later. "Day is not more different from night than the state of the garden as it was from its present utterly ruined condition."[34]

Fortunately by the time Joseph Hooker returned to Calcutta early in 1850, he found recovery well underway, thanks to the efforts of Wallich, once more in command, and his successor, John Falconer. The tropical climate helped: "The rapidity of growth is so great in this climate," Hooker noted, "that within eight months from the commencement of the improvements, a great change had already taken place. The grounds bore a park-like appearance; broad shady walks had replaced the narrow winding paths that ran in distorted lines over the ground, and a large Palmetum, or collection of tall and graceful palms of various kinds, occupied several acres at one side of the garden." There were new plantings of bamboos, evergreens of every sort, plantains, and screw-pines. The banyan was now sending out hundreds of props and the *Amherstia* thriving, thanks to a watering system making use of bamboo pipes sunk deep into the ground. Nevertheless, the expense of restoration had been enormous and "now cripples the resources of the garden library and other valuable adjuncts."[35]

Flowers were another potential problem. What role should pure aesthetics play in a botanical garden? Griffith did grudgingly allow for a flower garden during his stewardship, although he didn't care for floral borders along the paths. Kew itself faced the same pushes and pulls. An MP voiced his certainty "that where one person was interested in the botanical specimens, 100 were attracted by the flowers." In 1856 one of the Kew commissioners made known his displeasure with the "bad state of the flower-beds and the untidy appearance of the grass and the extremely bad condition of the walks in the Gardens," declaring, "I cannot suffer such things in the future." Thus reprimanded, Hooker dutifully planted flowerbed after flowerbed until three years later Kew counted some four hundred. Nevertheless, for years he subdivided his annual report into separate headings for "a place of beautiful recreation" and for educational, instructive, and scientific pursuits.[36]

Even flowers themselves were not neutral. Horticultural partisans battled over the role of bedding-out plants, massing by color, paths, and lawns, their dictates changing over time. Plantings at Kew were reviewed like the latest in music or fashion, with praise and rebuke meted accordingly. Where William Hooker was forced to accept the annual ritual of bedding-out flowers, his son and successor Joseph Hooker had to give in to the "passion for a blaze of gaudy colours," which William Morris labeled "an aberration of the human mind."[37] Farther from the horticultural epicenter, the Calcutta Botanic Garden nevertheless reflected changing tastes and changing demands. After the 1864 cyclone wiped out most of its trees and turned large areas into marsh, the director seized the occasion to redesign the whole, creating pools in which to show off the great South American waterlily, *Victoria amazonica* (also a star at Kew), and clusters of trees and shrubs owing more to aesthetics than taxonomic relationships.[38]

Botanical gardens, whether at home or abroad, were also expected to supply plants to nurseries and to the public, the more spectacular the better. So serious a problem had this become that when Lord Canning arrived in Calcutta as governor-general in 1856 he resolved to improve the garden, which although a "fine establishment . . . has been quite spoiled by the practices of giving plants to whoever wished for them." In the preceding ten months alone, some fifty thousand plants had been given away. If Canning did not quite end the practice—his own wife was writing home a few months later that the director was "most amiable in getting plants for me"—he sharply curtailed it.[39] On the other hand, a longtime superintendent of the garden at Saharanpur, in the foothills northwest of Calcutta, was quite happy to ignore the demands of science in favor of raising flowers and agricultural plants to stock the private gardens and parks from Lahore to Lucknow and Delhi. At the same time, he responded to the insatiable appetite for deodars (Himalayan cedars) in Britain with large shipments of seeds.[40]

Gardens in more temperate climes, such as Saharanpur and the higher elevations of the hill stations, offered opportunities that Calcutta could not match. Wandering through the serpentine walks bordered with English flowers and shrubs, Captain Mundy almost forgot he was in India, "an illusion, however, which was speedily dispelled by the apparition of my faithful elephant waiting for me at the gate."[41] Here European fruits and vegetables could thrive—an enterprising botanist even suggested growing hops in the neighborhood of Kabul to produce beer for the troops now penetrating into Afghanistan—and European flowers gladden the heart of expatriates. But these gardens also served the aims of economic botany. Initially a major focus had been on medicinal plants, a matter of growing importance with more and more troops stationed overseas. Drugs from Europe were not only expensive but tended to lose their potency on the long voyage east. They were also often of little help in treating tropical diseases. This led to a keen interest in "bazaar medicines," a term first used by John Forbes Royle. Royle, like many European botanists before the "rampant racism" of the later nineteenth century took hold, had a great respect for local knowledge, particularly local knowledge of materia medica. He considered that Indian works on the subject "were far advanced and embraced an extensive range of subjects before any progress had been made in Europe," and laid out a garden for medicinal

Fig. 27. Medical Garden, Darjeeling Botanical Garden
[Photograph by author]

plants at Mussoorie in the foothills of the Himalayas that included species commonly used by indigenous doctors.[42] A garden for medicinal plants is still a feature of the Darjeeling Botanical Garden (Fig. 27).

Quinine, Opium, and Tea

The most critical plant for survival in the tropics, however, was the cinchona tree, whose bark yielded quinine, the only known treatment for malaria. It was native to the Andes, and the more jealously the Spanish crown guarded its monopoly, the more other colonial powers tried vainly to smuggle out seeds and plants and grow them in their own dependencies, initially with little success. By the 1850s the British were spending more than £40,000 per year to supply the Bengal Presidency alone with quinine. Kew and the India Office combined forces to obtain seeds, germinating some of them in the United Kingdom but sending most on to the botanic garden at Ootacamund, where a Kew-trained gardener at last succeeded in getting large plantations to grow. The species established at Ooty as well as in Ceylon and Darjeeling proved nevertheless to have a much weaker concentration of quinine than that later found in Bolivia, but when seeds of this species were offered to Kew, Sir Joseph Hooker, distracted by the death of his father and his own illness, turned them down. They were snapped up by the Dutch consul-general in London, shipped off to Java, grafted onto older stock, and thrived so spectacularly that the Dutch henceforth dominated the world market. Whatever its source, by the end of the nineteenth century, one could buy a dose of quinine at any Indian post office for half a farthing; mixed with gin, it became the colonial "tipple" par excellence.[43]

Cinchona was only one of a host of "useful plants" the British tried to exploit commercially in India. Spices, indigo, cochineal, cotton, hemp, flax, teak, mahogany, rubber—the emphasis changed over time, mirroring changing markets in the outside world. Many were blind alleys. With a whole empire to choose from, the British found, for example, that sisal did better in East Africa, cloves in Zanzibar, and rubber in Malaya. Two plants, however, were to prove bonanzas—tea and opium—and their histories were curiously intertwined.

Marlene Dietrich once observed that the British "have an umbilical cord that has never been cut and through which tea flows constantly."[44] This recourse to tea in moments of both stress and ease is relatively recent. The beverage began its rise to preeminence as the national drink of England only in the early decades of the eighteenth century after beating out its rival, coffee. Like coffee, it was touted at first mainly as an exotic medicinal. Not only did it "delight the Palate," noted John Ovington, an early advocate, it also prevented gout, stone, and other complaints, especially those brought on by "a pernicious Excess of inflaming Liquors." Indeed a *Poem to Tea* contrasted its balm with the "turbulent Effects" of alcoholic drinks; tea, declared the poet, "does not run our Senses all aground." He concluded with a clarion call to the "sickly Souls, that languish on your Beds":

> *Call for the Kettle, and raise up your heads:*
> *Sip but a little of this Nectar rare,*
> *Expect it will your Health, and Wit repair.*

Nonetheless doubters not only challenged its therapeutic value but found it downright unpatriotic. John Wesley, the founder of Methodism, blamed his disorder of the nerves on twenty-six years of tea-drinking at breakfast and advised his fellow countrymen to leave off the alien beverage and content themselves with "*English* Herbs instead." Others denounced it as a destroyer of female beauty and a drain on the national economy.[45]

Opponents were fighting a losing battle. Before long, as its price dropped steadily, tea was "cheering the whole land from the palace to the cottage," a welcome picker-upper in the "foggy Air or fenny watery Places" of the British Isles.[46] At the same time, tea-drinking moved from coffee houses and taverns into the newly created pleasure gardens of Vauxhall and Ranelagh, gardens that brought the "elegant aristocratic parks of the countryside into the town," offering Londoners "a scintillating carnival of delight . . . ranging from the cultural to the carnal, seductively twinkling across the river" like the moonlight gardens of some Indian prince.[47] Here the middle classes came to see and be seen; here they promenaded, viewing the latest objects of curiosity, artistic or mechanical, and drinking tea. And, unlike coffee houses and taverns, the gardens were very much open to women and children. By midcentury tea had become a staple of working-class diets as well, affordable to the lowest farm-hand and, with the advent of the industrial revolution, the lowest millhand. It is hardly an exaggeration to say that tea changed both eating and social habits, accommodating to and even reinforcing the class structure of the nation.

Camellia sinensis originated in the remote hills of Yunnan in southwestern China, the cradle of so many plants. The tiny new leaves were plucked from wild trees by small peasant farmers. After being processed laboriously by hand in time-honored fashion, the tea made the long and tortuous journey to the port of Canton on the backs of human porters. Until 1833 the East India Company maintained a monopoly of tea imports into Britain. The figures are staggering: consumption climbed from 20,000 pounds in 1700 to more than 20 million pounds by the end of the century, or some two cups a day for every man, woman, and child—and these figures did not take into account the perhaps equal amounts of tea smuggled into the country.[48] The dizzying increase in consumption meant equally dizzying profits both for the Company and for the British Government, which taxed imports. Initially Bengal cotton was traded to the Chinese for tea, but when the Chinese improved their own cotton industry, tea merchants insisted on payment in silver. By the late eighteenth century, when tea had become the single most valuable item in the Company portfolio, supplies of silver were drying up, and the Company was desperate for another commodity acceptable to the Chinese. Opium provided the answer. If the demand was not insatiable at the start, it soon became so.

Opium had been grown in several parts of India long before the British arrived.[49] From the time of Babur, Mughal rulers and their courts indulged freely, often drinking the drug mixed with wine. The lion's share of Indian opium was produced in the Ganges plain between Patna and Benares. When the East India Company wrested control of the region from the Mughals in the second half of the eighteenth century, they also took over their predecessors' monopoly of the trade. As demand skyrocketed, huge areas of land were diverted from other crops to poppies, especially in Bengal. Hundred of workers were employed, many of whom became addicts themselves, either by choice or simply by exposure to the drug.

Kipling gives a vivid account of the factory at Ghazipur, some forty miles below Benares, "an opium mint" that so handsomely filled the coffers of the Indian government. Ironically, the city had been known earlier as the "Gulistan, the rose-bed, of Bengal" for its plain of roses "as far as the eye can see." They were made into the finest rosewater in the world.[50] Opium was a different matter. The entire process was tightly controlled from the moment regiments of a hundred jars, each holding one maund (about eighty pounds), began arriving in April. At every stage forms had to be filled out—"never was such a place for forms as the Ghazipur Factory"—certifying the quality and weight of each pot; woe betide anyone involved if a pot arrived tampered with or broken. Random samples were checked for adulteration, resulting in still more forms and registers. Once approved, the jars were emptied into huge vats, and then smashed and tossed into the Ganges. The contents of the vats were assayed yet again before the blend was transferred into smaller vats and worked by the feet of coolies, dangling from ropes and dragging their legs painfully through the slurry: "Try to wade in mud of 70° consistency, and see what it is like." Next, the opium was made into cakes, finally packed into chests, and dispatched to Calcutta. Kipling reckons the value of Ghazipur's huge godowns of opium at the beginning of the cold season at three and a half millions in sterling.[51]

Some of Ghazipur's opium was refined into morphia and other medicinal compounds, but the "real opium" was destined for the China trade, carefully tailored to meet the exacting requirements of the Chinese smoker. China itself had long produced opium, but it was uneven in quality, while that imported from Smyrna had characteristics that made it less desirable—hence the preference for Indian opium: "The Chinaman likes every inch of the stuff we send him," even boiling the shell in which it was packed.[52] Needless to say, the Chinese government watched with horror as more and more of its citizens became addicted: "For a pot of tea," Henry Hobhouse has written, "one could say, Chinese culture was nearly destroyed." This is a slight exaggeration, to be sure, since China continued to produce opium itself, and an unholy alliance of Chinese smugglers and corrupt officials made sure that the Celestial Empire's attempts to interdict the trade would be unavailing. In the face of growing protest in both China and Great Britain, the East India Company could plead innocence since it was not itself directly involved but sold the opium to private traders, including many Americans, who operated under Company license.[53]

The Opium War of 1838–42 had devastating and long-lasting effects on China while at the same time underscoring the vulnerability of British reliance on China for its national drink and the need to find other sources. The obvious place to look was India. Both Warren Hastings and Joseph Banks had had the foresight in the latter decades of the eighteenth century to propose acclimatizing the tea plant to the subcontinent, but the Company was too distracted by its wars of expansion—and in fact it was only these that brought under its dominions the mountainous areas that would prove suitable for tea cultivation. By the 1820s, however, interest was rekindled, stimulated by reports of wild tea growing in newly acquired, if remote, areas of Assam. The first seeds and plants sent to Calcutta were met with considerable skepticism—were they really tea or simply a flowering form of camellia? Given the uncertainty it seemed wiser to some to try to smuggle tea plants out of China, in spite of official Chinese embargoes and even death penalties. One misguided report argued that even inferior Chinese plants would be more likely to produce a marketable crop than would the "jungly stock" of Assam. In the mid-1830s the Assam plant was positively identified as true tea, inspiring the Tea Committee in Calcutta to pronounce the discovery "by far the most important and valuable that has ever been made in matters connected with the agricultural and communal resources of this empire." Nevertheless, it would be decades before less hardy Chinese hybrids, the "pests of Assam," were finally eradicated.[54]

Given the remoteness of Assam, the Company hoped to be able to stimulate local chiefs to grow tea, but this plan was quickly abandoned in favor of European "tea gardens." The problems were manifold. Europeans knew nothing about cultivating or processing tea, the elaborate sequence of drying, withering, rolling, and cutting to break down the leaf—the so-called CTC (cut, tear, curl) method.[55] They even labored under the mistaken assumption that black and green tea came from different plants. An early planter did learn serendipitously that tea trees grow faster when pruned—and a bush is much easier to pick than a ten-foot tree. Since the local populations were sparse and uninterested in plantation labor, planters turned to the Chinese for both labor and know-how. Naively assuming that "every Chinaman must be an expert in tea cultivation and manufacture," they shanghaied stray Chinese in the bazaars of Calcutta. Many had come from the sea ports of China and had never seen a tea plant in their lives. "Stuck in the middle of nowhere, surrounded by jungles full of herds of wild elephants, tigers so plentiful they were referred to as pests like the leeches and rats, far from their families, without women or recreation," the Chinese suffered heavy mortality and absconded whenever they could. Nevertheless, they provided much of the labor force into the 1860s, along with Indians rounded up by unscrupulous recruiters among the poor of Calcutta.[56]

Once the real Chinese experts were found, a veritable tea mania ensued, thanks to the promise of free land and dreams of unlimited wealth. European planters descended on Assam and later on other areas found suitable, such as Darjeeling, the Nilgiri Hills, the Western Ghats, and Ceylon. Inevitably this led to overexpansion and poor quality, with periodic crises throughout the century. The crash of 1867 was so severe that it prompted a rethinking of the industry and its methods from start to finish. Even with miserably paid "coolie" labor, Indian tea was more expensive than Chinese and Japanese tea produced by peasants earning even less. To compete successfully, science and capitalism would have to be applied to every stage of production. Although there was no way to mechanize planting, growing, and picking, they could be made more scientific, along the lines of British agriculture at home. Science could prescribe the best plants and the best soils, the optimum spacing between plants and rows, the best trees for shading and how they should be located, the appropriate seeds, fertilizer, and pesticides. The hand labor, still indispensable to pick the new leaves as they appeared, could be subjected to the same sort of time discipline and supervision that nurtured the industrial revolution. "The green world" became, in Alan Macfarlane's words,

Fig. 28. Tea plantation, Western Ghats
[Photograph by author]

"an extended factory, roofed only by the shade trees" (Fig. 28).⁵⁷ Gradually, machines were adapted to the processing of tea leaves, driven first by steam, later by electricity.

The end result was that Indian tea was a standardized product, consistent in quality—and cheaper than even the very cheap China tea that could claim to be neither. It helped as well that there was no export duty on Indian tea (in contrast to a 35 percent duty on Chinese tea), that there were few middlemen, and that Indian tea could now be shipped out by steamship or rail, rather than on the backs of humans. In 1884 imports of Indian tea into Great Britain exceeded those from China for the first time, and by the early decades of the twentieth century Chinese tea exports were negligible, leaving a millennia-old industry in tatters.⁵⁸

A curious coda to this story is the creation virtually ex nihilo of a tea-drinking public in India itself. Although surrounded by tea-drinking peoples, Indians had never taken to it except for small fractions of the population influenced by close contact with British culture. Coffee, in contrast, had been introduced into southern India much earlier by Arab Ocean traders and acquired many devotees. Nevertheless, a few champions of Indian tea foresaw a time when the huge Indian market would become avid consumers, with, of course, benefits for all concerned: for surplus agricultural labor, for mountain wastes that could now be brought under cultivation, for the government through increased revenue. The great plant explorer Robert Fortune declared already in the 1840s that tea would make the Indian and his family "more comfortable and more happy."[59] In fact, tea did not colonize India until the twentieth century—the familiar cry of the chai-wallah passing through the railway corridors, "Chai! Gurram, gurram chai!" is thus nowhere near as old as the railroads themselves—and then only as a consequence of a massive, well-financed advertising campaign carried out by the Indian Tea Association. The ITA literally canvassed the entire subcontinent, often sending tea-preparers door-to-door, as well as providing canteens for factory workers and soldiers. Their efforts were finally rewarded, as tea drinking filtered down even to the homeless on the streets of Calcutta and now seems as Indian as *lassis*. To be sure, along the way it has become indigenized by the addition of spices such as cardamom and ginger.[60] And like the invasion of Great Britain by curry, chai is now a staple in western coffee shops.

Botanizing in India

"A new frontier . . . seems an irresistible lure to a collector," observes Alice Coats in her lively book *The Quest for Plants*. "No sooner is a mud fort built, with a handful of native soldiers and two or three British officers in residence, than the botanist is there."[61] In India during the later eighteenth and early nineteenth centuries, the botanist was, more often than not, a Scottish surgeon in the employ of the East India Company. Scottish universities such as Edinburgh, Glasgow, and Aberdeen offered the best in medical education, and botanical instruction was an integral part of the training of every aspiring doctor, since plants were the primary source of medicinals. In India as elsewhere, the quest for plants focused initially on those that could profitably be added to the pharmacopoeia, drawing on the ancient and rich corpus of Ayurvedic medicine. Conveniently, Scotland had more than its share of sons on offer for empire-building: nine superintendents of the Calcutta Botanical Garden were born and educated in Scotland, along with myriad professional and amateur plant collectors, to say nothing of soldiers, administrators, and other personnel.[62]

Imperial plant-collecting in India has a long history, going back to Alexander the Great's Asian campaigns of 331–323 B.C.E. He took along a special corps to collect plants, animals, fish, and other specimens for the benefit of his tutor, Aristotle, who was writing a book on natural history. The book was never finished, but on his death in 322 his papers were passed on to Theophrastus, who did record the botanical finds of the expedition in his *Enquiry into Plants*. This remained the only source on Indian flora for the next two millennia. His first modern successor was the Danish surgeon Johann Gerhard Koenig. A Moravian missionary and botanist trained by Linnaeus himself, Koenig was stationed in Tranquebar, south of Madras, from 1768 to 1785. For a time he was naturalist to the *nawab* of Arcot before passing into the employ of the East India Company which also sent him botanizing in Siam and the Straits.[63] On his death, Koenig was followed in the field by a number of pioneering collectors.

Indeed, whatever their other failings, both Warren Hastings and, after him, Lord Wellesley were keen naturalists and sponsors of naturalist exploration; so were governors of Madras such as Lord Clive and Sir Thomas Munro.[64] Francis Buchanan, dispatched by Wellesley to carry out the exhaustive survey of the territories in southern India acquired with the defeat of Tipu Sultan, was, like so many other botanists, a Scottish surgeon. Earlier, he had roamed about Burma, Nepal, and Bihar and published a scholarly work on the fish of the Ganges and Bengal. He was an ideal field collector, but the mandate of this mission was even more ambitious than plant- or fish-collecting, as its title makes abundantly clear: *A Journey from Madras Through the Countries of Mysore, Canara, and Malabar: for the express purpose of investigating the State of Agriculture, Arts and Commerce; the Religion, Manners, and Customs; the History Natural and Civil and Antiquities.* His instructions, inter alia, were to send on to the botanical garden in Calcutta "whatever useful, or rare, or curious plants and seeds you may be enabled to acquire," with directions for their cultivation. Buchanan seconded earlier proposals to grow grapes and other fruits from the Cape of Good Hope in the higher elevations of Mysore.[65] After his successful return, Wellesley installed him as the first superintendent of his menagerie at Barrackpore, a scaled-down version of the governor-general's original intent to create an "Institution for Promoting the Natural History of

India." The menagerie limped along for just a few years after Buchanan went on leave and Wellesley was recalled for extravagance. Nevertheless, between them they left a legacy of some three thousand drawings of plants, birds, and animals from India and neighboring countries, now contained in the India Office Library.[66]

Other naturalists, including the superintendents of Indian botanical gardens, crisscrossed the length and breadth of the subcontinent as more and more territories came under British control. Some even trained elephants to pluck flowers from high branches and geological specimens from roadbeds.[67] Surgeons of the Company were soon joined by botanists sent out by Kew, by the Royal Horticultural Society, even by private nurseries, such as Veitch, and aristocratic estate owners, such as the Duke of Devonshire. But "Flora could be a melancholy muse"—plant collecting was dangerous work.[68] Banks personally selected many of the collectors dispatched across the world, preferring bachelors—who would, he argued, be less distracted from their tasks, but he might also have been hoping to avoid the bothersome problem of widows, for most of the men were of modest backgrounds and were woefully paid. Banks himself had lost several of his team in the South Seas with Captain Cook. Victor Jacquemont, bon vivant and inspired amateur collector, died in Bombay at the age of thirty-two; William Griffith died on the eve of his thirty-fifth birthday. Contemplating possible expeditions of his own, the young Joseph Hooker remarked to the taxonomist George Bentham, "Have not you Botanists killed collectors a-plenty in the Tropics?"[69] Isaac D'Israeli, father of the future prime minister, declared the plant hunters more worthy of remembrance than many a better-known hero: "Monuments are reared, and medals struck to commemorate events and names which are less deserving of our regard than those who have transported into the cold regions of the North, the rich fruits, the beautiful flowers, and the succulent pulse and roots of more favoured spots."[70] Reading accounts of their adventures one marvels that any survived. Whether in the arid Deccan or the malarial swamps of Assam and Burma or the bitter cold of the Himalayas, their devotion to the search for plants is humbling to the stay-at-home-in-comfort reader.[71]

The Himalayas were the last frontier of Indian botanical exploration. Extending some seventeen hundred miles from Afghanistan to Assam and China, from the arid Hindu Kush to the subtropical valleys of Kashmir, Nepal, Sikkim, and Bhutan, they offered a rich diversity of soils and microclimates and a treasure trove of plants: dense forests of many-hued rhododendrons and white magnolias, carpets of daphnes and poppies, primulas and potentillas, dazzling assortments of orchids, and clusters of Alpine flora clinging to the rugged outcrops. On their northern and western reaches, the mountains formed a botanical continuum with western Asia and Europe, while to the south and east the affinities were with India and China, a fact first noted by the seventeenth-century traveler François Bernier. The mountain kingdom of Nepal, some 500 miles long and 150 miles at its widest, formed the heart of the transitional zone between east and west. But if the Himalayas were a botanist's paradise, collecting was complicated not only by their ruggedness but also by the politics of the region, much of which remained beyond British control during the first half of the nineteenth century. Buchanan was forced to cut short his mission to Khatmandu in 1803 because of the hostility of its recently installed Ghorka rulers. To the west, Ranjit Singh determined who could and could not come exploring in the Punjab and Kashmir; to the east, the *dewan* of Sikkim frustrated Joseph Hooker's original plans to botanize in that kingdom, even going so far as to have his companion, Archibald Campbell, superintendent of Darjeeling, imprisoned and beaten. Hooker was of no political interest but loyally remained with his friend.[72]

Hooker was far from the first to be attracted to the Himalayas. Three quarters of a century before he set out, Warren Hastings had sent George Bogle on an embassy to the Panchen Lama in Tibet with instructions to learn all he could about the natural history of the mountains of Bhutan through which he passed. Even more appealing than any botanical finds was the shawl goat Bogle brought back to Calcutta, the animal Hastings tried unsuccessfully to acclimate to his English estate.[73] Thomas Hardwicke seems to have been the first to identify *Rhododendron arboreum* while botanizing in the Siwalik Hills on a military tour in 1796. He sent home seeds, little imagining the floodgates about to open. Indeed, few of the leading names in Indian botany could resist the lure of the Himalayas, but inevitably Hooker's name takes precedence over all the others.

Hooker's *Himalayan Journals,* chronicling his travels from 1848 to 1850, make exciting and beguiling reading (Fig. 29). They were an immediate popular success, as were the botanical works that followed in quick succession: *Illustrations of Himalayan Plants* (1855), the first volume of *Flora Indica* (1855), and, most eagerly devoured of all, *Rhododendrons of Sikkim-Himalaya*

(1849–51). Ten lithographed plates from this last had appeared to whet the public appetite while Hooker was still in the mountains. Kew's official botanical artist, Walter Hood Fitch, translated Hooker's sketches and dried specimens into lithographed plates. Ironically, some of the plates showed the rhododendrons in their natural habitats, a practice Hooker generally disparaged as unscientific (!). Amazed that such magnificent illustration could be produced in so short a time, a reviewer in the *Athenaeum* pronounced them "one of the marvels of our time." By the time the twenty-ninth and last appeared, both botanist and gardener had been captivated by the new species of rhododendron Hooker introduced.[74] Before long many of them had taken their place in English gardens, flourishing wherever acid soils prevailed—Hooker was surprised to find that the plants he collected grew even better on the Cornish Riviera than in their native Sikkim.[75] At Cragside in Northumberland his *Himalayan Journals* inspired Lord Armstrong to plant several hundred thousand, "forming impenetrable thickets, and blooming so profusely as to light up the whole hillside." At Kew itself they are displayed in all their May glory in Rhododendron Dell, a corner of the gardens landscaped originally by Capability Brown (who would probably not have approved).[76] Rhododendrons had more than their beauty to recommend them to British estate owners: layered in stands of trees, they provided an ideal cover for pheasants at just the time these were replacing partridges as the game bird of choice.[77]

Finding plants was only the beginning. Tons of living materials were gathered in the field, loaded onto the backs of human porters and humped back to base, often over the most difficult terrain. The problem was to get these cargoes to their final destinations alive. Originally plant boxes were simply flour barrels with holes cut in their sides for ventilation, with lath and tarpaulin covers. Ship captains begrudged the space, care during long voyages was often hit or miss, and plants had to be kept out of nibbling range of the livestock with whom they shared their quarters. Furthermore, no one was quite sure how exotics should be tended once they had been removed from their habitats. Seeds were less bulky and were even entrusted to the mails by midcentury, but they didn't always germinate on arrival. Wallich experimented with improved plant boxes. The real breakthrough came with the adoption of the Wardian case: a wooden box topped with glass, in fact a mini-greenhouse which insured a steady recycling of water vapor, sufficient

Fig. 29. Sir Joseph Hooker in the Himalaya. Engraved by W. Walter after Frank Stone [The British Library Board, P576]

light for photosynthesis, and relatively constant temperature. The Duke of Devonshire's plant collector, John Gibson, was the first to take the cases to India, and most botanists soon adopted them. So much did they reduce plant mortality that in 1851 Sir William Hooker was able to declare with satisfaction that "they have been the means, in the last fifteen years, of introducing more new and valuable plants to our gardens than were imported during the preceding century."[78]

Plants then had to be identified and preserved in some form. Botanists developed the technique of preserving them in herbaria by first drying and then pressing them between sheets of paper which were mounted on stiff paper or cardboard. As collecting gained momentum early in the nineteenth century, herbaria piled up at such a rate that it required whole teams to sort through them. Wallich alone arrived back in England on leave in 1828 with his entire herbarium packed up in thirty crates, together with chests of living plants and troves of seeds—more than eight thousand species assembled by not only his own efforts but those of an army of official and unofficial collectors in the field. He was generous in sharing his materials with other British and continental botanists—he distributed some 250,000 specimens to 66 individuals and institutions. While some British botanists attacked him for his "exotic liberalities," other colleagues reciprocated by collaborating on the Herculean task of sorting and labeling specimens, with the result that he was able to begin publishing installments of his monumental *Plantae Asiaticae Rariores* the very next year. Lest any doubts remained about the splendors of Asian flora, the first plate, *Amherstia nobilis,* supplied a brilliant "curtain-raiser" on the beauties to come.[79]

But important as herbaria were and still are to the taxonomist, much was lost when plants were dried—one critic even dismissed them quite unfairly as "dried foreign weeds" to which "barbarous binomials" were attached.[80] What was needed was a means to illustrate live plants and then to duplicate the illustrations. Woodcuts were the earliest form of illustration, used especially in herbals, but they were too clumsy to convey fine details, a matter of little importance until botany became a more exact science in the eighteenth and nineteenth centuries and had to face the huge influx of exotics. If botanists were going to classify plants and create a permanent record of an ephemeral object, they needed to be able to produce precise images showing the exact structure of the flower in bloom along with its seed. In time a standardized system evolved, showing the idealized form of the plant in isolation and emphasizing taxonomic details rather than context. Artists even found ways to resuscitate dried herbarium specimens sent back by the distant collectors, but the specimen was then useless, so that there had to be duplicates.[81]

Trained European illustrators were few in India, but there were indigenous artists aplenty. They had long demonstrated their aesthetic versatility in the employ of the Mughal court. Under the patronage of Akbar and his successors, painters, both Hindu and Muslim, synthesized the styles of Iranian masters of the miniature with a growing interest in European illustration. Akbar showed great curiosity for European printed books, first introduced by Jesuit missionaries in 1580, and commissioned paintings to accompany the *Baburnama,* his grandfather's classic memoir. What especially intrigued him was the European art of portraiture. He had likenesses painted of himself and of many of his grandees. His son, Jahangir, however, was more interested in the natural world. He and his wife, the formidable Nur Jahan, were passionate lovers of nature and great admirers of European botanical etchings and engravings. In his own memoirs, he describes instructing his foremost court painter, Mansur, to paint more than a hundred flowers blooming in the summer meadows of Kashmir.[82] Known as the "Wonder of the Age," Mansur produced exquisite studies of tulips, narcissi, and other blossoms, recording each with almost scientific exactitude but also capturing the "essence of the plant." Jahangir's son and successor, Shah Jahan, shared his father's love of flowers. During his reign they become the decorative motifs of choice in miniatures, textiles, and architecture. Best known are the studies contained in the *Dara Shikoh Album,* named for Shah Jahan's favorite son (see Pl. 13). True to the more flamboyant "floral imperialism" of Shah Jahan, these studies tend to be gaudier and more stylized than those of Jahangir's artists.[83]

Europeans for their part had been turning to Indian artists to paint scenes from Indian life virtually from the moment they arrived on the subcontinent in the sixteenth century. So great was the demand that by the eighteenth century families of artists came to specialize in subjects of interest to the British concentrated in areas such as Tanjur, Trichinopoly, Delhi, Murshibad, Patna, Calcutta, Benares, and Lucknow. They learned to adapt both style and technique to suit their new patrons, and began to work in watercolor rather than gouache. They also toned down the brilliant colors favored in Indian miniatures to suit British preferences for more muted hues. Some even experimented with one-point perspective and shading as well, without, however, entirely abandoning their own pictorial conventions. The best achieved a "hybrid vigour," rather like their counterparts in the garden world.[84]

All the major botanists working in India drew on this pool of skilled artists, initiating them with differing degrees of success into the conventions that had come to dominate the medium, especially the decontextualization of plants, their isolation from surrounding habitats. Roxburgh kept an

Indian artist "constantly employed" while still in Madras, for not only could he describe plants accurately, he could also add information on their uses gleaned from his own experience or from local testimony. Roxburgh continued the practice when he became director of the Calcutta Botanical Garden. Touring the garden in 1810, Maria Graham was delighted not only with the "great collection of plants from every quarter of the globe," including of course the fabled banyan tree, but also with the native artists she saw at work, drawing some of the rarest botanical treasures: "They are the most beautiful and correct delineations I ever saw," she declared, commenting that Hindus excel in miniature work. Eventually Roxburgh was able to forward almost seven hundred paintings to the Company for publication in his *Plants of the Coromandel Coast,* considered by Banks to be one of the finest Indian floras yet to appear. Lord Valentia was equally impressed with drawings by a native artist at the Bangalore gardens then tended by Benjamin Heyne, another surgeon-botanist. A few observers were more critical. When he selected the illustrations for his *Rhododendrons of Sikkim-Himalaya,* Joseph Hooker instructed the Kew artist to redraw them to correct "the stiffness and want of botanical knowledge displayed by the native artists who executed most of the originals."[85]

Perhaps Hooker's dissatisfaction stemmed from his relatively brief time in India. Others, such as Robert Wight, were able to form close and extended collaborations with Indian artists and plant collectors. Another of the East India Company's stable of Scottish surgeons, Wight made extensive collecting trips around South India, the Palni Hills, and Western Ghats in addition to official duties such as experimenting with the introduction of American long-staple cotton in the region of Coimbatore. To speed up the publication of his finds, he bought a press and taught himself lithography. Normally a relatively simple technique, environmental extremes in Madras made the process unpredictable, resulting in "innumerable failures, from the damp and heat of the climate, clumsiness and prejudice of the natives, warpings of presses, breaking of stones, moulding of paper, drying of printing ink, and cracking of rollers." Most important of all, the ink had to be of a consistent thickness if fine lines were to make an impression, and this was a constant struggle. Nevertheless, by the time he left India in 1853, Wight had published no fewer than 2,464 plates of Indian plants, claiming with justifiable pride that "the Indian Flora can now . . . boast of being more thoroughly illustrated than any other country under British [rule], Great Britain alone excepted."[86]

Unusually, the names of Wight's two principal illustrators are known. Rungiah worked with him for some twenty years, from about 1825 to 1845, and may have trained his successor, Govindoo. Even more remarkably, 711 of their original, labeled drawings have survived in the library of the Royal Botanic Garden Edinburgh, with a further store of works never published by Wight in the Natural History Museum in London. As they were Telegu-speaking artists in South India, their art probably owes little to the Mughal traditions of the north; they are much closer in style to the textiles of the Coromandel Coast, with their sinuously ebullient hand-painted floral motifs. If Hooker complained of stiffness in his artists, Rungiah is their polar opposite. His drawing of a climbing cucurbit (see Pl. 14), for example, fills the entire page with its exuberant flowering—as Henry Noltie comments, Rungiah has taken its stem not so much for a walk, as for a dance! On the other hand, his careful training in dissection and microscopic examination shows in the fine details of another work. An extraordinary Nilgiri orchid drawn by Govindoo is close to Rungiah's style, although the plant itself looks like something out of Edward Lear's *Flora Nonsensica*. In time Govindoo appears to have developed a style that was both bolder and cruder, perhaps recognizing that subtle effects would be lost in the lithographic process.[87]

Amateurs

The East India Company supported botanical researches, if sometimes grudgingly, in the hopes they might yield unexpected treasures that would gladden the hearts of stockholders. The Company's Scottish surgeons-cum-botanists, for their part, often found themselves playing a "double game": mindful of their contractual duties but also devoted to the disinterested pursuit of knowledge and the larger benefits it might bestow.[88] The same was true of other officials—and their wives. In the post-Company period, the naturalist and botanical artist Marianne North was often pleasantly surprised by the botanical knowledge and enthusiasm she encountered in her travels in India and Ceylon.[89]

William Jones has been pronounced "perhaps the most interesting person in the history of eighteenth-century British policy in India"; he is surely one of the most appealing of its amateur botanists. Nicknamed "Persian Jones" for his facility in Persian while still a young man, he was a brilliant linguist, a master not only of Greek and Latin but also of Arabic and eventually of Sanskrit and a host of other languages. As an Orientalist, he is best known for his pioneering studies of the genetic relationship between Sanskrit and the classical European languages, and for his compilations of Indian law. But his great delight was botany, "the loveliest and most copious division in the science of nature."[90]

Almost as soon as Jones arrived in Calcutta in 1784 to take up his duties as a judge on the Supreme Court, he and his wife, Anna Maria, fell in love with Bengal, "this wonderful kingdom, which Fortune threw into her [Britain's] lap while she was asleep." He soon decided to devote his vacations "to a vast and interesting study, *a complete knowledge of India,* which I can only attain in the country itself."[91] His goal was, in fact, to know India better than any other European had ever known it. As a first step he founded the Asiatick Society of Bengal to encourage the exchange of knowledge among like-minded expatriates and publication of researches in an annual journal. The Asiatick Society was to have "but one rule, namely, to have no rules at all," its aim to benefit both Asia and Europe through an interdisciplinary approach to the study of "Man and Nature."[92]

Jones immediately sought out pundits to teach him Sanskrit, to assist him not only in his official work of codifying Hindu law but also in translating classic works such as Kalidasa's *Sakuntala*. "Every day supplies me with something new in Oriental learning, and if I were to stay here half a century, I should be continually amused," he wrote to the botanist Patrick Russell a few months after his arrival.[93] He was fascinated by the natural world around him, although the actual practice of zoology repelled him. "I never could understand," he commented, "by what right, nor conceive with what feeling, a naturalist can occasion the misery of an innocent bird, and leave its young to perish in a cold nest, because it has gay plumage, and has never been delineated, or deprive even a butterfly of its nocturnal enjoyment, because it has the misfortune to be rare or beautiful."[94] Indeed, Jones and his wife shared a love of animals that went far beyond not wanting to stuff birds or pin butterfly wings to boards. On the voyage out, they had rescued several sheep intended for the pot, which subsequently formed the nucleus of herds kept at their house in Garden Reach, downriver from Calcutta. Here Anna Maria had "an excellent dairy which produces the best butter in India."[95]

Their retreat at Krishnagar was even more idyllic. As he described their

"Indian *Arcadia*" to his patroness, Lady Spencer, "it would bring to your mind what the poets tell us of the golden age; for, not to mention our flocks and herds that eat bread out of our hands, you might see a kid and a tiger playing together at Anna's feet. The tiger is not so large as a full-grown cat [it was about a month old at the time], though he will be (as he is of the royal breed) as large as an ox; he is suckled by a she-goat, and has all the gentleness (except when he is hungry) of his foster-mother." The tiger he named Jupiter; alas, one looks in vain for references to Jupiter's later life.[96] In Calcutta a friend reported that while dining with the Joneses, William at one point called for "Othello." Expecting a servant to materialize, the guest was startled to see instead a large turtle waddling over to his master's chair to be fed. Jones apologized that he would prefer to set it free but knew it wouldn't last long in the river.[97]

Unlike zoology, botany did not offend his almost Buddhist reverence for life; it soon became the great delight of his leisure hours, a delight shared by Anna Maria, who illustrated the specimens he found or had brought to him. He was soon exchanging letters and seeds with his fellow Harrovian Sir Joseph Banks, with Sir George Yonge, superintendent of the botanical garden on St. Vincent, and, closer to home, the pioneering botanist Johann Koenig, whose death in 1785 he much lamented. Like Banks and others, Jones hoped to identify plants with medicinal qualities as well as those that might go some way to remedying the awful famines that regularly ravaged India.

Jones preferred to study fresh plants. Rather than collecting specimens, he initially limited himself to describing them and trying to fit them into the Linnaean system. Sometimes this was successful, sometimes not. One morning Anna Maria brought home "the most lovely *epidendrum* that ever was seen," which "grew on a lofty amra, but it is an air plant, and puts forth its fragrant enameled blossoms in a pot without earth or water."[98] Nothing in Linnaeus corresponded to it. He asked Banks's help, too, in trying to find a Linnaean category for *cusha,* a plant celebrated in the Vedas. Another plant that he identified was *atimucta,* the favorite plant of Sakuntala, the heroine of Kalidasa's play. *Sakuntala,* he noted, calls it justly the "Delight of the Woods" for its fragrant and beautiful flowers.[99] There are also references in *Sakuntala* to the *madhavi,* about which Jones enthused, "If ever flower was worthy or paradise, it is our charming Ipomea."[100]

As Jones was able to identify more and more plants by their Sanskrit names, he proposed that the Linnaean system be altered to catalog Indian plants with their "Indian appellations," an innovation he maintained Linnaeus himself would have approved. His own practice was to provide names in both Roman and Sanskrit orthography, along with their Linnaean genera where ascertainable; this presentation he thought would be most serviceable to posterity. Within a few years of his arrival, he had collected the Sanskrit names for a thousand plants, including some three hundred to which medicinal properties—"virtues"—were ascribed.[101] Thanks to his linguistic facility, he was able to supplement field study with literary sources and vernacular identifications, often annotating Anna Maria's sketches with Hindi and Bengali vernacular names, descriptions, and indications of their use. One drawing, for example, represents a seven-leafed plant medicinal plant mentioned in *Sakuntala* with its Bengali and Sanskrit names in their respective scripts (Fig. 30).[102] For publication, Jones turned to professional Indian illustrators such as Zayn al-Din, whose drawings were then engraved by John Alefounder.

William Jones found in India happiness beyond any he had known in England: "I never was unhappy in England," he wrote a friend, "it was not in my nature to be so; but I never was happy till I was settled in India." His religion became a kind of floral pantheism: "We find a more exquisite lecture, on the being and attributes of God, in every flower, every leaf, and every berry, than can be produced by the mere wisdom or eloquence of man." He might well have been tempted to settle for good in India had it not been for the "incessant ill health" of his wife. Once he had put away enough money, he fantasized that they might retire to a country house in England, far from the intrigues of the capital, with pasture for horses and "garden ground enough for our botanical amusements, with which we are both in love."[103]

Lady Jones sailed for home in 1793, with the expectation that Sir William would follow within the next two years. In a supremely ironical twist of fate, he died suddenly in April 1794 at the age of forty-seven, while she lived on for another thirty-five years. Like his *Digest* of Indian law, his *Treatise on the Plants of India* was left unfinished at his death. Generations of botanists with better training and greater opportunities for travel completed the work he and Koenig and Russell had begun, but few could match Jones for the sheer breadth of his learning and eagerness to benefit both Europe and Asia with the fruits of his researches. His botanical memorial, as lasting as the obelisk in South Park Street cemetery, is *Jonesia asoca,* the "Sorrowless" tree under which tradition says Buddha was born.[104]

Fig. 30. Lady Anna Maria Jones, Botanical drawing
[Courtesy of the Royal Asiatic Society of Great Britain and Ireland, Jones Collection, 025.054.]

Anna Maria Jones was far from unusual in her devotion to botany and her application to botanical illustration. From the middle of the eighteenth century botany had become an increasingly fashionable pursuit in England, even a kind of "occupational therapy" for well-born ladies with little to do. Troubled not at all about the indelicacy of Linnaean metaphors, one writer declared that the study of nature "prevents the tumult of passions and provides the mind with a nourishment which is salutary by filling it with an object most worthy of contemplation."[105] In India Sir Elijah Impey, Chief Justice of Bengal, and his wife had anticipated the Joneses in their excitement with the flora and fauna of India. They maintained an assemblage of birds and animals in their Calcutta menagerie. While she does not seem to have done any illustrating herself, Lady Impey took the lead in commissioning more than three hundred paintings of their collection between 1777 and 1782. Three Indian artists were employed, both Hindu and Muslim, but all came from Patna where they had been trained in the Mughal tradition.[106] One of them was the Zayn al-Din, who, as we have seen, subsequently made botanical illustrations for Jones.

Early in the following century, Lady Amherst pioneered the study of Himalayan botany. During their ten-week stay in Simla in 1827, she and her daughter Sarah happily roamed the hills in search of new plants. *Clematis montana* and *Anemone vitifola* were among the flowers raised from seeds she sent home, and she also brought from her travels a trove of flowers to Wallich and the Calcutta Botanical Garden, where we have already encountered her in the beautiful *Amherstia nobilis,* one of the few good things to come out of Lord Amherst's Burma campaigns. Also a keen ornithologist, she returned home with large botanical and zoological collections, including two living Lady Amherst pheasants, also known as golden pheasants, beautiful creatures whose descendants can still be found strolling along the walkways of Kew.[107]

Wives of other officials also tried their hand at botanical exploration and illustration in India as elsewhere in the empire. Marianne Cookson, wife of a military officer, completed thirty folio-sized paintings of indigenous plants during her posting in 1834, and they were published the following year. They depicted a water lily, lotus, banyan tree, and cashew, some sufficiently detailed to show flower or fruit at different stages of development. Lady Emily Bourne collaborated with her administrator husband in collecting and cataloguing plants from southern India in the early twentieth century. She mobilized a posse of European amateur naturalists summering at the hill stations of Kodaikanal and Ootacamund to collect and illustrate the local flora. The results of their work can be found in an unpublished bound volume of some 225 illustrations in the Ooty Botanical Garden. Similarly, Diana Fyson illustrated her husband's *Flora of the South Indian Hill Stations,* published in 1932.[108]

The most memorable and the most accomplished of the women botanical illustrators in India, however, was Lady Charlotte Canning. Nineteen great leatherbound volumes containing her mounted watercolors reside in the Library of Harewood House, Yorkshire. One feels that an experience, most especially an experience of novelty, was not quite real for Charlotte Canning until she had drawn or painted it. When she first landed in Alexandria on her way to India in 1855, she was dazzled by the exoticism of the scenes around her, for which her earlier travels had done nothing to prepare her. "I long to draw and so regret being unable to sketch figures when everyone is so picturesque," she wrote Queen Victoria, "the land is like the richest gardens, and the view ranges over crops of rice, wheat, cotton and sugar cane, and wretched mud villages with their palm trees raised on mounds just high enough to escape the inundation." Far more isolated from both Indian and even English society than the Joneses had been ("isolated to a degree I never could have imagined") thanks to her high station as wife of the governor-general, to the increasing distance of ruler and ruled during the nineteenth century, and to the outbreak of rebellion in 1857, she found solace not only in her garden at Barrackpore but also in collecting and illustrating Indian flora.[109]

Lady Canning found something of a botanical heir in Lady Beatrix Stanley, whose husband was governor of Madras from 1929 to 1934 and briefly acting viceroy. As we have seen, Lady Beatrix was particularly knowledgeable about what plants were best suited to southern India, but she painted large numbers of watercolors of flowers from all over the subcontinent—a family photograph shows her sitting at her easel in Srinagar during a trip to Kashmir. She has been immortalized in both a lovely blue iris and a snowdrop.[110] Of a generation sandwiched between Canning and Stanley, Marianne North cut quite a different figure. She had no official position but very good connections. Altogether lacking in Canning's vulnerability, North was an intrepid, even imperious, artist with the means and independence to travel wherever she listed and to devote herself wholeheartedly to the depiction of the world's tropical flora, albeit more as a landscape painter since she did not stick to the rigid conventions of botanical illustration (Canning did both). Unlike

Canning she not only survived but also insured her own immortality by endowing a gallery for her art in the bosom of Kew.[111]

The World as a Garden

In 1889 a glasshouse, modeled after London's Crystal Palace, was built in the Bangalore Lal Bagh to commemorate the visit of the Prince of Wales and to serve as the venue for flower shows (see Pl. 15).[112] By this time the Lal Bagh was a "purely European pleasure-Ground," a public park in the heart of the growing city with bandstand, menagerie, aquarium, gravel paths, and a topiary garden along with the glasshouse. To be sure, there were "the gorgeous creepers, the wide-spreading mangos, and the graceful betel-nut trees," lest one forget that it was, after all, the East. Edward Lear delightedly labeled it the "Kew of India," and declared that he had never seen "a more beautiful place, terraces, trellises, etc., not to speak of some wild beasts. Flowers exquisite." The natives, wrote the wife of a British official, "seem fully to appreciate the gardens, and every evening numbers are there sitting under the trees, or looking at the flowers and animals."[113]

The Lal Bagh was part of a botanical network that spanned the globe, completing the process of plant transfers that had begun in antiquity, accelerated with the discoveries of the sixteenth century, and spiraled in the nineteenth.[114] J. C. Loudon, a leading garden writer in the first half of the century, estimated that 89 species of trees and shrubs were introduced into England in the sixteenth century, about 130 in the next, more than 490 by the eighteenth century, "whereas in the first thirty years alone of the nineteenth around 700 species were brought to England." When plants of all kinds were factored in, this meant about two hundred actively cultivated in England in 1500 compared with more than eighteen thousand by 1839. By this date imported evergreens had already transformed a landscape that had hitherto been dominated by deciduous native trees.[115] Well might the Reverend Henry Hill speak of England in 1838 as "a vase emerging from the ocean, in which the Sylvans of every region have set their favourite plants, and the Flora of every climate poured her choicest gifts, for the embellishment of the spot round which Neptune throws his fostering arms."[116] Still more revolutionary changes were to come: Himalayan rhododendrons, Chinese primulas, American redwoods, Australian eucalyptus, begonias from Assam.

Loudon's and Hill's perspectives were unduly insular, for the phenomenon of plant transfer was worldwide. Dapuri was a backwater, a minor Indian botanical garden near Poona in existence for less than thirty years (1837–1865), and yet an inventory of the plants illustrated by an unidentified native artist in the late 1840s includes species from Central and South America, from North America (including some collected by David Douglas in California and Thomas Drummond in Texas), from Africa, China, and western and southeastern Asia, as well as from other parts of India (Fig. 31). In its small way, too, Dapuri reflected the tug of war between science and government. Attached as many botanical gardens were to the governor's residence, its priorities were often trumped by the demands of the official household: for vegetables and flowers for the governor's table, for grass for the governor's horses.[117] Shades of royal Kew!

In the larger picture, botanical gardens were under pressure to justify their existence by seeking out and adapting "useful plants," plants with

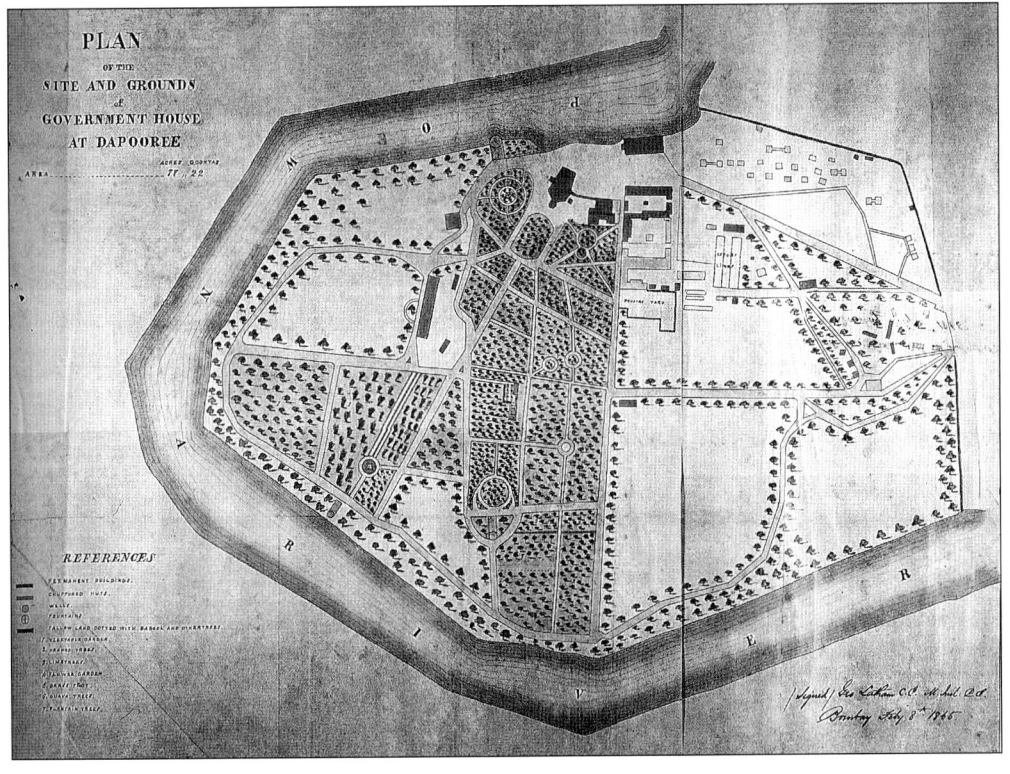

Fig. 31. Plan of the garden at Dapuri
[Royal Botanic Garden Edinburgh]

commercial potential, from all corners of the globe. If botanists were the foot soldiers of imperialism, Sir Joseph Banks was their captain (the "staunchest imperialist of the day," one admiring official called him)[118] and Kew their command center (H-Kew, we might say). Already in 1737 the frontispiece of Linnaeus's *Hortus Cliffortianus* (1737) showed Europe seated in the center with the key of knowledge in her right hand, while Asia (bearing coffee), Africa, and America wait to deliver their own gifts.[119] Botanists were even expected to engage in espionage and smuggling to serve national interests, for example, to thwart the Spanish monopoly on quinine or the Chinese on tea. There was an imperial dimension as well to the prerogative, increasingly insisted upon by botanists at home, that they, not those in the field, had the right to name a new species—even if they had never seen it growing wild—and in a tongue understood by few Europeans and almost no one anywhere else; metropolitan science trumped vernacular knowledge. Then the apotheosis: botanical illustration, "the final act in possessing a plant and the first act in civilizing it, whence multiplied by engraving it could pass into the worlds of learning and commerce." But it was Flora standing all alone, isolated from her natural habitat, her physiology stripped bare, rendered as a Platonic ideal form that might never have actually existed and that froze the species for all time. Europe dictated most emphatically how nature would be represented.[120]

Furthermore, while the exchange of plants and of botanical knowledge might ultimately benefit the rest of the world, European interests always took precedence. After ruining the indigenous cotton industry with cheap Manchester imports, for example, England was eager to expand the production of Dacca and later American cotton in India to feed its ravenous mills. At the same time, the world's botanical riches became status symbols for the high and mighty, who vied to be the first to coax blossoms from their *Amherstia nobilis* or *Victoria amazonica* in their chilly climes. It would be an oversimplification nonetheless to see botany as nothing more than the handmaiden of imperial commerce and power. Aside from those who devoted their lives to the acquisition of knowledge as an end in itself, the expanding repertoire of flowers and shrubs and trees brought disinterested delight to countless ordinary mortals. And thanks to nineteenth-century advances in glass and iron manufacture, one did not have to be the Duke of Devonshire to benefit from the bounty of exotics; even the middle-class homeowner in

Surrey could aspire to a greenhouse to bring on bedding plants or nurture tender tropicals.

Another aspect of plant collecting that was little noted at the time, however—one that now resonates all too conspicuously—was the ecological impact. When Robert Wight went on leave in England in 1831, he took with him a hundred thousand specimens, weighing two tons, and his was a relatively modest collection. Hooker shipped out even more tons of living plants from the Himalayas, including seven head-loads of a single species of orchid, the spectacular blue-flowered *Vanda caerulea*. Much of the material died even before reaching England, but simply by calling attention to the great value of these flowers—to orchids in particular—Hooker stimulated a rush into the field by other orchid hunters. He estimated that a collector might clear £2,000–3,000 in a single season from the sale of Khasia orchids.[121] Orchids were not the only casualty: whole districts were denuded of trees as well. In the search for one species alone, ten thousand plants were collected—but four thousand trees were cut down to obtain them. Then the camp of floral treasure-seekers moved on to start all over again.[122]

India's forests were indeed under threat from all sides. At the same time that collectors were stripping the subcontinent of its flora, planters were clearing forests for tea gardens and cinchona plantations: in Sikkim alone great swaths were lost to such plantations within thirty years of Hooker's explorations.[123] Earlier, naval demands for teak and the Company's interest in expanding land under cultivation to increase its revenues led to serious deforestation in both mountain and plain. When Lord Dalhousie arrived as governor-general in 1847, surgeon-botanists had been warning for half a century that the loss of India's forests was not only causing local shortages of wood for cooking fires and for house building but also might have far-reaching ecological and climatic effects such as lower rainfall, soil erosion, and silting up of rivers and streams. Dalhousie has not fared well at the hands of later historians, who have tended to overlook his precocious environmentalism in spotlighting his disastrous policies in other areas. Dalhousie, however, had a strong utilitarian bent and chanced to sail out to India with Joseph Hooker, not yet the despoiler of the orchids. After a visit to St. Helena and Ascension Islands, which thanks to Sir Joseph Banks had kept careful meteorological records, Hooker had become convinced of the relationship between forest cover and rainfall, subsequently promoting a program of tree planting on Ascension, an important British naval base in the south Atlantic.

Influenced by Hooker as well as by a host of reports by Company officials and by some modest projects already underway, Dalhousie established the first all-India Forest Department. He took as his model the precolonial policies of the recently conquered Punjab and Sind. Here forest reserves had long been administered by the central government, stressing conservation rather than reforestation. This was not ideal, to sure, in that authorities could decide just how lenient to be in granting access to timber, but it did focus attention on the problem. Later, there would be renewed pressure on India's forests with the huge appetite for wood for building telegraph poles and railway carriages.[124] In some areas the government also encouraged tree planting, although attempts at reforestation were not always well advised, as we have seen with the wholesale introduction of Australian blue gums in Ootacamund. "Improvement" could be a double-edged sword.

Finally, the human cost of plant collecting was often lost in what one might call the *furor florae*. Hooker's rich harvest of "2000 flowering plants . . . 150 ferns, and a profusion of mosses, lichens, and fungi," all within a ten-mile radius, was obtained at the cost of the lives of many local Khasias who had been driven over a precipice in their skirmish with the British, a "sanguinary conflict" that seemed to trouble the botanist very little.[125]

Pl. 1. Flower market, Kolkata

[Photograph by Genie Robbins]

Pl. 2. Victoria Gardens, Bombay

[Postcard, author's collection]

Pl. 3. William Simpson, *The Maidan, Calcutta*, 1860. Watercolor

[The British Library Board, WD 3840]

Pl. 4. James Moffat, *Government House, Calcutta*, 1804. Watercolor
[The British Library Board, WD 476]

Pl. 5. E. H. Locker, *The Governor's House at Barrackpore*, 1808. Watercolor
[The British Library Board, WD 3856]

Pl. 6. Lady Charlotte Canning, *The Governor's Villa, Parel, Bombay*, 1856

[Reproduced by the kind permission of the Earl and Countess of Harewood and Trustees of the Harewood House Trust]

Pl. 7. Lady Charlotte Canning, *Garden Reach at Barrackpore*

[Reproduced by the kind permission of the Earl and Countess of Harewood and Trustees of the Harewood House Trust]

Pl. 8. Lady Charlotte Canning, *Banyan Grove*
[Reproduced by the kind permission of the Earl and Countess of Harewood and Trustees of the Harewood House Trust]

Pl. 9. Nishat Bagh, Srinagar, Kashmir

[Photograph by author]

Pl. 10. Capt. George Bellasis, *The Club House, Ootacamund*, 1852. Watercolor

[The British Library Board, WD2301]

Pl. 11. Edward Lear Landscape Drawings, *View of Ootacamund*, 1874. Watercolor
[MS Typ 55.26(2275), Houghton Library, Harvard University]

Pl. 12. Banyan tree, Botanical Garden, Kolkata
Left to right: Ellie Weld, Bob Herbert, Eric Tilles, and Cathy Herbert
[Photograph by author]

Pl. 13. Exotic flowers and insects, *Dara Shikoh Album*, c. 1635

[The British Library Board, Ms.Add.Or. 3129, fol. 49v]

Pl. 14. Rungiah, botanical drawing

[Royal Botanic Garden Edinburgh]

Pl. 15. "Crystal Palace," Lal Bagh, Bangalore

[Photograph by author]

Pl. 16. Taj Mahal

[Photograph by Genie Robbins]

Pl. 17. Marianne North, *Taj Mahal*
[Reproduced with the kind permission of the Director and the Board of Trustees, Royal Botanic Gardens, Kew]

Pl. 18. *Babur Supervising the Laying out of the Garden of Fidelity,*
from the *Baburnama,* c. 1590

[© Victoria and Albert Museum, London]

Pl. 19. Thomas and William Daniell,
The Taje Mahel, Agra, View across the River, 1789. Aquatint
[The British Library Board, P 395]

Pl. 20. Kedleston Park, Derbyshire, England
[Photograph by author]

Pl. 21. Temple complex, Khajuraho
[Photograph by author]

The South West View

of a quiet little Residence at the Kootoob, as yet unhonored by a name. prettily situated and of convenient access whenever retirement or change of Air is desirable. It is but yet in its infancy — a few months will, I trust, perfect both its comfort and Beauty.

The North West View, with the Tomb of Adham Khan (vide Page 80) in the Distance.

Pl. 22. Thomas Metcalfe's tomb house at the Qutb Minar, Delhi, c. 1815, from the "Delhi Book"

[British Library Board, Ass.Or. 5475, fol. 82]

Pl. 23. Mughal Garden, Viceroy's House, New Delhi
[From Andreas Volwahsen, *Imperial Delhi*, 2002]

Pl. 24. Rajpath, New Delhi

[From H. Y. Sharada Prasad, *Rashtrapati Bhavan*, 1992, courtesy of the Publications Division, Ministry of Information and Broadcasting, Government of India]

Pl. 25. Interior of the Red Fort, Delhi
[Photograph by author]

Pl. 26. Brindavan Gardens, near Mysore
[Photograph by author]

Pl. 27. Lal Bagh with garden gnomes, Bangalore
[Photograph by author]

Pl. 28. Raj Ghat, New Delhi
[Postcard, author's collection]

Pl. 29. Lady Canning's grave, Barrackpore
[Photograph by author]

Pl. 30. Tollygunge Club, Kolkata
[Photograph by author]

Pl. 31. Imperial Hotel, New Delhi
[Photograph by author]

Pl. 32. Mumbai University, old campus
[Photograph by author]

CHAPTER 5

Gardens of Memory

Lucknow was a city renowned for its oriental extravagance, not to say decadence. To Victorian England it symbolized all that was wrong with India and all, as they came increasingly to believe, that they could set right. Lucknow and the surrounding province of Awadh (Oudh or Oude in contemporary British spelling) had been tributary to the Mughal emperor but gradually asserted its independence as Mughal power declined. The British preferred to maintain Awadh as a convenient buffer between their holdings in Bengal and the tumultuous kingdoms of the hinterland rather than to conquer it outright, counting on their Resident to influence policies appropriately—better to be the ever more intrusive presence behind the throne than to add another, possibly restive, territory to the empire. As long as they received revenues from the rich kingdom and dealt with reasonably compliant rulers, the British were content to humor the vagaries and corruption of the court. For reasons that have been much debated, this attitude changed in the 1850s and the Kingdom of Oudh was summarily annexed in 1856. A little over a year later, when a rebellion broke out among the Indian regiments in the Gangetic plain, Lucknow became an epicenter of the uprising and its besieged Residency a symbol of the struggle to maintain British supremacy in India. By the time the siege was lifted, only a shell of the building was left standing, its once verdant lawns and flowering shrubs covering the ravaged graves of its defenders, their families, and Indian servants. For Lucknow and its gardens, 1857 was a watershed of unforgettable proportions.[1]

The Residency

The British men, women, and children hastily buried in Lucknow's Residency garden did not choose to spend eternity there. They were, rather, the casualties of an event that soon took on a mythological life of its own in Victorian England. The ruined Residency, left defiantly in its shattered state with the Union Jack flying day and night, became an enduring shrine, "perhaps the supreme temple of British imperialism" (Fig. 32). Tennyson's truly awful poem telling of the siege and the relief that came at last immortalized Lucknow's heroism for every school child—the "handful of men . . . English in heart and in limb, / Strong with the strength of the race to command, to obey, to endure."[2] Twenty years later the Prince of Wales himself would make a pilgrimage to the site, his party touring the battlefield with its terrible memories framed almost unbearably by the "sweet English flowers" of the restored gardens: phlox, sweet peas, antirrhinums.[3]

Edith Cuthell, a post-uprising resident of Lucknow, tried to imagine an earlier time and the English sitting in their gardens of an evening: "Then fell the thunderbolt out of the blue. Their gardens knew them no more."[4] Of course the thunderbolt did not really fall out of the blue. There had been earlier mutinies, such as the ones at Vellore and Barrackpore, and a few voices continued to cry in the wilderness of complacency. Musing about the vulnerability of the handful of Europeans going about their polite amusements in Simla amid the much more numerous mountaineers "wrapped up in their hill blankets," Emily Eden had wondered, we may recall, that they did not "cut all our heads off, and say nothing more about it." Even closer to the mark, William Huggins, a Bengal indigo planter, had compared the "Seapoy army" on which the Raj depended to a "powder magazine" that might be touched off at any time by innovations "of themselves insignificant, but offensive on the score of prejudice."[5]

Fig. 32. Ruins of the Residency, Lucknow, NWP. Samuel Bourne, 1860
[The British Library Board, Photo 394(55)]

And, indeed, tensions long building erupted in May 1857 soon after the introduction of cartridges enclosed in paper greased with what was rumored to be beef fat (offensive to Hindus) or pork fat (offensive to Muslims) that had to be bitten open with the teeth before ramming them down their rifles; many saw this not only as polluting but as part of a more general British plot to forcibly convert native troops to Christianity. Revolt broke out first among the sepoys (native soldiers) in Meerut and quickly spread to other camps, especially in Awadh, where the lion's share of Indian soldiers in the British army had traditionally been recruited and which had been annexed just the year before. Europeans from outlying stations and from Lucknow itself fled to the Residency for safety, although it had no fortifications and could draw on only a small neighboring garrison for protection.

Like so much of Lucknow, the Residency was itself a hodgepodge of incongruous parts. Three years before the outbreak of violence, an American visitor had described it as "a large and lofty building [it was three stories high]

... surrounded by beautiful gardens"—not unlike other residencies scattered about India except that instead of being located in a quiet corner outside the city, it was situated in the midst of Lucknavi palaces and mansions and close to a major market or *chowk*.[6] Furthermore, the compound included, in addition to the Residency and banqueting hall themselves, a number of substantial bungalows and gardens belonging to officials, a treasury, barracks and mess hall, a small Gothic church, a post office, and tennis courts, plus several houses belonging to Indians, a sheep house, a slaughterhouse, two Sikh squares, two mosques, a Muslim saint's tomb, and a native hospital. At the height of the siege almost seven thousand people were penned inside the Residency and a few adjoining houses in the garden. They consisted of some three thousand Europeans, including of course the women and children who captured the public imagination, but also an even larger number of Indians: soldiers, servants, and camp followers. To his credit, Tennyson offered thanks to these "kindly dark faces who fought with us, faithful and few." When the successive sieges were finally lifted five months later, two thousand of those who had taken refuge were dead and the rest reduced almost to starvation.[7] In the fury of revenge that followed, many wanted to raze all of Lucknow to the ground and annihilate its citizenry. Though cooler heads eventually prevailed, suspected rebels were shot out of cannons, many neighborhoods were dynamited, and the entire center of the city redesigned in the image of Anglo-India. Post-uprising Lucknow became once more a city of gardens, but the gardens bore a very different stamp from those of the earlier city.

Lucknow as Orientalist Fantasy

Nawabi Lucknow was created by a family of Persian Shi'ite origin who had first deputized as rulers of Awadh for the Mughal emperor in Delhi and then gradually asserted their independence. In 1775 the court moved from Faizabad to Lucknow, ushering in a golden age, however curious a one. As Delhi and other Mughal capitals declined, Lucknow grew until it became the largest and most prosperous precolonial city in India, surpassed in population only by presidency cities of Calcutta, Bombay, and Madras. Poets, artists, musicians, scholars, and craftsmen came from all over northern India, lured by lavish promises of patronage and making it a center of Urdu letters and learning.

At the same time, the ruling *nawabs* and court elite became increasingly fascinated with European culture and most of all with European architecture as mediated by officials, traders, and soldiers of fortune. Preeminent among the last was Claude Martin, a Frenchman in the service of the East India Company, who was "nearly as Indianised as the Nawab was Europeanised." Martin's various building projects culminated in the fantastic pile which he called Constantia but which has since been known as La Martinière. A fortress-cum-tomb, it was an over-the-top combination of "Gothic towers, and Grecian pilasters." Governor-General Hastings thought the plan must have been taken "from those castles of pastry which used to adorn desserts," while Emma Roberts characterized it as "a grotesquely magnificent house." The English journalist W. H. Russell went further: the first view inspired him to exclaim, "How beautiful! What a splendid building"; the second, however, caused him to add, "Why it must have been built by a madman."[8]

Other structures were hardly less sensational as amalgams of indigenous and western. Since none of the *nawabi* elite had actually been to Europe, their notions were secondhand. They tended to copy plans in books and then to copy each other—what looked good on someone else's building might be just as impressive on one's own. Dilkusha, for example, built as a country residence for Saadat Ali Khan about 1800 by a former Acting British Resident, is a fairly authentic replica of Vanbrugh's Seaton Delaval in Northumberland, with a grand exterior staircase surmounted by Palladian columns, but there are ranks of stone urns atop the balustrades and the flanking octagonal towers are crowned with almost pagoda-like turrets. Oddly enough, the staircases within the towers are the only way to reach the upper floors or the roof. Dilkusha departed from traditional Lucknavi architecture in that it was a solid block of masonry, with no interior courtyards. The masonry consisted of brick plastered over with *chunam* rather than stone because there was no stone to be had in Awadh. It also differed in being set on a slight prominence "with some extent of lawn about it" and a large surrounding deer park with its "avenue of mighty trees." Here the *nawab* hunted with hawks and trained cheetahs. In contrast to Dilkusha, the huge Qaisar Bagh palace complex, completed only a few years before the British annexation of the kingdom in 1856, is ostensibly neoclassical in style, but the plan derives from earlier Central Asian walled enclosures with separate pavilions in the manner of Akbar's Fatehpur Sikri. Inside, however, it was lavishly furnished with European furniture, draperies, mechanical instruments, and toys.[9]

GARDENS OF MEMORY

As ornate palaces, country villas, and *imambaras* (Shi'ite religious establishments) proliferated, it became harder and harder to characterize the city. Was it "an 'oriental' city, with gilded domes (albeit over a wooden frame) and minarets, or an Indian version of a European spa"? No wonder visitors fell back on the *Arabian Nights* to convey their reactions. Honoria Lawrence had to admit that for all its "bad taste and inconsistency," Lucknow "comes nearer to anything I have seen to realize my early ideas of the Arabian Nights and Lalla Rookh." Emily Eden had the same reaction to the garden in the Chattar Manzil: "Don't you remember in the 'Arabian Nights,' Zobeide bets her 'garden of delights' against the Caliph's 'palace of pictures?' I am sure this was the 'garden of delights.'" Usually so harsh a critic, Eden acknowledged that this was the only Indian residence she ever coveted.[10]

The gardens of delight of pre-1857 Lucknow were as eclectic as the architecture. One Resident brought in an English botanist to instruct the king's *malis,* but he only lasted a few months. Other Englishmen were employed in the royal gardens from time to time. An avowedly English garden was created for the Anglo-Armenian wife of one *nawab,* although we know little about it beyond its exotic flowers and European trees; similarly, the Badshah Bagh boasted "a large and beautiful garden, laid out in the English style, and uncommonly delightful," again without details. Presumably "English" referred to a more informal arrangement, with lawns and shrubs surrounding European-type villas, rather than within enclosed courtyards—the Dilkusha garden, for example, was planted in front of its east facade. More enigmatic were the remains of what was referred to as an "English village" that Major Archer (Fanny Parks's father) came upon in the deer park around the Dilkusha. It contained the ruins of some mud huts, but otherwise "the spire, the elms and hedgerows, and whitewashed honeysuckled walls, were all left to the imagination"—had it ever existed, "the furious hot winds would have parched it immediately."[11]

Mostly, however, the palace gardens took Persian and Mughal prototypes as their starting point: interior courtyards with their symmetrical parterres of flowers and trees divided by watercourses and fountains, all enclosed with high walls so that royal ladies could not be seen by passersby. Royal palaces boasted their *lal bagh* ("red garden") and *gulistan-i-iram* ("rose garden of paradise"). As Lady Nugent described the garden of the Chattar Manzil some twenty years before Emily Eden's visit, "The place that was yesterday only a barren waste, was converted into a beautiful garden, filled with flowers, pavilions, temples, bowers, and fountains, all composed of coloured lamps, and different sorts of lights." She does not mention the flowers by name, but they would probably have included sweetly scented bushes such as rat-ki-rani, jasmine, and frangipani, along with roses, poinsettias, and exotics obtained from the Calcutta Botanic Garden.[12]

Nonetheless, her description also alerts us to the fact that *nawabi* gardens contained more than the usual trees, flowers, and water. They were just as cluttered as their palaces, not only with elaborate pavilions, steam baths, mosques, pagodas, and of course swings for the ladies in the *zenana* garden, but also with very un-Muslim statuary. Here, too, Claude Martin may have been the inspiration, with "the profusion of plaster lions, Grecian gods and Chinese figures" on the parapets and pinnacles of Constantia and in its French-style garden. Captain von Orlich clearly found the "many painted statues" in the Badshah Bagh rather vulgar. This was not the view of a newspaper reporter when the last king of Awadh, Wajid Ali Shah, opened the gardens of the Qaisar Bagh to the public for a brief moment: "The garden is tastefully laid out with marble statues, arranged in outré groupings, Venus and Cupid and in juxtaposition an English cow, not a bad specimen of the statuary's skill. Then we witness a magnificent marble reservoir where gold and silver fishes disport undisturbed [fish were a symbol of Awadh], also fountains of marble which play unceasingly." The war correspondent William Howard Russell, on the other hand, while praising the gardens of the Qaisar Bagh as "worthy of Kew," condemned the statues as "most hideous, ludicrous, and preposterous . . . Hindoo statues in imitation of Italian [classical?] subjects."[13]

The gardens were intended for more than "eating the air," as an Urdu phrase had it. Like the gardens of Mughal emperors before them, they were the center of elite social life. And like Ranelagh and Vauxhall in eighteenth-century London, Lucknavi entertainments were famous for their music and dancing, their sumptuous feasts, their elaborately theatrical displays of colored lights, fireworks, illuminated hot-air balloons rising into the air "like so many moons."[14] But Victorian England had turned its collective back on the frivolities and alleged immorality of Georgian and Regency pleasure gardens. Now, the extravagance and the alleged "decadence" of its rulers provided the public rationale for the annexation of Awadh and the deposition of its king: "The British Government would be guilty in the sight of God and man,"

GARDENS OF MEMORY

intoned the official declaration of February 13, 1856, "if it were any longer to aid in sustaining by its countenance an administration fraught with evil to millions." Their claim was buttressed by a succession of reports of misgovernment under increasingly weak and profligate rulers. A Resident who had advocated a British takeover for several years dismissed the king, Wajid Ali Shah, as totally uninterested in public affairs, aiming at nothing but "the reputation of being the best dancer, best versifier, and best drummer in his dominions." His inner circle allegedly consisted entirely of "poets, fiddlers, eunuchs, and profligate women." Another writer compared Lucknow in all seriousness to Sodom and Gomorrah. The 1929 edition of *Murray's Handbook of India* was only a little less censorious: "With the exception of Sa'adat Ali Khan [whom the British had put on the throne in 1798], no reigning dynasty of India ever showed such a series of vicious and incompetent princes." And yet the doyen of Lucknavi chroniclers maintains, "It is unlikely that anyone will question the statement that the late court of Awadh was the final example of oriental refinement and culture in India."[15]

When fighting broke out some fifteen months later, the city's palaces, *imambaras,* and gardens were in the thick of it. Opposing armies seized control of the palaces with their towers and walled gardens. For Russell, looking out over the city from the balustrade of the Dilkusha in the midst of the battle to regain the city in March 1858, the view was surreal: "How lovely Lucknow looks today! The sun playing on all the gilt domes and spires, the exceeding richness of the vegetation and forests and gardens which remind one somewhat of the view of the Bois-de-Boulogne from the hill over St. Cloud. But for the puffs of villainous saltpeter, and the thunder of the guns, with noise of balls cleaving the air, how peaceful the scene is!" A little later the British captured the Badshah Bagh, the "garden of the great king," which had been a rebel stronghold. "In the days of its full magnificence it must have been glorious. Such forests of orange-trees, such trickling fountains, shady walks, beds of flowers, grand alleys, dark retreats and summer-houses, all surrounded by a high and massive wall, and forming, as it were, the approaches to a snug little palace of pleasure." Here as elsewhere the soldiers were given free rein to loot and vandalize to their hearts' content, leaving most of *nawabi* Lucknow in the same ruined state as the Residency. "Lucknow used to be the finest city in India and beat Delhi into fits," commented a British officer, "but it is a most miserable looking city now."[16]

The Aftermath

Over the next two decades, Lucknow rose from the ashes, this time reincarnated in the image of the conqueror. Colonel Robert Napier of the Bengal Engineers drew up a plan for remaking the city that was carried out almost to the letter, a plan that Russell could only characterize as "imperial in conception." Broad, straight boulevards were rammed through the heart of the old city. "All the bazaar was cleared away," commented a local woman. "The English like grass better than bazaars." Buildings that could be of use to the military or civil authorities were taken over, albeit with large empty esplanades leveled around them. Thus the Chattar Manzil, Emily Eden's Arabian Nights palace, which had been badly damaged by artillery fire, was quickly restored and reincarnated as the very elegant home of the United Services Club. Similarly, the restoration of the Macchi Bhawan involved the razing of one courtyard and its replacement with grass and trees. To add insult to injury, the Jama Masjid was used as a storage depot for ammunition, the Great Imambara turned into a field hospital for wounded British soldiers, and the Asafi Imambara into billets for troops, with no thought of how the vision of soldiers trampling the sacred precincts, eating pork, and downing alcohol would look to the Muslim population—or perhaps there was all too much thought of this. Like Haussmann in Paris, Napier was determined to eliminate the narrow, winding alleys and cul-de-sacs that were so easy to barricade, even if he had to run roughshod over mosques, cemeteries, and neighborhoods to do it. In the end some two-fifths of the city was reduced to rubble in the name of security and hygiene.[17]

By the time the Prince of Wales visited the city in 1876, the transformation was complete. "Lucknow has fairly been improved off the face of the earth," noted Russell ruefully. He had covered the last stages of the uprising, but so great were the changes that he found it almost impossible to recognize many parts of the city. "Hundreds of acres once occupied by houses have been turned into market-gardens. Swarded parks, vistas and drives, far prettier than those of the Bois de Boulogne, spread out where once were streets, bazaars, palaces. They are like oceans beneath which thousands of wrecks lie buried." Victoria Street cut a swath through the edge of Chowk; other thoroughfares with names such as Canning Street, Havelock Road, Abbott Street—even the very long Napier Street—radiated away from the riverbank, the heart of the old city. Russell felt that the wholesale demolition had been carried too far and that it was sheer foolishness to store guns and ammunition in the *imambara* and to use mosques for Christian worship, warning, "If we ever lose India, it will be from 'want of sympathy.'"[18]

In addition to the gutting of much of the old city, a whole new civil station was built adjacent to the cantonment, this, too, insulated from the native areas by an expanse of open spaces. As a residential quarter for Europeans, the new Lucknow anticipated to some extent the New Delhi of the twentieth century (see Chapter 8). The basic unit, here as throughout British India, was the ample bungalow, standing in the midst of a generous plot of lawn and garden. A contemporary Indian writer remarked of the civil station, "It has a complete country appearance and though its architecture is not pleasing to the oriental eye, its numerous streets with parks and gardens interspersed everywhere, and an almost dustless atmosphere, have made Lucknow famous as the garden city of India." This was the Lucknow of garden parties and flower shows, of cricket matches and horse races, the Lucknow of the Carlton Hotel with its bagpipe band in dark red tunics over dark-blue trousers playing at teatime in the garden, the contrast of their dark uniforms striking against the green of the grass. It was no longer the Lucknow of *nautches* and illuminations and "whimsical piles."[19]

It was also the city that so pleased Lady Dufferin as "one of the nicest stations in India." She was delighted with the "great open park-like spaces, intersected with broad roads overshadowed by fine trees, and all the grass, shrubs, and leaves . . . so green and luxuriant"—perhaps oblivious to the fact that all these open spaces were dictated by military rather than aesthetic concerns and that they overlay what had once been vibrant native neighborhoods. She even liked the bungalows with their nice gardens. In fact "the whole place looks well-kept and rich, and is as neat as a gentleman's park at home." Observing Lucknow through a different lens in the next century, the city planner Patrick Geddes was appalled by the dreary lines of small brick houses assigned to lesser civil servants, finding them ill-adapted to the environment. They were saved only by "zealous garden and tree planting."[20]

Edith Cuthell's husband was posted to Lucknow late in the century. Her book *My Garden in the City of Gardens* is an invaluable month-by-month account of her own garden and of the city's garden heritage (until she flees the unbearable heat of June). From her we get a confirmation of the extreme redevelopment of the city: the broad roads blasted through the native city; the long wide Mall, shady with huge gnarled mango trees, running straight as an arrow through the center of the cantonment; the "suburbs well planted"; the Botanical Garden lying in an "immense stretch of ornamental grass, carefully watered and forested, behind the Civil Lines" ("some good ribbon-gardening, with the beds intersected with tiny gravel paths"). But she also loved to visit the ruins of the "lordly pleasure houses" and their gardens. Not far from the Botanical Garden was the Sikanderbagh, built by the last *nawab* for a favorite and the scene of particularly bloody fighting in 1857. On a November afternoon, however, it was "a glory of beautiful gardening, as are all the Lakhnao ruins," radiant with plumbago, bougainvillea, alamanda, and convolvulus. She couldn't resist a visit, also, to the high-walled, fortified gardens of the Chattar Manzil. Three lofty ornamented gateways led into "pleasant grounds, well planted with fruit and forest trees, and divided by gravel walks into parterres gay with shrubs." As she remarks, shade, water and green were the primary requisites for a garden "in lands where the sun has to be reckoned with." And "roses, roses everywhere!" Her only disappointment seems to have been with a moonlight garden party in Dilkusha. However romantic this sounded, the reality was that it was "abominably chilly" by mid-evening and everyone huddled around a huge bonfire listening to the "inevitable British infantry band playing in the inevitable *chabbutra* among the stiff flower beds."[21]

Cuthell's accounts suggest that the British were maintaining many of the old palace gardens, perhaps after their own fashion. Photography came in just too late to make before-and-after comparisons, but pictures dating from the 1860s and 1870s show vast stretches of open ground around surviving or restored monuments, albeit with some rather indistinct plantings. Some appear to preserve older patterns, while others show the unmistakable imprint of the conqueror. Cuthell includes a picture of the Lanka and its gardens in the Qaisar Bagh: gone are the rectangular parterres, watercourses, and fruit trees of earlier times, replaced by nonsymmetrical flowerbeds, shrubs, walkways, and lawns (Fig. 33). Other photographs show ranks and ranks of flowerpots, even in the *imambara* gardens that one might imagine to be more immune to British fashions. Flowerpots notwithstanding, however, Cuthell considered the Husainabad Imambara the ne plus ultra of native ornamental gardening, its roses and flowering shrubs and occasional annuals—marigolds most conspicuously—brilliantly lit up by thousands of tiny lights during the sacred Shia rituals of Muharram. "Of grass or lawn there was not a vestige," but over all there wafted that marker of the Indian garden, "an amber scent of odorous perfume."[22]

Nonetheless, of all the gardens in this city of gardens, one overshadowed all the others after 1857: the Residency garden (Fig. 34). "The Residency is the spot which all Englishmen will wish to visit first in Lucknow," asserts Murray's guidebook. "The gardens are beautifully arranged and perfectly kept, and the place now reflects that peacefulness which properly belongs to sad scenes long since enacted."[23] One entered through the arched gateway, the Baillie Guard Gate, through which the relief column had literally battered its way with great cannon balls after punching through the walls of the gardens along the south bank of the river. Inside was an "oasis of greenery and flowers," lawns of *doob* grass maintained with great care (and difficulty) and stands of bougainvillea, ipomea, and other brilliant flowering shrubs. Left to themselves, luxuriant creepers would soon have completely enveloped the pockmarked shells of buildings, turning them into picturesque ruins rather than the reverent monument to the gallantry of the defenders: the "beautiful but treacherous elephant creeper" half veiling the ruins and the orange venusta hanging "like a golden curtain from the pillars that once formed the verandah."[24] The challenge was to maintain a balance, to use the beauty of the natural world to transform the unsightly into something transcendent.

Lady Dufferin found the place "very pretty—gay flowers, picturesque ruins"—not perhaps the adjective those in charge most wanted to elicit, but she did add, "Seeing ruins made is a very different matter from contemplating them calmly years after the destruction is accomplished." Edward Lear found the flowers "stupendous; what oleanders, pomegranates, roses and creepers!" And yet the effect was wanting in the Sublime, "especially as there are vulgar cannon-balls everywhere." Edith Cuthell, too, was constantly reminded of the "sharp contrast between the present and the not-so-far-away past—the gay gardens round deserted palaces; the shot-riddled pleasure-houses, with loop-holed walls." And yet here were "laughing, chattering Englishmen and women riding and driving about them just as before," as if there had been no "awful interlude."[25] While the history of the siege in recent guidebooks has been whittled down from the nine pages in Murray's 1929 edition to a mere box in the most recent *Lonely Planet Guide,* it is impossible to think of Lucknow without the "awful interlude."

Fig. 33. Qaisar Bagh, post-1857
[From Edith Cuthell, *My Garden in the City of Gardens*, 1905]

Fig. 34. The Lucknow Residency restored
[From Edith Cuthell, *My Garden in the City of Gardens*, 1905]

The "awful interlude" finds a curious parallel in the history of Shi'ite Lucknow. Here, too, an even more distant past was part of the present. The Great Imambara is the largest religious complex in the world devoted to the rituals and cult of the martyred Imam Husain, the grandson of the Prophet who was killed in an ambush at Karbala by the Caliph Yazid in 680 C.E. (AH 61). The Passion of Husain, like the crucifixion of Christ, became the defining event of Shi'ism. Every year in the month of Muharram the faithful enact the sufferings and sacrifice of the Imam, sufferings and sacrifice that have "transcended time and space to acquire importance of cosmic magnitude."

> *Lucknow exists but to mourn Husain.*
> *Rightly it can be called the home of Husain.*

Since Karbala was too far for many to make the pilgrimage, Karbala and the mausoleum of Husain were re-created in India in the *imambaras* of Lucknow.[26]

Whether Europeans, caught up in their own history of suffering and sacrifice, would have made such connections is doubtful. In their telling and retelling of the story of the Uprising of 1857, Lucknow shared the tragic stage not with Karbala but with Cawnpore (Kanpur), forty-six miles to the south. If anything the horrors at Cawnpore surpassed those at Lucknow. A contingent of Europeans who had surrendered to the rebels was massacred at the riverside *ghat* where they had assembled with a promise from Nana Sahib (Nana Rao) of safe passage to Allahabad. Then a further group of surviving women and children confined in the Bibighar were butchered, the bodies of living and dead thrown down a well. These events unleashed a frenzy of vengeance on the part of the British, who cared little whether the innocent were struck down equally with the guilty. Nothing was left of the Bibighar (the *zenana* garden of a Hindu favorite in calmer times) when the viceroy, Lord Canning, held a *durbar* at Cawnpore in late 1859, but he commissioned both a memorial church and a monument for the site of the infamous well. His wife, Charlotte, drew up the design for a sculpture, *Angel of the Resurrection*, surrounded by a stone screen, which Carlo Marochetti followed with only a few changes.[27]

The garden laid out around the well was, if anything, lovelier than that of the Lucknow Residency; Constance Gordon Cumming wrote that it was "a

Fig. 35. Garden outside the well, Kanpur. Samuel Bourne, 1860
[The British Library Board, Photo 394(60)]

garden of such richness and beauty as to be exceeded by none in England," adding "It is little short of a miracle to see such a triumph of art over nature—to pass from the world of dust outside to those smooth green lawns, with masses of such roses as might excite the envy of a Devonshire rose-gardener" (Fig. 35). And not just roses: stands of golden bignonia, lilac creepers "more exquisite still," bougainvillea, "whose long sprays of delicate lilac leaves festoon each shrub that comes within reach." Lear described it as "a quiet and beautiful scene, the flowers lovely, and a sort of melancholy grandeur in that sad space." What made the garden possible was water from the great Ganges Canal that originated four hundred miles away in the Himalayas at the holy city of Hardwar and joined the "mother stream" at Cawnpore, transforming "a sea of dust into a peerless rose-garden with greenest turf." A decade after the uprising, the well and its gardens were visited more frequently than the Taj Mahal. But entry was forbidden to unaccompanied Indians (servants could drive their masters through the grounds at a stately pace) until after

World War II. Even then there were occasional reports of ghosts, such as a sighting of "two blonde boys running this way and that around the mouth of the well" as if "desperately trying to find somewhere to escape."[28]

Lucknow's history ran the gamut from farce to tragedy, with all the registers in between and with its gardens ringing in the changes. The pleasure gardens of its *nawabi* elite were places of indulgence and fantasy. When the Victorians condemned the sham and illusion of the city with the epithet "Vauxhallish," however, they were looking back, perhaps uncomfortably, to a more frivolous time in their own history, and indeed there were parallels between Regency excesses such as the Royal Pavilion at Brighton and the follies of the rulers of Awadh.[29] But Victorian values had little time to implant themselves in Lucknow before the savageries of the Uprising of 1857. What followed the recapture of the city was a radical transformation, every broad tree-lined boulevard and greensward intended not only to prevent future uprisings but to proclaim the hegemony of the English urban landscape. And most of all, its sacred ruin and garden of remembrance to create an imperial myth of heroism and sacrifice.

CHAPTER 6

The Taj and the Raj

Restoring the Taj Mahal

LORD CURZON served as viceroy of India from 1899 to 1905. One of the accomplishments of which he was proudest was the preservation and restoration of India's ancient monuments during his watch and with his active participation. And of none was he prouder than those in Agra—first and foremost, his beloved Taj Mahal (see Pl. 16). "If I had never done anything else in India, I have written my name here [in Agra]," he declared in 1905, "and the letters are a living joy."[1] Today's visitors to the Taj are apt to be so transfixed by the mausoleum itself that they remember little of the gardens, but this was far from the intent of its creators; for the Mughals, the garden setting was as important a statement as the tomb itself. "Restoration" is at best a slippery term, all the more so when applied to as ephemeral an art form as a garden. What did Curzon know of classic Mughal garden forms and to what extent did he set out to replicate them faithfully? If literal authenticity was not his goal, what sort of a garden did he aim to re-create, and why? While the viceroy's project was undoubtedly a labor of love, it was as freighted with imperial implications as Shah Jahan's original monument to his beloved wife.

At the same time, too, the restoration of the gardens of the Taj set the pattern for landscaping other Indian monuments.

The Taj Restored

Curzon had first fallen in love with the Taj on a visit to the East in 1887–88. Writing to his friend St. John Brodrick, he could scarcely contain his enthusiasm: "The Taj is incomparable, designed like a palace and finished like a jewel—a snow-white emanation starting from a bed of cypresses and backed by a turquoise sky, pure, perfect and unutterably lovely. One feels the same sensation as in gazing at a beautiful woman, one who has that mixture of loveliness and sadness which is essential to the highest beauty." In the same letter, he added, "I stood there and gazed long upon the entrancing spectacle, the singular loveliness of it pouring in waves over my soul and flooding my inner consciousness till the cup of satiety was full, and I had to shut my eyes and pause and think."[2]

So taken with the Taj was the young traveler that he devoted fourteen pages of his diary to it, viewing the monument in the early morning light, in the waning gleam of evening, and "under the full effulgence of the moon." He rhapsodized that it was "the most beautiful building raised by human hands in the world," adding that it is "difficult to exaggerate the extent to which the beauty of the garden contributes to and enhances that of the Taj. Alone it would be one of the loveliest gardens anywhere to be seen, being divided into numerous parterres, and detached lawns & plots, planted with brilliant flowers & shrubs, and gloriously shaded by the foliage of ancestral and umbrageous trees." Remarkably, he found the Taj in "perfect condition," as "free from blemish or defect as the day on which it was completed." Whatever damage the years had wrought, he observed, had been "studiously repaired . . . under the watchful supervision of the British government," which had spent several *lakhs* (hundreds of thousands) of rupees on its preservation, so that "we are able to gaze in its perfection upon the most perfect structure in the world."[3] Over and over he finds no other word to express his admiration but "perfect."

Curzon made three more trips to India before becoming viceroy, visiting the great monuments of the subcontinent. Small wonder, then, that their restoration became from the first an imperative of his administration. Small wonder, too, that he should have retreated to the tomb garden of the

Taj Mahal one last time before leaving India under a cloud in 1905: "I have learned to love this place more than any other spot in India. Here it is always peaceful and always beautiful."[4]

The actual work of restoring the Taj and its gardens was entrusted to the Archaeological Survey of India (ASI), but Curzon subjected its officials to a steady stream of directives. The mausoleum itself required little work except for the crypt, which had been despoiled of much of its inlay work during the Uprising of 1857,[5] but the viceroy had clear ideas about what needed to be done with the gardens and with the "dusty wastes and . . . squalid bazaar" outside the Taj Ganj, the main entrance to the complex. "A beautiful park takes their place; and the group of mosques and tombs, the arcaded streets and grassy courts that precede the main building are once more as nearly as possible what they were when completed by the masons of Shah Jahan" (Fig. 36). He made the same claims to authenticity with the garden itself: "Every building in the garden enclosure of the Taj has been scrupulously repaired, and

Fig. 36. Taj Ganj
[Photograph by Jim Glickman]

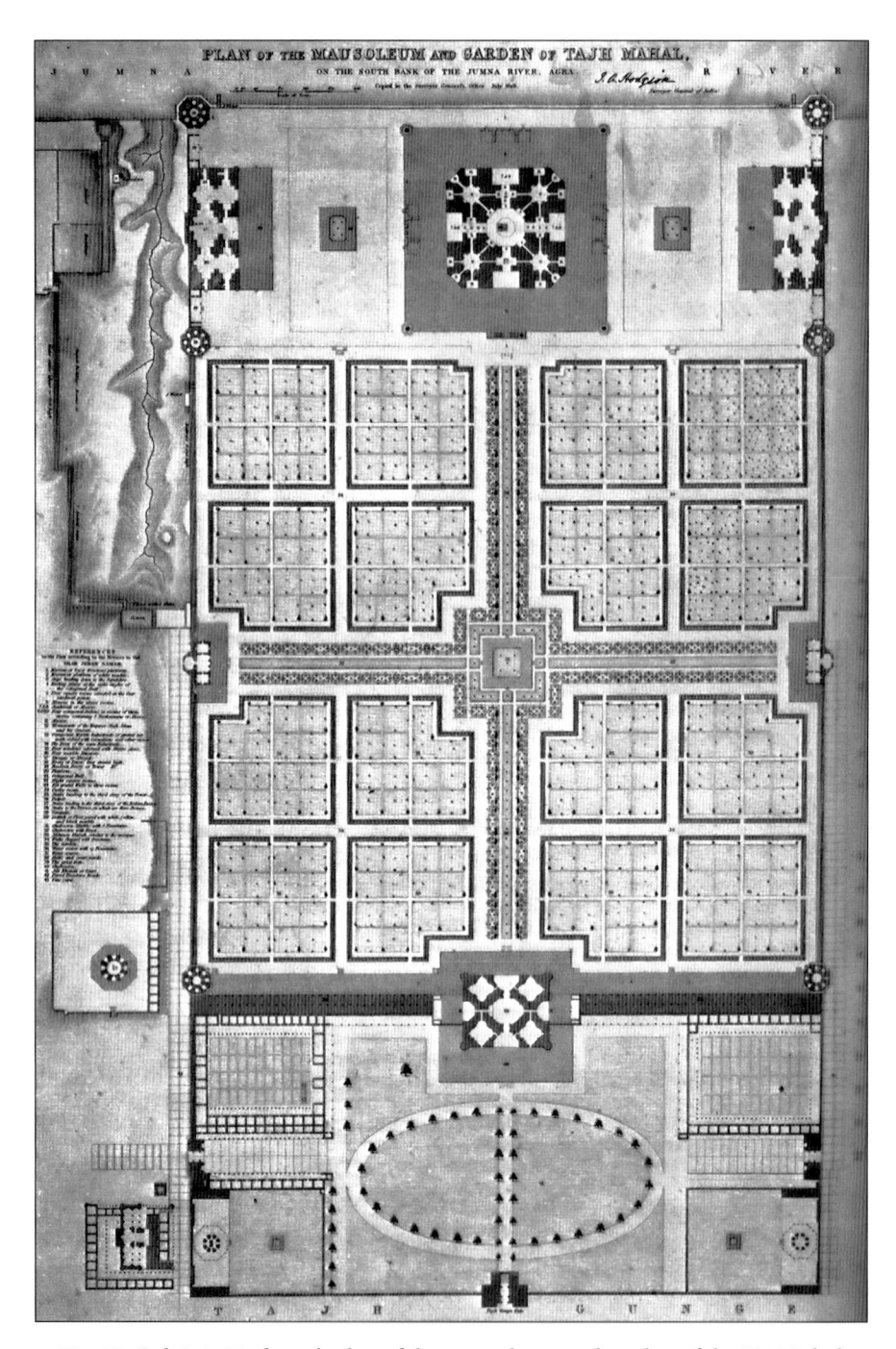

Fig. 37. Col. J. A. Hodgson's plan of the mausoleum and garden of the Taj Mahal
[*Journal of the Royal Asiatic Society*, 1843]

the discovery of old plans has enabled us to restore the water-channels and flower-beds of the garden more exactly to their original state."[6] The reference to "old plans" seems to be to the one drawn up in 1828 under the supervision of Colonel J. A. Hodgson, surveyor-general of India, but this is quite schematic and does not provide any detail about the plantings (Fig. 37). Curzon was familiar with François Bernier's valuable but incomplete description of the Taj garden in 1663 (discussed later in this chapter), nearly contemporary with its creation, as well as with the 1844 account of the British officer William Sleeman, for we find him citing both in debating the fine points of parterres of flowers and avenues of cypresses with Sir Antony MacDonnell, the lieutenant governor of the United Provinces, within whose jurisdiction Agra lay. At one point the exasperated official exclaims "I wish [Bernier] had told us what flowers were grown."[7] Curzon's proclaimed mantra was "to restore nothing that had not already existed, and to put up nothing absolutely new."[8] Did he in fact practice what he preached?

As far as architecture and its accoutrements were concerned, he and his lieutenants score high marks, except for the blatant example of the "Saracenic" lamp he commissioned in Cairo to hang above the crypt within the tomb and the "Mogul" uniforms decreed for the custodians of the site.[9] But the Taj garden was quite another matter. It has been "very capriciously treated in the past," he declared, "and what is wanted is continuity of treatment and artistic lines."[10] In consequence, "Agra . . . knew the fearful joy of five Viceregal inspections in six years," and after every visit, Curzon bombarded the ASI with instructions, micromanaging their restoration down to the last cypress tree and flower pot.[11] Already in December 1899, he wrote:

> I expressed a wish that the cypresses should be replanted, not, as before, at the sides or edges of the beds on either side of the stone causeway, nor in the two rows on each side, but in a single row on either side, the trees being placed in the middle of the beds. Thus there will be a single cypress avenue framing the Taj at the end. The garish English flowers which now fill these beds should be removed, and suitable dark shrubs or plants should be planted round the base of the cypresses. On either side of the central tank trellised archways have been made, the sides of which consist of red sandstone blocks standing on end, and the roof of creepers trained on wires. A visitor to

the Taj, subsequent to my tour, told me that it was in contemplation to remove these. This should not be done. I never even hinted at their removal, and *they are pretty, even if not very correct.*[12]

So the barrage of memos continued: "I think the removal of the flowers and the substitution of simple grass in the plots bordering the water-channel in the Taj is an improvement; but I think the cypresses are planted too thickly"; after a subsequent visit, the approving comment: "The Taj and its gardens were looking more beautiful than I have ever seen them; the green of the lawns was superb."[13] Nevertheless, adjustments were still needed: keep the cypresses as they are, he advised, with two instead of one in the longer beds, but they do seem small—isn't it possible to find larger ones? When MacDonnell appeared to look askance at Curzon's liberties, the viceroy bristled and the governor hastily retreated, assuring him that "the changes are all for the better" and that in his opinion "the present arrangement of a greensward is infinitely to be preferred [to that described by Bernier]."[14] Even as his term of office wound down, Curzon was still fiddling with the palms and debating whether more large trees should be removed to open up the view, as well as what to do with the quadrangles outside the gateway. His general principle seemed to be: when in doubt, plant grassy lawns, then decide whether shrubs or flowers should be added.

As the work neared completion, J. H. Marshall, chosen by Curzon as director general of the ASI, proclaimed with satisfaction: "The Taj Mahal, in particular, with its gardens and surrounding buildings, can hardly have looked more effective in the days of the Mogul Emperors than it does now." Echoing Curzon, he noted that "squalid bazaars have been cleared away from its gates, the colonnades flanking its approach have been opened out and repaired, and the untidy quadrangle that precedes its main entrance has been converted into a well grassed and peaceful court. Within the precinct of the tomb itself the gardens with their watercourses, fountains and flowerbeds have been restored more exactly to their original condition, and the stately mosque and *jawab* [guest house] have been structurally repaired and beautified by the renovation of their encrusted ornaments and sculptured panels."[15]

And yet Marshall himself acknowledged a different yardstick with regard to gardens as opposed to architecture. In his *Conservation Manual* (1923) he insisted that although it was important "to preserve the essential character of the original" in restoring Indian gardens, "it is not necessary to attempt to reproduce with pedantic accuracy the original appearance of the garden in all its particulars"—it was perfectly all right to substitute modern varieties of roses, for example, or "a far more beautiful lawn of grass" for "the old fashioned Indian beaten earth." In the final resort, "archaeological officers should therefore endeavor to observe the happy mean between antiquarian accuracy on the one hand and aesthetic beauty on the other."[16]

In truth, the garden was profoundly altered at the hands of the Curzonites. Before the restorations, it was much more densely shaded, it contained many more flowers, it was full of exotic fragrances, and it produced bountiful crops of fruits for the market. In 1792 the garden contained "thousands of orange trees, with their ripe fruit upon them," and a fortunate visitor was able to make his camp in this "grove of perfumes."[17] Fanny Parks, visiting the Taj forty years later, extolled the beauty of the gardens and the fine old trees. She noted that when the fountains were playing "of an evening . . . the odour of exotic flowers is on the air, the fall of the water has a delightful effect both on the eye and ear," and commented that "the produce in fruit is very valuable."[18] Or, as Edward Lear exclaimed in 1874: "What a garden! What flowers!" concluding simply, "The garden is indescribable."[19]

We can also illustrate the appearance of the gardens before and after Curzon visually. William Hodges was the first British artist to paint the Taj in 1783 (Fig. 38). He was followed six years later by Thomas and William Daniell (uncle and nephew) (Fig. 39). In both renderings the Taj is framed by dense foliage, partially blocking the view of the minarets and completely obscuring the mosque and *jawabs* flanking the mausoleum. In the foreground the clear water channel and its bordering walks lead the viewer's eye directly to the monument; Hodges' vantage point is closer to the Taj and, unlike the Daniells' versions, does not show the raised *chabutra* at the intersection of the waterways with its fountains.[20] The Daniells published a small book to accompany their prints of the "Taje," which includes a plan by James Newton. This lists beds of flowers along both the north–south and east–west channels of water, that is, within the lozenge-shaped parterres, while simply labeling the main squares as "gardens." The text refers to gardens "intersected with canals, paved walks, and avenues of umbrageous trees of various kinds; embellished likewise with alcoves, fountains, pavilions, &c. and interspersed with all the beauties of Flora."[21] A watercolor illustration entitled *The Taj Mahal with European*

Fig. 38. William Hodges, *The Taj Mahal,* c. 1783.
Gray wash and graphite on laid paper
[Yale Center for British Art, Paul Mellon Collection]

Fig. 39. Thomas and William Daniell, *The Taje Mahel, Agra, Taken in the Garden,* 1789.
Aquatint
[The British Library Board, P 395]

Fig. 40. The Taj Mahal at Agra, 1880s. Curzon Collection, photographer unknown
[The British Library Board, Photo 430/5(23)]

Sightseers from an Indian manuscript of about 1815 is more fanciful in its depiction of dense bushes, trees, and flowers. In Edward Lear's own watercolor of 1874, the Taj is an almost fairylike apparition at the end of lines of shrubs and tall cypresses dissolving into masses of dark woods. When the celebrated illustrator Marianne North visited the Taj in 1877, she chose an angle that emphasizes even more the exuberance of the bosky growth that blocks out the view of everything except the dome and minarets (see Pl. 17).[22]

By the late 1850s the new art of photography reached India, and from then on there are abundant black-and-white illustrations of the Taj. A photograph from Curzon's own collection dated to the 1880s was probably made during his first visit to the monument.[23] Taken from a raised point in the gateway, it shows masses of foliage that would have almost obscured the mausoleum when seen from ground level (Fig. 40). Nevertheless, this was the view that inspired such ecstasy on the part of the future viceroy.

Fig. 41. The Taj Mahal Agra, general view. Archaeological Survey of India, 1918–19
[The British Library Board, Photo 1007/16(3890)]

Little more than a decade later, however, Curzon set out to turn the Mughal garden into an English park, with a low avenue of cypresses and shrubs leading the eye along the primary, north–south water channel to the mausoleum, and above all with large expanses of lawn dotted with occasional trees and only modest beds of flowers, primarily roses (Fig. 41).[24] To be sure, the garden as he found it in 1899 was no longer the garden laid out by Shah Jahan, since the trees and shrubs had grown with tropical abandon—the poet Edwin Arnold referred to it as an "orderly wilderness"—barely kept in check, it appears, by the legions of gardeners.[25] While we do not know exactly what the original garden looked like, we can reconstruct its main outlines with reasonable certainty from what is known of other Mughal gardens, from contemporary miniature paintings, and from descriptions and plans recorded by European visitors.

The Mughal Garden

Mughal gardens in India, as we have seen, were always walled. The basic plan was that of the Persian *charbagh* or quadripartite garden. These were strictly geometric, laid out on a grid, divided literally into four parts or multiples of four; in the case of the Taj, there are four main squares each subdivided into four.[26] Water channels run at right angles, marking off the main divisions and meeting in a large tank in the center. Symbolically this layout invokes the garden of Paradise as described in Qur'an, with its intersecting rivers. Water is paramount in the design of the Taj as in all Mughal gardens, with lotus blossom–shaped fountains playing the length of the main canal. In the Taj garden a large stone platform (*chabutra*) rises at the confluence of the canals, around which runs the water channel; there are also *chabutras* on the east and west sides of the garden. Such raised platforms and pavilions were the social center of the Mughal garden. Here a ruler could entertain his guests, refreshed by the cool spray of the fountains and inhaling the perfumes of the garden. Scenes of pavilions spread with carpets were a beloved staple of Mughal miniature painters. They display an antiphony of art and nature: rugs depicted gardens, gardens invited rugs, and miniatures depicted both rugs and gardens.

The main walks of the Mughal garden were lined with trees, especially alternating cypresses and fruit trees, symbolizing life, death, and rebirth. The walks were always raised well above the channels of water and above the parterres planted with turf, flowers, and often a flowering tree at the corner. Looking down on the blossoms from above was like looking down on a floral carpet. Writing some twenty or more years after the garden was completed, François Bernier, the French physician who attended Aurangzeb, describes the main walk of the Taj as about eight French feet (about 2.5 meters, or 8.2 English feet) above the garden and so wide as to admit six coaches abreast (surely an exaggeration). It runs on either side of a canal "ornamented with fountains placed at certain intervals." To the left and right there were further pathways "covered with trees and many parterres full of flowers."[27] The East India Company agent, Peter Mundy, visiting the gardens of Agra even earlier (1632–33), notes that they are square, and then "againe devided into other lesser squares, and that into other like beds and plots; in some, little groves of trees, as Apple trees . . . , Orange Trees, Mulberrie trees, etts. Mango trees, Caco [cocoanut] trees, Plantan trees, theis latter in rancks, as are the Cipresse trees." Among the flowers to be found in the squares, Mundy lists roses, marigolds, poppies, carnations, and "divers other sortes of faire flowers which we knowe not in our parts, many growinge on prettie trees, all watered by hand in tyme of drought which is 9 monethes of the Yeare."[28]

The repertoire of flowers would also have included tuberoses, balsam, cockscomb, anemones, violets, and sunflowers, as well as the aromatics referred to in the Mughal chronicles. Sometimes homogeneous groups of flowers were massed together in a single parterre beneath a cypress or plane tree. Not surprisingly, flowers and trees were a favorite subject of Mughal artists as well as of poets, just as floral designs would dominate the decoration of the Taj Mahal. Mughal artists show us how bursts of flowers softened the strict geometry of a garden's layout: "Spring flowers grow informally from the exact turf plot, roses spray over the water-tanks, trees branch in their natural forms. The intellectual concept of the geometric order is wedded to the freedom of organic growth."[29]

The Mughal garden was intended to appeal to all the senses, but most of all to the sense of smell, with its fragrant trees, shrubs, and plants. Referring to one of the Babur's gardens, a contemporary chronicler burst into verse: "Sweet basil and fragrant hyacinth are in embrace with each other, / Rose flowers and Jasmine are shoulder to shoulder."[30] Emperor Jahangir declared: "From the point of view of herbs and fragrant flowers, India is preferable to anywhere else in the inhabited part of the world." The blossoms of one *champa* (white jasmine), he claimed "could perfume a whole garden."[31] The *A'in-i Akbari,* a compendium of everything imaginable related to the Emperor Akbar's household, listed twenty-one "fine smelling flowers," along with directions for making perfume.[32] In 1640 the Portuguese priest Fray Manrique strolled through the gardens of the Agra fort: "I saw several trees exhaling the sweetest odour and laden with many and varied flowers, whose sweetness fell most pleasingly on the sense of smell of all who entered."[33] When it came to scent, artists and poets could not match nature itself.

Curzon, to be sure, kept the core plan of the walled garden with its quadrants outlined by the channels of water with their lines of lotus-shaped fountains. But where the Mughal garden would have had patches of green, especially clover, with an overlay of flowers—the flowers and turf that give the impression of a carpet to the viewer on the raised walkway—and low fruit trees clearly marking off the corners of the quadrants,[34] the walkways now are only slightly raised and one looks down primarily on carpets of grass. Gone are the perfumes that delighted visitors from Peter Mundy in the 1630s to Fanny Parks two centuries later, the fruit trees with their abundance, the cacophony of birds, and the splashes of floral brilliance. The effect is to preserve the Mughal plan, exaggerating the rigidity of its geometry, without the softening effects of thicker plantings. As one writer comments, the seventeenth-century garden, "densely planted with beds of flowers and trees of different varieties, . . . must have had a greater sense of intimacy as well as greater color."[35] True, the new openness favors "endless beautiful views of the marble dome, the marble walls, and the marble minarets" but with the loss of the multisensory exuberance of the original.[36]

The reconstruction of the Taj Ganj, the entryway to the Taj Mahal, further alters the experience of the whole. Contemporary documents and the plan of 1800 make clear that the forecourt and series of *serais* and bazaars beyond it were intended as an integral part of Mumtazabad, the urban center at the heart of which was the tomb of Mumtaz Mahal. The forecourt or *jilokhana* provided a place for the faithful—rich and poor—to gather to observe the anniversary of the empress's death, the 'Urs.[37] Even in the 1830s Fanny Parks reported that the court was still used regularly for fairs, including the Muslim festival of Eid.[38] The gateway looks both backward and forward, bounding this public space and framing the view of the Taj. An unbroken line of sight stretches more than nine hundred yards along the main water channel, which itself is much wider than those of earlier Mughal gardens (as Bernier suggests) and allows for the reflection of the entire edifice in its shimmering water. The garden lies at a lower level than either the Taj Ganj or the mausoleum. The eye of the visitor is drawn along the watercourse to the raised marble reflecting pool in the center, following the rows of cypresses and the star-shaped parterres in which they are set.

In dismissing the Taj Ganj as little more than an Augean stable to be cleared as quickly as possible in order to focus on what really mattered, Curzon essentially decontextualized the monument, isolating the Taj from its original surroundings. John Dixon Hunt has emphasized the importance of the entrance to any garden: ideally, it fosters the "liminal" experience of "entering a special zone."[39] This was no doubt what Curzon himself aimed for in clearing the Taj Ganj, but he projected his own aesthetic perspective on the experience. The quite different purpose of Shah Jahan's builders was beyond his comprehension—that they very much intended the privileged visitor to enter from the noisy, dusty, bustling public space of bazaar and caravanserai, and then abruptly to be transported into a private world, a realm of quiet, the solemnity of the garden tomb as a foretaste of the Paradise promised to the faithful by the Qur'an.

Gardens and Empires

So much for the changes. The gardens as they once were and as they became under Curzon's guiding, even autocratic, hand offer clues to different visions of empire. For the Mughals gardens came first, historically speaking, followed by architecture, rather than the other way around. Much as the garden was a center of conviviality, it also played a highly political role. Armies camped in gardens; rulers were proclaimed in gardens; state visitors were received there with pomp and circumstance; Sufi poets declaimed their verses and musicians played their airs to the delectation of the elite. In the always separate *zenana* garden, the women of the court led a parallel but secluded existence. Under successive Mughal emperors the trend was toward increasing magnificence and complexity, mirroring the same evolution in government and imperial pretensions.

The progression began with Babur, the Mughal conqueror of India, hailed as the "Prince of Gardeners."[40] So great was his delight in gardens that he founded them wherever he went despite a life of constant warfare—legend had it that he would even pause in the midst of military campaigns to stake out gardens.[41] "He converted the world into a rose garden," commented a later Mughal chronicler.[42] A miniature depicts him dictating his memoirs in a garden,[43] a detail we may accept as metaphorically if not literally true. Another shows him directing work on the Garden of Fidelity in Kabul (see Pl. 18). When he first came to Agra, he wrote, "[I] scouted around for places to build a garden, but everywhere I looked was so unpleasant and desolate that I crossed back [over the Yamuni] in great disgust." Unpromising as the place was, however, "there was nothing to do but work with the space we had," and so he did.[44]

For Babur, always on the move, gardens marked out extensions of territorial control, imposing an alien sense of order on the landscape. Religious symbolism, however, was little emphasized.[45] Explicit associations of gardens with

Paradise appeared only during the reign of his son, Humayun (1530–1556). Obsessed with mysticism and religious symbolism, Humayun had few opportunities to translate these into gardens before being forced into a life of exile.[46] In situating his father's tomb in a garden, Humayun's son Jahangir combined associations of sovereignty, manifest in Babur's gardens, with statements of dynasty and its claims to permanence.[47] The garden was not conceived of as public space, just as government was not a public matter. It was imperial space, accessible only to the ruler, his court, and distinguished visitors. Nobles emulated the ruler by building their own gardens on a lesser scale, as a representation of their place in the imperial hierarchy. Where Babur had enjoyed the pure sensuality of his gardens—the luscious fruits and the exquisite blossoms—his great-grandson Shah Jahan, ruling a century later, was far more preoccupied with their symbolism, both political and religious, and with matching them to an imperial architecture. Indeed, Shah Jahan's reign (1628–1658) marked the apogee of imperial pretensions.

True to his Mughal ancestry, the emperor's gardens became a favored canvas for expressing this ideology—one writer refers to Shah Jahan's "flowermania."[48] A curious example of this: When Shah Jahan arrived in Srinagar in Kashmir in April 1640, he was disappointed to find that storms and heavy rain had destroyed all the almond blossoms he had looked forward so eagerly to seeing. But he took comfort in an iris plant in the garden on which he counted 212 flowers, both open and still in bud. The day before he had gloried in a red rosebush in the Shalimar gardens on which there were no fewer than 4,500 flowers and buds.[49] Of course, this is imperial hyperbole, but what is truly surprising is that the official chronicler of the emperor's reign deemed these tales worth recounting.

Although Babur himself wished only to be buried in a garden, his grave open to the skies, tomb building was part of the Timurid heritage of the Mughal dynasty. It is generally agreed that Humayun's tomb in Delhi provided the immediate model for the Taj Mahal as for other great Mughal tombs. Begun by his eldest widow after his death in 1560, it is the earliest Mughal garden plan that has survived without alteration: a classic Persian *charbagh* or four-part garden, in this case enlarged and divided by causeways so that there are thirty-two smaller plots or parterres (Fig. 42). Future tomb gardens would gradually widen its narrow rills of water until at the Taj Mahal the waterways are eighteen feet across.[50] How the parterres were planted we do not know,

Fig. 42. Humayun's tomb, Delhi, c. 1820. Opaque watercolor on paper
[The British Library Board, Ms.Add.Or.1809]

but we can imagine that, like other contemporary gardens, they were dotted with fruit trees and flowers according to the season.

Rulers and notables often designed their tombs during their lifetimes, enjoying the pleasures of the gardens while they lived. Then after their death a mausoleum replaced the pavilion at the center of the garden. The suddenness of Mumtaz Mahal's death at a relatively young age made this sequence impossible; her funerary garden was thus intended less to evoke the delights of this life than of the one to come. The architect of the Taj, however, introduced a radical innovation, one for which there was no precedent: The mausoleum is set not in the middle of the garden at the confluence of the water channels but at the far end, at the river's edge on a marble plinth, itself set on a raised sandstone platform. There are four freestanding minarets at the four corners of the tomb, and, flanking it, a mosque on the left and an almost identical building on the right, the *jawab* or guesthouse.

The positioning of the tomb at the end of the garden achieves several effects. First of all, it emphasizes the garden in all its forty-two-acre majesty, not just as setting for the tomb. Further, it shapes the visitor's experience of the architecture: as one progresses through the garden, the tomb itself appears to change, at first rising ethereally in the distance and then looming larger and larger as one approaches the plinth on which it sits. Finally, the siting makes the tomb visible from the Agra Fort, from the river itself, and from the opposite bank, a view much favored by painters and then by photographers (see Pl. 19). These multiple and shifting visions, so different from Humayun's tomb, for example, surely account in some measure for the unique place the Taj holds in the world's imagination.[51]

The architectural forms reflect the symbolism of the garden with their interplay of the square platform, circular dome, and octagonal base. "The square," writes Susan Jellicoe, "stands for the terrestrial order and man's earthly condition, the circle for unity, perfection and the eternal order; man's struggle for regeneration and his striving from the first state to the second is symbolized by the octagon—the circle squared."[52] The decoration of the buildings reinforces these themes. The walls of the Taj Ganj are covered with Qur'anic inscriptions. The last before one enters the garden reads:

> *O thou soul at peace,*
> *Return thou unto thy Lord, well-pleased*
> *And well-pleasing unto Him!*
> *Enter thou among My servants—*
> *And enter thou My Paradise!*[53]

The mausoleum, too, is decorated with Qur'anic inscriptions, as are the mosque and guesthouse flanking it.[54] The spandrels of the arches of these two buildings and of the Taj Ganj are decorated as well with floral arabesques of semiprecious stones (*pietra dura*) inlaid in the white marble that then burst into full bloom on the white marble walls of the Taj itself. Here a profusion of floral inlays and carvings alternates with borders of black calligraphy to cover almost all the surface (Fig. 43). Most exquisite of all are the two cenotaphs, that of Mumtaz Mahal and of Shah Jahan himself. Contemporary sources are silent as to whether he had from the start intended that the Taj should also be his tomb; his rebellious son Aurangzeb decreed it so. Nevertheless, the fact that he chose no other site during his lifetime may mean that this was his intention all along.[55] Other evidence reinforces this interpretation, as we will see.

Fig. 43. Taj Mahal: Floral relief and inlay, detail
[Photograph by author]

The flowers represented are above all spring flowers: bluebells, daffodils, tulips, lilies, irises, crown-imperials. The floral motifs are continued within the tomb, on the walls, the interior of the dome, and the delicately carved marble screen. Here, too, carpets would have covered the floor. The dome itself invokes the lotus through its form and decoration—the lotus a symbol of creation appropriated from Buddhist and Hindu iconography and repeated in the fountains along the watercourse. In essence, then, the Taj Mahal embodies a three-way conversation between architecture, garden, and decoration, all offering their testimony to the iconic themes of life, death, and regeneration and converging in the memorial to an empress who died in the act of giving birth.

Mausoleum and garden were paralleled by an equally audacious project: a mirror image of the Taj garden on the opposite bank of the Yamuna River, the Mahtab Bagh or Moonlight Garden. This garden was apparently abandoned when it proved too prone to flooding. It was only rediscovered in the late twentieth century, thanks to the work of Elizabeth Moynihan and her colleagues from 1996 to 1999, and was therefore unknown to Curzon (it is intriguing to think what he might have done with it had he known) or other visitors throughout the nineteenth and most of the twentieth centuries. Although the entire site could not be excavated, and in any case much of the brick and stone have long since been removed from the site and recycled by local people, the dimensions of the waterfront wall correspond almost exactly to the north wall and platform of the Taj. Above the landing and retaining wall was a raised terrace, in the center of which a large octagonal pool was so positioned that it reflected the Taj in the light of the full moon.

The primary purpose of the garden was to view the Taj. "One imagines the royal barge carrying the emperor from the fort to the garden, where he could sit in an airy pavilion and embrace the dramatic view of the Taj and its ethereal likeness," writes Moynihan. "Magically the image was disembodied by the fountain jets as they fell back in the pearl drop pattern—portraying water as a precious gift from the heavens. . . . Facing [Shah Jahan] was the north portal of the Taj with Sura 84 [of the Qur'an] 'Rending Asunder' wherein this world and the next are sundered by death. Here in his earthly paradise he could enjoy the pleasure of sorrow."[56]

The existence of the Mahtab Bagh lends support to those who argue that the Taj was intended to be Shah Jahan's tomb as well as that of his wife. The epitaph engraved in luminous calligraphy on his cenotaph refers to the emperor as "Rizwan," the guardian of paradise. The Taj complex "is his image of paradise, and he is the gatekeeper of that paradise. Surely Shahjahan envisaged this ultimate tomb at the ultimate crossing of the Four Rivers of Paradise."[57] Not only is the Taj complex anomalous in the canon of Mughal art if it ends with the tomb at the northern end of the garden, "it lacks the symmetry essential to the Mughal sense of order." This symmetry is restored if we look at the tomb instead as a centerpiece: the water channels in the two gardens are so aligned that they provide a single, long north–south axis, extending from below the Taj gateway to the raised tank in the center to the base of the plinth. There it disappears, once again to "[rise] joyfully in the fountains of the octagonal pool of the Mahtab Bagh, from which it falls in a cascade to the lotus pool, and overflows into a channel that runs into the central tank of the *charbagh*, an image of the pool within the Taj enclosure." Seen thusly, the river joins rather than separates the two gardens. "[W]hen reflected in the river, the Taj, as *axis mundi*, is transformed into an evanescent image above the crossing of the Four Rivers of Paradise. Only someone with [Shah Jahan's] vainglorious sense of himself could conceive such an audacious plan." The plan of the Taj is a "scheme of truly imperial proportions,"[58] nothing less than the emperor's "cosmic diagram," materializing the final lines of Sura 54 of the Qur'an, the "Moon":

> *Surely the godfearing shall dwell amid gardens and a river*
> *in a sure abode, in the presence of a King Omnipotent.*[59]

This was a hard act for Curzon and the British to follow. At every turn, they were conscious of the glory that was Mughal India, of living in the shadow of past greatness. To a degree that is difficult to define, Curzon identified himself with the Mughal emperors. Touring the monuments of Agra and Fatehpur Sikri with him one last time before he left India and noting his extraordinary absorption in every detail (he was still measuring the growth of the cypress trees at the Taj Mahal), his old friend Valentine Chirol suggested laughingly that were he, Chirol, a Hindu, he would "almost believe that in a former stage of existence [Curzon] must have been Akbar himself." Without a trace of humor, the viceroy responded, "I know nothing of former stages of existence, but I may tell you, my dear Chirol, that I can always feel myself to be living the very life of all the great men of whom I read in history."[60]

Both Mughal and Briton came from nations almost obsessively attached to their gardens. Both saw them as instruments of civilization, bringing order out of the chaos of nature. When Curzon boasted to the secretary of state for India, "What were then dusty wastes are now green parks and gardens," he was echoing the words of Babur as he set to work to tame the arid plains of Agra. On a visit to the Taj Mahal in 1834, Lord Bentinck, then governor-general of India, had reflected: "In a country where we have erected no monuments, it is a satisfaction to see that the Taj at least is cared for."⁶¹ Lord Curzon was not content to be a caretaker. Nevertheless, however much might be spent on restoration of the Taj—and the viceroy had allocated the then enormous sum of £50,000 for the monuments of Agra (nearly half the budget destined for restoration in the subcontinent as a whole)—he had neither the resources nor the power to match the opulence that has made "mogul" a byword for both.⁶²

Of necessity, then, his imperial aspirations took quite different form. His interest in preserving the archaeological and architectural heritage of India was genuine, but it was not disinterested; it was part and parcel of demonstrating the greatness of British civilization, its appreciation for the past of all peoples, and its civilizing role in India. During his viceroyalty he visited virtually every monument that fell under the aegis of the ASI. He saw himself not just as a "pilgrim at the shrine of beauty . . . but as a priest in the temple of duty . . . charged with their reverent custody and their studious repair."⁶³ One of his great triumphs was the passage of the Ancient Monuments Bill in 1904, "expiating the carelessness of the past, and escaping the reproaches of posterity."⁶⁴

Nowhere was this more conspicuous than with Agra and the Taj Mahal, although he unfairly minimized the role of his predecessors;⁶⁵ virtually all nineteenth-century visitors remark, like Bentinck, that the Taj and its gardens had been well maintained, whatever may have been the case with other monuments.⁶⁶ Curzon came to identify himself with these monuments and to bask almost personally in their greatness. As he wrote to Lord George Hamilton at the India Office: "The whole of the principal mosques, tombs, etc. have been surrounded with exquisite gardens or parks, and, by the time I leave India, I believe it may be said with truth that the Agra Monuments will be the best tended, *just as they are also the best and most beautiful body of architectural remains in the world.* [Excelling Egypt? Greece? Rome?] I have supervised and given orders upon every single detail myself for the local engineers who have to carry them out are destitute of the faintest artistic perception; and, if left to themselves, will perform horrors that make one alternately laugh and weep."⁶⁷ So possessive was he of the Taj that when Sir Herbert Baker, one of the primary architects of New Delhi, proposed to make alterations to the gardens long after Curzon had ceased to be viceroy, Curzon barked, "I won't have that African Baker interfering with my Taj garden." Baker backed off, wondering, however, whether Curzon felt for the Taj as a "lover or a child."⁶⁸

But why did he change the plantings so radically? It is true that the trees had become so overgrown as to block many of the views, and yet at the moment he first fell in love with the Taj on his visit in late 1887, when the foliage was at its densest, he had praised the gardens without qualification, both for their own beauty and for their enhancement of the Taj itself. And he couldn't resist adding, "It is to the credit of England that this garden is mainly the product of English hands, a burly Yorkshireman named Smith having been its custodian for some 20 years." Rather smugly he noted, "Had I not been made aware of this, the existence of a rose garden and the universal prevalence of that plant would have been sufficient to prove the dominion of English ideas"—quite unaware, it appears, of the Mughal passion for roses.[69]

The Taj as Curzon first saw it was much the same as that which had captivated artists from the Daniells to Edward Lear and Marianne North. It was quintessentially "picturesque"—one might even label it "oriental picturesque," with the ethereal form of the white marble sepulcher rising bit by bit out of the mass of semitropical vegetation. "Nothing is lost," Lord Hastings insisted in 1815, "by this temporary interruption of a distinct perception of all the parts." When the pure white marble of the dome became visible at last, it contrasted "advantageously" with the green of the treetops.[70] As *The Times'* war correspondent William Russell described the experience in midcentury:

> Before us lay beautiful walks, lined by dense rows of umbrageous cypress trees, which divided the ground into squares filled with flowers and fountains, rose and orange trees, and an infinity of oriental shrubs. A few native gardeners moved quietly along among the bushes, drawing water from the long reservoirs and canals which run by the side of each plot of ground. . . . We started onwards towards the Taj, which was now altogether hidden by the trees. But suddenly striking to the right we came out in front of it, and there it stood in its queenly beauty and astonishing perfection, rising above us from a lofty platform of marble, of dazzling whiteness.[71]

Clearly what had appealed to the youthful Curzon (he was in his late twenties when he first saw the Taj) no longer appealed to the proconsul; "picturesque" was not the image he wanted to project. For a view of the mausoleum and other structures that revealed itself only gradually through the foliage as one moved along the central axis, he substituted the starkly uncluttered vista of today.[72] At best one can only speculate on the factors at play, both cultural and personal, in this change of attitude toward the Taj garden.

First of all, there was the residue of eighteenth-century landscape design in England, the legacy of Capability Brown, which emphasized expanses of lawn dotted with a few majestic trees that swept right up to the great houses, relegating gardens to the margins.[73] Curzon himself was raised at Kedleston, one such great house, and perhaps saw it as a model—the proper way to integrate nature and the works of man. Both house and grounds had been designed by Robert Adam in the Palladian manner, intended to rival Chatsworth, the home of the dukes of Devonshire. But unlike Chatsworth, Kedleston has never been noted for its flower gardens; rather, the estate seems even today frozen in eighteenth-century time, with its sweeping park, artificial pond, sheep grazing beyond the "ha ha," and the iron gates leading to the austere entry way (see Pl. 20).[74]

Victorian England, however, had moved away from the artificially contrived nature of the preceding period. Conservatories made of iron and glass abetted the passion for growing exotic plants from all over the world just as peripatetic colonials were carrying their gardens to the corners of empire. Like Akbar watering his apple tree for nine months of the year, the British in India could count on an army of *malis* to water and trim each blade of grass—to *force* it to grow against all odds. But nineteenth-century England was also marked by a succession of battles over competing historical styles, bedding plants, topiaries, and herbaceous borders. Curzon, however, seems to have been quite oblivious of the garden wars raging around him. There is no evidence that he was familiar with the work of William Robinson or Gertrude Jekyll or of any other prominent English gardeners—none is mentioned in the back-and-forth about the Taj and other Agra gardens; indeed, his approach seems to have been entirely empirical and personal, not beholden to any contemporary theories of landscape or garden design.

A. E. P. Griessen, who worked closely with Curzon in the restoration of the Taj gardens, later defended the decisions taken. He insisted that they had "gone into the matter very carefully in an attempt to get back to the historical gardens of India," but that the problem had been a difficult one. They were perfectly aware of the importance of fruit trees in the old gardens of both Muslims and Hindus, the fruit trees that Bernier and Tavernier had so much admired. But these visitors saw the garden only in its infancy, when the trees were small and did not obscure the causeway and the views of the mausoleum. "If big trees had had to find their way there, as they had found their way in the early nineteenth century the whole of the beautiful vista of the Taj and adjoining buildings would have been masked." They chose therefore to plant trees which would not replicate the earlier "afforestation which some people had admired and blamed Lord Curzon for not adopting."[75] View trumped historical exactitude, a subordination of garden to architecture that might well have baffled the Mughals. Besides, the produce from fruit trees had defrayed the costs of maintaining Mughal gardens, something the British did not even consider.

Curzon had other champions as well. One of his correspondents, for example, commended Curzon for substituting lawns for the "tiresome little flower beds of no particular form or beauty" at one of the other Agra sites.[76] Defending him against charges of overrestoration, especially of Mughal monuments, his obituarist declared: "Lord Curzon, had all the cultivated Briton's love of clearing away incongruous accretions which make a comprehensive view of a monument, and of setting the jewel again in an environment of greenery. This praiseworthy passion can be over indulged. But what Lord Curzon did to open out the Taj and restore its garden is generally approved." Perhaps all too revealingly he added: "Indian accretions are usually neither medieval nor picturesque, but recent, squalid, and noisome. The Viceroy was very well aware at the outset that in dirt and stench the spirit of the East finds little incongruity or offence."[77]

The problems faced by Curzon in Agra were dwarfed by those with other antiquities. At least at Mughal sites—not only the Taj but also the tombs of Humayun, I'timad ud-Daulah, and Akbar—there was an outline of the original and historical sources to draw on in restoring gardens. In the case of non-Muslim monuments, such as the Buddhist site at Sarnath or the great Hindu temple complex at Khajuraho, there was little to go on. Sarnath is sacred as the place where the Buddha preached his first sermon to his five companions in a deer park. Over time it became a center of Buddhist learning. Under the patronage of local rulers a great *stupa* or dome-shaped shrine was built, as well as extensive monasteries for disciples and pilgrims. Buddhism declined in India in the later first millennium C.E., and the site was gradually deserted. Muslim invaders delivered the coup de grâce in the twelfth century. An engraving from the 1840s shows a desolate brick *stupa* with rank vegetation growing out of its cracked crown and sides.[78] Excavation and restoration have been ongoing for over a century, but there has been no attempt to re-create a Buddhist meditation garden, which would typically have featured large shade trees and water; instead the landscaping is that of an archaeological site, with open lawns (such as they are), a circuit of walkways, and a few trees, but adjoining all this is a large deer park and a splendid museum housing Buddhist sculpture from the site, including the great lion capital. If not a meditation garden, Sarnath is a welcome island of serenity only a few miles from the hurly-burly of Varanasi.

At Khajuraho in what is now Bundelkhand, a vanished dynasty created a stunning assemblage of Hindu and Jain temples, many of them featuring a dazzling array of sculptural ornamentation.[79] The Chandella kings dominated the region from the eleventh through the fourteenth centuries, successfully repelling Muslim invaders from the north. Legend has it that they built some eighty-five temples, devoted to the entire constellation of Hindu deities. With the decline of the dynasty, the entire area reverted to bush. In spite of this it was recognized as a major monument and documented by an eminent Indian photographer as early as 1886. The accompanying text describes it as "a wretched deserted place," showing that the task of clearing had barely begun. Nevertheless, the writer pronounced the surviving group of some thirty temples to be "the most beautiful in form as well as most elegant in detail of any of the temples now standing in India," a judgment not wide of the mark. Excavation and restoration are still in progress more than a century later; there is, in fact, a thriving workshop nearby where artists keep alive the craft of stone carving. The main temple complex comprising the western group is more extensively landscaped than Sarnath: there are large swaths of green, trimmed hedges along stone walks, low bushes and flowering shrubs, and a few shade trees to provide some refuge in the intense heat of summer (see Pl. 21). The guiding principle seems to be to maintain open, unobstructed views of the temples. Of course we have no idea what the surroundings would have looked like during the golden age of Chandella rule—when the temples were rediscovered by a British army engineer in 1838, they had long since been swallowed up in jungle—but one suspects that originally the precincts would have included more tanks than at present and certainly gardens to provide the flowers indispensable to Hindu worship.

Overwhelmed by the sheer number of the country's monuments, the ASI has had its hands full with the Herculean task of rescuing them from ruin and restoring them as best they could. As for showing them off to best advantage, what could surpass an inviting greensward and a few trees for shade?

The Taj as English Park

For the British, the Taj Mahal was always a place of enchantment. Captain Sleeman's wife declared, "I would die to-morrow to have such a tomb." An awestruck official could only invoke the cliché that "the Moghuls designed like Titans and finished like jewellers." Nonetheless, this did not stop Britons from turning the Taj and its gardens into an oriental Vauxhall (not unlike the Lucknavi palaces they so deplored) throughout much of the nineteenth century. Fanny Parks found it detestable that European ladies and gentlemen danced quadrilles in the garden with a band playing on the marble terrace of the tomb, but hers seems to have been a minority opinion. Emily Eden describes "a pretty fête" given for the hundred people in her party. They dined in what once had been a mosque. She explains that it had been "desecrated" years earlier. "Still I thought it was rather shocking our eating ham and drinking wine in it, but its old red arches looked very handsome." She does not seem to have minded that on another occasion two gentlemen played hop-scotch "with all their old Westminster rules" in the gardens, one of them "the image of Pickwick," whose hopping and jumping and panting "filled the afternoon very well." The visit of the Prince of Wales in 1876 inspired far grander entertainments: "Seven thousand guests came to look at the Prince of Wales looking at the Taj!" A band entered the illuminated precincts playing "Vedrai carino" from Mozart's *Don Giovanni,* and then struck up dance music, which was accompanied by the "clank of spurs and sabers on the complaining marble." Yet none of this, Russell claims, marred the loveliness of the peerless mausoleum—but, thank goodness, no fireworks![80]

Mercifully, Lord Curzon put an end to these revelries. Constance Villiers-Stuart, one of the first to write authoritatively about Mughal gardens in India, rightly gave Curzon his due for rescuing "many magnificent old Indian buildings and works of art." But while she was glad that he had cleared Mughal gardens of "much accumulated overgrowth and rubbish," she tactfully regretted the lack of any "serious attempt to revive the old garden-craft in its artistic and symbolic aspects."[81] Above all, she deplored the sacrifice of Bernier's "gay parterres" in favor of "the fixed belief [of English landscape gardeners] in the universal virtue of mown grass" and their penchant for substituting "grass-plots and scattered trees" for the brilliance and fragrance of the old gardens.[82] What was lost was any semblance of intimate gatherings on carpeted turf where one could listen to the poet, breathe the fragrance of fruit trees, and enjoy the cool spray of the fountain. In their place were emblems of a past fitted into the Procrustean bed of British hegemony. Where Shah Jahan could invoke the Qur'anic template of Paradise itself for his gardens, Paradise was, for his successors, only a metaphor, a metaphor often translated into what William Dalrymple has dismissed as "sterile English lawns."[83]

At the same time, the viceroy looked upon the Taj, like other great monuments of India, as a historical site, fixed forever in a past time. He recognized that control of history is in some measure control of the present. Historical monuments were also public spaces; they became a variant of the public park, an innovation in nineteenth-century England.[84] Vast numbers of tourists would come, whose gaze could be carefully directed from the moment they approached the entrance. When he ordered that mahogany trees, palms, and other trees be removed or pruned, it was to open up specific vistas of the mosque and *jawab* and most of all to present a "glorious view" of the Taj itself from all angles.[85] They would see what he chose to have them see and how he chose to have them see it, just as Shah Jahan had aligned the Mahtab Bagh to direct the gaze of his nobles across the river to his soaring funerary memorial or marvel at its inverted reflection in the octagonal pool.[86] If Curzon could not create a comparable tour de force nor redesign a whole imperial city such as Paris or Rome—to say nothing of Shahjahanabad—he could put his improving stamp on single sites.

To be sure, Curzon was at a further disadvantage. The Mughals *knew* what a garden should look like, smell like, and sound like. By Shah Jahan's reign the model had been in place for a century. Its rules were malleable enough to fit terrain as mountainous as Kashmir and as flat as Hindustan, and they allowed for the imperial embellishments that culminated in Shah Jahan's fluidity between architecture and garden. They invoked an age-old love of flowers and fruits, enhanced by Sufi ideas of oneness with nature and Qur'anic visions of Paradise. Shah Jahan could even draw on a recently imported European vocabulary for more realistic visual representation of the natural world. By contrast, Curzon was a child of a more secular time, in which notions of what made a proper garden were constantly in flux and prey as much to individual taste as to cultural traditions. In focusing on a single sense, sight, he ignored the appeals to nose and ear that played such a large part in Mughal (and Hindu) kingship and made gardens so central to its expression.

What Lord Curzon shared with Shah Jahan, however, was a genuine love of beauty wherever it might be found. "After every other Viceroy has been forgotten," declared Jawaharlal Nehru, "Curzon will be remembered because he restored all that was beautiful in India."[87] They also shared an unquestioned faith in empire. Three years before he became viceroy of India he dedicated his *Problems of the Far East* to "those who believe that the British Empire is, under Providence, the greatest instrument for good that the world has ever seen."[88]

Postscript: The Victoria Memorial

For most of his viceroyalty, Curzon had to content himself with a vicarious imperial glory from the restoration of the Taj. But Fate provided the opportunity to rival Shah Jahan in the creation of a funerary monument when Queen Victoria died in January 1901. Within weeks Curzon had conceived of a memorial to her in Calcutta, a memorial to symbolize the greatness of British India and at the same time to legitimize British rule by incorporating the Indian contribution. This became the Victoria Memorial Hall, supported, Curzon always maintained, entirely by *voluntary* donations from both British and Indians.

The parallels with the Taj are intriguing. Both honor a dead queen, indeed an extremely fertile queen, although Queen Victoria did not die in childbed. While Curzon stoutly resisted Indianizing the Victoria Memorial—the Taj was of course on everyone's mind—there are a few resemblances. At the viceroy's insistence, it was built of the same marble as the Taj, hauled from the distant quarries of Rajasthan at great expense. The great dome, the octagonal *chhatris,* the plinth on which the building stands, even the domed corner terraces—all echo the Taj Mahal. Well satisfied, he extolled it as "by far the finest structure that has been reared in India since the days of the Moghuls, and the most splendid concrete monument of British rule." A later viceroy remarked that "although nominally a memorial to Queen Victoria," it was "a no less striking memorial to himself [Curzon], as exemplified by his statue

Fig. 44. Statue of Lord Curzon, Victoria Memorial Hall, Calcutta
[Photograph by author]

placed in front of the memorial and overshadowing all the statues of previous Viceroys" (Fig. 44). Or, as another commentator remarked, it was "the nearest the British ever came to erecting a funerary monument to their rule."[89]

Whatever the case, the gardens bear no resemblance whatsoever to Mughal models. True, there are two pools of water to reflect the brilliance of the marble facade, but the hall, built in Italian Renaissance style by William

Emerson, is set in an expanse of green. Entering from the south, one passes first through the Curzon lawn (with its statue of the viceroy) and then the Edward lawn, named for Edward VIII. Both are edged with neat strips of shrubbery and flowerbeds, very much like the approach to an English manor house. In front of the great entrance archway looms the seated bronze figure of the Queen-Empress as she was at the time of the 1897 Jubilee.

The most ironic parallel lies in the fact that just as Shah Jahan moved his capital to his new city of Shahjahanabad ("Old Delhi") even before the Taj Mahal was completed, so the Government of India moved its capital to a new city, New Delhi, before the Victoria Memorial could be finished. Curzon had hoped with the memorial "to have bequeathed her [England] something that will conquer Death, and be better than gold," a reference to Kipling's poem on Calcutta.[90] When it was dedicated by the Prince of Wales in 1921, twenty years after the queen's death, however, the Victoria Memorial was already a relic of fading empire.

A century earlier, the British surveyor J. A. Hodgson, gazing upon the Taj Mahal through the long vista of trees that bordered its canal of fountains, had pronounced it "one of the most perfect and beautiful buildings in the world." But when he reflected that only 130 years had passed since the death of Aurangzeb, the son of Shah Jahan, he was inspired to reflect on the "instability of dominion in Hindostan" and the fleeting "power of the mighty monarchs who erected so many magnificent buildings in their dominion."[91] Curzon might well have pondered his words.

CHAPTER 7

Imperial Delhi

City of Gardens

GAZING OUT upon Delhi in 1838, Fanny Parks beheld a vast panorama of gardens, pavilions, mosques, and burial places. But the "once magnificent city" was now "nothing more than a heap of ruins."[1] When the British became masters of Delhi in the opening years of the nineteenth century, they had found it a city of gardens and a city of ruins, the two often intertwined. The plains were dotted with crumbling walls of palaces and tombs, often cannibalized by later conquerors, and even more with the faded, weed-infested gardens in which earlier kings, nobles, and saints had once taken their pleasure or their solace (Fig. 45). The last Mughal emperors were of a piece with their diminished surroundings, eking out a threadbare existence until the dynasty finally collapsed in wake of the events of 1857–58. The British were then left to decide just where the city fit into their imperial agenda. The more the Mughals receded into history, the safer—and more tempting—it became for the Raj to style themselves as their heirs in everything from gardens to rituals.

Fig. 45. The Ruins of Delhi, with Humayun's tomb in the background:
from an early sketch by Capt. R. Elliot, RN
[From Charles Lewis and Karoki Lewis, *Delhi's Historic Villages*, 1997]

Delhi Before Shah Jahan

Unlike the presidency towns of Madras, Calcutta, and Bombay, Delhi was not a British creation. Its serial incarnations—"as numerous as the incarnations of the God Vishnu"—stretched back into protohistoric times, from Indraprastha to Shahjahanabad, from the era of the *Mahabharata* to the glory years of Mughal rule.[2] The city lies within a large triangle, bounded on the east by the river Yamuna and on the west by a series of jagged ridges running north and south. Whoever held Delhi, tradition had it, held India. Neither the ridges nor the river provided much protection; the "bride of peace was ravished" by wave after wave of foreign invaders from Central Asia, spilling through the mountain passes to the northwest onto the great plain of northern India. Some came simply to loot and massacre, others to stay and found dynasties of varying duration. In truth, foreigners dominated Delhi for so much of its history that its final incarnation as a British imperial city was hardly an anomaly.

The earliest Delhi was the semilegendary Indraprastha, dating from the Later Vedic period (c. 1000 B.C.E.). In historic times, Rajput kings were followed by a series of Muslim invaders: Turks, Afghans, and finally Mughals, descendants of Timur (Tamerlaine), who had ravaged Delhi in 1398. Most raised new cities, monumental buildings being the time-honored way to proclaim power and prestige. They chose their sites either because they seemed to be defensible (warfare was endemic) or because they might catch the northern breezes (Delhi summers are scorching). Rarely did they show any interest in conserving the works of predecessors. An exception was Firoz Shah Tughlak (d. 1388), who anticipated the Archaeological Survey of India (ASI) in his concern for the preservation of the past. He brought a pillar of Ashoka to his new city of Firozabad. Already fifteen hundred years old, the pillar recorded Ashoka's project of planting trees along the main roads of his empire, along with digging wells and establishing *serais* for travelers, all of which Firoz Shah himself emulated.[3] The ruler also dedicated himself to protecting forests and made the first attempt to afforest the Ridge, to the north of the capital, where he maintained a hunting preserve.[4]

When Percival Spear reminisced that "Delhi was always a city of gardens and greenery for me, even more than of monuments," he was thinking above all of the Mughal period, still so evident when he first arrived in the city in 1924.[5] But gardens predated the Mughals, although descriptions are few and the sites ephemeral. Kingship was proclaimed through gardens as well as palaces and new urban centers. Thus 'Ala' al-Din Khalji (1296–1316) built gardens in the royal city of Siri, both within and around the palace and at Hauz Khas, the tank he had constructed to supply water to his city. Inclined no doubt to hyperbole and a touch of sycophancy, the great poet, musician, and Sufi mystic Amir Khusrau (1253–1325) described the Delhi of this time: "It can well be compared to the Garden of Aram in Paradise. . . . Gardens surround it for three kilometres and the river Yamuna flows nearby."[6] A mid-fourteenth-century Arab writer from Damascus refers to gardens extending for twelve thousand paces on three sides of the city (the fourth side was the rocky ridge with its many ravines). About the same time the poet Mutahar of Kara extolled Firoz Shah's Delhi: "There is verdure everywhere and hyacinths, basils, roses and tulips were blooming," while Zia-Barni, the Sultan's chronicler, declared: "Sultan Firoz had a great liking for the laying out of gardens, which he took great pains to embellish. He formed 1,200 gardens

IMPERIAL DELHI

in the vicinity of Dehli [sic].... All gardens received abundant proofs of his care, and he restored thirty gardens that had been commenced by ['Ala' al-Din].... In every garden there were white and black grapes."[7] To be sure, we must take these figures with a grain of salt, and it is unclear whether the gardens were mostly intended to produce fruit for court and market or whether some also served as places of pleasure.

That they also grew flowers, however, is implied not only by the poets' encomia but also by the traveler Ibn Battuta's account of the importance of flowers in funeral rituals in fourteenth-century Delhi. He describes a cemetery outside one of the city's twenty-eight gates: "This is a beautiful place of burial; they build domed pavilions in it and every grave must have a [place for prayer with a] *mihrab* beside it, even if there is no dome over it. They plant in it flowering trees such as the tuberose, the *raibul* [white jasmine?], the *nisrin* [muskrose?] and others. In that country there are always flowers in bloom at every season of the year." When his own baby daughter died while in Delhi, he carried out the appropriate rituals: on the third day after burial, they spread carpets and silk fabrics on all sides of the tomb and placed on it the flowers mentioned in the preceding passage. In addition they set up orange and lemon branches with their fruits, together with dried fruits and coconuts.[8]

Delhi, then, had long been a city of tombs and tomb gardens when Babur captured it in 1526 and established Mughal rule in India. Indeed, on his first tour of inspection he lists nothing but tombs, culminating with those of the most recent Lodi rulers, Sultan Bahlul and Sultan Iskander, both of which had gardens attached. Apparently they did not impress him, for, as we have seen, Babur dismissed all the gardens he found in Hindustan, lumping Muslim and Hindu indiscriminately in his blanket indictment.[9] Later writers take issue with this verdict. They argue that gardens were an important part of Sultanate culture before the Mughal conquest and not as miserable as Babur suggests. In practical terms, of course, they provided food and income to their owners, but on a symbolic level they provided a foretaste of paradise, settings for mausolea and palaces, and retreats for leisure and relaxation. The Mughals may in fact have borrowed from the Delhi sultans their preference for situating family tombs in gardens, a practice that their Timurid forebears had not followed.[10] Nevertheless, it seems quite likely that the gardens of pre-Mughal Delhi lacked the formal, ordered structure that typified the Mughal *charbagh*.

Then, too, Babur's own preference as a man of the mountains was for hillside gardens, with sparkling streams carefully straightened and channeled to run down the terraces, something that could hardly be replicated on the level plains of Delhi.[11]

In India riverfronts had to substitute for streams and springs, and gardens were adapted accordingly. Babur chose Agra rather than Delhi for his capital even though it was just as flat and, if anything, hotter and dustier. His very first act was to create a garden on the banks of the Yamuna for his residence—true heir of Timur, he was more at home in the open than confined within fort or palace. Members of the imperial family and notables soon followed his example, so that both shores of the river were lined with gardens during his reign (he died in 1530) and the reigns of his successors as royals and nobles vied with each other in the magnificence of their creations. As Sylvia Crowe writes, "gardens . . . were in fact open-air rooms on a lavish scale," often with colorful tents hung with tapestries pitched on the lawn or carpets unrolled on the clover and grass. "Just as [Mughal] camps on the march were laid out as if in a garden, so their gardens served as a form of encampment."[12] Francisco Pelsaert, factor of the Dutch East India Company in Agra from 1621 to 1627, during the reign of Babur's grandson Jahangir, noted that anyone who aspired to be someone had a garden along the river, giving the city a curiously narrow, elongated form. He listed thirty-three gardens by name, noting that the "luxuriance of the groves all round makes it resemble a royal park rather than a city."[13] A map of Agra made for the Maharaja of Jaipur in 1720 shows the banks of the river in detail, identifying the gardens depicted, including those of the Taj Mahal and the tomb of I'timad-ud-Daula, Jahangir's powerful father-in-law.

Because land could only be inherited in rare cases, elites had little incentive to build extravagant palaces that the owners could not bequeath to their heirs but reverted at death to the crown, to be redistributed to a member of the royal family or to another noble. The same inheritance laws apparently applied to gardens unless they contained tombs. This encouraged the practice of creating luxurious pleasure gardens during one's lifetime, gardens which, Pelsaert observed, "far surpass ours . . . for their gardens serve for their enjoyment while they are alive, and after death for their tombs, which, during their lifetime they build with great magnificence in the middle of the garden."[14]

During more than a century of rule in northern India, the Mughals virtually ignored Delhi in favor of Agra and Lahore and, for a time, Akbar's new city of Fatehpur Sikri. True, Babur's son, Humayun, moved the capital back to Delhi for a brief period late in his life, intending to build a new palace and a new city in the time-honored tradition. The hapless ruler had managed to lose most of the territory conquered by his father before being overthrown by the Pashtun Sher Shah and forced into exile. After years as a "wanderer in the desert of destruction,"[15] he at last regained his throne, only to die a few years later in a fall from the library in the Purana Qila as he was rushing to answer the muezzin's call to prayer. Humayun had always been not only devoutly religious (as his father never was) but inclined toward mysticism; at the same time he was intensely superstitious and in thrall to his astrologers, unable to make a move without consulting the stars.[16] Like most of his family, he was addicted to alcohol and opium, but unlike them he had little interest in gardens or things horticultural even though important events of his reign continued to take place in gardens as they had under Babur.[17] It is more than a little ironic, therefore, that his magnificent garden tomb became the prototype for the genre itself.

Shahjahanabad

In 1638, more than a century after Humayun's false start, Shah Jahan decided to move his capital definitively to Delhi. This may seem strange in view of the attention and resources he had lavished on the fort at Agra—and even stranger when one remembers that the Taj Mahal, the memorial to his beloved wife Mumtaz Mahal, was well underway in Agra and would be completed by the time the new capital was built. The reason given for the move was the ruler's pique at the merchants of Agra for their refusal to allow him to open up the narrow, congested streets of the city—"irregular, and full of windings and corners"—so that stately processions with their legions of elephants could pass through.[18] A Pyrrhic victory for the merchants: the rise of Delhi meant the decline of Agra.

Shah Jahan entered his new city by the river gate on April 8, 1648, a day chosen as auspicious by the royal astrologers.[19] Shahjahanabad was intended to outshine anything that had gone before. The emperor called upon the finest craftsmen of the day: architects and garden designers, stonecutters and

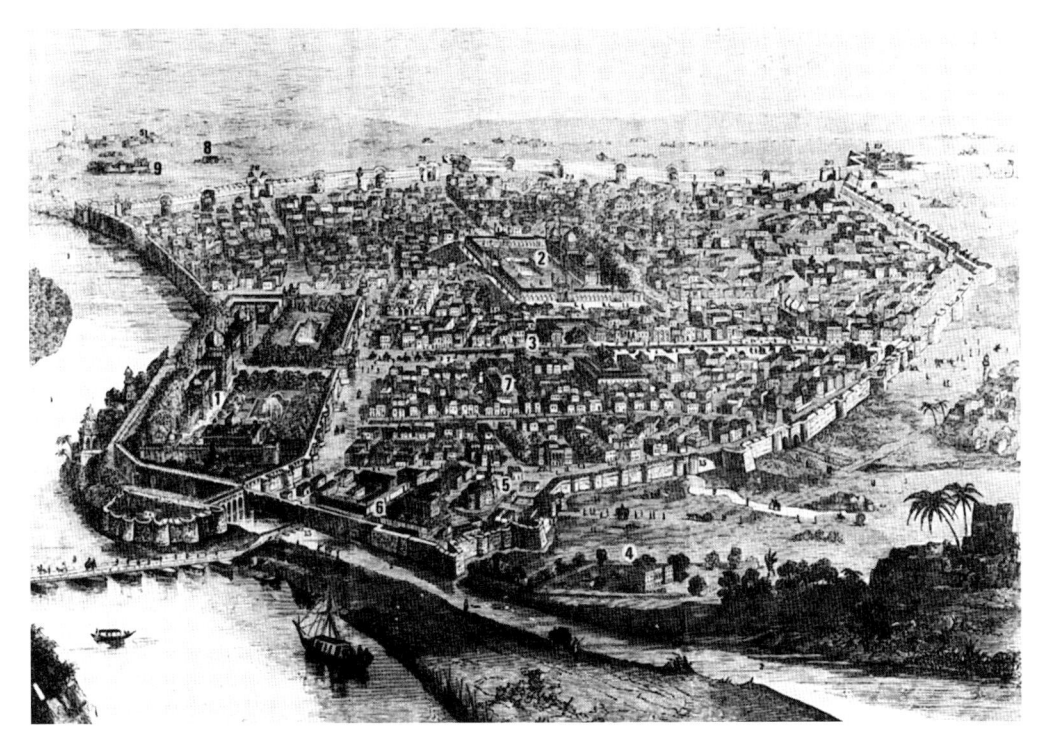

Fig. 46. Panorama of the Walled City of Delhi, c. 1856
[From Anthony King, *Colonial Urban Development*, 1976]

carvers, masons, carpenters, and jewelers. Its fame reached all the way to Europe, thanks to the accounts of François Bernier, the youthful Venetian courtier Niccolao Manucci, and the jeweler Jean-Baptiste Tavernier, who cast an expert eye over the jewel-encrusted Peacock Throne; their reports "created the legend of the Great Mogul."[20] Measuring some four miles around, the planned portions of the city, laid out as symmetrically as the site allowed, included the Friday Mosque and other mosques, boulevards and bazaars, an elaborate system of water channels, and several extensive gardens lining Chandni Chowk, the primary artery (Fig. 46).[21]

At its heart was a huge complex, the Qila-e-mubarak, the Exalted Fort, later known as the Red Fort from the red sandstone of its walls and gateways (Fig. 47).[22] It was surrounded with a moat on the three sides that did not face the river and, beyond the moat, a garden "filled at all times with flowers and green shrubs, which, contrasted with the stupendous red walls, produce a beautiful effect."[23] There was in fact a succession of gardens ringing the fort:

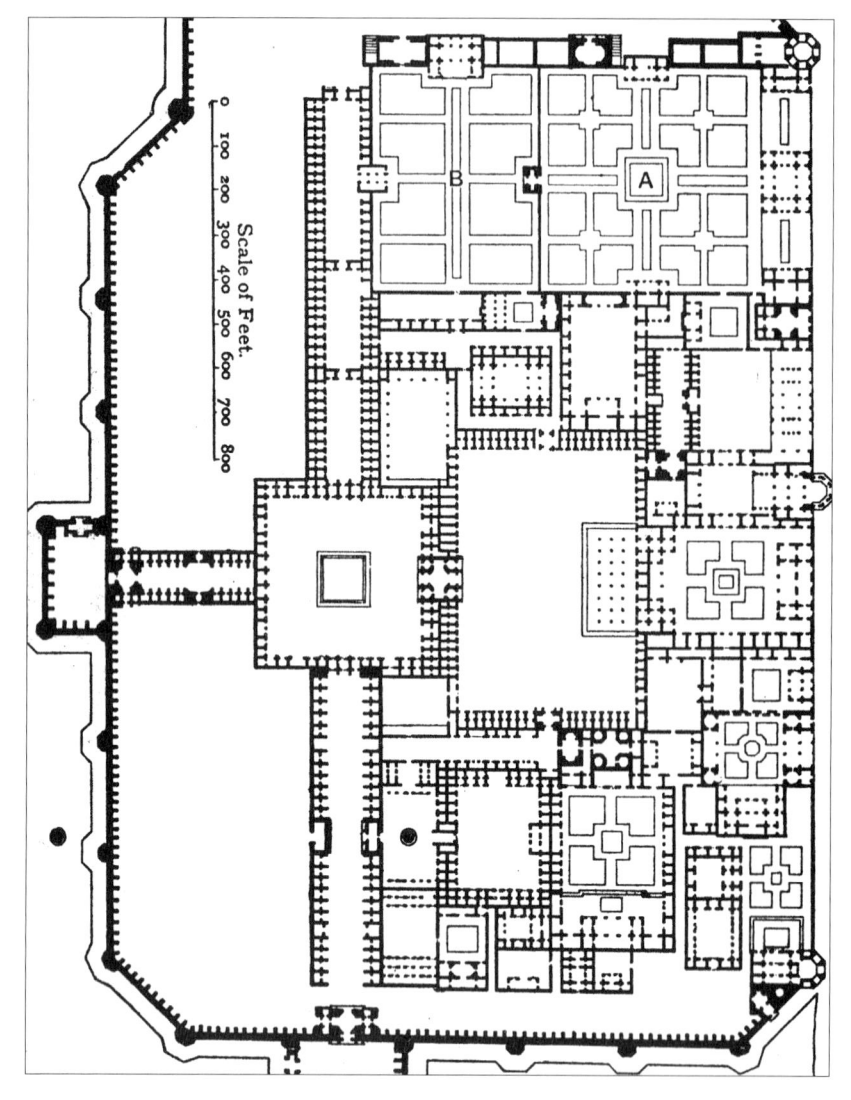

Fig. 47. The Delhi Palace before 1857
[From Constance Villiers-Stuart, *Gardens of the Great Mughals*, 1913]

the Rose Garden in front of Lahori Gate with its adjoining Grape Garden and the High Garden before the Delhi Gate. From the principal gates one entered what was a walled world to itself, the administrative and military hub of the empire but also a center of manufacturing and commerce, and above all the residence of the emperor and his seraglio. Larger than any European palace of its time, the fort's inner, private quarters alone encompassed an area five times that of Spain's Escorial.[24]

The palace fortress was built on the banks of the Yamuna, where it could benefit from both the defenses and the easterly breezes the river provided. It represented the culmination—and endpoint—of the modular riverfront plan that evolved from Babur's earliest gardens. Gardens occupied more than half the area of the Red Fort: "The garden is to the buildings," reads the main inscription, "as the soul is to the body, and the lamp to an assembly."[25] Like the waterfront gardens in Agra, major pavilions and halls within the fort were constructed on terraces facing a canal on the riverfront. In front of each, was "a garden . . . of perfect freshness and pleasantness," whose vegetation is so exuberant that it draws "a veil across the green sky and the sight is presented to the eyes of the beholder like the highest paradise."[26] Bernier describes spacious alcoves facing flower gardens, embellished with small canals of running water, reservoirs, and fountains. He was not allowed into the *zenana*, the women's quarters, but he was told by some of the eunuchs that on every side the apartments opened onto "gardens, delightful alleys, shady retreats, streams, fountains."[27] The last of the series of *zenana* buildings on the riverfront was known as the Khurd Jahan, the "Little World." The origin of the name is uncertain, but it may have been chosen to suggest that within were collected all the flowers and trees to make it a "microcosm of the world."[28]

Most of the gardens within the fort were domestic spaces intended for the ruler, his immediate family, and their servants, private places of pleasure and relaxation but encoding their own message of dominion for all that. As absorbed with garden design as with architecture, Shah Jahan oversaw the dazzling integration of both. Because most of the pavilions were single-story and were often extended out by awnings, screens, and arcades, boundaries between art and nature, exterior and interior, dissolved. "In most of the private imperial areas, there was no strict boundary between built and open space. Space flowed into the building from the outside through the open arches—in the views that it provided of the court or garden, in the sound of birds, in the scent of flowers and trees, and through cool breezes . . . The garden was carried into the building by decorating the floors and the walls with inlaid flowers of semi-precious stones."[29] Tiny mirrors set in plaster intensified the illusion of shifting and infinitely permeable boundaries.

The two largest gardens in the northern portion of the inner palace were the Hayat Baksh (Life-giving) and the Mahtab (Moonlight)—"two separate enclosures treated in one design"[30]—while the southern half was devoted to the harem gardens described by Bernier.[31] The Hayat Baksh was the ultimate *khanah bagh* or house garden, Shah Jahan's masterpiece. A classic square measuring five hundred feet on a side, the garden surrounded a central water tank with a summerhouse in the middle, 49 silver fountains surrounding it, and another 119 bordering the four rims of the tank. The avenues extending from the tank to the walls of the garden were bisected by canals of water, also set with fountains that cast spray high into the air. At the northern and southern ends of the avenues were two more pavilions, mirror images built in marble, with porticoes opening to the east and west. They were named, appropriately, after the Hindu monsoon months of Bahadun and Sawan. The emperor's artists decorated the southern one with paintings of herbs, trees, and flowers; water rushed in one side of the house and out the other, bringing the coolness for which its monsoon namesake was noted. Niches in the wall held gold vases filled with flowers during the day and wax candles at night, like "stars and fleecy clouds . . . lighted under the veil of water."[32]

The gardens themselves were planted with flowers and fruit trees. Muhammad Waris, a court historian, declared: "A heaven-like garden in this state of flourishing has not appeared before on the face of the earth. He [Shah Jahan] took pains so that every work was the rarest and beyond computation. A variety of fresh plants and fruitful trees grew to a great height. . . . The pleasantness of the garden area . . . and the colorfulness and greenness and abundance of the narcissus and sambal and the loveliness of the flowers caused this area to be the envy of the heavens." Hyperbole, yes, but not entirely: the accounts preserved for the construction of the palace underscore the extravagance of the Hayat Baksh and its neighboring bath.[33] And added to this was their upkeep through the parched non-monsoon months. The "Moonlight Garden" was smaller and less ambitious, planted with pale flowers such as lilies, narcissus, and jasmine that would fill the night air with their fragrance.[34]

Ebba Koch sees the Hayat Baksh as a major innovation in the representation of Mughal imperial power. Not only was it of unprecedented size, it employed the vocabulary of art to make the garden itself an expression of Shah Jahan's self-image as ruler of the world. Forms such as the baluster column and the curved *bangla* roof that had hitherto been used only for "palatial architecture of the highest ceremonial order, namely the marble *jharokas* [balconies] and baldachins in which the emperor appeared before his subjects," now appeared in the pavilions of the garden. Only the emperor was allowed to use motifs of plants in art and architecture, and he did so with a vengeance. As at the Taj Mahal, flowers adorned the walls and ceilings of the garden buildings, inlaid with semiprecious stones (*pietra dura*), carved in marble relief, gilded and painted: "different kinds of odiferous plants and flowers and various kinds of designs and pictures so colourful and pleasing that . . . the artisan Spring . . . itself is pierced by the thorns [of envy]."[35] The pictures became "virtual flower gardens" and Spring itself comes off second best to the emperor's artists. As a metaphor of the entire palace, the Hayat Baksh "epitomized its concept as a garden." Shah Jahan's ever-blooming gardens symbolized his claims to have made Hindustan indeed "the rose garden of the earth," in the words of the chronicler, and his reign a golden age of prosperity and unending spring.[36] The inscription over the Diwan-i-Khas was intended as no idle boast: "If there is a paradise on the face of the earth it is this, it is this, it is this."[37]

Koch's argument is compelling, given her profound knowledge of the art and architecture of the period, and yet it contains a certain paradox. If the Hayat Baksh garden and its attendant buildings embodied a statement of kingship audacious even by Mughal standards, this would nevertheless have remained invisible to most of the world since the garden was the most private of spaces within the palace. For whose eyes was it intended?

Louis XIV's Versailles was almost contemporary with Shah Jahan's Red Fort and provides a comparable example of "garden imperialism." With its vast size, its unswerving geometry, its architecturally trimmed shrubs, its army of fountains, Versailles was meant to overwhelm, to broadcast the power of the sovereign. If one needed reminding that he was the Sun King, there were statues of Apollo throughout the garden.[38] Two rulers staking their claim to dominion over nature through gardens, the one as Sun, the other as Spring. For most of us, the Mughal garden, with its more human scale, its flowers and fruit trees, its cooling breezes and soft carpets, is the more beckoning.

Unlike Agra, the Delhi riverfront itself was imperial territory, reserved for the emperor alone and a few favorites such as his son Dara Shikoh.[39] Others had to build their gardens and houses inland, especially along the Paradise Canal. But build they did during Shah Jahan's reign and after, dotting both city and suburbs with gardens large and small. The largest by far (almost fifty acres) was the Sahiba Abad Bagh, also known as the Begum Bagh, bordering the Chandni Chowk, designed by Shah Jahan's favorite daughter, Jahanara, who also oversaw the construction of the most beautiful mansions and gardens within the harem area of the Red Fort. Sahiba Abad was fed by one branch of the canal (the other ran down the middle of Chandni Chowk) on its way to the palace-fortress. Part of the garden consisted of an opulent caravanserai and bath intended for wealthy Persian and Uzbek merchants, but a greater portion was filled with flowers and fruit trees and reserved for women and children of the royal household, a "private, intimate space in the middle of the city—a cool, green area" refreshed by the spray of myriad fountains and waterfalls.[40] One can only imagine the delight of an outing to this glorious garden for those usually confined day and night, year after year, to the *zenana*.[41]

Outside the city walls, about four miles to the north, one of Shah Jahan's wives built the Shalimar Bagh, a very large if rather conventionally laid out garden. Here Shah Jahan entertained and here Aurangzeb crowned himself king after locking up his father and doing away with his brothers. Bernier refers to it as the "King's country house" but judged it inferior to French counterparts such as Fontainebleau or Versailles.[42] Nor could it match its namesakes in Lahore and Kashmir for sheer beauty. It did, however, serve as a convenient staging post for royal progresses to the north. Even in the latter half of the seventeenth century, the Mughals had not given up the habit of assembling in gardens, whether for war or peace. When Aurangzeb camped here for six days in 1664 to prepare for his upcoming expedition to Lahore and Kashmir, his retinue of military, officials, and assorted camp followers totaled perhaps a hundred thousand, accompanied by some hundred and fifty thousand animals, if Bernier's account is reliable.[43]

Nobles and members of the royal family constructed two types of gardens: the traditional *charbagh* (a garden divided into quadrants) and the house garden, *khanah bagh*.[44] The latter, modeled on the Hayat Baksh in the imperial palace, was domestic space, serving only the pleasure of the families and servants of the elite. Impressed nonetheless with the magnificence and size of these establishments, Bernier wrote in 1663: "A good house has its courtyards, gardens, trees, basins of water, small jets d'eau in the hall or at the entrance.... They consider that a house to be greatly admired ought to be situated in the middle of a large flower-garden."[45] The *charbagh*, on the other hand, might be open to the public on certain occasions, and, like the royal Shalimar Garden, it often functioned as a country retreat.

The *charbagh* might also, as we have seen, be the site of a future tomb. A number of these were built by women. Among them was the Roshanara Garden, containing the tomb of the younger sister of Jahanara. Jealous of her sister's influence with their father, she sided with her brother Aurangzeb in his successful struggle against both father and brothers. Roshanara created the garden twenty years before her death. Jahanara, in contrast, asked only for a simple grave with green grass around it, writing as her epitaph:

> *Let nought but the green grass cover the grave of Jahanara*
> *For grass is the fittest covering for the tomb of the lowly.*[46]

But Jahanara was the rare exception; most rivaled each other in the magnificence of their garden tombs.

As Mughal power declined in the century and a half following the death of Aurangzeb in 1707, however, tombs fell into decay and gardens into neglect. Approaching the city from the northwest in 1793, William Franklin, a lieutenant in the Bengal infantry, was struck by "the remains of spacious gardens and country-houses of the nobility" now "nothing more than a shapeless heap of ruins."[47] Such descriptions of a landscape in ruins run as a leitmotif through travelers' accounts of Delhi from the late eighteenth and nineteenth centuries.

Delhi and the Raj

In 1803 the British captured Shahjahanabad (which they always referred to as Delhi or some variant thereof) and gained control over the diminished estates of the Great Mogul. Ruling under the auspices of the East India Company, they claimed to bring peace and order after a long period of bloody turmoil that saw Delhi despoiled by a series of foreign invaders. In 1739 the Persian Nadir Shah had sacked the city, carrying off the fabled Peacock Throne and leaving the poet to lament, "The lovely buildings which once made the famished man forget his hunger are in ruins now. In the once-beautiful gardens where the nightingale sang his love songs to the rose the grass grows waist-high around the fallen pillars and ruined arches."[48] In the wake of Nadir Shah came Afghans, Mahrattas, and Jats, to say nothing of internecine struggles among the Mughals themselves.

After conquering Delhi, the British left the emperor nominally in power, a puppet ruler pottering about his crumbling palace with a multitudinous retinue of dependent relatives, servants, and hangers-on, or, in the case of the last Mughal, Bahadur Shah (r. 1837–1857), composing verses in the Roshanara Gardens.[49] He had little influence outside the walls of the Red Fort; even here, he had to accept British ways and British intrusions, on view like an animal in the zoo. Most British travelers were curious to glimpse the ruler in his fabled palace, but the word that most captured their impressions was "melancholy." Bishop Heber, for example, "felt a melancholy interest in comparing the present state of this poor family with what it was 200 years ago." He found the royal pavilions still lovely, with their white marble and inlay of flowers in precious stones. The gardens attached to these buildings, he wrote, "are not large, but, in their way, must have been extremely rich and beautiful," adding, "They are full of very old orange and other fruit trees, with terraces and parterres on which many rose-bushes were growing, and, even now, a few jonquils in flower. A channel of white marble for water, with little fountain-pipes of the same material, carved like roses, is carried here and there among these parterres, and at the end of the terrace is a beautiful octagonal pavilion, also of marble, lined with the same Mosaic flowers as in the room which I first saw, with a marble fountain in its centre, and a beautiful bath in a recess on one of its sides." But everywhere the effect of all this loveliness was spoiled by debris, gardeners' sweeping, walls stained with droppings of bird and bat; "all . . . was dirty, desolate, and forlorn," flowered inlays and carvings defaced, doors and windows in a "state of dilapidation," old furniture strewn about, torn hangings dangling in archways.[50] Emily Eden, sister of the governor-general, records much the same impression from her audience with Bahadur Shah in 1838: "The old king was sitting in the garden with a chorybadar [mace bearer] waving the flies from him; but the garden is all gone to decay too, and the 'Light of the World' had a forlorn and darkened look."[51]

Things were even worse by the time the American traveler Bayard Taylor visited in 1853. The garden pavilions were tumbling down, green scum covered the fountain basins, rank weeds infested the walks; old trees were a tangle of parasitic plants, and unpruned rose bushes ran wild. Still, a walk in the garden was a relief after the decay of the imperial halls and the great quadrangle leading into the palace, which he compared to "a great barn-yard, filled with tattered grooms, lean horses, and mangy elephants" and called "a miserable life-in-death, which was far more melancholy than complete ruin."[52]

For those British actually living in Delhi in the first half of the nineteenth century, the view was not so grim. They could not, of course, occupy the fort, as they had done in Agra, nor were they initially allowed to own land. Instead they took over Mughal palaces and mansions, especially in the prestigious area around Kashmir Gate, and adapted them to their purposes.[53] Sir David Ochterlony, Resident at the time of Heber's visit, appropriated a portion of a palace that had once belonged to Dara Shikoh, Shah Jahan's favorite son and heir-apparent, remodeled it and restored the large garden, "laid out in the usual formal Eastern manner, but with some good trees and straight walks."[54] Subsequently a very long extension was added running along the length of the garden. As a result the building was no longer centered on the garden but on a new curved driveway that led past a spread of lawn to a porticoed entry in a tripartite Palladian gateway. As if to underscore the intrusion of English styles, a stately staircase was affixed to the entrance of the building, echoing Government House in Calcutta.[55]

The Shalimar Gardens outside the city also became a favored retreat for Ochterlony and his fellow officials, as they had been for their Mughal predecessors. After years of neglect, the wilderness of trees and undergrowth was cleared, the old pavilions refurbished, and the pools restocked. The results did not impress Emma Roberts, who sought in vain to recognize the "paradise of flowers and foliage" of Shah Jahan.[56] Nevertheless, Ochterlony loved the garden and often took refuge in it. Here, too, another Resident, Sir Charles Metcalfe, built a simple house where he could live secretly with his Indian wife and half-caste family.[57] Ochterlony, in contrast, had no such inhibitions, openly flaunting his Indian family. One of the fabled sights of Delhi was the evening outing with his thirteen wives, each on her own elephant, around the walls of the Red Fort. A short distance south of Shalimar Bagh, he bought a large property that he named Mubarak Bagh after one of these *bibis*. Here he built his tomb, a "wonderful hybrid monument" with a cross surmounting a dome and a forest of minarets clustered on the side wings.[58]

In due time Charles Metcalfe's younger brother, Thomas, also Resident in Delhi, built "the last of the princely riverine palaces," a mansion that rivaled those of the Mughal *amirs*.[59] A huge rectangular building, Metcalfe House overlooked the river and the eighteenth-century Qudsia Bagh that lay between the house and the city walls. Perhaps the best description is provided by the novelist Flora Annie Steel, who knew India well. The parklike grounds around the house were laid out in the manner of an English garden, but with broad verandahs full of rare plants. At their height in the late winter months, the gardens bloomed in all their glory: "There was not a leaf out of place, a blade of grass untrimmed. Long lines of English annuals in pots bordered the broad walks evenly, the scentless gardenia festooned the rows of cypress in disciplined freedom, the roses had not a fallen petal, though the palms swept their long fringes above them boldly, and strange perfumed creepers leaped to the branches of the forest trees." On a raised dais near the house, a regimental band played. Very English, to be sure, but the scene was leavened with oriental touches: a splendid marquee of Kashmir shawls and Persian carpets, luxurious divans for reclining, a polyglot assemblage of Delhi's elite, both Indian and European.[60]

Metcalfe also converted a tomb adjacent to the Qutb Minar into a country house; the space allotted for coffins made a nice dining room, and off of it he grouped an octagonal set of rooms (see Pl. 22).[61] "Round the house he laid out a very pleasant garden, and built three or four rooms for the accommodation of gentlemen in the garden," wrote his daughter Emily. "Our house was called the Dil-Koosha (the delight of the heart) and was constantly lent by my Father to bridal parties for their honeymoons. It was a most enjoyable spot in itself, and had also the additional charm of being close to the beautiful Kutub Minar, the great historical tower, and all the wonderful ruins surrounding it. The grounds on which the tower and ruins stood had been laid out, at my Father's suggestion, as a beautiful garden, and the place was kept scrupulously clean and in excellent repair." After Metcalfe's death in 1853, this, too, fell into ruin and became known as "Metcalfe's Folly."[62]

Because they settled into a preexisting walled city, the British in the first half of the nineteenth century could not very well segregate themselves as in the presidency towns of Madras and Calcutta; there was no separate "Black Town." Company officials rented and refurbished houses, living and working with Indians in a confined area. Their country residences outside the city gates depended on grants of land bestowed by the Mughals. The older generation, personified by such men as Ochterlony, James Skinner, and William Linnaeus Gardner, openly embraced an oriental manner of life and married Indian women. This became less and less common and more and more frowned upon (witness Charles Metcalfe's secret life). At the same time, housing became increasingly segregated as the British presence grew and attitudes changed. The so-called Civil Lines gradually expanded in a triangle bounded by the river, the Ridge, and the northern wall of the city. Here Europeans lived in "detached houses, each surrounded by walls enclosing large gardens, lawns, out-offices," a pattern already anticipating that of New Delhi.[63]

Nevertheless, there was still considerable interaction between the British, Muslim, and Hindu populations in the daily life of Delhi in the period before 1857. The court was the cultural center, diminished though it might be; Hindus dominated the commercial sphere; and the British ran the administration. Briton and Mughal shared a common love of hunting. Mughal princes, Hindu bankers, and British officials with wives in tow attended official garden parties at Metcalfe House. On the Indian side, Begum Samru "was wont to give superb entertainments and receive the highest mark of respect from her European visitors" in her mansion at the upper end of the Chandni Chowk, "in the centre of a spacious and stately garden." The Begum was the immensely rich and powerful widow of a German adventurer and commanded her own private army. When she converted to Catholicism, she built a church on the model of St. Peter's in the small principality that she contrived to keep out of British hands after the conquest of 1803.[64] As for religious ecumenism, the Muslim court celebrated the Hindu holidays of Dewali and Holi, while "Hindus were almost as proprietary of Mohurram ceremonies as Muslims."[65] And, important for future generations, Europeans and Indians joined together in 1847 to form the Delhi Archaeological Society, ancestor to the ASI. Its first publication was an account of Delhi's historic monuments, written by a Muslim scholar and dedicated to Thomas Metcalfe.[66]

The Uprising of 1857

The British made little attempt to change the face of the city during the early decades of their dominion.[67] On the administrative level, however, the conviction grew that the "dual mandate" of emperor and Company could not be maintained indefinitely, but attempts to negotiate an end to Mughal rule with Bahadur Shah went nowhere. Known by his poet's name of Zafar, he had little interest in anything besides poetry and gardens (he oversaw the layout of two). Besides, a court astrologer had predicted long before that he would be the last of his family to occupy the throne, so what was the point of negotiating?[68]

The future of Delhi and of the dynasty was abruptly and brutally altered by the events of 1857.[69] The spark of mutiny touched off in Barrackpore and Meerut eventually spread to Delhi and much of the Gangetic plain. The eighty-two-year-old Bahadur Shah was forced to accept nominal leadership of the rebellion. Mutineers held the Red Fort over the summer before the British succeeded in relieving the siege of the city and restoring their rule. Both sides committed horrendous atrocities during the conflict, but these paled in comparison with the savage reprisals after victory. British troops were given license to loot the city and did so with abandon; mass executions were the order of the day. Theophilus Metcalfe was so enraged by the despoiling of his father's house that he set about killing Indians indiscriminately. When the governor-general (now styled viceroy) at last imposed some restraint on the retribution, he was reviled in the press as "Clemency" Canning.

The most extreme voices called for the total destruction of Delhi itself—or failing that, the razing of the Red Fort. In the end, Muslim Delhi suffered severely: "Delhi was made to forget that it was a Mughal city."[70] The great mosque, the Jama Masjid, barely escaped demolition, only to be turned into soldiers' quarters as a deliberate act of desecration. Barracks also took over large areas of the rest of the city: "Where is Delhi?" lamented the poet Ghalib, "By God, it is not a city now. It is a camp. It is a cantonment."[71] The fort was not demolished, but many of its buildings, already damaged by British shelling, were reduced to rubble and barracks built within its precincts with no regard to existing architecture or gardens. The *zenana*, which had encompassed the southeast quadrant of the fort, was almost entirely torn down and replaced by military quarters; one of the few pavilions left standing, the terraced Mumtaz Mahal overlooking the river, was used as a prison and later as a sergeants' mess. The military also took over much of the Hayat Baksh, Shah Jahan's "life-giving garden."[72]

Twenty years later the botanical artist Marianne North lamented, "Alas, alas! The hideous barrack buildings and other atrocities introduced by my countrymen."[73] With the benefit of almost a half-century of hindsight, the ASI, too, acknowledged the "severe treatment" meted out to the buildings of Shahjahanabad and the conversion of the fort into a cantonment. "On the west," a report lamented, "all traces of the Mahtab Bagh [Moonlight Garden] have long since been entirely swept away and hideous barracks erected in its stead."[74] In less restrained language, William Dalrymple refers to them as "the most crushingly ugly buildings ever thrown up by the British Empire—a set of barracks that look as if they have been modeled on Wormwood Scrubs."[75] Nor did the surviving parts of the palace go unscathed: Emily Metcalfe's diary refers to soldiers using the ends of their bayonets to pry out leaves and petals of the flowers inlaid in precious stones in the marble walls of the most important imperial buildings. They also removed plates of gold from the domes of the beautiful Pearl Mosque, the Moti Masjid, and sold them; fountains were stripped of their silver finials.[76]

Even before 1857 the British had encroached on garden areas within the city, especially the public gardens along the river front and Daryaganj. After the uprising, the royal gardens and retreats that had once lined the river and extended onto the Ridge were confiscated. Those immediately outside the fortress walls were swept away completely, along with adjoining mosques, shops, and mansions, and turned into a defensive area 450 yards wide, virtually an island isolated from the city.[77] Inexplicably, the tree-lined canal running down the center of Chandni Chowk was covered over by a footpath. The Shalimar Garden was sold off for commercial cultivation, its original footprint now barely visible. The vast gardens laid out on the north side of the Chandni Chowk by Begum Jahanara were renamed Queen's Gardens, in honor of Queen Victoria, but more commonly viewed as the "Hyde Park" of Delhi. The *serai*'s walls and pavilions, built for visiting merchants, were leveled and replaced by a town hall and library, across from which rises an incongruously Gothic clock tower.[78] The Qudsia Gardens, enclosed within a monumental three-story wall, had the misfortune of housing a British gun battery during the siege. It was badly damaged and much of the garden was later taken over for a bus terminal and tourist campsite. Just outside its southwest corner, the Nicholson Garden commemorates the grave of General Nicholson, killed during the rebellion.[79] As Constance Villiers-Stuart remarked apropos of the tomb of Safdar Jung, few Mughal gardens have survived British rule and those that have are invariably associated with tombs: "Respect for a tomb seems to have been the only protection for its garden."[80]

The reconstruction and modernization of Delhi after the rebellion brought far-reaching changes to the city, inevitably affecting its spatial layout generally and its gardens specifically. A railroad line ran across Salimgarh and the adjacent corner of the Red Fort, leading to a station that destroyed large sections of the city north of Chandni Chowk. By the early twentieth century, seven lines radiated out from Delhi, making it the most important transportation and commercial center in northern India.[81] Roads, too, changed the face of the city. "It is the new roads more than anything else," lamented Villiers-Stuart, "which have ruined the gardens like the old pleasance of the Princess Roshanara, or the Queen's Gardens in Delhi City; the winding drives which give a sense of restlessness and exposure as they cut up the garden with their broad bare gravel sweep and make the flower borders, however large, look mean and unrelated to each other."[82] Only a few Mughal gardens, such as the Talkatora Bagh on the lower slopes of the Ridge, preserved something of their original form thanks to their isolation, but it was almost hidden beneath a tangle of scrub and thorn bushes.[83]

Modernization and neglect were the twin ills afflicting the gardens and monuments of Delhi; and yet "restoration" was itself a mixed blessing. Serious concern for the conservation and restoration of the country's heritage as a whole did not begin until the turn of the century with Lord Curzon. In Delhi attention focused primarily on Humayun's tomb and the Red Fort. The walls surrounding Humayun's tomb had collapsed and much of the garden was planted in tobacco. Curzon ordered the reconstruction of the walls and the clearing and replanting of the gardens, which in turn required the repair of the system of channels and tanks that watered the garden.[84]

The Red Fort posed more serious problems. Its appropriation by the military had led not only to the rampant demolitions and erections of barracks, but also to the intrusion of roads that served the military but destroyed the carefully designed spatial relationships of Shah Jahan's palace. In considering restoration, the ASI faced a multitude of questions. Should its goal simply be conservation of old buildings still in good enough shape to be worth saving? Should it aim more ambitiously to rebuild what had been there before, and, if so, how could anyone be sure what this was? How should gardens and other open spaces be treated? Here, too, there was a lack of detailed information about original plantings and hydraulic systems. Those who had carried out the "fearful piece of Vandalism" after 1857, declared the British architectural historian James Fergusson, had not even thought it "worth while to make a plan of what they were destroying or preserving any record of the most splendid palace in the world." True, some of the finest buildings had survived the onslaught, but situated in the midst of a "British barrack-yard, they look like precious stones torn from their settings in some exquisite piece of Oriental jeweller's work and set at random in a bed of commonest plaster."[85] And hovering over all these dilemmas loomed the perennial shortage of funds and the conflicting claims of the military.

Curzon himself, as was his wont, gave specific instructions. He ordered that the garden between the Diwan-i-Am, the Hall of Public Audience, and the Rang Mahal reproduce the lines of the rectangular garden that had once existed there. As for the Diwan-i-Khas, the Hall of Private Audience, whose original plinth had sunk into the ground so that the bushes in front obscured the view of the facade, he directed that the flowerbeds lining the paths be totally eliminated and a new garden laid out along with the adjoining garden areas. Pathways, he directed, should be constructed "on the same level as the lawns and not above them"—an odd proposal since he was familiar with Bernier's account of pathways raised well above parterres. When the ASI set to work on the Hayat Baksh, it lay under some three feet of earth, roads, and debris. Excavations turned up two marble tanks with inlaid bottoms. Still, those "hideous barracks" remained; rather pathetically, an iron rail was erected to fence off the area being restored from the barracks which continued to occupy almost half of the original garden.[86]

Once again the ASI adopted a double standard, aiming for the greatest authenticity possible for architectural restoration, all the while adopting a much more casual attitude toward gardens. It was not necessary to reproduce the original plantings exactly, they insisted, since horticulture had made immense strides in later times and tastes had changed as well.[87] As a result "pleasing lawns and shrubbery" came to define the destroyed gardens, courtyards, and colonnades. Sometimes they were at least an improvement on the intrusive roadways and buildings of the military, but elsewhere they were stunningly out of place, as in the forecourt of the Diwan-i-Am. "The vastness of the courtyard," proclaimed the official archaeologist with evident satisfaction, "wherein a throng of courtiers daily assembled before the 'Great Mughal' is now suggested by a pleasant stretch of lawn and the gorgeous colonnades decked out in rivalry by the nobles of the realm, by screens of flowering shrubs."

As Anisha Mukherji explains, this misses the "effortless spatial integration of the original design, wherein open spaces formed the necessary prelude to built structures; and built structures in turn provided a focus to, or defined, the open space in front of them." The Diwan-i-Am, in fact, would have stood in a paved courtyard, the climax of a carefully orchestrated passage through exterior gateway and intervening passages and buildings.[88] Where gardens *were* appropriate, they consisted of little more than the same English formula of lawn and shrub. Gone were "the fruit trees, parterres, and cypresses," only to be "replaced everywhere by turf and gravel paths."[89]

The Delhi *Durbars*

The belated attention paid to the Red Fort, misguided though it might sometimes have been, was inspired by more than antiquarian interest. Much had changed since 1857–58. Increasingly the British assumed the mantle of the Mughals, whom they had once disdained as weak and decadent. Now they were happy to seize upon the rituals of empire of their erstwhile enemies, rituals that required noble spaces resonant with past glories. Chief among these were *durbars*. A Persian word, the *durbar* had been indigenized by the Mughals along with many other Persian customs (and words). The durbar took many forms, but the one seized upon by Lord Canning as a means of reasserting British authority in the aftermath of the uprising had as its focus the public submission of subjects amid an exchange of gifts and pageantry. In the winter months from 1858 to 1860 Canning and his entourage of twenty thousand toured northern India with a succession of grand levees at which local notables reaffirmed their allegiance to the viceroy as representative of the queen.[90]

Splendid as they were, these traveling durbars were dwarfed by the imperial Delhi assemblage of 1877. It was the brainchild of the viceroy at the time, Lord Lytton, who had a flair for the theatrical as well as strong Tory leanings. He proposed that Queen Victoria be proclaimed Empress of India, arguing that the title would "place her authority upon the ancient throne of the Moguls, with which the imagination and tradition of [our] Indian subjects associate the splendour of supreme power."[91] Although she dearly loved Indians, the queen decided against coming herself, no doubt still put off by the "heat and the insects."[92]

The durbar lasted for two weeks, attended by some 84,000 people, housed in a sea of camps, with Indians carefully segregated from Europeans, and everyone sorted out by their place in the social hierarchy from maharajas to sweepers. The Indian and European camps were a study in contrasts. The former were so arranged that each ruler was responsible for disposing of his allotted space as he chose. To western eyes, they were "cluttered and disorganized," a jumble of cooking fires, people, and animals. The European camps "were well ordered, with straight streets and neat rows of tents on each side. Grass and flowers were laid out to impart the touch of England which the British carried with them all over India." All of which demonstrated why the British were the rulers, the Indians the ruled, at least in the view of Sir Dinkar Rao. On the other hand, the Indian camp looked more colorful, livelier, and altogether more inviting to many Europeans.[93]

The viceroy held court in an enormous tent, sitting on the viceregal throne, behind which a stern portrait of the monarch, dressed all in black (she was still in mourning), oversaw the proceedings. At last, at noon on January 1, 1877, he rode into the great amphitheatre to the strains of Wagner's "March from Tannhäuser," mounted the throne in front of the imperial pavilion decked out in red and gold, and announced that henceforth "Empress of India" would be added to Queen Victoria's Royal Styles and Titles.[94] In Lord Salisbury's view, the durbar had to be "gaudy enough to impress the orientals" while at the same time concealing "the nakedness of the sword on which we rely."[95] Somewhat more oddly, it was replete with medieval imagery because that was what appealed to Lytton and seemed to him, in much romanticized form, well suited to pomp and ceremony. It did not appeal to the artist Val Prinsep, who had been brought along to paint a huge picture of the scene for Victoria. Prinsep was aghast at the whole "circus." He found the imperial pavilion a real monstrosity; the frieze hanging from the canopy was decked with, inter alia, an Irish Harp, the Lion Rampant of Scotland, the Three Lions of England, and, oh, yes, the Lotus of India. It "outdoes the Crystal Palace in 'hideosity,'" he wrote. Even the viceroy's wife had to agree that it was indeed "all in rather bad taste."[96]

Bernard Cohn cites the 1877 durbar as a prime example of the "invention of tradition." It was neither authentically European nor authentically Indian, nor even "Indo-Saracenic," a style that was rapidly catching on as the appropriate architectural idiom of empire.[97] But whatever the eclecticism of its content, the 1877 durbar did put Delhi on the world map.

Twenty-six years later, another durbar celebrated the coronation of Edward VII as Emperor of India. The then viceroy, none other than Lord

Curzon, saw it as the climax of his proconsulship. Far more knowledgeable about India and far more sophisticated in his tastes, Curzon dismissed Lytton's "medieval" frumpery: "So far as these features were concerned, the ceremony might equally have taken place in Hyde Park."[98] His durbar was to be emphatically Indian. The great amphitheater constructed for the occasion was crowned with a "Saracenic dome" and adorned with other ornaments of Mughal inspiration. The whole arena, he declared, was "built and decorated exclusively in the Mogul, or Indo-Saracenic style."[99] In addition, the genius of Indian civilization would be on display in a major exhibition of crafts set up in the Qudsia Gardens: carpets, jewelry, paintings, and gold and silverware.[100]

But while Curzon's durbar—and it was very much Curzon's durbar—put the spotlight on the glory that was India and the grandeur of the Mughals, it was even more a celebration of the British Empire and all it stood for: "the outward sign of an ideal, the heavenly pattern of an Empire to which his life was devoted." The pageantry, the great ingathering from all over the subcontinent, was meant, as Curzon put it, to be an "overwhelming display of unity and patriotism."[101] The King-Emperor would not be attending; he had "done" India in 1875–76 as Prince of Wales and did not share his mother's enthusiasm. In his stead he sent a pair of lesser royals, the Duke and Duchess of Connaught, who were unlikely to upstage the viceroy.

As the king's representative, Curzon set about planning for it with the same meticulous attention to detail he bestowed on all his projects. To begin with, he vetoed "Onward Christian Soldiers," the hymn chosen for divine services during the durbar, not because most of the soldiers present were non-Christians (it was in fact a general favorite) but because it contained the lines "Crowns and Thrones may perish, Kingdoms rise and wane"—hardly the note he wished to strike.[102] Then he turned to the layout of the vast camp. Like his predecessor Lord Lytton, he was acutely aware of the symbolism of the city to be created for the thousands of visitors, a city, indeed, as large as Greater London.[103] The 1877 durbar had provided a precedent, its "camp spread over a large tract of country transformed for the time into a pleasure ground, with lawns, flower-gardens, triumphal arches and gay pavilions."[104] The 1903 durbar would match this and much more.

The viceroy's camp alone boasted some fourteen hundred tents covering ninety-three acres just south of the Ridge that had been carved out of a "howling wilderness of jungle scrub" (Fig. 48). It was bisected by a broad avenue,

Fig. 48. The Durbar Camp, Delhi: Main street of the camp
from the roof of the circuit house. Niele and Klein, December 30, 1902

[The British Library Board, Mss.EUR F111/270(55)]

"bounded on each side by hundred-foot-wide lawns decked with palms, potted ferns, flowerbeds, and by side streets named after British proconsuls or heroes of the Raj."[105] The new building erected for the viceroy and vicereine in a commanding position on the slope of the Ridge faced a lawn and fountain at some distance from the road that led to the central avenue of the camp, and in the center of another expanse of turf towered the forty-foot-high viceregal flagstaff. Spread out close by and also in a sea of grass were suites of tents housing the Duke and Duchess of Connaught and other notables, as well members of the viceroy's staff.[106] Specially constructed ducts brought water from the Najafgarh Canal to maintain the vast acreage of lawns and gardens.[107] With three polo grounds also demanding turf, the planners had to commission a local dairy farmer to set up a grass-farm near the camp.[108] Nothing was left to chance: once the festivities were underway, coolies flicked the dust off all the flowers with feather dusters.[109]

As before, Indian rulers were provided acreage for their camps and left to dispose of it as they would. With more time for planning than in 1877, the results were more varied, providing a microcosm of the country itself. And this time around the native chiefs were not going to be caught without gardens. Because the state color of Hyderabad was yellow, there were yellow flowers in the garden to match the yellow flags and banners and livery of the Nizam's men. The four Rajput camps were grouped around a small circular garden where a band played. There were also bands in the "tastefully laid out gardens" attached to the Begum of Bhopal's camp. Maharaja Scindia combined the old and the new in his camp: "Like the beautiful Jai Belas Palace at Gwalior itself, [it] was enclosed in an elaborate and well laid-out garden. It was difficult to believe that, only a few weeks before, this trim and well-cultivated plot, with its fountains and palm trees, had been nothing more than a field of wheat." The Maharani had her own enclosed winter garden. The Nawab of Junagadh in the Kathiawar Peninsula, famous for its forest of Gir, the only place in the country where the Indian lion was still to be found, produced a "fine display of garden flowers" that had all been brought from his home. The Maharaja of Jaipur was also eager to show that he was a man of the world, able to combine tradition with a cosmopolitan taste. Although his camp followed the time-honored Rajput defensive plan of concentric circles, it also boasted "the refinement and elegance" of a "carefully-planned Italian garden."[110]

All of these gardens were overshadowed, however, by those of the Punjab chiefs. Because their camps were situated close to plentiful supplies of water, they were able to bring their "groves and gardens to a greater perfection than those of any other camp." The star among them was the young Maharaja of Patiala; "[His camp] was surrounded by a hedge of orange and rose bushes, and over six hundred palm trees . . . planted in the gardens, in which a dozen fountains were continually playing. Two colossal statues of knights in armour, bearing electric lights, guarded the entrance to the camp, which at night was illuminated by a profusion of lamps, arranged to form legends expressive of devotion to the Sovereign, while Urdu and Persian mottoes, written in letters of gold, and breathing the same sentiments, were visible by day."[111] No one was going to dismiss these camps as "jumbled and disorganized"!

The full fortnight of scheduled events ran like clockwork, from the state entry into Delhi with Lord and Lady Curzon and the royal party riding on borrowed elephants, to the Coronation Proclamation in the great amphitheater, to the state ball held in the Red Fort. For many the ball was the highlight of the entire affair—"the greatest entertainment ever given in the Indian Empire."[112] The Diwan-i-Am had been enlarged to three times its original size (Curzon himself tended to the architectural details) and decorated for the night with palm trees and flowers. Here four thousand invited guests, European and Indian, danced the night away. At 10 p.m. the vicereine, Lady Curzon, made her spectacular entrance clad in a gown of peacock feathers with emeralds in the eyes of the peacocks, outshining even the Indian princes "simply smothered in jewels." Dinner was held in the Diwan-i-Khas, "with its marble pillars inlaid with jade and cornelian and much gold tracery," one guest wrote, adding "You must try to imagine a fairy palace, for that is what it was like." And above it all, the inscription in Persian letters: "If there is a paradise on the face of the earth. . . ."[113]

The viceroy's enemies, and he had quite a few, referred to the extravaganza as the "Curzonisation" Durbar. They criticized him as too preoccupied with his own importance, sitting rigidly on the viceregal throne (unaware that he suffered from curvature of the spine and had to wear a steel corset padded with leather); Lytton's critics had condemned *him* for just the opposite—sitting sprawled on the throne in much too casual a manner (unaware that he suffered from hemorrhoids).[114] Nevertheless, Curzon was probably correct when he declared on New Year's Day 1903, "Nowhere else in the world would such a spectacle be possible as that which we witness here today." One hundred rulers of separate states, an outpouring of loyalty, whether genuine or politic, on a scale unimaginable before or since.[115] "I'm sure the world has seen nothing like it before," declared the painter Mortimer Menpes, "and I could weep to think that it may never look upon the like again."[116]

Fate decreed otherwise. Edward VII, having waited so long for his mother to die, reigned less than a decade. In 1911 it was time for another Coronation Durbar. Curzon had had the better part of two years to plan his durbar; Lord Hardinge had less than a year. But with the example of two Delhi durbars behind him, he had a good idea of what must be done. Needless to say, lawns and gardens would once more loom large in the overall design. As Hardinge notes in his memoirs, one of the most unusual sights to greet him on a planning visit to Delhi was "that of hundreds of native gardeners sitting on their hams in long serried lines sowing blades of grass to make out of waste land polo grounds and lawns, all of which were glorious green lawns by the end of the rains."[117] The two polo grounds, fashioned out of cornfields, were provided with three pavilions and sunken gardens with carefully ordered terraces. The king's camp, stretching over eighty-five acres, "was beautifully laid out with red roads, green lawns and rose gardens with roses from England"[118]—a rather superfluous touch, one would think.

If Hardinge could not match the sheer splendor of the 1903 durbar, he did have several trump cards to play. For the first time, a reigning monarch would attend the durbar. George V had in fact insisted that it be held once more in Delhi, resisting the very vocal demands that it was Calcutta's turn—Calcutta was, after all, the capital of India. Furthermore, the Hayat Baksh was finally ready to host a garden party for durbar guests (Fig. 49). Previous durbars had made use of the main pavilions of the Red Fort only at night, no doubt counting on darkness to mask the sad state of much of the palace and the ubiquitous barracks. Curzon had made a start with the restoration of the Hayat Baksh and the Diwan-i-Khas, as well as the questionable enlargement of the Diwan-i-Am, but with his departure in 1905, funds dropped off and the fort reverted almost to the state described by visitors earlier in the century. Thus, when Hardinge inspected its interior in the spring of 1911, he found it a shambles. This would not do. The viceroy found more money for the ASI and "gave orders that the whole of the interior of the Fort should be cleaned up and laid out as a garden with lawns, shrubs and water, and that the jungle outside the Fort should be cut down, drained and turned into a park."[119]

Nine months later, all was ready for the durbar: "The inside of the Fort was a lovely garden with flowering shrubs, fountains, lawns and runnels of fresh water." Outside the walls was a green park dotted with fine trees that had been concealed by the tangle of overgrowth. The Hayat Baksh, the jewel of Shah Jahan's palace gardens, had been lowered to its original level, but planting could not begin until hydraulic engineers finally solved the problem of irrigation by sinking electric pumps in the old wells and installing pipes, rebuilding something of the old system of channels and conduits that had served the Mughals so well. Its pathways repaired, its channels restored, its ornamental beds reconstructed, and a somewhat incongruous screen of conifers planted to hide the iron railing and barracks beyond, the Hayat Baksh was finally presentable after centuries of neglect and desecration.[120]

The garden party was one of the last and most enjoyable functions of the

Fig. 49. Garden party in the Fort, Delhi. Vernon & Co. December 13, 1911.
Wilberforce-Bell Collection
[The British Library Board, Photo 1/14(26)]

durbar. Hardinge could write with satisfaction and echoes of Babur that the Hayat Baksh "had been transformed from a dusty waste into a lovely garden." The party reached its climax when George V and Queen Mary donned their crowns and royal robes and took their seats on the battlements "so that the crowds below could cheer them"—a hundred thousand strong, passing by "in huge masses and in perfect order."[121] One could almost imagine the king as the reincarnation of Shah Jahan seated cross-legged in the *jharoka,* performing the ritual of *darshan,* the viewing; the queen, however, should by rights have been sequestered behind a lattice screen, seeing but unseen.

Constance Villiers-Stuart was happy to see the Hayat Baksh, the "Life-Giving" garden, brought back to life, no matter how inauthentically. Alas, she could not easily tune out the ugly intrusions that even a viceroy was powerless to dislodge: "Looking across the garden from the river terrace a range of hideous barracks forms the background, towering over the exquisite little Bhadon

IMPERIAL DELHI

and Sawan pavilions, and barrack buildings cover the Moonlight Court. The whole effect of the reception held here during the Imperial Durbar festivities was spoilt till the kindly dusk shut out the iron railings and the ugly red and yellow walls. Then as the fire-fly lamps lit up the trees and the lights of the two pavilions gleamed under the falling spray, the old palace garden seemed once more a fitting place for an Indian king to greet his people."[122]

The king and his close advisers had had a particular reason for insisting that the Coronation Durbar be held in Delhi, one that remained a secret until announced by the monarch himself: the city would henceforth be the capital of India. "The ancient capital of the Moguls is to regain its proud position," proclaimed the *Illustrated London News,* "its dead glories are to live again."[123] A new city, a garden city, would rise from the plain of ruins.

CHAPTER 8

Imperial New Delhi

The Garden City

AS A child growing up in New Delhi in the 1930s, Patwant Singh could not have asked for more. "The magnificent sweep of this imperial city which the British were building, with a passion which matched that of India's Mughal rulers, was heaven-sent for us." He recalls the "gracious vistas of King's Way . . . with its broad well-cut lawns and lines of trees extending as far as the eye could see." Much as he and his playmates loved watching the pageantry, their greatest joy was climbing the trees along the wide boulevard for the succulent fruits of *jamun* or racing their bicycles through the water of the canals that paralleled its grassy margins. What a contrast to the "noisy, grilling heat of the old Indian city." It was a grandiose reimagining of the English garden city, "Hampstead enlarged on a giant scale and transposed to Asia."[1]

The Imperial Capital

At the great durbar of 1911 King George V announced that the British, too, would now leave their stamp on Delhi in the form of an imperial capital that would overshadow in brilliance even that of their Mughal predecessors. But where the Mughals had made a habit of shifting capitals, the British in India had known only one, Calcutta, so that the decision was abrupt and, in many quarters, unpopular. It took almost twenty years to complete New Delhi, in contrast to the less than a decade required for Shah Jahan's capital. Furthermore, the Mughal emperor could draw on a ready lexicon of forms and spaces, one that allowed for innovation and experimentation, as in the case of Akbar's Fatehpur Sikri, but mainly for perfection, as in the case of the Red Fort. The riverfront site chosen for Shahjahanabad marked the apogee of a tradition begun by his great-great-grandfather Babur over a century earlier. The emperor could mobilize the finest artists and craftsmen, but he could also overrule them if he chose to; if there was opposition to any of his decisions or horror at his extravagances, we do not hear of them.

As heirs to nineteenth-century historicism, the British had all too much choice. They also had to reckon with diffused authority, with commissions and bureaucracy and Parliament, to say nothing of the vociferous opposition of Calcutta's partisans, including Lord Curzon himself. There was a king, with very definite ideas, but also a viceroy (and viceroy's wife), with equally definite ideas; there were a host of architects and city planners, some already with long experience of India, others entirely unfamiliar with the subcontinent, all of them eager to put their stamp on the great work at hand. Events, too, intruded: domestically, the escalating pace of Indian nationalism; internationally, a world war, then a worldwide depression.

The decision to relocate the capital had been almost accidental, with minimal consultation and no planning. It was pointed out that Delhi had time-honored associations with imperial rule, Mughal and pre-Mughal, that it was more centrally located than Calcutta, and that it was much closer to the summer capital of Simla. These arguments did little to appease the diehards in Calcutta who were dismayed at losing their privileged economic and political position as second city of the empire. Invoking the cadences of the Old Testament prophet, an English-language newspaper warned that those making the move would suffer "the swamps and heat, the boils and blains, the snakes and insects"—as if Calcutta could not match Delhi plague for plague.[2] "They are going to Delhi, the graveyard of empires to be buried there," commented one Bengali, sounding a note that would be oft repeated.[3] Ramsay Macdonald, the first Labour prime minister, who had visited the city in 1909 and 1912, had been struck by its resemblance to a "vast churchyard." "For what reason Providence only knows," he declared, "the Government decided to build new palaces and offices and bring itself bag and baggage to this city of ruins and of tombs." To escape from the raucous clamor of Bengali nationalists, "we determined to regild the thrones of the Moguls and sit down upon them."[4]

Although Curzon himself had idly considered moving the capital to Agra and had not hesitated to choose Delhi for his Imperial Durbar, he led the charge against the transfer. He was motivated partly by a genuine love of Calcutta (unfathomable to most Britons), even more by pique that his new Victoria Memorial, intended to be the architectural jewel in the colonial crown, would now be marginalized. Delhi, he argued, was a backwater, "a cemetery of dead monuments and forgotten dynasties." The East India Company had sacked Lord Wellesley for his extravagance in building Calcutta's Government House over a century earlier, but that would be a mere "bagatelle," he insisted (correctly as it turned out), compared to the expense involved in the new undertaking.[5] There were, indeed, so many second thoughts after the decision was announced that had not work already started and considerable sums already been spent, the outbreak of World War I might well have dealt a deathblow and caused the whole idea to be scrapped.[6]

But proceed it did, albeit with many questions still to be answered. Where would it be situated? Who would design it? Should it reflect Indian styles or European? For whom was the city to be designed? Would it be a collection of administrative buildings or a place to live? What would be its relationship to Shahjahanabad and all the other Delhis? How, for that matter, could the builders pick their way around all the ruins? And could even the hardiest planners create an oasis of greenery on the dusty plain?

Two days after the Coronation Durbar, George V had laid a foundation stone (rumored—erroneously—to have been a hastily acquired tombstone) on the durbar site. This spot, however, proved to be far from ideal, and a location to the south was finally chosen as more suitable to the grand vision that was unfolding. Government House was to crown Raisina Hill, a spur of the Ridge, with opposing Secretariat Buildings slightly below. An almost two-mile avenue would terminate in a monumental arch, the War Memorial, beyond which (later) stood the statue of George V and the ruins of the Purana Qila, the alleged site of the protohistoric Indraprastha. Radiating out from this were residential zones for civil and military personnel and the huge numbers of workers required for the machinery of government. In contrast to Babur and Shah Jahan, the British were so fixated on an acropolis-like eminence that they ignored the riverbank in the debates about possible sites. To be sure, the Yamuna had meandered to the east in the intervening centuries and no longer lapped at the battlements of the Red Fort.

Grand processional avenues were a hallmark of capitals. In another time Edwin Lutyens, the presiding genius of the imperial city, need have looked no farther for inspiration than Shahjahanabad's Chandni Chowk, where elephants once progressed in stately ranks from Fatehpur Mosque along a "very wide and straight" street to a "great square" before the gates of the Red Fort.[7] But in the aftermath of the Uprising of 1857, mosque, avenue, and fort were sad shadows of their former selves. As for London as model, late Victorians felt embarrassed about the lack of broad avenues and triumphal vistas in the city—nothing to rival Haussmann's Parisian boulevards and the Champs Elysées. In the decade following the queen's death in 1901, the Mall was redesigned as a more imperial processional way, with the newly erected Admiralty Arch at one end and a statue of Queen Victoria in front of Buckingham Palace at the other. Not much could be done with that unprepossessing pile of a palace, but it did benefit from a facelift and a reconstruction of the facade to focus on the balcony where the king and queen could make their own version of *darshan*. This project was completed just as planning was underway for New Delhi.[8] Since Lutyens had the rare opportunity of creating a new capital from scratch, however, he was inspired far more by examples such as Washington, Canberra, and Pretoria (built by Herbert Baker, who would be his primary collaborator on New Delhi). Here, with almost unlimited land and largely untrammeled by history, he could fashion a city truly worthy of an empire.

The overall plan of the new city consisted of a complicated interplay of equilateral triangles and hexagons, intersected by several cross avenues at right angles and an abundance of roundabouts.[9] This plan was inspired, according to Lutyens, by the viceroy's command that one avenue should lead to Purana Qila and another to the Jama Masjid, the most important mosque. In other words, there should be an antiphony between the old city and the new. While Lutyens had a very low opinion of Mughal architecture (he dismissed it as "piffle"), it suited his Beaux-Arts aesthetic to use major monuments to provide "visual accents" to the main axes of the new city. Dotted amid the green parkland, they might, with some imagination, evoke the pavilions and gazebos of an English garden. The myriad lesser monuments, on the other hand, he considered simply "nuisances" and not worth zigzagging around when they got in the way of his geometry: "Imagine the Place de la Concorde with tombs anywhere or everywhere about it, in the middle of the road, half on & half off pavements." In fact, even the Purana Qila is off-center as the endpoint of the Kingsway, thanks to the "inflexible rigidity" demanded by the symmetry of the master plan.[10]

The House on the Hill and the Garden Imperial

The focal point for all the geometry is Government House, later renamed Viceroy's House, atop Raisina Hill. A huge structure whose facade is exactly the length of Buckingham Palace, it dominates the surrounding plain, as it was intended to do.[11] King George made it clear that he would like to see a heavy Mughal flavor to the capital "if it were not dreadfully expensive."[12] Lord Hardinge as viceroy stated his preference more generally as "Western architecture with an Oriental motif."[13] After Lutyens was chosen as its architect, Hardinge sent him to tour major Indian monuments—Agra, Indore, Mandu, Sarnath—in hopes he would be inspired to create an architectural synthesis of East and West.

These tours did nothing to shake Lutyens's conviction that India had "no real architecture and nothing is built to last, not even the Taj." The Taj had charms, he acknowledged, as did some other tombs: "They are empty of people, quiet, square, simple and green, and this is only when money is spent on repairs, upkeep, etc. When in ruins the buildings, especially the Mogul, are bad and have none of the dignity a ruin can have that has been the work of any great period." By moonlight, he conceded to his wife, "the patterns [of the Taj] disappear and the architectural forms merge into a fog of white reflection, leaving the great turnip of a dome as a bubble posed in space"; "It is wonderful," he allowed, "but it is not architecture and its beauty begins where architecture ceases to be." Inspired by nothing grander than carpets, it could never stand comparison with the great works of the Greeks, Byzantines, Romans, or of later giants such as Mansard and Wren.[14] In the end he did incorporate more elements of Indian architecture and decoration into his work than he cared to admit, all the while insisting on his primary allegiance to the classical tradition and its western heirs, above all Christopher Wren.[15]

However strongly he rejected Indian architecture, Lutyens found Indian gardens more to his liking. Those of the Taj Mahal, he declared, were "delicious—clear western skies, gorgeous colours and dark glossy trees and the pools and water channels full," and he added, "We spent a good deal of time with the gardener looking at trees and shrubs and finding out what will and will not do at Delhi."[16] Here at least was an Indian art form he could embrace. Lady Hardinge had fallen in love with the Mughal gardens of Srinagar in Kashmir and wrote Lutyens of her desire for such a garden at the new viceroy's house, with "terraces to start from the very top of the Ridge and come to the house." She had arranged to have the Kashmiri gardens carefully photographed for his "edification," adding, "I can only tell you it was a *dream of loveliness*."[17] Both she and Lord Hardinge were familiar with Constance Villiers-Stuart's pioneering work on Mughal gardens, a book intended to influence the planning of New Delhi as much as to make the forgotten treasures of Indian garden craft better known. Back in London, Villiers-Stuart had mobilized the Royal Society of Arts to support an "Indian Garden"—"a Royal Garden of Unity," as she termed it.[18]

The stepped terraces fell victim to the shift in site from Ridge to Raisina Hill—the slope was simply too slight—but on other matters Lady Hardinge found a ready listener in Edwin Lutyens. And a knowledgeable one. For over twenty years he had collaborated with Gertrude Jekyll, the influential English writer and designer who "affected the gardening habits of two generations."[19] Lutyens had met Jekyll in 1889 when she was forty-five and already a formidable figure in the garden world and he an unknown, awkward, and largely self-taught architect of twenty. So successful was their partnership that over the next twenty-five years they worked together on more than a hundred projects, perfecting what Jane Brown has referred to as the "peculiarly English art" of creating "dream houses and their even more magical gardens." Lutyens knew nothing—and cared to know nothing—about horticulture (and never had a garden of his own); he happily left the selection and arrangement of plants to Jekyll. But he was as concerned with the *design* of the garden as with the architecture that accompanied it and with harmonizing both.[20]

Perhaps because he was self-conscious about his lack of formal education, more likely because he thought visually rather than verbally (he had an almost infallible visual memory), Lutyens avoided committing his theories to paper or to the lectern. A rare exception comes in some remarks prepared for a meeting of the Architectural Association in 1908: "A garden scheme should have a backbone—a central idea beautifully phrased. Thus the house wall should spring out of a briar bush—with always the best effect, and every wall, path, stone and flower bed has its similar problem and a relative value to the central idea." If this has strong echoes of Jekyll's phrasing, it is hardly surprising since she had helped him put his thoughts together the previous weekend.[21] Mostly, however, he was an incessant doodler, jotting sketches and notes on any scrap of paper at hand, often flavored with puns—he was an inveterate, not to say compulsive, punster.

Through Jekyll's connections and then through his own after he married a daughter of Lord Lytton, viceroy of the 1877 durbar, Lutyens became one of the most sought-after architects of the day. For the Edwardians, "'a Lutyens house with a Jekyll garden' was . . . the outward symbol of good taste and financial success."[22] At first associated with the "Surrey style" of his home region, before long he was designing and remodeling houses for the well-to-do from Cornwall to Northumberland. His work often appeared in the pages of *Country Life* (for whose editor he designed or renovated several houses), epitomizing the tastes of the "golden afternoon," the last era in which wealthy clients could afford to commission large country houses and gardens and the staffs to maintain them—Jekyll's own Munstead Wood, by no means a palatial estate, depended on the labor of seventeen gardeners, and she was a hands-on gardener herself.[23]

How then did a man known primarily for picturesque villas land the most audacious commission ever for imperial architecture and city planning? Lutyens seems to have bested his rivals through a combination of Lytton family influence, well-connected clients of his own, and a knack for charming highly placed people when it most counted—for example, King George and Lady Hardinge.[24] It also helped that he had designed the Central Square of Hampstead Garden Suburb, an early foray into city planning. India itself held little appeal for him, neither its people nor its culture (India "makes one very Tory and pre-Tory feudal," he confessed to his wife), but it promised the chance to realize ideas and forms that had been dancing in his head in the twenty years since he had drawn a Castle in the Air to amuse his patron,

Barbara Webb; all that it needed now was the "dome from St. Paul's and a Palladian portico"—and a garden worthy of a castle.[25]

It must have been an enormous relief for Lutyens to turn to the gardens at last during a visit to India in the winter of 1917 after five years of incessant wrangling over almost every detail of the Viceroy's House and the surrounding capital. The Government of India, he wrote his wife, have "commanded a Mogul garden which means terraces, water ways, sunk courts, high walls, etc. etc. and have at the same time allocated sufficient money to plant a certain area with shrubs and no more. It is too Alice in Wonderlandish for worlds. However it will come in time."[26] Lady Hardinge, the chief inspiration for the garden, had died suddenly in the summer of 1914, leaving him without her sympathetic presence and warm support in his battles with almost everyone. To be sure, the world war had hugely complicated matters, but he was not a man to show much patience with opposing views or with red tape: "When God created the world he started a bureaucracy which he could not control and which Newton called gravity."[27]

The garden waited on the house. Then there was a great rush to complete it as the time drew near for Lord and Lady Irwin, the current viceroy and vicereine, to move in. Fortunately Lutyens could count on a topnotch assistant to take charge of the planting. William Robertson Mustoe was a Kew-trained horticulturalist attached to the Punjab administration until seconded to New Delhi for the crucial years 1919–1931, and Lutyens got on very well with him. It is not clear whether Jekyll herself offered any suggestions for the enormous flower borders—she was by now almost blind and unable to stir far from home—but they were planted very much according to her precepts and color harmonies.[28] Like Jekyll, Mustoe served as an alter ego, someone who complemented Lutyens's sense of garden design with a thorough knowledge of plants and who could carry on in his absence.[29]

Lutyens came out to India almost every winter. In January 1929 he was breakfasting daily with Mustoe. "[He] has done extraordinarily well with the gardens," Lutyens enthused. "Last winter they were a desert," strewn with debris. "Now full of roses and beautiful roses. The tanks run and reflect and ripple and my rainbow in the deep fountain has come off—a vivid rainbow and children *can* find its start."[30] In the butterfly garden, the mignonette perfumed the air. The Irwins came frequently to survey both house and garden, proving to be ideal "clients": Lord Irwin pronounced the garden "too lovely for words." The Indians, too, were appreciative, calling the gardens "Gods own Heavens."[31] Then, disaster: at the very end of the month frost killed many of the plants. "Mustoe was in tears. His car wouldn't start and he couldn't get to the gardens before sunrise to pour cold water on them to present ice thawing too quick and the Indian Mallis [*malis*] he found standing around doing nothing."[32]

Fortunately, by the time of the official inauguration in February 1931 they had recovered. Emily Lutyens accompanied her husband for the festivities, her first visit to the site of his long labors. During those two decades she had been estranged, living in her own Theosophy-obsessed world as a disciple of Annie Besant. But the attractions of theosophy had finally faded and, if she had never been much interested in her husband's architecture, she had to recognize at long last the magnitude of his achievement. She was enraptured with the garden: "Though so formal, yet everything has grown up so quickly, and flowers are set in such masses, producing a riot of colour and scents, that, with the fountains playing continually, there is not the least sense of stiffness."[33]

When completed, the gardens of the Viceroy's House covered some fifteen acres, stretching a half-mile from the west loggia of the house to the potting sheds at the farthest end (Fig. 50).[34] Its whole configuration could only be seen from west windows of the house (or from the air) because of its raised position above the plain and its surrounding walls. An early drawing had depicted a state garden flanked by privy gardens, but this was abandoned in favor of just the state garden with its strict geometry of paths and watercourses.[35] Beyond this was a narrower garden with an enormous stone pergola down the center, a high-walled "purdah garden" that blocked off tennis courts to right and left and led to the circular butterfly garden with its round pool, so that the whole complex ended "in the shape of a ping-pong bat."[36]

The state or Mughal garden (sometimes also referred to as the Indian garden) was rectangular, measuring 200 by 175 meters (656 by 574 feet) (see Pl. 23). Two parallel channels ran north and south—in contrast to the single central channel typical of Mughal gardens—intersected by two running east and west from square basins immediately below the house. At the intersections were six fountains consisting of three tiers of red sandstone disks, from the center of which rose hexagonal fountains that sprayed foam to a height of twelve feet, before it fell onto the disks that were perforated so that the water could seep gently from one layer to the next. (Some of these fountains proved

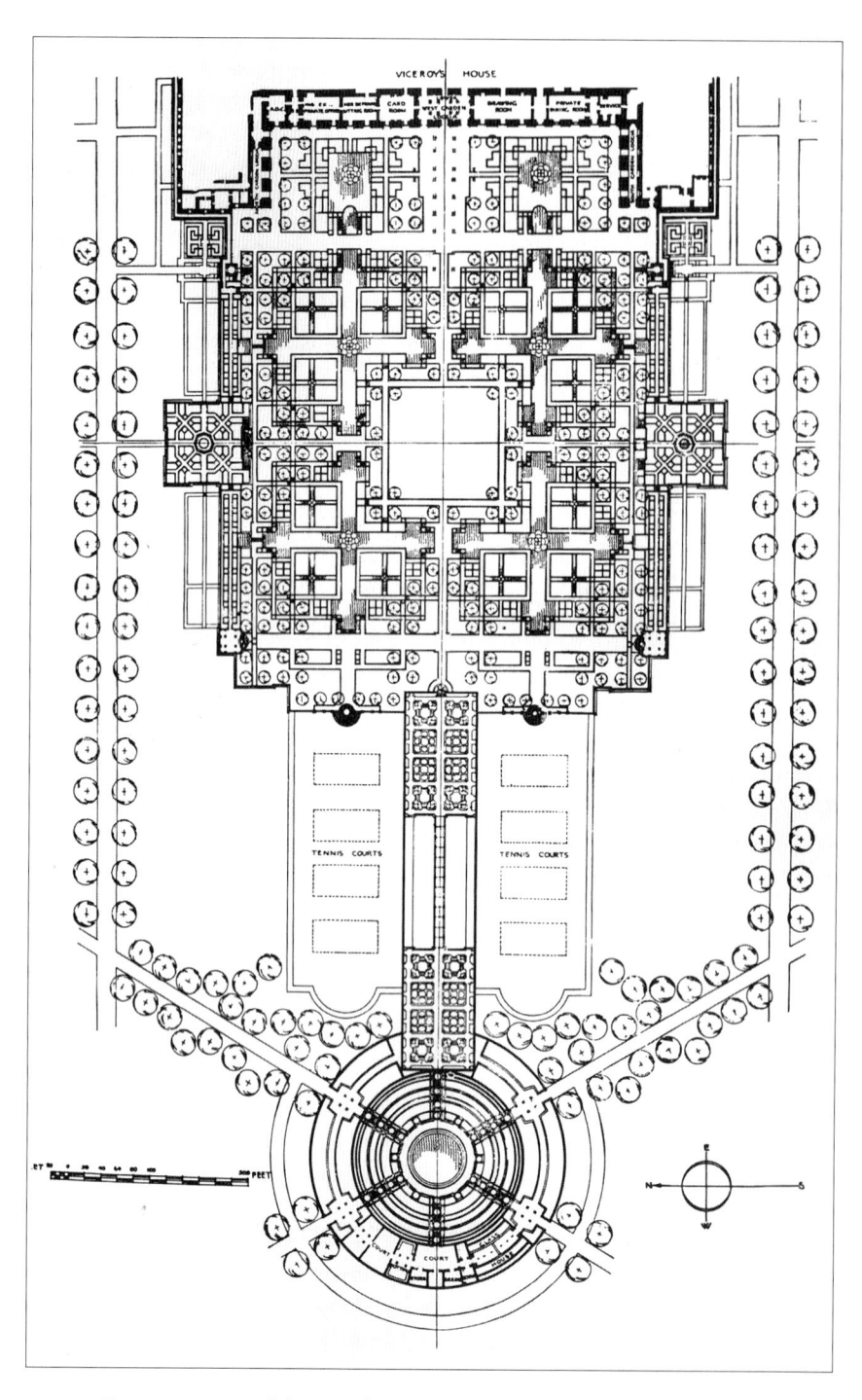

Fig. 50. Layout of the Mughal garden, Viceroy's House, New Delhi
[From A. S. G. Butler, with George Stewart and Christopher Hussey, *The Architecture of Sir Edwin Lutyens*, 1950]

Fig. 51. Mughal garden, Viceroy's House, New Delhi, 1934
[Sir Andrew Buchanan]

recalcitrant or exploded like a geyser when finally coaxed into action.)[37] A network of lesser channels, pools, steps, bridges, and raised walkways accentuated the grid pattern of the garden, enclosing plots of lawn and flowerbeds. There were stone planters strategically set along the watercourses. An early photograph shows purple violas in stone planters bordering a pool (Fig. 51).[38] Flowerbeds, too, were coped in stone, "profusely planted in the English fashion, so that the flowers, grown to twice their English size," spilled out over their margins, nicely softening the rigidity of the chessboard patterns of the overall plan.[39] In the garden proper, the slope was too gentle for the more dramatic cascades of water Lady Hardinge had loved in Kashmir, but Lutyens took advantage of the high retaining walls to create a twenty-foot waterfall from the North Fort to a basin below.[40]

Flowers depended on the season; some were massed in low beds, others set out in combinations of varying heights and textures "to create a pyramid of colours." They were the classics of the English garden: dahlia, poppy, larkspur, verbena, chrysanthemum, Sweet William, cosmos, sweet pea, aster, stock, lupin, petunia, daisy, marigold, carnation, even bulbs such as narcissus, freesia, lily iris, and daffodil. Gaillardia, sunflowers, cosmos, and zinnia braved the harsh heat of summer. Roses—perhaps the largest variety in the world (more than 250)—were the glory of the garden. They bloomed throughout the year, but reached their peak soon after they were pruned in October.[41] "I have never seen better roses anywhere in England than those in New Delhi," declared Lady Beatrix Stanley, vicereine during a brief interregnum in 1934.[42] In contrast to the flowers, the garden's trees, shrubs, and creeping vines were primarily native species or tropical imports. When the garden was first opened for public view, they had not yet had time to mature. Most conspicuous were the evergreens, such as the *moulsri,* a typically Indian tree which bloomed in May and June, spreading a "mild sweet fragrance throughout the garden." It was pruned in a mushroom shape. There were two large lawn areas, one adjacent to the building, the other, much larger one in the center of the garden. They were planted in *doob* grass, originally brought from Belvedere House in Calcutta. It had a coarser texture than the classic English grass and had to be removed once a year before the monsoons: then new top soil was spread and three weeks later a new crop of grass sprouted.[43] As Christopher Hussey points out, this "Viceregal lawn" lies on the axis of the dome of the house, enclosed by "jeweled parterres," and was intended for the garden parties and receptions "which were the social *raison d'être* of the garden."[44]

Most observers were not fooled by the "Mughal" garden, so ardently dreamed of by Lady Hardinge. Robert Byron stated the obvious when he referred to it simply as "the Mogul garden, brightened with English flower beds and borders." Lord Irwin, the first tenant, thought it the ideal setting for the house, "with the combination of its Oriental design of water and lawns and formal trees with the riot of colour from the best of Western flowers."[45] Closest of all to the mark is the comment that it was "'Mughal' as seen by a man famous for the very English gardens he created with Gertrude Jekyll."[46] This was not really surprising considering that the Mughal gardens Lutyens inspected—the Taj Mahal in Agra, the Shalimar Garden in Lahore, and the gardens of the Red Fort and Humayun's Tomb in Delhi—had all been heavily restored (not to say "Curzonised") in the English manner (the gardens he much appreciated at Lucknow were post-Mughal in any case). While Lord and Lady Hardinge were familiar with Villiers-Stuart's work, we can't be sure Lutyens even looked into it, given his lack of intellectual curiosity about Indian culture generally, to say nothing of the fact that he was not much of a reader.

Nevertheless, he would have found the basic formulae of a Mughal garden congenial precisely because in so many ways they matched his own precepts of garden design. He shared the Mughal passion for order and symmetry, expressed through rigid geometry; he could happily accept a space enclosed in stone, constructed on a pattern of grids around a unifying plan of waterways, with squares of turf, flowers, and trees. As for water as a focal point of gardens, his partner Gertrude Jekyll had written the book on water gardens—quite literally—although she preferred a more natural layout to one employing modules and symmetry, choosing when possible to build her gardens along riverbanks and around ponds. She loved to stock her pools with water lilies (real ones), and with the abundance of new varieties "an important modern pleasure ground is scarcely complete without its lily tank."[47] Lutyens was equally fond of water. On his first visit to Delhi in the spring of 1912 he had gone early to the Red Fort and arranged to have the fountains turned on so that he could observe both sound and sight of cascading water (in the Hayat Baksh?—unfortunately no one mentions just where in the Red Fort this took place).[48]

The large, tiered disks in Lutyens's fountains are sometimes referred to as lotus leaves but in fact are modeled not on the dainty lotus but on the giant leaves of the *Victoria amazonica* water lily, a native of South America.[49] The lotus, as Lutyens was surely aware, was a sacred flower to both Buddhist and Hindu, a symbol of creation. The lotus motif was adopted by Muslims in northern India well before it was widely used in Mughal art to symbolize fertility. The fountains of the Taj Mahal take the form of lotus blossoms, lotuses encircle the base of the dome and crown its top, lotus flowers etched in *pietra dura* adorn its walls. In stylized form the plant was carved into the scalloped edges of the octagonal pool—perhaps the pool had once been full of lotuses themselves.[50] Plinth patterns derived from the lotus are common in the Red Fort, and the domes of the Moti Masjid are surmounted by marble lotus petals.[51] For good measure, there was the example of Lady Curzon, who had worn a dress of white satin embroidered with lotus leaves for her first "Drawing Room" (a reception for some five hundred ladies)—the "only part of the Indian India that Mary chose to embrace."[52]

Lutyens was happy to incorporate the lotus motif elsewhere. The Jaipur column is a prime example, with its imperial orb, lotus flower, and hexagram. The five-petaled lotus flower inlaid in marble in the vestibule of the great

Durbar Hall may have been intended to echo the splendid lotus on the floor of the Rang Mahal in the Red Fort.[53] (Lutyens was also taken by the *peepal,* a sacred tree in India, whose leaf he adapted in an intricate pattern for the underside of the *chajjas,* the projecting stone slabs providing shade for the Viceroy's House.)[54] So, why the sandstone water lilies in the garden rather than lotuses? It may of course have been a statement of imperial hubris—the *Victoria amazonica* (née *Victoria regia*) was the pride of British horticulturists and indelibly linked with the Empress of India herself—but Lutyens was not as imperial-minded as many others, including his colleague, Herbert Baker.[55] Could it simply be that the irrepressible punster was indulging in a private joke?

Be that as it may, the mantle of the "Mughal" garden sat lightly on Lutyens's shoulders. He did not feel the need to raise the walks well above the parterres, nor to plant fruit trees for fragrance and produce. The Long or "Purdah" Garden has twelve-foot walls that even a voyeur mounted on an elephant would not have been able to see over, but there is no *zenana* attached, no harem provided for the viceroy's ladies, only the flanking tennis courts.[56] Everywhere one finds imports from the many gardens he had created with Gertrude Jekyll: terraces, pergolas, *oeil de boeuf* ovals pierced through stone walls, topiaries, gazebos, herbaceous borders, and lawns.[57] At the central intersection of the water channels in the classic Mughal garden there would have been a raised stone platform, the *chabutra,* with a pavilion or simply a silken tent furnished with carpets and cushions. Here the ruler and his guests could catch the breezes from the water and the fragrances of flower and tree. In Lutyens's design there was no central intersection, but instead a large lawn between the channels, which Jane Brown has aptly pronounced "a symbolic triumph for the English way of gardening," as well as "a carpet for the vice-regal garden party tent."[58]

The quintessential Lutyens/Jekyll touch, however, was the sunken butterfly garden at its farthest end. It was a "secret garden," a private retreat, entered through an iron gate in the sandstone wall, down sets of stone steps to a large round pool set in banks of flowers enclosed within a round wall. Here are the mignonettes and roses, jasmines and verbenas—everything to delight the butterfly. Ten years earlier he had designed just such a garden for Lady Sackville, filling it only with butterfly-luring blossoms, so that from a distance the shimmer of their wings looked "like brilliant patches of flowers."[59]

Behind the scenes, another world existed to care for the garden. It required a staff of 418, fifty of whom were assigned solely to scaring off predatory birds (unlike the resident peacocks which ranged freely), and another twenty to flower arrangement. Hidden from general view, too, was a sixteen-acre "utility garden." It provided cut flowers for the palace, vegetables and fruit in season for the kitchen, and rosebushes to replace three thousand annually. The garden staff was only part of the more than two thousand needed to run the miniature city that was the Viceroy's Palace and for whom quarters were discreetly tucked away at the northwest corner of the compound.[60]

Lutyens and Mustoe counted on the passage of time to bring their garden to maturity. What they hadn't reckoned with were the depredations of Lady Willingdon, successor to the agreeable Lady Irwin as vicereine. Lady Willingdon fancied herself a gifted decorator and made numerous "improvements" to house and garden without consulting Lutyens or anyone else. She redid many of the rooms in her favorite shade of mauve, provoking Lutyens to refer to her as "the mauvey *sujet*"—a more appropriate sobriquet than he realized, since she left a trail of mauve not only through the Viceroy's House but across the entire subcontinent. She also hung a huge chandelier in the Durbar Hall, turned the stone elephants at the gates into garden gnomes, and cut down a number of gum trees, replacing them with cypresses. Lutyens prevailed upon Queen Mary to protest, but to no avail. When the Willingdons came home on leave, Lutyens confronted her in person. "I told her that if she possessed the Parthenon she would add bay windows to it. She said she did not like the Parthenon." Fortunately, the next viceroy, Lord Linlithgow, invited Lutyens to undo the damage. Accompanied by a stenographer and the faithful Mustoe, Lutyens took an inventory of Lady Willingdon's "vagarious vagaries" with an eye to correcting them. His letters to his wife overflow with diatribes against "that Willingdon Bitch." In one he even drew a design of a fountain to commemorate her reign: a very vulgar pair of buttocks with legs sticking up in the air and water spurting out of its private parts. He noted with malicious pleasure that his drawing enjoyed so much success that he made a number of copies. The lions were returned to their perches in the forecourt, the "silly cypresses" uprooted, and the garden restored to its earlier state.[61]

The renowned traveler Freya Stark was a guest in the Viceroy's House toward the end of World War II. The viceroy was away and had arranged for the gardens to be open to the public in February and March (as they still are), at the peak of their winter bloom. "It was extraordinary how alive and agreeable it made them," she wrote. "There is no point in having pomp unless there is a crowd to enjoy it."⁶² Pomp indeed.

The Green City

Christopher Wren, the builder of Hampton Court for William III, was, in Jane Brown's words, "the last *compleat* architect in terms of masterminding the whole concept, the total visual effect of house and grounds as much as construction details." But even Wren was thwarted in his bid to build London anew after the Great Fire of 1666. Lutyens accomplished what was denied his "spiritual mentor," not only building a great palace and garden but also laying out a new city. He oversaw "every aspect of the construction, from the shape of the doorknobs in the Viceroy's palace to the types of flowers suitable for planting in the roundabouts."⁶³ This was the commission he had longed for all his life, but he could hardly have imagined in the early days of 1912 that it would consume so much of his life and bring as much disappointment as success. "In a trite sense, Delhi proved a perfect example of the old warning: be careful what you wish for, for it might come true."⁶⁴ During an exasperating argument about both design and money, he declared that the new city should be called "Bedlampore": "It is like composing an opera when they leave out the fiddles and all but one wind instrument, and leave you a banjo with one string."⁶⁵

The durbars had provided a rehearsal for city planning. Hardly had the dust settled from the festivities of December 1911 when the entire durbar area north and west of the city was transformed into a temporary capital to which flocked thousands of administrative emigrants from Calcutta. They were housed in bungalows or substantial well-furnished tents, set in beautiful gardens. So impressed was the Delhi Planning Committee with their enthusiastic gardening that its final report declared, "If in future the inhabitants in the new capital area pay as much attention to their gardens as many of the inhabitants have during the period of construction, the results should be a gorgeous blaze of colour and a riot of bloom."⁶⁶ The Circuit House, built originally for Curzon's use at the 1903 durbar, served as the interim residence for the viceroy until the palace was ready for occupancy in 1929 and could boast an already well-established garden. Rechristened Viceregal Lodge, it was a "typical Indian bungalow of the grander sort writ large." Lady

Reading, the viceroy's wife, wrote home in wonder about the garden, intentionally or unintentionally repeating a phrase from the report: "Holly hocks much taller than I am, the herbaceous border a blaze of colour and all for Christmas!"[67]

To the south in what had once been the small village of Raisina, the imperial capital was gradually—very gradually—taking shape. Unlike Wren, Lutyens and his fellow planners were not faced with a densely populated warren of narrow streets and impossibly complex property claims. It was mostly agricultural land, the price was low, and there were no vocal business interests to resist the government's appropriation of ten square miles for the new city and fifteen for the cantonment, an amount attacked as extravagant at the time.[68] The 440-foot-wide avenue leading from the Viceroy's House to the War Memorial and the statue of King George was the rigid spine of the city (see Pl. 24). Bordered by a series of rectangular lawns and pools of water, it was intended as a purely ceremonial way, not as a residential or a commercial thoroughfare. Unlike Chandni Chowk in Shahjahanabad, the "bazaar" at Connaught Place was offset at some distance to the north.

Kingsway, later rechristened Raj Path, was the embodiment of dominion. The palace stood at its apex, with the Secretariats flanking the Great Court. Off to one side as something of an afterthought was the circular Council House for the legislative chambers. Lutyens originally designed four cultural buildings appropriate for the avenue, but only the India Record Office was actually built. The other structures lining the way between the Secretariats and the Arch are guest houses for members of parliament. Of course the Indian princes wondered where they fit into the picture. The answer was: peripherally. The most important, such as Hyderabad and Baroda, were given sites on Princes Park, around the statue of King George, others were distanced according to their place in the pecking order.[69]

Most of the area extending to the north and south of Kingsway was set aside for the residences of officials, although some staff had houses on the vast viceregal estate itself. They were housed by rank and race. Thus bungalows of junior European officials ("thin white") stood on higher ground above junior Indians ("thin black"), with houses of senior officers ("rich/fat white") still higher. Even individual roads were segregated by rank, so that those in the know registered exactly the grade of the residents in the bureaucratic pyramid.[70] Lutyens and his colleagues built more than five hundred bungalows, each set in a spacious lawn (how spacious, of course, depending on one's status).[71]

With so much land at his disposal, not only could Lutyens mete out residences to each according to his station, he could also realize his own vision of the garden city. Both Hardinge and Herbert Baker claim that at the same time plans were made for the new capital, they were also made for the improvement of the old city: remedying the defective sanitation system, laying out gardens and lawns, repairing roads, and beautifying the surroundings of famous monuments such as the tombs of Humayun, Safdar Jung, and the Lodi emperors, along with "many smaller tombs and old gardens with their baradaris," which "we were able to embrace in our plans for the larger city; and by restoration and care of their gardens, groves, and fountains, as far as the limitations of water and cost would allow, to bring back some of their former glory."[72] Foremost among these sites was Lady Willingdon Park, named for Lutyens's nemesis, which incorporated the Lodi Tombs. After independence it was renamed Lodi Garden.[73]

Nevertheless, the new city was built entirely separate, indeed, insulated, from the old, an echo of the White Towns and Black Towns of the early presidency cities.[74] A glance at photographs from the 1930s to the present—and even more graphically a satellite view via Google Earth—makes vividly clear not only the contours of the imperial city but also how it contrasts with Old Delhi: low housing density, wide streets, and, above all, trees (Fig. 52). Kingsway was a vast park, laid out with reflecting pools in the Great Place filled to the brim; broad canals stretching the length of the avenue; riding paths reminiscent of Hyde Park; trees providing shade for the tracts of greensward.[75] The European quarter, stretching from Connaught Place in the north to Safdar Jung's tomb in the south, "presents the aspect of a forest," as Robert Byron wrote already in 1931. "Each house is set in a compound of two to three acres, whose trees have matured in ten years and will become enormous in twenty."[76]

Lutyens and Mustoe oversaw the selection of trees for the major avenues with the same care bestowed upon the viceroy's gardens, but probably unaware that tree-planting, imperial or otherwise, had a venerable history: "Plant a tree, dig a well, write a book, and go to Heaven," ran the folk adage.[77] European travelers in Mughal India remarked on the trees that lined the major routes leading from Agra and Delhi. The road from Agra to Lahore,

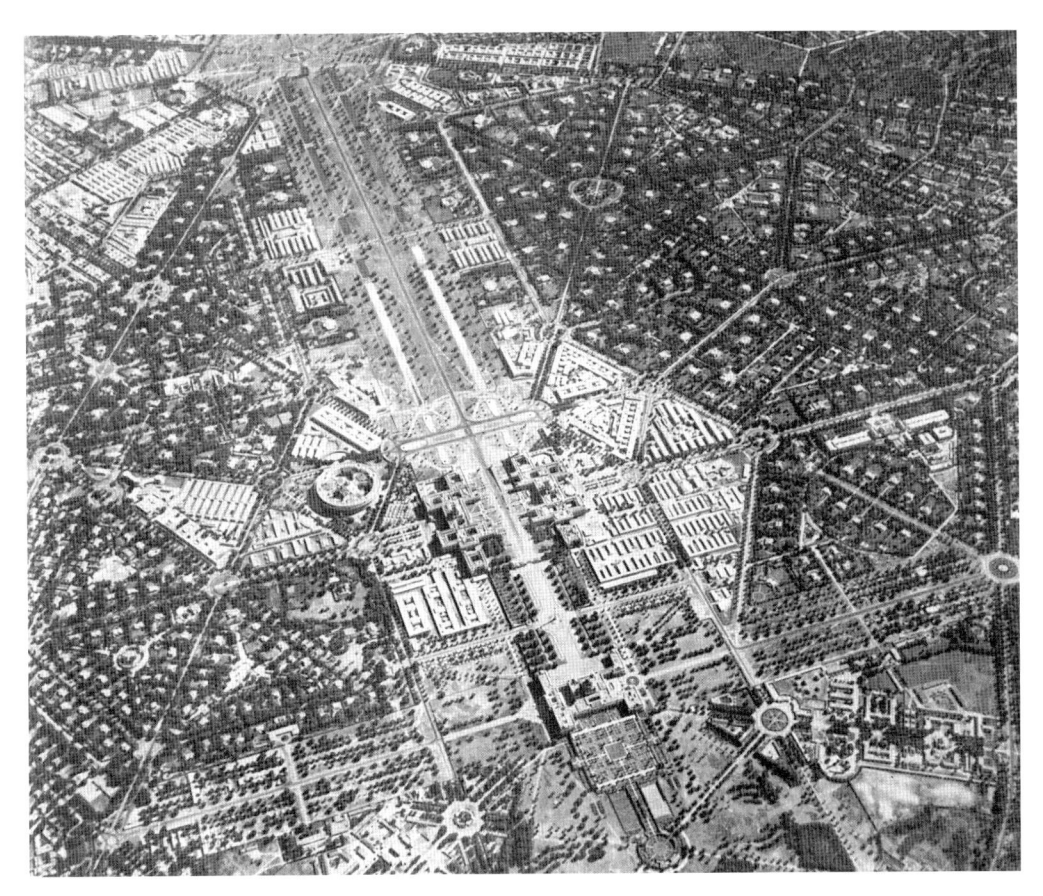

Fig. 52. Aerial view of New Delhi
[Center for South Asian Studies, Cambridge University]

noted Roe, was planted on both sides with trees "like a delicate walke."[78] They do not mention the types of trees chosen, but Jean-Baptiste Tavernier comments that not all survived. In fact, it was not easy to find species adapted to the climate of northern India, trees that could provide maximum shade but also adapt to Delhi's extremes of temperature, the dust, and the "loo," the hot, dry winds that blew from the deserts of Rajasthan. A nursery was created at the Talkatora Gardens, once a small Mughal garden but in a tumbled-down state until Mustoe took charge. Here he experimented with various trees, and tried them out in gardens of larger government houses before planting a whole avenue. Walter George, an architect and landscape designer who worked closely with Mustoe, has left a fascinating account of how avenues, buildings, and trees were designed together as much as possible—and the fiascos that resulted when they weren't. Inevitably, there were many frustrations. For one thing, the planters could not get the engineers to decide how far apart to place street lights. For another, allowances had to be made for roundabouts, most of which had been determined by then, but also for the gates of individual plots, which had not.

When they began their work, New Delhi had no unfiltered water supply. Mustoe had to reopen old wells that had been filled in, using bullock carts and *bhistis* (water carriers) to transport the water to the trees. Next he had to devise a system of six-foot-long taper pipes, three of them sunk around each tree, so that the water would reach all the way down to the roots; watering on the surface alone would cause the roots to turn upward. He also had to take into account that fill had been used in many places and that this would be apt to settle. His solution was to observe plots through at least one monsoon season, preferably two, before planting any trees, to see how much settling occurred. "In this manner," George explains, "road by road, the tree-planting of New Delhi was done, beginning in the cold weather of 1919/20, and was mainly completed by the cold weather of 1924/25, except for certain roads which had not yet been formed, because the area was not free."[79]

In the end only eight kinds of trees were chosen for the main thoroughfares; none was native to Delhi except for the *amaltas* planted later along Akbar Road. Almost entirely missing were many North Indian favorites such as mangoes and *shisham*.[80] Perhaps the most unusual, and controversial, aspect of New Delhi's tree planting was the decision to plant a single species per avenue. For the Processional Way, the planners' preferred term for Kingsway, Lutyens wanted the biggest tree available to match its monumental scale. The *imli* or tamarind was the initial choice but was turned down in the end in favor of the *jamun* or its close relative, the *rai jamun*.[81] It is a tall spreading tree that takes about eighty years to reach full maturity and produces small fruit. Tamarind trees, with an expected lifespan of five hundred years, were planted along Akbar Road, although their small leaves did not provide much shade; other favored trees were the *neem, ficus, peepal,* and *arjun.*

George defended the practice of using a single type tree along Kingsway against critics who charged that it was monotonous:

> If the intention is to create the impression of spaciousness, or unlimited space, and of order within that space, then such a scheme as this

will produce it as no other will. In my opinion, and in that of other Horticulturalists, this is a most masterly piece of planting. From any point in the area, the eye is free to range to infinity, and is not confined between long rows of trees; everywhere, the eye sees groups of trees, with specimen trees standing free, showing their full shapes, but still there remains an indefinable feeling of order, although the order cannot be identified; the effect produced is of freedom within order, the highest possible achievement in design, comparable with Shakespeare's blank verse or even with the freedom within order which is the secret of the universe.

Later he adamantly opposed proposals to increase plantings—maybe even add peach trees—along the Processional Way: "If the main characteristic of New Delhi, which is spaciousness, is to be preserved, then 'hands off.'" Further encroachment of any sort, he warned with perhaps some exaggeration, and "the finest street in Asia" would turn into another Chandni Chowk, "a narrow crowded street confined by slums."[82]

George did acknowledge that elsewhere the roadside trees were sometimes a bit too uniform, allowing that it would have been nice to have more variety but that "what was known and available had to be planted."[83] As it was, some of the species did not thrive or grew so thickly that they blocked views of Safdar Jung's tomb or the radial approaches to the Secretariats. The problem was compounded by the unchecked planting and rampant growth of shrubberies, which in time contended all too successfully with the roadside trees, hiding the houses behind them and in the end making all neighborhoods look so much alike that the stranger was hard put to it to find his way.

Public gardens compensated for the lack of variety in tree planting along the avenues. In more sheltered locations it was possible to grow trees not suitable for exposed spaces. Thus, at the center of Connaught Place's concentric circles of shops a large lawn was laid out with a fountain in the middle and an array of trees, many of them with brilliant blossoms: flamboyants, *gulmohurs, ashupals,* and *maruls,* as well as the ubiquitous *jamun.*[84] There were lawns and flowerbeds in the Viceroy's Court, in the Great Court between the two Secretariats and in their north and south approaches; gardens within the circular Council Hall; and gardens around the War Memorial. Roundabouts often served as mini-parks, sometimes protecting historic monuments.[85] An awed visitor described the imperial capital as he found it during the monsoon season in 1937: "The layout is superb. . . . Its beautiful roads lined with trees from all parts of India, its long vistas of lights at evening, down roads that seem never ending—its velvety lawns and wealth of gorgeous flowers all combine to makes a memory picture and must be seen to be believed."[86]

Official and princely houses matched the public display. Residents added flowers and shrubs and trees to their bungalow sites with just the zeal anticipated by the Planning Committee's report. The Chief Engineer for Imperial Delhi, Teja Singh Malik, included in his spacious garden examples of each of the trees chosen by Mustoe and Lutyens for the city's avenues, as well as lawn and flowers and potted plants.[87] During the Second World War, a nurse billeted with a family on Akbar Road described the beautiful garden where she often chose to sleep: "I enjoyed those long still nights in the garden with the scent from the flowers—nicotine, stocks, flowering frangipani—perfuming the air." Like Hindu and Mughal gardens of old, it had evidently been planted for both day and night. In the loveliness of the moonlight, white flowers were dazzling and all other colors whitened.[88]

Mustoe's agenda also embraced the afforestation of the Ridge. In 1911–12 there were no trees on the Ridge, only scrub; the rest was bare rock. Lutyens had it all declared a Forest Area, protected against any cutting without permission, and Mustoe set to work finding trees that could withstand the harsh conditions. He at last settled on Mexican Morn as more drought resistant than any Indian species. Once this became established, other species could be planted. By 1939 virtually the entire Ridge had been planted.[89]

"A Majestic Garden"

"Sifting the layers of memory," Christopher Hussey observes, "gardens form the connecting background rather than the buildings in [Edwin Lutyens's life]; the lovely sequence from Miss Jekyll's at Munstead Wood to the enameled carpets of Delhi, gardens of which the geometry left nothing to chance yet the forms and colours of nature were given their freedom, and the shapes of trees seen to greater advantage for their harmonized surroundings." These elements, he adds, were Lutyens's "first love . . . and remained a prime inspiration of his creative invention." Delhi itself might be seen as a "majestic garden," presaging the aging architect's vision of a new London rising from the ashes of the Blitz in World War II.[90]

It may seem strange to characterize thus the man who created the world's greatest imperial capital. Although the early Surrey houses of the Lutyens/Jekyll partnership have an intimate and domestic atmosphere that is remote from the Viceroy's House in New Delhi, certain aesthetic principles remained constant threads in his work. Most importantly, the triad of house, garden, and site form an organic whole. Ideally, the site inspires the initial concept, then, "gardens spring from the doors and windows of the house"—from the rear, since the front was designed primarily as an introduction to the house. Then both gradually revealed themselves, with elements of architecture such as pergolas reappearing in the garden. Brown writes of "that magic point where the house met the garden, and the beguiling could begin. In stepping on to the terrace, the multi-dimensional, sensual world of the garden began to assert its power."[91]

Indeed, the terrace was a central feature in Lutyens's gardens. Not only did it "settle" a house into its site, but it also provided just the right venue for tea, as indispensable a convention in India as in Surrey.[92] In the Viceroy's House, one steps out from the West Loggia onto the grassy terrace with a paved walk down the center leading to an intimate patio, the terrace serving as prelude to the formal vastness of the state garden. In practice, the western exposure must have limited al fresco tea parties to the winter months; at other times, tea could be taken in the West Loggia, the great verandah designed to provide the transition from house to garden. Other smaller loggias within the palace opened onto interior courts, and there were views of the Mughal Garden from the State Dining Room and State Ballroom, but the West Loggia was the most important, occupying the center of the west or garden front. With an enormous sixty-five-foot-long barrel vault ceiling, it faced the garden through a row of coupled columns; between them fountain basins were set in the sills. Intended as the intersection of house and garden, it is in Hussey's view "the most enchanted of all these architectural lungs that interpenetrate the palace."[93]

It is tempting to compare the loggia with Mughal pavilions that serve much the same purpose as zones of transition. Perhaps because the nomadic Mughals began with gardens and temporary structures, only gradually evolving toward stone pavilions, the buildings of the Red Fort have a lightness and openness entirely lacking in the loggias of the Viceroy's House—Anisha Mukherji aptly refers to the former as "flexible stone tents." The Red Fort is dominated by one-story pavilions, connected to each other by colonnades and gardens, rather than by a single freestanding palace (see Pl. 25). Formerly, awnings and canopies extended the pavilions into the garden, enfolding its fountains and runnels of water and providing coolness and shade in the Delhi heat. Screens and water in turn projected shifting patterns and reflections which made external space function virtually like a building. The result was permeability between interior and exterior, an interpenetration of house and garden, so that it was hard to tell where one ended and the other began. All of which contrasts with western concepts of the relationship between a palace and its gardens, where the boundary between outside and inside is "more definite and acute" even when views and openings are carefully calculated.[94] As we have seen, Shah Jahan enhanced this effect by carrying the garden right into the buildings of the fort: decorating floors and walls with inlaid floral patterns. Lady Willingdon, for her part, accentuated the westernness of the Viceroy's House by glazing the loggias.[95]

Capitals of Empire

The imperial impulse to build monumental capitals has a long history. What seems surprising, indeed, is that Mughal and Briton came to it so late in India. Calcutta, Madras, and Bombay just grew, with little coherent planning, as did most other colonial cities.[96] Bangalore was an exception, being both a "garden city" and, to a large extent, a planned city.[97] Of Mughal emperors, Babur and Jahangir were far more interested in creating gardens, for both aesthetic and political reasons. True, Akbar had expressed his catholic tastes in architecture and religion in his short-lived capital of Fatehpur Sikri, but it was left for his grandson Shah Jahan to implement an actual vision of urbanism in the service of court life and imperial spectacle. Sylvia Crowe characterizes the city of Shahjahanabad as "magnificent in scale, highly sophisticated in character, and executed with a wholly imperial disregard of cost."[98] The same might be said of New Delhi, although to Lutyens's frustration the cost could not be wholly disregarded. Shahjahanabad drew on an architectural vocabulary reaching back to Cyrus's garden at Pasargadae (sixth century B.C.E.), refined in Persia, and stamped with the Mughals' own fusion of Muslim and Hindu elements.[99]

Shah Jahan was looking over his shoulder at Shah Abbas's capital of Isfahan, just as Lutyens could not ignore Washington. Both Shahjahanabad and New Delhi are laid out according to rigid patterns of geometry and conceived of as new creations in the landscape rather than reconstructions of older centers, although New Delhi nods in passing to the remnants of earlier cities.

In keeping with their roots in the Western classical tradition, however, the planners of New Delhi chose an acropolis-like height, even if Raisina Hill is not as lofty as they might have wished. This was intended to guarantee that it would be the focal point of city planning and that it would not be blocked or overshadowed by any neighboring structure. In Shahjahanabad, it is the Jama Masjid that rises above the surrounding city, tangential to the major thoroughfare, the Chandni Chowk, which leads to the Red Fort. The riverfront location of the fort provides not only a modicum of protection but also ensures that nothing can rise behind it to detract from its preeminence. Equally important, it places the fort squarely in the Mughal tradition of the riverfront garden.

But there are other major differences between the cities that relate especially to the disposition of open spaces and gardens. Shah Jahan began planning for his new city by acquiring large tracts of mainly agricultural land around the future fort. He then gave gifts of land as rewards to his favorites, keeping some of it as royal properties. Much of it was planted in gardens and orchards that were exempt from taxation, effectively creating a green belt around the built areas. To provide water for irrigation, he supervised the construction of a vast network of canals, repairing and extending the skeleton already in place. Once the fort was completed, princes and *amirs* built great houses with their walled gardens, and larger gardens were added throughout the city. Most of these gardens, like the gardens within the Red Fort, were private, but they were opened at certain times of the year. There were no suburbs as such, but rather large royal and aristocratic preserves, gardens and hunting lodges outside the city walls.

Within the city, bazaars, workshops, mosques, and private residences coexisted cheek-by-jowl. There was no real segregation between rich and poor. The luxurious houses of the rich could be found in virtually all parts of the city, interspersed with the mud and thatch houses of the poor. François Bernier saw both great opulence and great squalor when he visited in 1638. Those who were neither very rich nor very poor lived in *havelis* that tightly lined the narrow lanes leading to the wider streets of the bazaars. Typically, the upper stories of these houses projected out over the street, almost meeting their neighbors across the way and providing welcome shade and protection from rain. Invisible from the street, verandahs opened onto interior courtyards usually planted with trees, creating what one writer has termed "an introverted Garden City."[100]

Contrast this pattern of high-density urbanism with the low density of New Delhi, where *all* the streets were wide, not only the vast, parklike main thoroughfares. Reflecting British ambivalence toward "trade," commerce was banished to Connaught Place, and industry and manufacturing were absent altogether. There was no provision for the poor save for the army of servants attached to the Viceroy's House. It was ostentatiously a city of administrators, living in self-contained residential "colonies" that were virtual bowers of greenery. One-story villas were detached from each other and set well back from the street in the midst of a lawn with garden behind. Roads were clean and quiet, conspicuous more for automobile than pedestrian traffic. Once Mustoe's trees had matured, they helped to compensate for the heat-absorbing expanses of black asphalt. Nowadays many residents of New Delhi live in flats rather than bungalows, but as Sunand Prasad observes, the design of the flats "subscribes to the same values as the villas," that is, a preoccupation with "space, light and greenery and display." They differ from the older *havelis* in their freestanding, outward orientation—curiously public in contrast to the private, inward orientation of Mughal urban architecture.[101]

One of the main critiques leveled against New Delhi as conceived and executed by Lutyens and Baker and their associates was that it was not really a city at all but a glorified cantonment, with its civil and military "lines," its government house, and its clubs, set apart, as cantonments always had been, from India itself. Yes, its avenues were verdant oases in the best tradition of the "garden city," but they were also devoid of street life because there was little to attract it. Such was the lack of urban vitality that "at night dogs come out of the houses to sleep in the streets where they are guaranteed an undisturbed peace." Another critic refers to the "Crusoe-like individualism of the scattered and formless bungalow compounds." Kingsway might be grand for ceremonial pomp and circumstance, but it led nowhere anyone wanted to go.[102] At best, it was very much like England on a Sunday, with families picnicking on the greensward while their children vied with the monkeys for the fruit of the *jamun* trees, walkers bestrode the footpaths, or equestrians cantered on the bridal trails.

Even Patwant Singh, who had such happy memories of growing up in 1930s New Delhi (his family was very much involved in the construction of the city), acknowledged that it lacked the "pulsating life of a typical Indian city with its *kuchhas, katras,* and *mohallas* (traditional neighbourhoods and meeting places); its *galis* and *havelis* (narrow lanes and old houses with their interior courtyards); its tantalizing temptations and spaces teeming with life, leavened with history and offering continuity as well as emotional and nostalgic fulfillment." For this, one had to go to Chandni Chowk in the old city: "so chaotic, so crowded, so colorful, so demented, so full of life and excitement and so noisy, so marvelously cacophonous—the very antithesis of the Raj Path," in the words of the architectural critic Peter Blake. "Nobody had designed it, and yet it was the only place really worth being in. . . . It was what urban life was all about."[103]

For all their differences Lutyens and Shah Jahan found common ground in their love of imposing symmetry and geometric patterns on the landscape, and in treating house and garden as one. Hussey saw the Mughal Garden in the Viceroy's House as a "wonderful affirmation of the power of intellect over nature, in this case an arid, treeless, rocky, and inhospitable nature."[104] Here Lutyens created a mosaic of plants, trees, water, walkways, and lawn that Babur might have recognized when he set out to tame the disordered and dusty wastes of Hindustan. But gardens were not mere "pleasaunces." They also encoded notions of what it meant to be civilized and justified the rule of one people over another. Shah Jahan was an imperialist to the marrow, giving the Mughal ideology of "garden imperialism" its most extreme expression. His palace was a garden wherein he threw down the gauntlet to Spring itself, perhaps even to Paradise.

Lutyens, on the contrary, was an indifferent imperialist, unlike his erstwhile partner, Herbert Baker. He was first and foremost a folly builder—and in Nikolaus Pevsner's view the Viceroy's House "beats any other folly in the world." Only to the extent that his ideas of gardens and their place in domestic and public space distilled a very English synthesis of tradition, and to the extent that he believed this tradition could and should be imposed on subject peoples, could he be called an imperialist. As Robert Byron observed, "If the Viceroy steps out to pick a rose, he can look up to find the very horizon in deferential alignment with himself. Such is a proper setting for a ruler." "But," he adds, "the architect has given his heart to the pansies as well."[105] If, in the end, Lutyens did incorporate elements of indigenous architecture and garden design—Ridley refers to his style of Indian motifs within the framework of western classicism as a variant on "Hobson-Jobson" (the Anglo-Indian argot)—he was drawn as much to Buddhist architectural forms as Islamic or Hindu, although Buddhism had long since disappeared from India. But his criteria were above all aesthetic, not political. He was in fact supremely apolitical all his life. Nevertheless, as work on the capital dragged on through the 1920s, even he could not escape doubts about the longevity of the British imperium in the face of escalating nationalism.[106]

The creation of New Delhi was without question a monumental achievement. The architectural critic Peter Blake labeled it a "vast, overwhelming, mindboggling statement about who was who and what was what—a staggering demonstration of British imperial power."[107] And a staggering demonstration of cultural hubris as well in imposing the alien aesthetics of the English garden city on India, from the majestic Kingsway, essentially sterile for all its trees and greenswards and canals, to the "gigantism" of the Viceroy's House and garden, to the myriad bungalows on their oversized plots of lawn. By the time New Delhi was formally inaugurated in 1931, the triumphalism of December 1911 already seemed the echo of a distant age. Sixteen years later the era of the Raj would end and New Delhi would join the roll call of earlier imperial capitals that had risen and fallen in India.

CHAPTER 9

The Legacy

THE ENGLISH garden legacy put down roots in India long before that nation achieved independence in 1947. In 1843 Baron von Orlich noted that the rajah of Bhurtpore, installed and educated by East India Company officials, had laid out "an uncommonly pleasant villa, surrounded by four small flower-gardens . . . solely for the use of the English who visit him." Other rajahs followed his lead, no doubt aware that this was a good way to curry favor with their rulers but perhaps intrigued also by exotic motifs, as Lucknow's rulers had been. Maharaja Sayajirao III brought over a gardener from Kew to design the gardens for his Indo-Saracenic palace of Laxmi Vilas in Baroda, described by one commentator as "laid out like a Willow Pattern tea set": neat walkways, flowerbeds, and a trelliswork summerhouse inspired by Victorian glass conservatories (Fig. 53). In 1927 the Nawab of Rampur held a garden party for the viceroy, Lord Irwin, who in fact hated garden parties. Irwin commented that the Nawab had delusions of grandeur, laying out gardens on the scale of Versailles with "great vistas of lawn and trees and fountains and what not."[1] The novelist Louis Bromfield

Fig. 53. Laxmi Vilas Palace, southeast view, Baroda, 1895.
Curzon Collection, photographer unknown
[The British Library Board, Photo 430/24(16)]

knew whereof he wrote with his word-picture of the Maharaja of Ranchipur's palace park: "The park itself, with banyans and mangoes and eucalyptus trees and palms taking the place of the elms and oaks and cedars of an English park, was no less fantastic than the palace. In the beginning the Scotch gardener employed by the Maharani had tried, stubbornly and with heroism, to make English plants and shrubs and trees grow in the reddish heavy soil, but in the end India would have none of them and one by one they shriveled and died beneath the burning sun."[2]

Gardens as Public Spaces

From princely garden to public park proved a short step. By the time the grounds of the Victoria Memorial Hall were opened in 1921, the idea of the public park was no longer a novelty. The gardens of precolonial India had been the resort of elites, both Hindu and Muslim, open at very rare times to the public, such as the anniversary of Mumtaz Mahal's death in the case of the Taj. In Great Britain access to the great gardens was largely a nineteenth-century phenomenon. When Paxton's gardens at Chatsworth were open to all on bank holidays, special trains brought visitors from all over the Midlands. Civic-minded Victorians went beyond this, creating public parks in London and throughout the provinces as places of wholesome recreation, with sports grounds and lakes for boating, vast greenswards, and acres of brilliant carpet bedding.

In India it became the mark of an enlightened ruler to follow suit. Maharaja Ganga Singh of Bikaner, for example, laid out a thirty-five-acre public park early in the twentieth century. Like English parks, it had its monuments: at the same time that a Tower of Glory recalled the past feats of Bikaner arms, the Queen Empress Gates, Minto Terrace, and Egerton Tank (Egerton had been the Maharaja's old tutor) reminded strollers of present colonial realities. Baroda, too, boasted a public park, described by Sir Edwin Arnold in 1886 as "a charming expanse of flower-gardens, lawns, and pools, established for the use and enjoyment of the citizens." In Jaipur, Maharaja Ram Singh surrounded Swinton Jacob's Indo-Saracenic Albert Hall—a "vast and awful museum"—with lovely ornamental gardens.[3]

The Sajjan Niwas Bagh in Udaipur began as a private park-cum-botanic garden but was opened to the public about the same time as that in Bikaner. The garden consisted of formal beds running along an extensive, if problematic, lawn, and it pioneered the introduction of English annuals and vegetables to Rajasthan. It had the quasi-obligatory hall commemorating Queen Victoria's Jubilee, as well as a bandstand, fountains, and a pond created expressly for the *Victoria amazonica*. Annual flower shows encouraged local interest in horticulture.[4] Perhaps the most spectacular public garden, however, is Krishnaraja Sagara (Brindavan Gardens), named for the Maharaja of Mysore and part of an ambitious irrigation scheme. It was the brainchild of the engineer Sir Mokshagundam Visvesvaraya, who built the dam in 1924, and Sir Mirza Ismail, who subsequently laid out the hillside garden with its blend of Mughal and English plantings and its colorful fountains (see Pl. 26).[5]

After independence many of these public parks, along with the botanical gardens (which doubled uneasily as parks), fell on hard times for lack of funds. Visiting Jaipur where he had once been prime minister, Sir Mirza found it "heartrending to see what should have been one of the most beautiful parks in India sadly neglected, and fast becoming a wilderness once more." Earlier he had had to defend himself against charges of extravagance for his support of the Brindavan Gardens and beautification projects elsewhere. Invoking the clean, well-kept roads, the tidy gardens and trimmed hedges of England, the great open spaces in crowded London, he exhorted: "How many cities in India can boast of such parks?" And yet public parks and private gardens are both vital to "a full and happy life," and thus "slum clearance and housing of the poor must go on *pari passu* with the beautification schemes; they are inseparable." And, he insisted, amenities can pay for themselves, citing the Brindavan Hotel and Gardens as a prime example. Ironically, the Brindavan Gardens themselves subsequently went through a long period of poor maintenance, with weeds invading the flowerbeds and its illumination and fountains in a "pathetic state" until the provincial government belatedly commissioned a facelift in 2004.[6]

Sir Mirza's views were very much those of a cosmopolitan Indian and were not shared by all. In a heated exchange in Chennai as late as 2000, a city planner charged that proposals for public spaces by a civic group were not "in synch with local attitudes," maintaining, "We don't go to parks like foreigners, we don't have Saturdays and Sundays free, as they do. We don't take walks for recreation, it's not part of our concept of health. For leisure, we spend time with our families." In rebuttal, others argued that if Indians did not use parks, it was because they were in such miserable condition, not because they were "foreign" things.[7] In fact, one of the most profound legacies of the Raj may be the gradual reorientation of urban Indian family life from courtyard to park, from private to public space, in tandem with the democratization and redefinition of notions of leisure. Any nice Sunday finds flocks of Indians, in families, in couples, in random groupings, strolling and picnicking on the lakeside terraces of Mughal gardens in Kashmir, the neat lawns of the Victoria Memorial, the ample greenswards of the Raj Path, and the Disneyfied Lal Bagh of Bangalore (Figs. 54, 55; see Pls. 9, 27).

Thanks in large part to Curzon and his heirs, India's monuments themselves are as much public parks as historical sites. They draw millions of domestic as well as foreign tourists. Their preservation is often a subject of political wrangling, pitting different ideologies and constituencies against

Fig. 54. Victoria Memorial Hall gardens, Kolkata

[Photograph by author]

Fig. 55. Sunday on the Rajpath

[Photograph by author]

each other. The Taj Mahal is only the most conspicuous—and most contentious—example. Since the early 1980s it has been in the eye of a succession of storms that have not yet abated. For almost a century the placid stretches of lawn and orderly rows of cypress remained pretty much as Curzon had ordained, but Agra has grown into a grimy, congested industrial city of 1.3 million, with pollution levels so high that WHO has identified it as a "pollution intensive zone." In 1982 UNESCO designated both the Taj and the Agra Fort as World Heritage Sites, mandating that the government repair existing damage and protect them from future threats. By a neat sleight of hand, the state authorities outsourced the problem to the giant Tata Group, which agreed to keep the monuments in repair in return for permission to develop the two-kilometer strip between them as a "heritage corridor" with restaurants, shopping malls, cyber cafes—all the trappings of a modern tourist Mecca. And no touts, beggars, or snake charmers.

Simultaneously, faculty and students in the Department of Landscape Architecture at the University of Illinois came up with a no less mindboggling plan for a Taj Mahal Cultural Heritage District: a proposal to link the Taj and Agra Fort with other cultural sites such as the Mahtab Bagh (Moonlight Garden) and the tomb of I'timad-ud-Daulah in an expanse of "green parks, orchards and gardens." As tourists moved along the corridor, they would experience constantly unfolding visions, highlighting the "mystery and grandeur of Taj against a changing sky, floating above the waters, and silhouetted against the fields." At its most ambitious, the plan imagined an earth-mound amphitheater with breathtaking views of the Taj as backdrop and a cleaned-up river on which tourists could glide by boat from site to site, like Mughal grandees of old.

Just as Lord Curzon aimed to control the visitor's experience of Mughal masterpieces by imposing his own very English green-park vision, the University of Illinois planners seem to have been equally obsessed with the viewer's "dynamic experience in time." Whatever the nods to mango orchards and peasant farmers, their own "green aesthetic" reflected a late twentieth-century ecosensibility that has been attacked as no less culture-bound than Curzon's, an Orientalist fantasy based on superficial site visits. Why not just dig up the manicured lawns and bougainvillea planted by the "misguided and ill-informed" British, argued a Delhi architect, and replace them with something more like the original shrubs, trees, and flowers? For now, however, all that remains of the showpiece riverfront promenade is the remnant of wall built before a decision by India's Supreme Court halted both plans in 2003; below it lie eighty acres of derelict wasteland. What tourists viewing the Taj Mahal from Agra Fort see is "heaps of stinking garbage, carcasses, graves of children dotting the structure and mounds of rubble that invite mosquitoes, dogs, snakes, crows and vultures."[8]

But this is hardly the end of the Taj saga. The latest scheme calls for two ropeways with gondolas, the first stretching from the Taj across to the Mahtab Bagh, the second from Agra Fort to the Mahtab Bagh to link the Taj to neighboring historic buildings. Ever eager to increase the number of tourists even beyond the 2.5 million who visited in 2008, local officials want to cap the "visitor experience" with a view from a giant Ferris wheel modeled on the London Eye. "Tourism is not everything," protests O. P. Jain, an adviser to the Indian National Trust for Art and Cultural Heritage. "The people who come to see the Taj are not the kind of people who like to go by ropeway or see it in front of a Ferris wheel."[9] It remains to be seen whether the Supreme Court and the Archaeological Survey of India (ASI) will agree. Meanwhile, shrinking greenbelts, massive highway projects, and a falling water table continue to plague the Taj and other Agra monuments. As dust levels rise they cause microscratches in the marble surfaces; these retain moisture and attract pollutants. In effect dust-laden winds from nearby construction sites and the more distant Rajasthan desert are sandblasting the Taj and threatening to turn its pure white marble an unappealing yellow.[10]

Debates surrounding the Taj Mahal have exposed broader conflicts over the meaning of public as well as of "heritage," since they have often arisen over preservation issues, such as the maintenance of temples and monuments, as well as issues of mourning and remembrance. When the Raj Ghat was laid out in New Delhi as a memorial to the recently assassinated Mahatma Gandhi, it no doubt seemed natural to situate the black flower-topped marble platform marking the spot where he was cremated in 1948 within a larger park (see Pl. 28). In time memorials to other national leaders were added, including Jawaharlal Nehru, his daughter Indira Gandhi, and her two sons, along with other prime ministers and presidents of the Republic. They are surrounded by beautiful lawns and plantings and a forest of peace, all designed by Sydney Percy-Lancaster, an Englishman who was born in India and spent his life there as an eminent horticulturalist.[11]

Later memorial parks have become more entangled in India's turbulent politics, religious and secular. Such, for example, is the MGR Memorial Arch overlooking the Chennai marina. One enters through a great curved double arch leading into a small manicured lawn and beyond that a grassy *maidan* over which presides the sculpted bust of the prominent film star turned politician M. G. Ramachandran, known simply as MGR, who served as chief minister of Tamil Nadu from 1977 until his death ten years later. The memorial is awash with political and religious symbolism, all the more complicated because MGR's body is actually buried on the site rather than simply his ashes—his religious views were always ambiguous. Beyond the sacred flame, the open lotus and other icons of traditional religious and political identity, however, it is striking that the setting is a westernized one of landscaped grounds with walkways and serpentine paths meant for strolling and relaxation as well as veneration.[12]

Lucknow, on the other hand, weathered the tumultuous years following independence surprisingly unruffled. As it grew into a sprawling, polluted city of over two million, it lost any claim to being a garden city, but tourists have continued to flock to see the crumbling ruins of *nawabi imambaras* and palaces and, most of all, the pockmarked ruins of the Residency. On August 15, 1947, the day India declared independence from Great Britain, nationalists pulled down the banner that had flown night and day since 1857, but otherwise no one seemed to have a problem with maintaining the Residency and its memorial gardens as a "heritage site" until 2007, the 150th anniversary of the Uprising. On that occasion a furor erupted when a small group of British tourists and scholars, by no means uncritical apologists of empire, came to the city to commemorate the events of 1857. For once Muslims and Hindus were united in their outrage, with more extreme voices calling for Tennyson to be banned entirely from school textbooks in retaliation for his poem extolling the bravery of the defenders of Lucknow.[13] In Cawnpore the gardens are no longer a memorial to the British massacred at the Bibighar: rechristened Nana Rao Park, they now honor the memory of the leaders of the uprising and specifically the man blamed for the massacre of women and children at Satichaura Ghat and then at the Bibighar. Marochetti's *Angel of the Resurrection* and its surrounding screen have been moved to All Souls' Memorial Church for safekeeping. The infamous well has been cemented over.[14]

New Delhi and its gardens have had a mixed legacy. In the turmoil following partition in 1947 the Purana Qila and Humayun's Tomb became huge refugee camps for those fleeing sectarian violence. The camps remained open for some five years during which the gardens suffered extensive damage. Thanks to the Aga Khan Trust, the ASI has been able to embark on an extensive program of restoration not only of its structures, but also of the grounds with their water channels, fountains, and the inevitable lawns, so that the complex is now in far better condition than many of the city's other monuments.[15]

With independence the Viceroy's House was rechristened Rashtrapati Bhavan. The first Indian heads of state were men in the Gandhian mold and found themselves out of place in the vastness of its imperial spaces. President Rajaji lamented, "I am in a zoo and a circus." He found solace in the garden and its flowers: "I never before possessed this wealth . . . but now that I had it for a time I feel sad when I see the little things fade and wither before their harsh father the sun." Dr. Zakir Husain, too, found the garden the only reward for living in what he termed "the belly of this leviathan."[16] And yet the very existence of these gardens contradicted nature, since in the harsh climate of Delhi they lay dried up and lifeless for much of the year.

If palace and garden have largely defied time, Delhi itself has been changing. Most of the city walls were finally pulled down in the decade after independence. The sixty-foot statue of the King-Emperor that crowned the majestic Raj Path (formerly Kingsway) lies forgotten in Coronation Park, once the scene of three imperial durbars, now "an Arthurian wasteland of swamp, mud and camel-thorn."[17] Nevertheless, the lawns along the Rajpath still fill with festive crowds following Republic Day celebrations (held on January 26). But Lutyens's city is showing signs of decay. The legions of trees planted by William Mustoe and Walter George throughout the city have reached the end of their normal life spans; at the same time, volunteer but unwanted *peepal* trees are carving toeholds in the masonry of the Secretariats.[18] And where as late as the early 1980s there was not a skyscraper in sight, now the city is expanding wildly outward and upward. A gleaming high-rise in glass and steel now looms up behind the Rashtrapati Bhavan. The "green lungs" of central Delhi make it the only city center in the world that is several degrees cooler than its periphery, but these will inevitably give way, William Dalrymple warns, to "a miasma of new concrete." Just as the Indian National Trust is proposing to have Lutyens's Delhi designated a UNESCO World Heritage Site, rampant development is destroying both the bungalows of the new city and the *havelis* of the old.[19] Mahatma Gandhi Marg, the noisiest and most polluted stretch of the Ring Road, cuts the Red Fort off from the riverbank. In less than a century, the population of the city has increased from about a quarter of a million to more than 14 million, choking much of the time on dirty air in spite of widespread conversion of buses to CNG (compressed natural gas) and the construction of a widely heralded metro system. Early in the new millennium WHO listed Delhi as the seventh most polluted city in the world; other estimates rank it even worse.[20]

The feverish preparations leading up the Commonwealth Games held in October 2010 conjured up images of Imperial Durbars--indeed some may well have longed for the autocratic hand of a Curzon to bring order to the chaos. The entire city was turned into a construction site; heavy equipment vied with hand labor, bulldozers with women in saris carrying loads on their heads; piles of old debris and new bricks were everywhere. In its plans to ensure a "greener look" for the city, the government out-Mustoed Mustoe: The horticultural department arranged to have some 500,000 plants, from a pool of 41,000 species, ready to bloom during the period of the games. Major thoroughfares were spruced up with luxuriant medians bedecked with flowers. In all, the master plan covered 84 main roads, 19 flyovers and bridges, and 198 traffic circles, all embellished with a variety of plants, shrubs, and grasses drawn from the Roshanara Bagh nurseries: plumerias, bougainvilleas, lantanas, cassias, *neems, ashokas,* hibiscus and many more. When the mayor of Delhi herself went to Bangalore, she was so taken with the Laxmi taru or paradise tree (*Simarouba glauca*) that she ordered four thousand of them to be brought from their native South America, pointing out that they also produce an edible oil. While existing parks were given a facelift, the focus was on beautifying the various sports venues with sixty *lakhs* of potted plants, or 6 million plants. And at the center of it all: Nehru Stadium, a latter-day Rashtrapati Bhavan.[21]

The professed aim was to make Delhi a world-class city, but it also had aspects of a Potemkin village. The municipal government launched a scheme to screen out slums and garbage along the roads to the games with fast growing bamboo trees. More drastically, large tracts of slums along the banks of the Yamuna River were demolished wholesale, their residents resettled twenty-five miles from the city center, if at all. At the same time environmentalists protested the felling of large tracts of trees in the Siri Forest to make way for construction of sports facilities.[22]

And what of the Ridge, so lovingly afforested by William Robertson Mustoe? Like Firoz Shah's before him, Mustoe's labors have largely counted for naught. The Ridge lost its government protection, and what was intended as Delhi's other "vital green lung" has been ruthlessly opened up to speculation and development: a stadium-cum-theater larger than the Roman Colosseum and rarely used, a wireless station, and a network of roads. Two new parks were created without regard for the ecological consequences, uprooting much of Mustoe's carefully nurtured vegetation. Patwant Singh noted: "This self-sustaining ecosystem—a proud friend and benefactor—has been grievously wounded by those it reached out to help. The sight of the Ridge bleeding to death is not only an agonizing reminder of the happy days we spent there, but also of the predatory ways of man." Singh's lament for the Ridge could stand as a lament for much that has been lost in the unchecked development of Delhi in the last decades. Whether a recent Supreme Court injunction against further building on the Ridge will succeed remains to be seen.[23]

The garden legacies of other towns and cities have also faced problems as they have navigated the transition from colonial rule to independence. The shabby, weed-infested Pankot in Paul Scott's *Staying On* catches the down-at-the-heels emptiness of the immediate post-independence period in Simla (now Shimla) and other hill stations. As the remnant of retired colonial personnel died or went back to England, however, these quintessential outposts of Englishness began to take on a new life as holiday destinations for the burgeoning Indian middle class. Now the roads are clogged with Indians escaping from the heat of the "burning plains." No longer the summer capital of the Raj, Shimla has become the year-round capital of the state of Himachal Pradesh, adding to the overbuilding and congestion that were already a problem a century ago. The Viceregal Lodge currently houses the Indian Institute of Advanced Study in its still-stately grounds with their breathtaking views, and *malis* still start tender flowers in its greenhouses.

The brutal history of Kashmir both before and after Indian independence has made a mockery of both Mughal and British paeans to this paradise on earth—a paradise for some, to be sure, but a purgatory for others. Conquered by Akbar, then by Afghans and Sikhs, the land of Lalla Rookh passed into British hands as part of the spoils of the First Sikh War in 1846. The British promptly sold it to the Dogra Maharaja Gulab Singh for 75 *lakhs* of rupees (£750,000) as a reward for turning against his former overlord. A century later many expected it to join Pakistan because of its predominantly Muslim population. This did not happen, nor did a mandated United Nations plebiscite ever take place. Instead Kashmir has been the scene of almost constant conflict and violent repression in the sixty-plus years since. Basharat Peer describes the capital, Srinagar, as a "city of bunkers"—no city in the world, he claims, has a greater military presence.[24]

The princely gardens dotting the hillside shores of Dal Lake have not escaped the turmoil. The Pari Mahal, Dara Shikoh's "Fairies' Palace," was for a time "the world's most beautiful paramilitary camp." Two of the domed chambers in its rough stone walls were converted into barracks; on a higher terrace stood sentries with automatic rifles in a sandbagged watchtower. In a desperate effort to attract foreign tourists, scared off by continued unrest, the government has restored many of Kashmir's gardens, including the Pari Mahal. But if the barracks are gone, the military are still ubiquitous, and the sight of armed soldiers strikes an incongruous note amid the natural and man-made beauty of the surroundings. The gardens retain their original Mughal plan, adapted to set off the spectacular setting: low-walled enclosures (no need to worry here about voyeurs on elephants peering down into *zenana* gardens) with a series of terraces rising from the shore, water-chutes dotted with fountains running down the center, and pavilions straddling the water at each level (see Pl. 9). While lovely old chenars (Oriental plane trees) remain in some of the gardens, one misses the Mughal favorites, the almonds and apricots and quinces that would have delighted eye, nose, and palate. Many of the flowers would still be familiar, but not so the very English arrangements of beds—a far cry from the scatter of spring flowers among fruit trees and cypresses—and the low hedges and topiary; unbroken stretches of lawn have replaced the geometric quadrants of earlier times.[25]

Like the Delhi Ridge, all of the hill stations suffer from the deforestation that began during the Raj and has if anything accelerated since. In Kashmir timber smuggling is a major problem, making its magnificent deodars increasingly rare (and therefore increasingly valuable). No longer can one find wild orchids in the Nilgiri hills; tea and market gardens have replaced meadows and *sholas*. Even the giant silvery eucalyptus and blue-green wattles, both imported from Australia and planted once upon a time by men of the old Madras Army, have been chopped down in what Ooty's memorialist likens to the final act of Chekhov's *Cherry Orchard*, although there have been subsequent attempts at reforestation. Ooty's lake has been shrinking; always a sewer, it is now an even smaller sewer. Luxury hotels dot the hillsides, shopping malls and arcades the town center.[26]

In Madras Lord Clive's sumptuous Government House and its Kew-inspired gardens were rescued once from neglect by Charles Trevelyan in the mid-nineteenth century, but there was no one to save it from the haphazard growth that enveloped it a hundred years later. When Trevelyan's descendant visited it in 1983, the "wilderness" had disappeared, replaced by "typically municipal flowerbeds of love-lies-bleeding and marigolds." Nothing was left of the deer park, and skyscrapers blocked the views of the river.[27] Thomas Munro's beloved Guindy Lodge survives in much better shape as the official residence of the governor of Tamil Nadu, thanks to its distance from the city center and location within a national park, unkempt though it may be (see Fig. 8). Barrackpore has not been so lucky. The gardens have been completely swallowed up—the irony is all too obvious—by barracks, military academies, and firing ranges. When I visited in 2008, it took the determination of a very persistent guide and driver to ferret out the grave of Lady Canning: a small patch of green above a firing range for women soldiers on the river's edge, with cows browsing all about. An equestrian statue of Lord Canning completes the scene, although he is buried far away in England (see Pl. 29).

In spite of the Communist dominance of Bengal politics, Calcutta seems surprisingly comfortable with its imperial past. British Calcutta's favorite watering place, the Tollygunge Club, thrives under new management, now catering to Indian elites (see Pl. 30). The statues of Lord Curzon (fore) and Queen Victoria (aft) welcome strollers to the neatly manicured lawns and colorful flowerbeds of the Victoria Memorial Hall. On a Sunday afternoon one may catch a concert by a bagpipe band, its bandsmen bright in their woolen tartans. Even the gardens of Tagore's youth have been tamed and Jorasanko converted into a family museum and art school.[28]

There are, however, other legacies that are more subtle. In Ooty the Botanical Garden provides an oasis, with its verdant slopes, exotic trees, and floral map of India. Above it, near the greenhouses, is another Rashtrapati Bhavan, once the summer residence of the governor of Madras, now the retreat of the governor of Tamil Nadu. When I visited in 2003, the gardens at Government House were undergoing a welcome restoration. Incidentally, the Ooty Hunt Club, the only hunt club left east of Suez, still rides to hounds, its committee members resplendent in the knee-length scarlet coats with green collar designed in 1907 by a British army officer. The club's membership is 95 percent Indian, the quarry is the jackal rather than the fox, and it is billed as probably the world's fastest hunt.[29] The neighboring station of Coonor may not have a hunt club, but amid the tourist development Lady Canning's Seat remains a popular destination for walkers—the outcropping she so loved for its richness of vegetation, its panorama of hills and distant plain. These days the hills are covered with tea plantations, and Lady Canning herself may be as little known to Coonor's visitors as she is to Calcutta's. Meanwhile, the ghosts of many an English gardener still haunt the Indian countryside, like the old English lady who used to live in a cottage in Ooty and is still seen occasionally, "an unalarming phantom pottering approvingly among the flowers."[30]

Paradoxically, Bangalore has moved from garrison town to high-tech capital of India without losing its preeminence in the garden world. The Lal Bagh is still the leading botanical garden in the Deccan, proudly boasting of its founding by Tipu Sultan; plant-lovers from all over India still flock to its biannual flower shows and order stock from its nurseries. Visitors entering the main gate are greeted by a flower clock and a bevy of garden gnomes (see Pl. 27). In England, the presence of garden gnomes was taken as an almost sure sign of Tory sympathies, but it is not clear what they signify here.[31] Although most of Bangalore's idiosyncratic bargeboard bungalows have fallen into disrepair or been replaced with apartment blocks, some Indian gardeners, such as Mrs. Subbanna, have stoutly carried on the city's horticultural traditions. Her award-winning garden at Lalitadiri is a riot of flowers set in a neatly trimmed lawn; minute silvery cascades ripple down from a miniature waterfall and red lotus dot the serene lotus pond. Ferns and orchids trail from pots hanging on the verandah and she has made a rose garden behind the house.[32]

The "heritage gardens" of top-range hotels have capitalized on Raj nostalgia. No Indian hotel with any pretensions is without its lawns and neat flowerbeds, preferably stocked with English flowers. The Imperial Hotel in the heart of New Delhi boasts of its three acres of "lush greens" (read: struggling *doob* grass), Royal palms, ferns, flowers, shrubs, and legions of potted plants (see Pl. 31). The Taj West End in Bangalore goes this one better by advertising twenty acres of landscaped gardens. In Shimla the more modest garden terrace of the old-fashioned Clarke's Hotel at the eastern end of the Mall clings to the precipitous hillside. One of the most appealing of the

Raj-era gardens, however, is that of the cozy Savoy Hotel in Ooty, with its inviting lawns, cheerful flowers, and trellised doorways—to be sure, showcase lawns and familiar flowers are a good deal easier to lay on in the hills than on the plains. In Rajasthan hotel gardens are more apt to invoke Mughal models; witness the Lake Palace in Udaipur and the Rambagh in Jaipur, both converted palaces.

The English garden aesthetic has also been perpetuated in such Raj imports as courts of law and the campuses of colleges and universities, with their eclectic but essentially British architecture and landscaping. As the novelist and essayist Pankaj Mishra describes Varanasi University: "Set in the middle of large lawns and gardens, the buildings look like products of an extravagant imagination . . . all jumbled together in stone." If anything, the old campus of Mumbai University is the product of an even more extravagant imagination (see Pl. 32). The modern information technology campuses spreading across the country are heir to these universities, boasting manicured lawns and plantings, to say nothing of putting greens and recreational facilities that universities could never dream of. The website for India's National Aerospace Laboratories (NAL) proclaims that one of its great joys is its gardens and that "a picturesque garden supplements an ideal workplace." On the main campus there is a rose garden in front of the administrative block, "well-mowed . . . lawns and the dense collection of big trees opposite the systems block." A subsidiary campus is wilder, with a park built around a historical temple. Every year, the site declares, the NAL gardens receive a host of prizes from the Bangalore Urban Art Commission.[33]

Just as they once were indispensable attributes of palaces, gardens have become badges of corporate modernity in contemporary India. Borrowing from the almost formulaic models of ASI-landscaped monuments, they feature verdant expanses of green, graveled or cemented paths lined with flowerbeds or low hedges, and occasional trees and flowering shrubs. By extension the same is true of new megatemples, such Delhi's Akshardham Temple on the south bank of the Yamuna River adjacent to the Commonwealth Games athletes' village. Completed in 2005 with major corporate support as well as the volunteer efforts of thousands, it is dedicated to the memory of Bhagwan Swaminarayan, whose life and teachings are celebrated in a state-of-the-art two-hour multimedia presentation, along with a resolutely nationalist overview of Indian history. While the complex invokes traditional Hindu motifs

THE LEGACY

with an infinitude of carved reliefs and colonnades, it bears little resemblance to classical Indian temples such as the great Meenakshi Temple in Madurai. Where Meenakshi encloses a modest garden framing a pool around which extends a labyrinth of shrines to individual deities, the Akshardham *mandir* (temple) sits in the midst of a vast hundred-acre site with the by now clichéd "beautifully manicured lawns." In the midst of these are gardens, fountains, a colossal eight-petaled "lotus-shaped creation," and sixty-five bronze statues of India's great men, women, and children: "child gems, valorous warriors, national figures and great women personalities." Indeed, Akshardham is as eclectic in its spirituality as in its landscaping.[34]

Gardens as Private Spaces

Gardens are not always motivated by politics or appeals to heritage. They may not even be politically correct. Take, for example, the case of Jawaharlal Nehru, the man with the signature red rose in his lapel. Nehru spent much of the 1930s in various prisons as a result of his agitation against British rule in India. During a term in Almora jail in 1934–35 he developed an interest in the natural world. "Latterly," he wrote, "I have felt drawn more and more towards nature—to plants and animals. Maybe it is a relief and an escape from human folly, human cowardice and human knavery." The possibilities for gardening were limited in the dusty plains of the United Provinces where he first found himself, but when he was later jailed at Dehra Dun, in the foothills of the Himalayas, he again turned to gardening. With official permission, he transformed a portion of the prison yard into a flower garden and was able to grow from seed a variety of classic English flowers: sweet peas, hollyhocks, nasturtiums, candy-tuft, lupines, stocks, and dianthus. Fellow prisoners helped him in his labors—he was amused by their mangling of English names: hollyhock, for example, came out as "Ali Haq." He loved gardening, he confessed, not just for the beauty of the flowers but for the contact with the "soft warm earth." Only three years after his last imprisonment, he found himself living in Teen Murti House, built two decades earlier as the residence of the British commander-in-chief in Lutyens's New Delhi. It was all rather too imperial for his tastes even as prime minister of the now-independent India, but the cabinet insisted that he have an appropriate residence. His consolation was an unimpeded view of its lovely lawns and gardens from his study window.[35]

Nehru's love of English flowers and gardens has been shared by many of his fellow citizens; how many it is impossible to say. In Coorg in the 1970s, the travel writer Dervla Murphy found an Indian coffee planter's wife who, starting from bare ground, created "what can only be described as a mini-Kew."[36] Another devotee is C. P. Sujaya, a retired civil servant who divides her time between Delhi and Shimla. Sujaya fell in love with English gardens and English flowers as a child. She explains that Agatha Christie was one of her great inspirations, for "her books may be about murders but she had a fondness for writing about flowers, especially sweet peas, the vicar's wife always won first prize." Indeed, she recounts, an "addiction to English novels as a young child (as a part of the colonization process!) growing up in Kerala had sowed the seeds of pansies and sweet peas . . . snapdragon and larkspur, stock and carnations, daffodils, etc., in my mind long, long before I had a glimpse of them when I went up North after my marriage." None of them grew in the south, so that when she actually saw these flowers for the first time she was "absolutely bowled over."

When Sujaya retired in 2003 there was at last the leisure to create a garden in the small plot surrounding her new house in Shimla, but it has not been smooth sailing, with much trial and error. Azaleas, "always reminiscent of Daphne Du Maurier and *Rebecca*," have proven recalcitrant, but she hopes to see them flower some day. She has a great many pots and hanging baskets, filled especially with giant pansies and freesias, although they require a lot of attention. Primroses flourish in the spring, just when she is in Delhi to escape the cold of Shimla, but in September one has the rare treat of pansies blooming. The gardener's life is much easier in the south, where luxuriant perennials just keep growing; as she notes ruefully, "it is certainly much more burdensome to have a garden in a temperate clime—you have to plan much more." She has tried importing crotons all the way from Bangalore, hoping they would thrive in the atrium of their home, with its protective roof of transparent polycarbonate. Alas, they didn't survive the winter, but the primroses and chrysanthemums put on a good show. For sweet peas, she relies on seeds from her daughter in the United States and some from the United Kingdom.

Finding a reliable *mali* has been a nightmare. She has discovered that Indian *malis* suffer from a lack of self-esteem, feeling that working outside is much inferior to working inside—that, equal though the skills demanded may be, it is a far, far better thing to work in the kitchen than in the garden.

The same young man who serves her guests with panache when they drop by in the evening is miserable when working in the garden, hating every minute of it. "So in spite of the Brits leaving us this special legacy of 'English' flowers," she comments ruefully, "they haven't empowered the *malis*."[37]

Perhaps we should leave the final word about the legacy of English gardens to a character in Indian literature, Mrs. Mahesh Kapoor in Vikram Seth's novel *A Suitable Boy* (1993). Decent, kind, affectionate Mrs. Mahesh Kapoor, bullied by her husband, without even a name of her own. But in her garden she is the gentle monarch, a Queen Victoria in her floral realm, although she may have some small differences with her *mali* over level versus uneven expanses of grass. The sweet English flowers she grows in the beds at Prem Nivas flank green springy lawns, the envy of her rivals, whom she routinely bests at flower shows. They coexist with the native flowering trees that add their own brilliance and perfumes to the air. Impatient with her during her lifetime, Mahesh Kapoor finds the garden his only refuge after her death: "a nameless, wordless one, with birdsong its only sound—and it was dominated, when he closed his eyes, by the least intellectualizable sense—that of scent."[38]

CONCLUSION

Garden Imperialism

THUS FAR the focus of this book has been on the life and afterlife of British colonial gardens in India. Now it is time to put them in a larger context and try to tease out what they may tell us about British imperialism itself.

A passion for gardens was by no means limited to India or to the British. Rival powers, such as the French and Dutch, put their own stamp on their imperial landscapes, but none did so on the scale or with such lasting effect as the British. They created botanical gardens that doubled as public parks from Melbourne to St. Vincent, from Zomba in Nyasaland to Aburi in the Gold Coast. Thanks to the garden in Entebbe and its horticultural training programs, Nairobi and Kampala were in the years immediately after independence "the most lavishly flowered towns in the world," in the view of an eminent British garden historian. Where fever-ridden colonials in India retreated to the Himalayas and the Nilgiris, in Malaysia they sought out Penang, in Africa the Jos Plateau of Nigeria and the Eastern Highlands of Southern Rhodesia. In a sense, Kenya's Happy Valley, the White Highlands, was the ultimate hill station, inhabited not by birds of passage but by a perpetual population of self-proclaimed elite. Following the lead of New Delhi, planners dreamed up new "garden city" capitals in Canberra and Lusaka. And as late as 1955 a full-fledged durbar met the young Queen Elizabeth and her consort on tour in northern Nigeria, prompting her hosts to undertake the "thankless task" of growing grass on the hard-baked grounds and planting out geraniums in window boxes alongside the royal dais. After the durbar, with its display of mounted warriors in chain mail and "tribal" dancers, the Royals greeted a thousand guests at a garden party on the lawns of Government House in Kaduna.[1]

In the remotest corners of the empire colonials great and small lovingly tended their own approximations of English gardens—including Scots and Irish (but less commonly Welsh), who were very much part of the empire-building project and just as partial to "English" gardens. At Grote Schur, outside Cape Town, Cecil Rhodes ignored the advice of both Francis Bacon and Gertrude Jekyll that a garden should be in intimate proportion to the house and planted an acre of hydrangeas far from shade and water. Sir Stewart Gore Browne carved an imposing estate out of the Northern Rhodesian bush, with terraced lawns, a walled ladies' garden, roses, and an avenue of cypress trees (Fig. 56). Ordinary colonials simply tried to grow lawns and a few flowers from home amid the jacarandas and bougainvilleas. Expatriated to Egypt with her banker husband, Penelope Lively's mother created a garden that was "unashamedly English in design—it had lawns and a lily pond with a willow, pergolas and formal beds and a rose garden"—but the drive to the house was lined with thirty-foot eucalyptuses. More ambitiously, the Egyptian Delta Land and Investment Company laid out the garden city of Maadi early in the twentieth century, transforming a swath of countryside into an "English township, with neat little roads lined with vine-covered houses, each with its large garden filled with trees and flowers and surrounded by a hedge." Settled by a large colony of Anglo-Egyptians, it also attracted "highbrows addicted to gardening."[2]

In northern Nigeria, Muriel Bennett's garden was home to a flower-loving monkey. Every morning he took her hand as she made her rounds and climbed trees to help her gather sprays of blossoms beyond her reach. Roses held a special place in the hearts of those far from home. The Kenyan novelist Ngugi wa Thiong'o describes the gardens of a high colonial official with their flame lilies, morning glory, sunflowers, and bougainvillea. "However, it was

Fig. 56. Front garden at Shiwa Ng'andu, Zambia, 1950s
[Photograph by Jo and Charles Harvey]

the gardens of roses that stood out in color above all the others. Mrs. Margery Thompson had cultivated red roses, white roses, pink roses—roses of all shades." Alas, it was common wisdom in Africa that "planting roses was sure to lead to transfer."[3]

One of the few spots on the imperial map that appeared ungardenable was Aden, a bastion of solid rock guarding the sea route to India, but even here Baron von Orlich found "indefatigable" English officers importing mold from Arabia in an attempt to grow flowers and bananas in the mid-nineteenth century. After the British acquired Ascension Island, halfway between Africa and Brazil, the Royal Navy brought in tons of earth and innumerable trees "to soften the volcanic landscape." According to tradition, every officer posted to the garrison added some useful plant to the garden of roses, geraniums, and English vegetables. Indeed, the taste for English flowers overflowed the

GARDEN IMPERIALISM 305

bounds of formal empire. On a plant-hunting expedition to remote areas of Tibet, Frank Kingdon-Ward was surprised to find a courtyard "gay with hollyhocks, asters, sunflowers, dahlias, pansies, geraniums, poppies, stocks and nasturtiums." The Dzong-pen (local governor) had brought back a tin of Sutton's seeds from a trip to Calcutta. Tibetans were very fond of such flowers, especially for monastery gardens. In fact the government requested Kingdon-Ward to send seeds for the Dalai Lama to grow in his private garden, "which he tends with loving care."[4]

When one power redirects the economy of another to produce tea or cotton or opium primarily for the benefit of the rulers, no one disputes the term "imperialism." But can we justify the term when speaking of the colonization of the world with English gardens? After all, this phenomenon was a composite of many elements, not least of them homesickness, nostalgia, love of nature, the pleasure of seeing things grow, a delight in beauty itself. The expatriate wife in Sara Duncan's *The Simple Adventures of a Memsahib* (1893) went down to the garden simply to "talk of home to her friends in the flowerbeds," commending their bravery in toughing it out so far from England. Or, as Leonard Woolf's sister Bella so aptly remarked, "It takes a primrose in the tropics to give one true nostalgia."[5] Nevertheless, sometimes consciously, sometimes unconsciously, these gardens in form and content contained an ideological message that reflected both individual personalities and cultural values. It may be a leap to argue that they were an integral part of the template of power relations, the ability of the British to govern so many with so few—at the height of the empire no more than 165,000 Europeans ruled 300 million Indians, for example, and the same ratios held elsewhere—but they were one of the most *visible* manifestations of British presence and British civilization. Perhaps John Mortimer was only half jesting when he commented that the herbaceous border, along with British law, Shakespeare, Wordsworth, and Lord Byron, was "one of our great contributions to the world."[6] For the colonials themselves gardens were, more often than not, a means of keeping the "other" world at bay, of creating an oasis of Britishness in an alien if not a potentially hostile land.

Conversely, subject peoples aiming for acceptance aped the ways of the British, not least of all their gardens. Just as Rajput princes had earlier adopted Mughal gardens, then English parks, so Madhur Jaffrey's very middle-class father oversaw his family garden in twentieth-century New Delhi, with "vast lawns, a badminton court, a tennis court, a rose garden, mixed flower borders edged with sweet peas"—indeed an array of gardens growing just about any flower that might be made to flourish in a subtropical climate, from cannas to lupins. While the women in the family might stick to more traditional fare, he relished his breakfasts of fried eggs, toast in a silver toast rack, and jams in proper silver-lidded cut-glass jam jars; for a special treat, there was ham, bacon, or sausages. It was all part of the package, the colonial heritage that ran the gamut from public to personal.[7]

"A perennial theme running throughout Britain's imperial experience," notes the historian P. J. Marshall, "has been the relationship between the ideas about the ordering of society at home and ideas about the ordering of the empire overseas." However obvious may seem to be the difficulties of imposing this order on very different societies, "generations of British people have tried to do precisely this." Gardens are but one instance, and, as the garden historian John Dixon Hunt warns us, "we should not let all that 'nature' seduce us from registering their cultural self-construction." If extensive greenswards and neat flowerbeds and banks of shrubbery were the ideal of civilized living at home, they were all the more so abroad, where the danger of losing one's compass was so much greater and the need to set an example for subject peoples so urgent. "It was the Cotswold ideal, transplanted to the equator inflated in scale, and without the servant problem."[8]

Were one to look down from the air on almost any British enclave in India, or indeed anywhere in the world, during the imperial heyday, there would have been no mistaking its identity. First of all, one would have been struck by contrasts: on whatever high ground might be available, spacious lawns and gardens surrounding ample bungalows, whether of officials or planters; clubs with their manicured golf courses, polo grounds, and tennis courts; on lower ground, tucked out of sight at some distance and packed closely together, the huts and bazaars of the indigenous population. One would also see Government House, with its "borders, beds and shrubberies and lawns and avenues." Botanical gardens and public parks extended these attractions to the populace at large. And, with the advent of the automobile age, tree-lined thoroughfares interspersed with quintessentially English roundabouts, bedecked with flowers and greenery, in the city center (see Fig. 16).[9] The irony of the whole scenario was that from start to finish it was totally dependent on a virtual army of "natives" to make it run.

This was the footprint of empire in India at high noon. But it had evolved from an earlier period of informal empire conspicuous in the layout of the presidency cities and their offshoots. Europeans were fewer, but they aspired both to grand city houses in the Palladian manner and garden houses on the model of country estates in eighteenth-century Britain, with their fine prospects and artfully positioned copses, streams and lakes. An aerial view would have underscored the contrast between high-density urban habitations and low-density suburban or rural, but without the full complement of clubs, playing fields, and other amenities so typical of later colonial life.

Alongside the gardens themselves, garden metaphors and metonyms have a venerable history in the rhetoric of politics to express ideals and failures of government; the well-kept garden is the symbol of good stewardship, the unkempt tangle, of anarchy. Shakespeare's Richard II found England a "sea-walled garden...

> *full of weeds, her fairest flowers chok'd up,*
> *Her fruit-trees all unprun'd, her edges ruin'd*
> *Her knots disorder'd and her wholesome herbs*
> *Swarming with caterpillars*[10]

Mughal rulers progressively extended images of gardens and flowers to the language of politics. As Akbar's manifesto in occupying Kashmir proclaimed: "The sole idea of wise kings is day by day to refresh the garden of the world by the streams of justice, and assuredly this design is accomplished whenever extensive countries come into the hands of one who is just and of wide capacity."[11] On another occasion, he insisted that "cleansing of the four *bangs* of India [a reference to the Mughal division of India into seven climes] ... and the sweeping away of the weeds and rubbish from this garden ... did not proceed from self will and self-indulgence, and that we had no object except to be kind to mortals, and to obliterate their oppressors."[12] Given his own views, it is not implausible to read Kipling's "Glory of the Garden" with its famous opening lines, "Our England is a garden," as an allegory of empire. Its reminder that "the Glory of the Garden lies in more than meets the eye," that it depends on the unsung toilers in potting shed and dung-pit—"Told off to do as they are bid and do it without noise"—can refer just as well to the unsung sahib or BOR (British

Other Ranks: enlisted men), insuring, as the poet would have it, that the empire as glorious garden "shall never pass away."[13]

The long-serving district officer Henry Sharp invoked the metaphor of the garden to characterize the stages of British rule in India from mercantile to imperial. At first, he points out, they did not try to interfere with the natural flora of the land, but gradually all that changed: "The scorching beams of centralized authority withered its hardiest growth. Moreover the gardeners themselves consciously and deliberately began to interfere with the natural flora and, in the hope of making improvements, to sow the seeds of exotic plants." Some of these proved beneficial but others either perished or choked out "useful native herbs and sometimes bore fruits which disagreed with the inhabitants. Thus the whole nature of the garden began to change." Taking leave of India, Sharp returned to the garden metaphor, hoping that the new India will find "a pleasance more natural to their bent and nearer to their heart's desire." When asked by a *nawab* what the use of a viceroy was, another official ventured the epigram that "India was the plant and the Viceroy the flower."[14]

The question remains: Why are gardens so much a part of English identity, why are the English such "plantaholics"? Some four-fifths of households in Britain have their own garden or access to one, by far the highest proportion of any European country. "Is there something peculiarly English in their response to nature?" asks the garden historian Edward Hyams, answering in the affirmative.[15] It is worth remembering, however, that the English garden did not really come into its own until the eighteenth century. Although garden historians make much of earlier styles—Tudor, Jacobean, Queen Anne—these were largely beholden to continental designs and even continental designers, with just a little tweaking here and there to suit national tastes. What came to distinguish the *jardin anglais* were the great expanses of verdant parkland with well-placed clusters of trees and copses, streams and ponds, a neatly unnatural simulacrum of the "natural" in which flowers and flowering bushes played a minor part. Only toward the end of the century did flowers stage a comeback, leading to the full-fledged Victorian and Edwardian gardens with their various configurations of beds and shrubs, all set in extensive and neatly trimmed lawns. "Green lawns and flower-beds with superb trees which obscure the view, that is what the English like, and what one finds everywhere here," remarked the Duchesse de Dino with some wonderment on a visit to England early in the nineteenth century. It was a green and pleasant land with a vengeance, so much so that when Flora Annie Steel remarked to Walter Pater on the loveliness of the green fields around Oxford in the spring (which would have struck her with particular force after her years in India), he replied, "Don't you think they are almost offensively green?"[16]

A number of commentators have argued that the eighteenth-century English park encoded an ideology of liberty in contrast to the autocratic constraints of, say, the French formal garden. Paradoxically it also coincided with the most expansive phase of empire-building and was financed to some degree from imperial revenues. The multiple incarnations of the nineteenth-century garden, on the other hand, are an ideological jumble; they encode a confusing welter of ideas, from free trade (the flood of exotic plants and exotic styles), to the ascendancy of the middle classes (every villa set in its own garden), to the wanton historicism of the age, with one revival after another. In the free-for-all of expanding democracy, garden professionals fought as fiercely over contending styles as any politicians on the hustings. Perhaps the underlying message is simply that gardens matter, just as politics matters.

Like the democratization of British public life, too, the democratization of gardening was a gradual process, although it moved a good deal more quickly than parliamentary reform. By the beginning of the nineteenth century, Keith Thomas maintains, there was "no country in which flower-gardening had as socially wide an appeal as in England." The working classes regarded gardens almost as a right. In fact, Thomas makes the provocative claim that "the preoccupation with gardening, like that with pets, fishing and other hobbies, even helps to explain the relative lack of radical and political impulses among the British proletariat." In any random catalog of what constitutes "Englishness," gardens would surely be right up there with fair play, roast beef, and Thomas's "sentimental view of animals." And hot baths.[17]

The farther one ventured from home, the more such traditions gained in intensity—Maria Graham and others, we may recall, did remark on the excessive chauvinism of her countrymen in Calcutta, a sentiment echoed by Lady Henrietta Clive, who could not restrain herself from exclaiming "What a wonderful people we are really, having the command of the whole world." Others, too, have noted the tendency of the English abroad to carry with them the "habits and customs of their own country." As Byron's friend Lady Blessington observed, "It would appear they travel not so much for the purpose of studying the manners of other lands, as for that of establishing and displaying their own."[18] This was surely true of expatriate gardens that visually proclaimed the superiority of their owners, individually and culturally. And if the adoption of gardens and gardening could "civilize" the British working classes, the same should be true of subject populations, guided by the example of their colonial masters.

Although at home notions of what constituted an "English garden" were both ever-changing and hotly contested, at a distance they tended to resolve themselves into more generic forms: the parklike gardens of the eighteenth century yielding to variations on the classic Victorian in the period of high colonialism. There is little evidence that the "eclectic bandwagon" of styles vying for acceptance in nineteenth-century England had much resonance in India.[19] There was always a time lag, for one thing; for another, most colonials were too impermanent in their postings to sink time and money into an fashionable garden; for a third, they had enough to do simply to get the flowers of home to grow in an alien land without worrying about the latest fad in topiary or balustrades or weeping willows. The British gardens that characterized high-colonial India and survived the end of empire, however precariously, tended therefore to be variations on the basic Victorian pattern of lawns, defined flowerbeds with as many English flowers as possible, and ranks and ranks of potted plants. Shrubs and trees of necessity were indigenous rather than imported from home.

As far as I know, only the Mughals matched the British in the intensity of their love of gardens and certainty in their own models (although the British—some British—have had a sense of humor about their horticultural addictions that seems quite lacking in the Mughals).[20] One is hard put to it, however, to explain why two such different peoples should share this obsession: in the one case, restless invaders from the uplands of Central Asia, in the other, merchant adventurers morphing into civil servants from a small boreal island. There were of course differences, both in outcomes and in ideological underpinnings. The British came to see gardens not only as aesthetically pleasing but also as a means of moral improvement for all classes at home and all peoples under the Union Jack, an idea that would have seemed quite alien to their Mughal forebears. Moreover, Mughal gardens were essentially male domains, although a few highborn women such as Nur Jahan, the wife of Emperor Jahangir, oversaw the design of several. The Victorian rulers of India, it has been remarked, personified a masculine ideal, the public school ethos writ large. They lived, worked, and played in a largely male environment, married late, and often experienced long periods of separation from wives and children. Gardens, however, were a largely female contribution to imperial life—one might even say that gardens were to empire as women were to men, softening and taming the excessive masculinity of the enterprise.[21]

But why create a garden at all? "Logically the pleasure garden has no excuse for existence," comments one writer, "but the charm of living plants seems to respond to some basic human need." Or divine need: as Bacon reminds us, "God Almighty first planted a garden." Robert Pogue Harrison has mused that the existence of gardens means that there are aspects of our humanity that nature by itself does not fully accommodate—we must go nature one better. For some the garden has provided a sanctuary from history, either a referent to the prelapsarian world we have lost or to the Paradise that we hope awaits us.[22] For others, the garden is an "exercise in memory," a way of getting to a past that may be one's own or more distantly related. A garden is also a very tangible display of wealth and power. Just as there are many reasons one creates a garden, there may be many reasons one chooses its form and content. The Rajut princes of Udaipur and Amber who laid out Mughal-inspired gardens may have wanted to curry favor with their Mughal overlords, as did later Indian elites in adopting British architectural and garden styles, along with cricket, Marmite, and public-school educations. The Kew-trained gardener became a fixture, along with the English tutor. One might even label gardens the "soft face" of imperialism, a manifestation of power by other means and part of the agenda stated most baldly by Thomas Macaulay in his famous "Minute" on education of 1835, namely to form a "class of persons, Indian in blood and colour, but English in taste, in opinions, in morals, and in intellect."[23]

Still, we should not overdetermine the matter. Cultural boundaries are immensely permeable, and one should also recognize that the delights of other garden traditions have appealed to many for purely personal motives. To think otherwise is to sell the Nehrus, the Sujayas, and the Mrs. Mahesh Kapoors short. Their love of English gardens and English flowers was and is genuine. On the British side, the exceptions may be as interesting as the stereotypes. What accounts for the openness of a James Forbes or William Jones? One can to some extent understand the insularity of an Emily Eden, cocooned as she was in the protocol enveloping the entourage of her brother, the governor-general, but what are we to make of Charlotte Canning's quite opposite response, although she was even more isolated and straitjacketed in her contacts? Or Fanny Parks, who started out with the usual prejudices but allowed herself ultimately to be caught up in all that India had to offer? To be sure, Parks spent much longer in the country, but it was nevertheless highly unusual for a woman to go off traveling on her own as she did so happily. Just as Edward Lear was to find the picturesque he so eagerly sought in the luxuriance of India, others on both sides of the imperial equation have been able to separate the wheat from the chaff in their colonial heritage. Perhaps no one offers a better example of cultural openness than the "white Mughal," Colonel William Linnaeus Gardner. Passing his twilight years with his beloved Begum, he summed up the recipe for his happy life: "New books, a garden, a spade, nobody to obey, pyjamas, grandchildren, tranquility: this is the summit of happiness, not only in the East but the West too."[24]

True, such boundary-crossing figures as Gardner became scarcer in the bureaucratized India of a later generation. Nevertheless, Constance Villiers-Stuart was such a one. She saw in the study of Indian garden craft a larger purpose than mere antiquarianism. In urging that an "Indian garden" be part of the plan for the Viceroy's House in Delhi, she held out the hope that gardens might bridge the divide between peoples, not only between East and West but also within India, voicing a Gandhian ideal of social harmony:

> In a vast continent where temples, churches, mosques, forts, and even palaces but serve to mark off and divide men and creeds, all might yet meet in a garden. Hindu and Muslim might both recognize their own symbols there, where the fountain mists and whispering trees would murmur to us of that power, the *bhakti,* which for all our restless Western cleverness we miss. . . . The Lilies of Our Lady and the Lotus of the Good Law would share the gardens with the pink rose of the Persian poets and the red rose of England. . . . New needs and our modern wealth of flowers would give fresh life and added beauty to ancient symbols and ideas, charms to rival and surpass all the older Shalimars.[25]

The history of British colonial gardens in India shares with imperialism itself the lack of a clear theoretical basis, even clear aims. While not really created in a fit of absentmindedness any more than was the empire, they happened piecemeal, reflecting changing views at home, changing circumstances abroad, and individual taste. As an historian of empire has observed, "what was distinctly English about the enterprise was not peoples' motives for going where they did but what they believed themselves to be doing when they got there."[26] And what they did almost from the first moment was to lay out gardens. Calcutta itself mirrors this, with its evolution from garden houses to bungalows, and the constant redoing of the gardens of Government House and Barrackpore, but always with the imprint of individual tenants. The acquisition of the Himalayas and Nilgiris opened up gardening possibilities undreamt of in the plains, making exile both more familiar and more acceptable. The long reach of Kew catalyzed the founding and expansion of botanical gardens with their impact on both England and its outposts, but here, too, policies and practices varied with individuals. Without Curzon's autocratic intervention, India's monuments would not be landscaped as they are today. New Delhi is at one and the same time an abstract vision of Empire, a very finite translation of English ideas about garden cities circa 1910, and the work of individuals such as Sir Edwin Lutyens and William Robertson Mustoe—even at several removes, the influence of Gertrude Jekyll. Sometimes the forces at play were more impersonal. The insatiable demand for tea in the United Kingdom simultaneously stimulated the ruthless industrialization of opium production and the spread of a plantation economy from the Western Ghats to Assam and Ceylon. Had it not been for the Uprising of 1857, neither Lucknow nor Cawnpore would have been etched on the British memory through their memorial gardens.

There is a historical contingency about particular gardens but less so about the *need* to have gardens; conversely there seemed to be a horticultural response to just about every historical contingency. By the nineteenth century if not earlier, gardens and gardening seemed bred in the English bone; like tea, they offered colonials reassurance in situations of stress and cemented a community of shared interests. And those who aspired to join this heaven-born host might hope to do so through the garden gate.

COMMON TREES, SHRUBS, AND PLANTS IN INDIA SOUTH OF THE HIMALAYAS

Many botanical names are disputed. I have not given botanical names of most flowers because of the many species and cultivars.

TREES AND SHRUBS

NATIVE

Aam/Amri/Ambi (Mango) (*Mangifera indica*)
Amaltas (*Cassia fistula*)
Amlaki/Amla (Indian gooseberry) (*Phyllanthus emblica*)
Amrood (Guava) (*Psidium guajava*)
Anjan (Indian blackwood) (*Hardwickia binata*)
Arjun (*Terminalia arjuna*)
Ashok (*Polyalthia longifolia*)
Babul (*Salvadora persica* and *S. oleiodes*)
Baheda (Belleric) (*Terminalia bellirica*)
Bahr (Banyan) (*Ficus bengalensis*)
Champaka (*Michelia champaca*)
Chenar (*Platanus orientalis*)
Coconut palm (*Cocos nucifera*)
Dhak (Flame of the forest) (*Butea monosperma*)

Dhauldhak (Coral tree) (*Erythrina variegata* and *E. suberosa*)
Harshingar (Night-blooming Jasmine) (*Nyctanthes arbor-tristis*)
Imli (Tamarind) (*Tamarindus indica*)
Jadi (*Ficus amplissima*)
Jamun (*Syzigium cumini*); *Rai jamun* (*Syzigium nervosum*)
Jarul (Queen's crape myrtle) (*Lagerstroemia speciosa*)
Kadam (*Neolarmarckia cadamba*)
Katthal (Jackfruit) (*Artocarpus heterophyllus*)
Kewra (Screw pine) (*Pandanus fascicularis*)
Khirni (Ceylon ironwood) (*Manilkara hexandra*)
Lantana (*Lantana camara*)
Laurel fig (*Ficus microcarpa*)
Maharukh (Tree of heaven) (*Ailanthus excelsa*)
Mahua (*Madhuca longifolia* var. *latifolia*)
Mari (Jaggery or toddy palm) (*Caryota urens*)
Maulsari (*Mimops elengi*)
Morpankhe (Laurel tree) (*Kalmia latifolia*)
Mowa (Indian Butter tree) (*Bassia latifolia*)
Neem (*Azadirachta indica*)
Peepal (*Ficus religiosa*)
Pilkhan (*Ficus virens*)
Putranijiva (*Drypetes roxburghii*)
Ramdhan Champa (*Ochna obtusata*); *Champ* (*Michelia champaca*): both referred to as Golden Champak in English
Sagwan (Teak) (*Tectona grandis*)
Semal (Silk cotton tree) (*Bombax Ceiba*)
Shisham (Indian rosewood) (*Dalbergia sissoo*)
Siris (*Albizia lebbeck*)
Sita-Ashok (Sorrowless tree) (*Saraca asoca*, formerly *Jonesia asoca*)

INTRODUCED, PRIMARILY BY MUGHALS AND EUROPEANS

Almond (Middle East)
Baobab (*Adansonia digitata*) (Africa)
Bougainvillea (*Bougainvillea spectabilis*) (South America)
Chinese Fan Palm (*Livistona chinensis*)
Crape Myrtle (*Lagerstroemia indica*) (China)

Custard-Apple (*Annona reticulata*) (Central America and West Indies)

Cypress (*Cupressus sempervirens*)

Eucalyptus (Australian)

Frangipani (*Plumeria rubra* and *P. obtusa*) (Central and South America)

Fruit trees: orange, lime, citron, quince, cherry, apple, pomegranate, plum, apricot, pear, mulberry

Gulmohur (Gold Mohur) (*Delonix regia*) (Madagascar)

Jacaranda (*Jacaranda mimosifolia*) (Brazil)

Mexican Morn (*Prosopis juliflora*) (South America)

Pineapple (*Ananas comosus*) (South America)

Sausage tree (*Kigelia africana*) (East and Southern Africa)

Weeping Bottlebrush (*Callistemon viminalis*)

Yellow Oleander (*Thevetia peruviana*) (Mexico and West Indies)

FLOWERS, SMALL SHRUBS AND CREEPERS

NATIVE OR INTRODUCED VERY EARLY

Amaranthus

Chandni (Moonflower)

Henna

Hibiscus: *Hibiscus rosa-sinensis* and *H. mutabilis*

Impatiens balsamina

Jasmine: many varieties, including *madhavi, mogree,* and the tree form, *Harsinghar* (see above)

Lotus (*Nelumbo nucifera*): red, white, blue

Tuberose

Tulsi (Holy basil)

INTRODUCED BY MUGHALS OR EUROPEANS

(Plants common in Mughal gardens may have been reintroduced by the British or introduced as different varieties.)

Agapanthus	Balsams	Chrysanthemums
Anemones	Belladonna Lilies	Clarkia
Annual Gaillardias	Camellias	Coreopsis
Auricula	Carnations	Crown imperial

Cyclamen	Oleander	Salvias
Dahlias	Peony	Stocks
Heliotrope	Pansies	Sweet William
Hollyhocks	Petunias	Tulips
Honeysuckle	Phlox	Verbena
Hyacinths	Polyanthus	Violets
Larkspurs	Primulas	Wallflowers
Marigolds	Ranunculus	Zinnias
Mignonette	Roses	

POTTED PLANTS

Begonia	Hoyas
Crotons	Pelargoniums
Ferns	Salvias
Fuchsias	

FLOWERS IN THE BEDS AND BORDERS OF THE "MUGHAL GARDEN," RASHTRAPATI BHAVAN, IN 2003

(See http://presidentofindia.nic.in/S/html/mughal.htm)

Alyssum	Godetia	Ranunculus
Anemone	Gomphrena	Roses
Aster	Ice plant	Rudbeckia
Calendula	Iris	Salvia
California poppy	Ixora	Statice
Carnation	Lilies	Stock
Chrysanthemum	Lupin	Sunflower
Cockscomb	Marigold	Sweet pea
Cosmos	Mignonette	Sweet William
Dahlia	Narcissus	Tuberose
Daisies	Nemesia	Tulip
Freesia	Nicotiana	Verbena
Gardenia	Pansy	Viola
Gladiolus	Portulaca	Zinnia

NOTES

PREFACE

1. Lively, *A House Unlocked,*113ff.; Lively, *Oleander, Jacaranda,* 28, 31.
2. Kipling, "The Glory of the Garden," in *Complete Verse,* 735–36.
3. Quest-Ritson, *English Garden Abroad,* preface (n.p.).

INTRODUCTION

1. Lutgendorf, "All in the (Raghu) Family," 224; Knighton, *Elihu Jan's Story*; Goody, *Culture of Flowers,* 339ff.
2. Russell, *Prince of Wales's Tour,* 116, 120, 518; Dufferin, *Our Viceregal Life,* 2:18; Wilson, *Letters from India,* 414; Lawrence, *Indian Embers,* 171–72. Cf. Postans, *Western India,* 1:109.
3. Forbes, *Oriental Memoirs,* 1:121, 126–27, 138–39; Goody, 181.
4. E. Roberts, *Scenes and Characteristics of Hindostan,* 1:126–27; cf. Parkes, *Begums, Thugs and White Mughals,* 43.
5. Srinivas, *Landscapes of Urban Memory,*142.
6. Cuthell, *My Garden,*135; Villiers-Stuart, *Gardens of the Great Mughals,* 232–36.
7. Goody, 332–34, 342; Desmond, *European Discovery,* 25; Arthur, *Mission to Mysore,* 91; Parkes [Parks], *Begums, Thugs and White Mughals,* 126–27; Villiers-Stuart, *Gardens of the Great Mughals,* 177, 231–32, chap. 11; D. Lentz, "Botanical Symbolism," 52. For a comprehensive study of the lotus in Indian culture, see Malhotra, *Lotus*. Malhotra shows how the lotus has been adopted by all the major religions in India, including Christianity in Goa and Kerala, but the book's forewords also underscore the politicization of the symbol. Most recently, the Bahai Temple, completed in 1986, takes the form of a lotus blossom. The brilliant animated film by Nina Paley, *Sita Sings the Blues* (2008), provides a gentle spoof of the ubiquity of the lotus motif in Indian life.

8. Desmond, 25; Goody, 327ff.

9. Goody, 327ff.

10. Tulsidas, *Rámáyana of Tulsi Dás,* chaupái 231.

11. Sinha, *Landscapes in India,* 58ff.

12. Ali, *Courtly Culture and Political Life,* passim, quotations on 77, 147–48, 236.

13. Forbes, 2:231–32; Dyson, *Various Universe,* 184; Husain, *Scent in the Islamic Garden,* 180–81.

14. Babur, *Baburnama,* 335; Grover, *Islamic Architecture,* 122–23; Dalrymple, *City of Djinns,* 235.

15. Heber, *Narrative of a Journey,* 3:234–35.

16. Villiers-Stuart, "Horticultural Club Lecture on Indian Garden Craft," 337; Villiers-Stuart, *Gardens of the Great Mughals,* 255ff.; Babur, 344ff., 363ff.; Forbes, 1:152–53; Tod, *Annals and Antiquities of Rajasthan,* 1:568.

17. Wilson, 32; Marquess of Hastings, quoted in Dyson, 338; Forbes, 2:230; cf. E. C. Archer, *Tours in Upper India,* 1:204; Parkes, 275; Nugent, *Journal,* 1:317–18; Dyson, 81, 338, 341. See Dyson, 110–11, for an overview of European reactions to Indian music and dancing, and her Appendix B for selections from journals and memoirs on the subject.

18. Parkes [Parks], *Begums, Thugs and White Mughals,* 110, 254–55, 317–18; Knighton, 18, 23–24; Villiers-Stuart, *Gardens of the Great Mughals,* 234; Bowe, "Indian Gardening Tradition," 194.

19. Desmond, 24–25; Uglow, *Little History of British Gardening,* 24, 34ff.; Scott-James and Lancaster, *Pleasure Garden,* 18, 20; Chaucer, *Canterbury Tales,* "General Prologue," line 668; Goody, chap. 8 passim. Cf. Hamlet, 4.5.145: "There's rosemary, that's for remembrance..."

20. Quoted in F. Jekyll, *Gertrude Jekyll,* 141; Forbes, 1:332; William Hodges, quoted in Archer and Lightbown, *India Observed,* 77; T. Bacon, *Orientalist,* 62; Dyson, 89; Elwood, *Narrative of a Journey,* 1:387.

21. Havell, "Indian Gardens," 213; Elwood, 1:369; Kindersley quoted in Dyson, 63; Forbes, 1:60; Shields, *Birds of Passage,* 216; Graham, *Journal,* 21–22. Cf. Maitland, *Letters from Madras,* 25.

22. Jekyll quoted in Jennifer Potter, review of David E. Cooper, *A Philosophy of Gardens, Times Literary Supplement,* 22 and 29 Dec. 2006, 35.

23. Thomas, *Man and the Natural World,* 234. Cf. Endersby, *Imperial Nature,* 304–5.

24. P. Coats, *Flowers in History,* 266; Veblen, *Theory of the Leisure Class,* 133–35.

25. Harrison, *Gardens,* x.

CHAPTER 1. FROM GARDEN HOUSE TO BUNGALOW, NABOBS TO HEAVEN-BORN

1. Babur, *Baburnama,* 364.

2. Ibid., 353.

3. For a wide-ranging and readable history of the Company, see Keay, *Honourable Company.*

4. Ibid., 96; Koch, "Influence of the Jesuit Missions" and Koch, "Jahangir and the Angels"; Dye, "Artists for the Emperor," 109ff. Hawkins's embassy was also accompanied by two musicians, Lancelot Canning, a virginal player (and distant kinsman of a later viceroy), and Robert Trully, a cornetist. The latter was enthusiastically received, converted to Islam, and

performed at courts throughout India. Virginals were, alas, too chaste for Mughal tastes and Canning is said to have "dyed of conceit."

5. The quotation is from Gleig, *Memoirs*, 1:25.

6. Keay, *Honourable Company*, 394–95; Keay, *India Discovered*, 19.

7. Tipu's fame abroad was such that he served as a bogeyman to frighten a generation of English children into good behavior; he has been immortalized in a mechanical tiger devouring a red-coated British soldier, now in the Victoria and Albert Museum.

8. Judd, *Lion and the Tiger*, 33; Keay, *Honourable Company*, 363, 397; Philip Mason, introduction to Beames, *Memoirs of a Bengal Civilian*, iii.

9. G. O. Trevelyan, *Competition Wallah*, 113.

10. Beames, 252; Judith Brown, "India," 423–27.

11. Quoted without identification in Sharp, *Good-bye India*, 3.

12. "The Song of the Cities," in *Complete Verse*, 174.

13. Llewellyn-Jones, *Engaging Scoundrels*, 156; Spear, *Nabobs*, 5.

14. Forbes, *Oriental Memoirs*, 2:479–80.

15. E. Roberts, *Scenes and Characteristics of Hindostan*, 1:186.

16. G. C. Mundy, *Pen and Pencil Sketches*, 1:8.

17. Eden, *Up the Country*, 122; Emily Eden in H. Brown, *Sahibs*, 37; Bence-Jones, *Palaces*, 138.

18. Shields, *Birds of Passage*, 127.

19. Keay, *Honourable Company*, 170.

20. In Fisher, *Visions of Mughal India*, 118–19.

21. Lawson, *Memories of Madras*, 241.

22. Ibid., 264; Maitland, *Letters from Madras*, 17; Mrs. Bowring, in L. B. Bowring, *Eastern Experiences*, 368.

23. Neild, "Colonial Urbanism"; Hare, *Story of Two Noble Lives*, 2:38.

24. Love, *Vestiges of Old Madras*, 1:281ff., 420, 553n2.

25. Charles Lockyer, quoted in Spear, 4–5.

26. Ibid., 17; Love, 1:476, 2:614, 617; Lawson, 240.

27. Dyson, *Various Universe*, 134; Thomas Williamson, *East India Vade Mecum*, 1:137–38; Morris, *Stones of Empire*, 49–50; Valentia, *Voyages and Travels*, 1:337; Neild, 224ff.; Lewandowski, *Migration and Ethnicity*, 50.

28. I. Butler, *Viceroy's Wife*, 126–27.

29. Valentia, 1:336. Cf. Maria Graham's similar comment: Lawson, 264.

30. Steevens, *In India*, 292.

31. E. Roberts, 2:220; Fay, *Original Letters*, 170. Cf. Lawson, 294, 295; and Orlich, *Travels in India*, 2:216–17.

32. Dyson, 133.

33. Hare, 2:37.

34. Hickey, *Memoirs*, 108, 110; Valentia, 1:337.

35. Bence-Jones, 28.

36. Ibid., 28–30; Love, 2:462, 3:525–26; Jasanoff, *Edge of Empire*, 190ff.; Nilsson, *European Architecture in India*, 107–8, 121; Lawson, 136; Shields, 186, 302, and passim.

37. R. Trevelyan, *Golden Oriole*, 331ff.

38. "Raj Bhavan, Chennai," www.tnrajbhavan.gov.in/History-Chennai.htm.

39. Gleig, *Sir Thomas Munro*, 2:296–97, 300–302.

40. Dufferin, *Our Viceregal Life*, 2:94.

41. Lord Irwin to Lord Halifax, quoted in A. D. King, *Colonial Urban Development*, 167.

42. Dalrymple, *White Mughals*, xxxviii, 90–93, 218, 255–62; Bence-Jones, 82.

43. Kipling, "Madras," *Complete Verse*, 174.

44. Dalrymple, *White Mughals*; Ghosh, *Sex and the Family*, introduction; Judith Brown, "India," 425–26. It has been estimated that there were only eighty-five European women and children in Madras in 1771; Colley, *Ordeal of Elizabeth Marsh*, 164.

45. Graham, *Journal*, 133, 136.

46. Kling, *Partner in Empire*, 46–47. Cf. Duncan, *Simple Adventures*, 164.

47. Dufferin, 1:13; cf. Bence-Jones, 32.

48. E. Roberts, 1:56–57.

49. Quoted in Hilton Brown, *Sahibs*, 73.

50. Forbes, 1:476–77.

51. Quoted in Hilton Brown, *Sahibs*, 74.

52. Parkes [Parks], *Begums, Thugs and White Mughals*, 212, 245.

53. D. Arnold, *Tropics and the Traveling Gaze*, 60.

54. Ibid., 123.

55. Pott, *Old Bungalows*, 14–16; Lady Amherst, Journal, 18 Aug. 1827.

56. On the bungalow and British communities in India generally, see esp. A. D. King, *Colonial Urban Development*; A. D. King, *Bungalow*, chap. 1; Davies, *Splendours of the Raj*; Edwardes, *Bound to Exile*; D. Kincaid, *British Social Life*; Morris, *Stones of Empire*; G. O. Trevelyan, *Competition Wallah*, 34–35; and Pott, passim.

57. Dalrymple, *City of Djinns*, 75.

58. Davies, 77, 104.

59. Lear, *Indian Journal*, 71–72.

60. Orlich, 2:85–86, 119, 126; Taylor, *Visit to India*, 108; E. Roberts, *Scenes and Characteristics of Hindostan*, 1:37–38; Cuthell, *My Garden*, 86; Hooker, *Himalayan Journals*, 64; D. Arnold, 62; Woodrow, *Hints on Gardening*, preface; Churchill quoted in Sassoon, *Siegfried's Journey*, 119.

61. Diver, *Englishwoman in India*, 69–70; [C. Lang], *English Bride in India*, 84.

62. Gilmour, *Ruling Caste*, 173; R. Trevelyan, *Golden Oriole*, 232, 405–6.

63. Dufferin, 2:227. Cf. E. A. King, *Diary of a Civilian's Wife*, 1:95; Gordon Cumming, *In the Himalayas*, 229–30; Sharp, 17; Cuthell, 71; Edwardes, 153.

64. Pogson, *Indian Gardening*, 18ff.; Temple-Wright, *Flowers and Gardens in India*, 11–12; Harler, *Garden in the Plains*, 3, 145.

65. See, in addition to Woodrow, Pogson, Temple-Wright, and Harler: Speede, *New Indian Gardener*; Firminger, *Manual of Gardening*; Grindal, *Everyday Gardening in India*; Percy-Lancaster, *Gardening in India*; D. Kincaid, 161. Quotation from Harler, 16–17.

66. Cuthell, 11.

67. Villiers-Stuart, *Gardens of the Great Mughals*, 56.

68. Grindal, 129. He did allow that pots had their uses in flower shows and in hill stations where there was so little land for gardens (130–31).

69. Steel and Gardiner, *Complete Indian Housekeeper*, 129, 146.

70. Eden, *Up the Country*.

71. Roche, *Childhood in India*, 39.

72. Wilson, *Letters from India*, 135.

73. I. Butler, 82. Cf. Dufferin, 2:217; R. Trevelyan, *Golden Oriole*, 103; MacMillan, *Women of the Raj*, 88; Steevens, *In India*.

74. Harler, 220, 275.

75. Godden and Godden, *Two Under the Indian Sun*, 115.

76. Stanley, "Gardening in India."

77. E. Roberts, 2:33; Orlich, 2:44; Lear, 48; Allen, *Plain Tales*, 77; Duncan, *Simple Adventures*, 165; Monica Campbell-Martin quoted in MacMillan, 153.

78. I. Macfarlane, *Daughters of the Empire*, xxxv, 137, 232; Barr, *Dust in the Balance*, 127.

79. Cuthell, 12, 14ff., 23, 25, 69–70, 219, and passim.

80. Ibid., 5; E. Roberts, 2:134.

81. E. Roberts, 1:107–9; E. C. Archer, *Tours in Upper India*, 2:114–15.

82. R. Trevelyan, *Golden Oriole*, 7; Stanley, 392.

83. Dufferin, 1:19; Grindal, 4–5; Temple-Wright, 8–9.

84. Forbes, 1:476; Quest-Ritson, *English Garden Abroad*, 15.

85. Cuthell, 11.

86. Percy-Lancaster, 20–21; Grindal, 4–5, 57ff.; Harler, 203; Temple-Wright, 3, 8–9, 11–12.

87. Steel and Gardiner, 142.

88. Keay, *Honourable Company*, 76.

89. Tindall, *City of Gold*, 87; Pal and Dehejia, *From Merchants to Emperors*, 198; Sidhwa, introduction to *City of Sin and Splendour*, xii; Mehta, "A House Divided," 118, and Khanna, "I Went Back," 110–11; Bence-Jones, 173.

90. Quraeshi, *Lahore*, 31–33.

91. Tindall, 200.

92. E. A. King, 1:266, 267.

93. D. Kincaid, 245; D. Arnold, 123; Godden and Godden, 20–21.

94. Steevens, 255.

95. D. Kincaid, 270.

96. Taylor, 124.

97. Valentia, 1:81.

98. Tytler, *Englishwoman in India*, 82.

99. Parks, *Wanderings*, 313; Villiers-Stuart, 171. In the house, furniture legs were set in pots of water and indigo used to ward ants off of textiles.

100. Allen, *Kipling Sahib*, 84.

101. Steel, *Garden of Fidelity*, 189–90; Wilson, 6; Barr, 58; Elwood, *Narrative of a Journey*, 1:383, 385–86; Harler, 8.

102. MacMillan, 151.

103. Steel, *Garden of Fidelity*, 73, 108–9

104. Stanley; Godden and Godden, 21; Cuthell, passim.

105. E.g., Harler, 4.

106. Ibid., 17–18.

107. Forbes, 1:477–79, 2:207; Dyson, 182–98.

108. E. Roberts, 2:124–35.

109. Parks, *Wanderings of a Pilgrim*, 1:57, 308–19; Dyson, 294–95. Dalrymple's edition abridges this section of the journal. He also prefers to spell her surname "Parkes." In the notes I have used "Parks" when referring to the *Wanderings*, "Parkes" when referring to Dalrymple's edition.

110. Lady Amherst, Journal, 30 Sept. 1827, 2 Dec. 1827. For Lady Canning, see chapter 2.

111. Desmond, *European Discovery*, 296–97; Dyson, 186; Lawson, *Private Life of Warren Hastings*, 146–47, 166; Gleig, *Memoirs*, 3:362–63.

112. M. Archer, *Early Views of India*, 230–34; Desmond, *European Discovery*, 296–97.

113. Cuthell, 204; Forbes, 1:21; Parks, *Wanderings*, 1:318; Maitland, 27; Steevens, 253; cf. T. Bacon, *Orientalist*, 62.

114. Steel, *On the Face of the Waters*, 15, 22–23, 25, 27, 52, 57.

115. Graham, 174; Maitland, 47, 58, and passim; Dalrymple, *City of Djinns*, 88; Morris, *Farewell the Trumpets*, 401; MacMillan, 13; Scott-James and Lancaster, *Pleasure Garden*, 9; Elwood, 1:365; Cuthell, 119, 135; I. Macfarlane, 66, 69; Edwardes, 69.

116. Deborah Dring, quoted in Allen, *Plain Tales*, 88–89; A. D. King, *Colonial Urban Development*, 142; BBC, *The Lost World of the Raj* (three-part documentary series, 2007).

117. Dyson, 250–51, and passim; Fenton, *Journal*, 37–38, 50; Lear, *Indian Journal*, 37; Sharp, *Good-bye India*, 15.

118. Lear, *Indian Journal*, 43, 61–69, 98, 105, 107, 134, 145, and passim. Cf. J. Lang, *Wanderings in India*, 286, for another traveler "in search of the picturesque."

119. Fowler, *Below the Peacock Fan*, 45. Roberts quoted in Dyson, 114; Arthur, *Mission to Mysore*, 56, 185; Kipling, "In Springtime," in *Complete Verse*, 77.

CHAPTER 2. CALCUTTA AND THE GARDENS OF BARRACKPORE

1. Ironically, the chain reaction that led to the large-scale uprising had begun in the Barrackpore cantonment with Mangal Pandey's attack on his British commander.

2. Desmond, *European Discovery*, 52.

3. Cotton, *Calcutta, Old and New*, 7. It was also said that after his wife's death Charnock sacrificed a cock annually at her mausoleum; Sharp, *Good-bye India*, 208.

4. In P. T. Nair, *Calcutta in the Eighteenth Century*, 4.

5. Ibid., 5.

6. Desmond, 52.

7. P. T. Nair, 220.

8. E. Roberts, *Scenes and Characteristics of Hindostan*, 2:205.

9. Cotton, 72.

10. Desmond, 52.

11. Cotton, 73, 255.

12. Spear, *Nabobs*, 42.

13. Huggins, *Sketches in India*, 4.

14. P. T. Nair, 191.

15. Edwardes, *Warren Hastings*, 53, 144; D. Kincaid, *British Social Life*, 110.

16. Quoted in Cotton, 278.

17. Ibid., 80–81.

18. Kindersley in P. T. Nair, 145.

19. Valentia, *Voyages and Travels*, 1:192.

20. G. O. Trevelyan, *Competition Wallah*, 169.

21. Moorhouse, *India Britannica*, 4.

22. Mitchell, quoted ibid., 99.

23. Twining quoted ibid., 276.

24. Fenton, *Journal*, 198; J. Roberts, "English Gardens in India," 118–19.

25. Gibbes, *Hartly House*, 59–60, quotation from the poet Isaac Bickerstaff. *Hartly House* is fiction, but Gibbes's son had served (and died) in India, and she was well briefed on Anglo-Indian life in Calcutta.

26. Heber, 1:23.
27. Eden, *Letters from India,* 2:87.
28. Desmond, 273.
29. Hare, *Story of Two Noble Lives,* 2:375; Russell, *Diary,* 1:198.
30. Lear, *Indian Journal,* 51.
31. They would also fall prey to English racial bias: in the early twentieth century certain parts of the garden were off-limits to Indians. Chaudhuri, *Autobiography of an Unknown Indian,* 384.
32. Steevens, *In India,* 66–71.
33. Moorhouse, *Calcutta,* 150. And to top it off, as William Russell, a *Times* correspondent covering the Sepoy Mutiny of 1857, noted approvingly, one could count on a "glorious tub" at day's end in the Bengal Club; Russell, *Diary,* 1:99.
34. Heber, 3:238.
35. Eden, *Letters from India,* 2:89.
36. Ibid., 1:205–6.
37. In Chaudhury and Mukhopadhyay, *Calcutta: People and Empire,* 133–34; Hare, 2:375; Valentia, 1:36.
38. Desmond, 273–74.
39. E. Roberts, 1:19.
40. Cotton, 20.
41. Sophia Goldborne [Phebe Gibbes], quoted in Dutta, *Calcutta,* 51.
42. Heber, 3:235.
43. E. Roberts, 2:217–18; Eden, *Letters from India,* 1:215–16, 234; Kling, *Partner in Empire,* 46–47; Dutta, 90–94; Orlich, *Travels in India,* 2:186.
44. Tagore, *My Reminiscences,* 16–17.
45. According to Chaudhuri, the garden Tagore describes was typical of city gardens of Calcutta's élite in the early decades of the twentieth century (395).
46. Moorhouse, *Calcutta,* 6–7; Maya Jasanoff, *Edge of Empire,* 316–18.
47. R. Trevelyan, *Golden Oriole,* 196; Llewellyn-Jones, *Engaging Scoundrels,* 148; Hermann Kisch, *Young Victorian,* 159, 205–6. A tigress escaped from the menagerie, swam across the Hughli to the Botanical Garden, mauled an employee, and then went into hiding in the dense undergrowth. It was finally discovered and shot.
48. Kipling, *Wee Willie Winkie, City of the Dreadful Night, American Notes,* 252–55.
49. E. Arnold, *India Revisited,* 244.
50. Heber, 1:23.
51. Steevens, 67.
52. Dutta, 66.
53. Curzon, *British Government in India,* 1:235.
54. Russell, 1:100.
55. Hare, 2:51.
56. Steevens, 69. Russell had noticed this trend as early as 1860 (1:189).
57. Cotton, 220.
58. Ibid., 196.
59. Ibid., 264; Duncan, *Simple Adventures,* 257.
60. E. Arnold, 251.
61. Duncan, 308.
62. Cotton, 196.

63. Steevens, 67.
64. Curzon, 2:11.
65. Ronaldshay, *Life of Lord Curzon,* 2:258.
66. Curzon, 1:91.
67. Ibid.
68. Ibid., 1:60.
69. Ibid., 1:64.
70. Valentia, 1:191–92.
71. Heber, 3:238.
72. Allen, *Glimpse,* 24.
73. Lutyens, *Lyttons in India,* 31; Bence-Jones, *Palaces,* 142.
74. Curzon, 1:81; quotation from Lady Canning in Hare, 2:74.
75. Graham, *Journal,* 136.
76. Curzon, 1:73.
77. Ibid., 1:85.
78. Ibid.
79. Emily Eden, quoted ibid., 1:84.
80. Losty, *Calcutta,* 95–99, figs. 55, 56, 57.
81. Eden, *Letters from India,* 2:137.
82. Hare, 2:65–66.
83. Steevens, 67.
84. E. Roberts, 2:107.
85. Curzon, 1:84.
86. Ibid., 1:73, 81; Chaudhuri, 278; E. Arnold, 245; Curzon, 1:84–88.
87. "Tea not being known to Manu, was non-caste: Hindus and Muslims could sit together at a table here and sip tea which they could not do together anywhere else. By some curious convention the food as well as the tea seemed to be exempt from caste protocol." Spear and Spear, *India Remembered,* 43–44.
88. Curzon, 1:85.
89. Ibid., 1:141; Edwardes, 182; Tobin, "English Garden Conversation Piece." I think Tobin misinterprets the painting, however, by failing to recognize Hastings's very individual relationship to the Indian landscape.
90. Curzon, 1:139–45. Hastings House was said to be one of the few haunted houses in India.
91. Ibid., 1:77.
92. Ibid., 1:8, 2:4–16.
93. Graham, 142, 144; Pope, "Epistle IV," 138–39; Colchester quoted in Curzon, 2:18; "Naufragus," quoted in Curzon, 2:12; Graham, quoted in Curzon, 2:10.
94. Eden, *Letters from India,* 1:95.
95. Cotton, 208.
96. Heber's sketch depicts Lady Amherst taking her morning airing. He identifies the large tree in the center as a *peepal* sacred to Siva but with an evil spirit believed to be lurking under every leaf. In the foreground left is an aloe, on the right a cotton tree whose flowers resemble roses when in bloom. In the background is a banyan to the right of a stand of bamboo. Heber, 3:287–88; Curzon, 2:1; Lady Amherst, Journal, 1823–24, 1:147.
97. E. Roberts, 2:205–8.
98. Curzon, 2:41–42.
99. Lady Amherst, Journal, 2 Dec. 1827; Desmond, 273.

100. E. Roberts, 2:205–10. Oddly enough, Roberts insists that elsewhere it was "infra dig" to take any exercise on foot, although this is contradicted by many other sources.

101. Desmond, 272.

102. Lady Amherst, Journal, 2 Dec. 1827; cf. ibid., 9 Feb. 1827.

103. Barr, *Memsahibs,* 10–11; Eden, 1:70, 2:52. Eden was aided by John Gibson, a gardener sent out by the Duke of Devonshire to gather exotics from the Himalayas. While waiting for the monsoon to end, Gibson helped lay out the garden at Barrackpore; see A. Coats, *Quest for Plants,* 154.

104. Tytler, *Englishwoman in India,* 14–15.

105. Hare, 2:60–63; Heber, 3:229.

106. Hare, 2:16–17, 2:63, 2:99; letter to Queen Victoria, quoted in Allen, *Glimpse,* 17; It is ironic that Lady Canning relied on an abundance of imported chintz to give Barrackpore the feel of an "English country-house" when chintz was originally an Indian textile, subsequently produced industrially in England.

107. Hare, 2:124, 2:289–90; www.highcliffecastle.co.uk.

108. Hare, 2:121.

109. Ibid., 3:54, 2:289, 3:55, 3:54.

110. Ibid., 2:121.

111. Ibid., 2:488.

112. Ibid., 2:431.

113. Quoted in Allen, *Glimpse,* 102.

114. Hare, 2:80.

115. Allen, *Glimpse,* 118; Surtees, *Charlotte Canning,* 265–66.

116. Allen, *Glimpse,* 39, 155–56.

117. Quoted in Allen, *Glimpse,* 156; Hare, 3:64 (Lord Canning to Viscount Sydney.

118. 15 Sept. 1861, quoted in Allen, *Glimpse,* 156, 158.

119. Quoted in Bence-Jones, *Viceroys,* 180.

120. Ibid., 161.

121. G. O. Trevelyan, *Competition Wallah,* 190. After Charlotte's death, her friend Emily Bayley, with whom she had passed some of her happiest days at Barrackpore, prepared a leather-bound memorial volume, now deposited in the British Library. It includes flowers removed from Lady Canning's grave as well as press notices of her death and funeral, photographs, letters, sketches, and a fold-out map of her travels in India.

122. Lutyens, 90.

123. Dufferin, *Our Viceregal Life,* 1:23, 28–29.

124. Goradia, *Lord Curzon,* 146–47.

125. Curzon, 2:35–36.

126. Steevens, 68.

127. Curzon, 2:45.

128. Ibid., 2:42.

CHAPTER 3. OVER THE HILLS AND FAR AWAY

1. Quoted without attribution in Cuthell, *My Garden,* 251.

2. Bernier, *Travels in the Mogul Empire,* 247.

3. Gordon Cumming, *In the Himalayas,* vi.

4. Parkes [Parks], *Begums, Thugs and White Mughals,* 119–20.

5. Heber, *Narrative of a Journey*, 2:98; Postans, *Western India*, 1:13; Tindall, *City of Gold*, 116.
6. Kipling, *Kim*, 52.
7. Quoted in Archer and Lightbown, *India Observed*, 108.
8. Kennedy, *Magic Mountains*, chap. 2 passim, 118. See also D. Arnold, *Colonizing the Body*.
9. MacMillan, *Women of the Raj*, 182.
10. Parkes, 327.
11. E. C. Archer, *Tours in Upper India*, 1:210.
12. Hooker, *Himalayan Journals*, 81.
13. Parkes, 328.
14. Westlake, *Introduction to the Hill Stations*, 64.
15. Kanwar, *Imperial Simla*, 71. Val Prinsep, commissioned to paint the Durbar of 1877, complained that the Order of Precedence made no mention of artists, leaving him in social limbo; see Buck, *Simla Past and Present*, 168.
16. Wright, *Hill Stations*, 249.
17. Sinha, *Landscapes in India*, 3; Bhasin, *Simla*, 2.
18. Wright, 112, 115.
19. Stewart, *Places in Between*, 161.
20. Kipling, *Kim*, 279.
21. Jahangir, *Jahangirnama*, 332; V. S. Naipaul, *Area of Darkness*, 97.
22. Crowe et al., *Gardens of Mughal India*, 74–120; Bernier, 275.
23. Moore, *Lalla Rookh*, 299.
24. Quoted in Steel, *Garden of Fidelity*, 95.
25. Morris, *Stones of Empire*, 54.
26. Quoted in Pubby, *Simla Then and Now*, 15.
27. The changing responses to mountains in the English literary, theological, and philosophical traditions are explored in great detail in M. H. Nicolson, *Mountain Gloom and Mountain Glory*.
28. Lady Amherst, Journal, 31 Mar. 1827.
29. Parkes, 328. As Wordsworth suggested in his *Guide to the Lakes*, travelers had come to anticipate the experience of the sublime; see M. H. Nicolson, 372.
30. Quoted in Dyson, *Various Universe*, 152.
31. E. C. Archer, 1:244–45.
32. Kennedy, 46–47; Parkes, 327–28; Lady Amherst, Journal, vol. 6 passim; Dufferin, *Our Viceregal Life*, 2:30; Lear quoted in Dehejia, *Impossible Picturesqueness*, 24
33. Eden, *Up the Country*, 125, 127.
34. Quoted in Pubby, 20–21.
35. Lutyens, *Lyttons in India*, 42.
36. Lady Amherst, Journal, 1 Apr. 1827; Eden, 31, 38, 248; Westlake, 22.
37. Bernier, 359–60.
38. Pubby, 42; Lutyens, 48; Tunzelmann, *Indian Summer*, 161–62.
39. Kennedy, 14; Kanwar, 40.
40. Eden, xv–xvi, 248; Westlake, 21–22.
41. Cuthell, 284; Gilmour, *Ruling Caste*, 227.
42. Archer quoted in Bhasin, 27.
43. Spear, *Twilight of the Mughuls*, 167–68.
44. A. D. King, *Colonial Urban Development*, 167. Cf. E. C. Archer, 1:207–8, 336.
45. G. C. Mundy, *Pen and Pencil Sketches*, 1:229–30; J. Lang, *Wanderings in India*, 302; Skinner, *Excursions in India*, 1:217, 315; Hooker, 74. As a trained scientist, Hooker noted,

however, that even the familiar flowers differed from their English cousins and were accompanied by various tropical growths.

46. Eden, *Up the Country*, 164.
47. Hooker, 328, 365; Waddell, *Among the Himalayas*, 18. Cf. I. Butler, *Viceroy's Wife*, 41.
48. Parkes, 327, 330, 339. Cf. E. A. King, *Diary of a Civilian's Wife*, 2:57.
49. Gordon Cumming, *In the Himalayas*, 312–13. Cf. Eden, *Up the Country*, 125.
50. Hare, *Story of Two Noble Lives*, 3:106, 110–11; Lear, *Indian Journal*, 122–23, 133.
51. Lloyd, *Narrative of a Journey*, 146, 192.
52. Harrop, *Thacker's New Guide*, 164–65.
53. Eden, *Up the Country*, 129, 139, 164–65.
54. Dufferin, 1:168, 171–72, 181–82.
55. Mason, *Guardians*, 194–95.
56. D. Kincaid, *British Social Life*, 235.
57. Buck, 23–24.
58. Kaye, *Sun in the Morning*, 26. Cf. Gordon Cumming, 300.
59. E. A. King, 57–58.
60. Duncan, *Other Side of the Latch*, 8, 44.
61. Ibid., passim; quotations 7–8, 46, 92–93, 168, 176, 97, 199. Lady Anne Wilson and her husband had the good fortune to occupy Duncan's house and garden just a few years later; see Wilson, *Letters from India*, 320–21.
62. Duncan, 230–31.
63. Buck, 14.
64. Eden, 169; Kennedy, 93. Elsewhere Eden puts the European population at only 105 (294).
65. Buck, 54–55, 91; Morris, *Stones of Empire*, 54; Harrop, 34. The ballroom was decorated in eastern Moorish style by Lockwood Kipling, father of Rudyard.
66. Buck, 117–18; Edwardes, 178; Keay, *India: A History*, 457–58.
67. Eden, *Up the Country*, 128–29, 180.
68. Bhasin, *Simla*, 36, 55; Bhasin, *Viceregal Lodge*, 11; Lutyens, 38–39.
69. Dufferin, 1:131
70. Bence-Jones, *Viceroys*, 143; Halifax, *Fullness of Days*, 129.
71. Bhasin, *Viceregal Lodge*, 14–15; Dufferin, 2:179. To this day, women are conspicuous as laborers at building sites.
72. Dufferin, 2:288, 297.
73. Allen, *Kipling Sahib*, 268–69.
74. Dufferin, 2:294–96.
75. Bhasin, *Simla*, 56; Bence-Jones, *Viceroys*, 143.
76. Bence-Jones, *Palaces*, 142. Quotation from Audrey Harris in Bhasin, *Simla*, 58.
77. Bhasin, *Simla*, 57.
78. Bence-Jones, *Palaces*, 188–89.
79. Buck, 48, 53; Barr and Desmond, *Simla*, 39.
80. Hardinge, *Indian Years*, 28; Harrop, 50.
81. I. Butler, 41–42; Kanwar, 225, 234; Fowler, *Below the Peacock Fan*, 265–66.
82. Buck, 48, 174; Bence-Jones, *Viceroys*, 244; Bhasin, *Simla*, 59–60, 183; I. Butler, 41.
83. Bence-Jones, *Palaces*, 142–43; Wilson, 322–33; Sharp, *Good-bye India*, 134.
84. Wilson, 323; Buck, 63–64, 181–82; quoted in A. Hodges, *Lord Kitchener*, 175–76. Kitchener's mansion was destroyed to make room for a hotel. This later burned down, but in 2000 a new luxury hotel opened, claiming to remain "true to the spirit of the original

bungalow in its external aspect" and building methods; see www.oberoihotels.com/oberoi_wildflowerhall/travel_guide/discover.asp.

85. Dufferin, 1:189–90; Bhasin, *Simla*, 75, 185; Buck, 176; Bence-Jones, *Viceroys*, 181; Bence-Jones, *Palaces*, 142–43.

86. Allen, *Glimpse*, 38–39, 155–61.

87. Gordon Cumming, 484, 505, 515.

88. I. Butler, 28.

89. Hardinge, 26; Gordon-Cumming, 484.

90. Dehejia, 38.

91. Parks, 331, 338.

92. Dufferin, 2:154–55.

93. Kennedy, 126–27; the BBC documentary *Lost World of the Raj*, part 3; Bond and Saili, *Mussoorie and Landour*, 29.

94. Waddell, *Among the Himalayas*, 41.

95. Dufferin, 1:131.

96. The quotation is from Burton, *Goa and the Blue Mountains*, 277. Ooty is now officially known as Udhagamandalam.

97. Ibid., 353.

98. Quoted in H. Brown, *Sahibs*, 27.

99. Panter-Downes, *Ooty Preserved*, 74–75; Gleig, *Sir Thomas Munro*, 2:305. Panter-Downes and Price, *Ootacamund*, provide the most extensive histories of Ootacamund, but see also Baikie, *Observations on the Neilgherries*, for an exhaustive early account, and Burton for a more jaundiced view. For an illustration of the *Strobilanthes callosa* by an Indian botanical artist, see Noltie, *Dapuri Drawings*, pl. 59. The plant has also been labeled *Strobilanthus kunthiansus*.

100. Baikie, 5; Burton, 283.

101. Baikie, 72–73; Price, 123; Hare, 2:437.

102. Panter-Downes, 31.

103. Price, 42, 44, 75, 258–59; Pal and Dehejia, *From Merchants to Emperors*, 188.

104. Noltie, *Robert Wight and the Illustration of Indian Botany*, 16.

105. Baikie, 121–22; Hare, 2:448; Price, 79, 84, 496; Molony, "Indian Hill Station," 627–38; Panter-Downes, 79.

106. Price, 102–3, 112–19, 130–33, 327–28, 303–4; Surtees, *Charlotte Canning*, 260; Panter-Downes, 31, 62, 73–74, 108; Kenny, "Climate, Race, and Imperial Authority," 704–5.

107. Surtees, 257–60; Hare, 2:442; Allen, 99–100.

108. Campbell, *Old Forest Ranger*, 70.

109. Lear, 193–97; Dehejia, 45–47, 105.

110. Molony, 639.

111. Gleig, 2:306.

112. Price, 68–69, 126, 253, 475–76; quotation, 495–96.

113. Burton, 277–78; Price, 68–69.

114. Burton, 201.

115. Ibid., 278.

116. Kennedy, chap. 3 passim.

117. Ibid., 175.

118. Mitchell, *Indian Hill Station*, 127–28; Price, 521; Panter-Downes, 107–8; Bond and Saili, 22; Wright, 26–27.

119. Wilson, *Letters from India,* 50.

120. Lawrence, *Indian Embers,* 290.

121. Pubby, 7, 88.

122. Eden, 293–94.

123. The quotation is from Kipling, "The Return," *Complete Verse,* 482: "If England was what England seems, / An' not the England of our dreams, / But only putty, brass, an' paint, / 'Ow quick we'd drop 'er! *But she ain't.*"

124. Morris, "Hill Stations," 51; Dalrymple, *City of Djinns,* 315.

125. Kesevan, *Looking Through Glass,* 274.

126. Lloyd, 141.

127. Duncan, 258.

128. Scott, *Towers of Silence,* 207, 283, and passim.

129. Dharma Vira, foreword to Hasan, *Bangalore Through the Centuries,* vii; Randhawa et al., *Famous Gardens of India,* 1; Bowring, *Eastern Experiences,* 9.

130. Shields, *Birds of Passage,* 142–43; Michaud, *History of Mysore,* 19; Arthur, *Mission to Mysore,* 140.

131. Buchanan, *Journey from Madras.*

132. Shields, 147.

133. Davies, *Splendours of the Raj,* 107–8; Pott, *Old Bungalows,*; Jayapal, *Bangalore,* 59ff.; Lear, *Indian Journal,* 176; cf. Hare, 2: 427. Both Davies and Pott include illustrations. Pott also discusses a number of individual houses, with interviews with their present owners.

134. Maitland, 138–39, 142.

135. I. Butler, 124; Pott, 48 and passim; Jayapal, 58; Davies, 106ff.; Lakshmi Reddy Bloom, personal communication, 29 May 2010.

136. Srinivas, *Landscapes of Urban Memory,* 57; Hasan, 214; Bowring, 9.

137. Jayapal, 184–85, 189ff.; www.indtravel.com/bang/places.html.

138. See http://nitpu3.nic.in/rajbhavan/thebuilding/gardens/htm; http://rajbhavan.kar.nic.in/history/comm-residence.htm.

139. Quoted in Bhatt, *Resorts of the Raj,* 83.

140. J. Nair, *Promise of the Metropolis,* 61; Bowe, "Indian Gardening Tradition," n40.

141. Bowring, 451; cf. 14, 371.

142. Cuthell, 75; Parks, 358–61; Mir Taqi Mir, quoted in Dalrymple, *City of Djinns,* 65: "What matters it, O breeze, / If now has come the spring / When I have lost them both / The garden and my nest?" Eden quoted in H. Brown, *Sahibs,* 241.

143. Beames, *Memoirs of a Bengal Civilian,* 225–28.

144. John N. Hawkins to Arthur Hawkins, 28 Aug. 1929, and photographs from 1922 and 1934. I am grateful to Arthur Hawkins's grandson for sharing these with me.

145. Most of these houses and gardens have long since fallen to the jackhammer or been put to other uses, but a glimpse of how they once looked can be had on a website created by "Ron, the Bangalore Walla" and devoted to Richmond Town quarter. www.geocities.com/Athens/Olympus/5024/roads.htm; Pott, passim.

CHAPTER 4. EASTWARD IN EDEN

1. Jayapal, *Bangalore,* 26, 174–75; Buchanan, *Journey from Madras* 1:46–47.

2. Dalrymple, *White Mughals,* 60.

3. Bowring, *Eastern Experiences*, 56. Lady Henrietta Clive thought the paintings "most viley done... without the least regard to perspective," but it was probably the reality of Baillie's defeat that most offended her; see *Birds of Passage*, 181.

4. E. Roberts, *Scenes and Characteristics of Hindostan*, 2:223.

5. Michaud, *History of Mysore*, 83. See also Jasanoff, *Edge of Empire*, 158ff.

6. On Haidar Ali, Tipu Sultan, and the Lal Bagh, see, in addition to Jayapal and Michaud, Randhawa et al., *Famous Gardens of India*, 2ff.; Forrest, *Tiger of Mysore*, 101, 255; Hasan, *Bangalore Through the Centuries*, 212; Drayton, *Nature's Government*, 46; M. D. L. T., *History of Hyder Shah*, 48, 74.

7. Desmond, *Kew*, xiii; Shields, 180–81.

8. Lear, *Indian Journal*, 177.

9. On the history of botanical gardens, see, in addition, to Drayton, Desmond, *Kew*; Desmond, *European Discovery of the Indian Flora*; Brockway, *Science and Colonial Expansion*; McCracken, *Gardens of Empire*; and Carlton and Carlton, *Significance of Gardening in British India*, chap. 4.

10. Drayton, 14–19; Philip H. Oswald, review of Charlie Jarvis, *Order out of Chaos: Linnaean Plant Names and their Types*, *Times Literary Supplement*, 14 Mar. 2008, 24. Classification criteria are still being refined: see Geldhill, *Names of Plants*. Some biologists are turning away from binomial nomenclature entirely, using DNA barcoding instead; Elizabeth Farnsworth, personal communication, 15 Oct. 2008. See also "DNA Barcoding All Our Flora and Fauna," *Telegraph* (UK), 21 Oct. 2006.

11. McCracken, viii, 2; Drayton, 72–74.

12. Desmond, *Kew*, 32ff.; Drayton, 42–43.

13. Desmond, *Kew*, chap. 6; Drayton, 67.

14. Desmond, *Kew*, chap. 6, quotation on 98; Drayton, 94–95. The *Bounty*'s mutinous crew threw the breadfruit trees into the sea, but Bligh was able to make a successful transfer of the plants a few years later; see McCracken, 102.

15. Darwin, *Botanic Garden*, part I, canto IV, line 561.

16. Drayton, 49–50, 108, 115.

17. Desmond, *Kew*, 101, 145.

18. Ibid., quotation on 141; Drayton, chap 5.

19. Desmond, *Kew*, 132, 141ff.; Drayton, 134–35, 153–69.

20. Drayton, chaps. 5–6; Desmond, *Kew*, xiii–xiv, chaps. 9–10, and passim; Endersby, *Imperial Nature*; Brockway, 6–7; quotation from McCracken, viii. Drayton takes issue with Desmond and Brockway over how clear William Hooker's imperial ambitions for Kew were when he first took over (171–72).

21. Drayton, 156–57.

22. According to Maria Graham, in Lawson, *Memories of Madras*, 265.

23. Quoted in Brockway, 75; see also Grove, *Green Imperialism*, 335ff., 403–4, Drayton, 117–18.

24. Desmond, *European Discovery*, 57–58; Drayton, 115ff.

25. Cotton, *Calcutta, Old and New*, 786–89.

26. Keay, *India Discovered*, 275; Desmond, *European Discovery*, 59–60; Desmond, *Kew*, 98–100, 117ff.; Kumar, *Science and the Raj*, 36ff.

27. Valentia, *Voyages and Travels*, 1:39; Cf. Graham, *Journal*, 145–46.

28. Milton, *Paradise Lost*, bk. 9, lines 1099ff.

29. Heber, *Narrative of a Journey*, 1:52–54; Lady Amherst, Journal, 3 Dec. 1824, 9 Feb. 1827;

Desmond, *European Discovery,* 84; Uglow, *Little History of British Gardening,* 210. The giant baobab fell victim to the great cyclone of 1867 with a crash that made the earth tremble for a distance of hundreds of yards; see McCracken, 100–101.

30. Cotton, 295; http://en.wikipedia.org/wiki/Amherstia; Wulf and Gieben-Gamal, *This Other Eden,* 233.

31. Heber, 1:52.

32. Cotton, 789–90; Desmond, *Kew,* 399

33. Desmond, *European Discovery,* 59–60, 90–91, 106–7, 281

34. Valentia, 1:39; Hooker, *Himalayan Journals,* 464–67; Desmond, *European Discovery,* 95–96.

35. Hooker, 466–68; Axelby, "Calcutta Botanic Garden."

36. Desmond, *Kew,* 181–83, 221–22, 228–30, 369;

37. William Morris, *Hopes and Fears for Art,* quoted in Robinson, *English Flower Garden,* 3.

38. Desmond, *European Discovery,* 101.

39. Hare, *Story of Two Noble Lives,* 2:116, 145. Cf. Desmond, *Kew,* 134–35, 229–30.

40. Desmond, *European Discovery,* 111.

41. G. C. Mundy, *Pen and Pencil Sketches,* 1:127–28.

42. Desmond, *European Discovery,* 111, 220. See also Schiebinger and Swan, *Colonial Botany,* on early European respect for indigenous botanical knowledge; the quotation is from ibid., 121.

43. Desmond, *Kew,* 214–15; Carlton and Carlton, 66–67.

44. *Marlene Dietrich's ABC,* quoted in Macfarlane and Macfarlane, *Green Gold,* 167.

45. Griffiths, *History of the Indian Tea Industry,* 25–26, 30–32. Wesley's indictment is contained in *A Letter to a Friend concerning Tea* (1748).

46. Isaac D'Israeli, quoted in Macfarlane and Macfarlane, 27–30.

47. Macfarlane and Macfarlane, 80; Gillian Darley, review of Tim Richardson, *The Arcadian Friends, Times Literary Supplement,* 23 Nov. 2007, 23.

48. Macfarlane and Macfarlane, 69–75, 99.

49. For a comprehensive history, see Booth, *Opium.*

50. T. Bacon, *Orientalist,* 51–52; Heber, 1:349.

51. "In an Opium Factory," in *City of the Dreadful Night,* 325–35. Kipling's essay dates from about 1891.

52. Quoted ibid., 334.

53. Booth, 109–10; quotation from Macfarlane, 112.

54. Macfarlane and Macfarlane, 33–38, 100–101, quotation on 131; Griffiths, chap. 4 and 110.

55. For a good description of tea growing and processing see www.alanmacfarlane.com/tea/Tea_manufacture.pdf, with accompanying film at www.alanmacfarlane.com/tea/av.html. The processing is now highly mechanized, although tea is still picked entirely by hand.

56. Macfarlane and Macfarlane, 135–39; Griffiths, 50–51.

57. Macfarlane and Macfarlane, 195.

58. Griffiths, 119, 124, 143; Macfarlane and Macfarlane, 189–201. But see Thomas Fuller, "A Tea from the Jungle Enriches a Placid Village," *New York Times,* 21 Apr. 2008, A9, for an account of the revival of interest in wild tea in China.

59. Macfarlane and Macfarlane, 115–16.

60. This story is well told in Collingham, *Curry,* chap. 8.

61. A. Coats, *Quest for Plants,* 172.

62. Ibid., 145; Desmond, *European Discovery*, vi.

63. A. Coats, 143–45; Desmond, *European Discovery*, 39–40; Noltie, *Robert Wight and the Illustration of Indian Botany*, 11.

64. Lord Clive was the son of Robert Clive, victor of Plassey. The elder Clive had a pet tortoise, which may have been the one on view in the Alipore Zoo, Kolkata, until its death in 2006; www.timesonline.co.uk/tol/news/world/asia/article744557.ece .

65. Buchanan, 1:xii–xiii, 47. Cf. Michaud, 195.

66. M. Archer, "India and Natural History"; Keay, *India Discovered*, 267–68, 275.

67. A. Coats, 157.

68. D. Arnold, *Tropics and the Traveling Gaze*, 67.

69. Desmond, *Kew*, chap. 8 passim, 212; D. Arnold, 62–63. After midcentury, Kew stopped sending out its own collectors, relying on its international network, other botanical gardens, and private nurserymen; see Desmond, *Kew*, 212.

70. Quoted in A. Coats, *Flowers and their Histories*, ix.

71. See, for example, A. Coats, *Quest for Plants*, passim.

72. Desmond, *European Discovery*, provides an excellent chapter on botanizing in the Himalayas. See also Keay, *When Men and Mountains Meet*, 179–80.

73. M. Archer, *Company Paintings*, 97–98, with illustration; Gleig, *Memoirs*, 1:411–13; Desmond, *European Discovery*, 123.

74. Desmond, *European Discovery*, 138ff.; Mabey, *Flowers of Kew*, 140–43; Endersby, 121ff.

75. Hadfield, *Gardening in Britain*, 17.

76. Elliott, *Victorian Gardens*, 195; Desmond, *Kew*, 208; Hadfield, 230.

77. Tom Williamson, *Polite Landscapes*, 138.

78. Desmond, *European Discovery*, 318–20.

79. Saunders, *Picturing Plants*, 7, 141; Desmond, *European Discovery*, 88–90; Noltie, *Robert Wight and the Illustration of Indian Botany*, 14; Kumar, 38.

80. Quoted in Endersby, 294–95.

81. Saunders, passim. See also Endersby, 118–36, for a detailed discussion of debates about botanical illustration.

82. Jahangir, *Jahangirnama*, 333.

83. Stronge, *Painting for the Mughal Emperor*, chap. 1 passim, 100–103, 172–73; Dye, "Artists for the Emperor," 104; Desmond, *European Discovery*, 144–47.

84. Mildred Archer is the preeminent scholar of Indian painting for the East India Company and other British patrons; see esp. her introduction to *Company Paintings*. The "hybrid vigour" quote is from Noltie, *Robert Wight and the Illustration of Indian Botany*, 23. See also Saunders, 12–14, 80. In Thanjavur (Tanjur) they also made natural history drawings of birds and animals from his menagerie for the ruler, Serfogi; see M. Archer, *Company Paintings*, 44.

85. Maria Graham, 145–46; Valentia, 1:356; Mabey, 88–91; Desmond, *European Discovery*, 65, 68, 144, 148–51.

86. On Wight, see esp. Noltie, *Robert Wight and the Illustration of Indian Botany*, but also Desmond, *European Discovery*, 116–18.

87. Noltie is paraphrasing Paul Klee's *Pedagogical Sketchbook* in his comment about Rungiah's treatment of the stem. Noltie has published two hundred drawings by Rungiah and Govindoo in *Robert Wight and the Botanical Drawings of Rungiah & Govindoo*.

88. The phrase "double game" is Noltie's (*Robert Wight and the Illustration of Indian Botany*, 24).

89. North, *Vision of Eden*, chapters on Ceylon and India, passim.

90. Quotations are from Mukherjee, *Sir William Jones*, iv; Desmond, *European Discovery*, 53. See also Cannon, *Letters of Sir William Jones*; A. M. Jones, *Works of Sir William Jones*; Shore, *Memoirs*; Cannon, *Life and Mind of Oriental Jones*; Cannon, *Oriental Jones*; Desmond, *European Discovery*, 52–57; Head, "Divine Flower Power Recorded."

91. Cannon, *Letters of Sir William Jones*, 2:813, 848.

92. Jones, *Works*, 1:6.

93. Shore, 251.

94. Quoted from *Asiatick Researches* 4 in Desmond, *European Discovery*, 53.

95. Cannon, *Letters of Sir William Jones*, 2:743.

96. Cannon, *Letters of Sir William Jones*, 2:755, 783–84; Shore, 309.

97. Thomas Twining, in Sykes, *Calcutta Through British Eyes*, 125.

98. Shore, 354–55.

99. Jones, *Works*, 2:91.

100. Quoted in Dyson, *Various Universe*, 183. It is more likely that the *madhavi* was a variety of jasmine.

101. Cannon, *Letters of Sir William Jones*, 2:771; "The Design of a Treatise on the Plants of India," repr. in Jones, *Works*, 2:2–8. In the same vein, Lady Henrietta Clive emphasized in a letter to her husband that trees she was sending to him had "Malabar" names attached and that care should be taken to preserve them; see Shields, 243.

102. Jones Collection, 025-036/18: XXIX. See Head, *Catalogue of Paintings*, and Head, "Divine Flower Power Recorded," for reproductions of botanical illustrations by Lady Jones and artists commissioned by William Jones.

103. Arberry, *Asiatic Jones*, 22; Cannon, *Letters of Sir William Jones*, 2:902, 897.

104. Cannon, *Life and Mind*, 352; http://en.wikipedia.org/wiki/Asoka_tree. The tree has been reclassified as *Saraca asoca*; see glossary under *Sita-Ashok*.

105. Thomas Martyn, introduction to a translation of Rousseau's *On the Elements of Botany Addressed to Ladies* (1785), quoted in Mabey, 37.

106. M. Archer, *Company Drawings*, 97.

107. A. Coats, *Quest for Plants*, 151; M. Archer, *Company Paintings*, 134; Desmond, *European Discovery*, 88; http://en.wikipedia.org/wiki/Amherstia. Specimens of the golden pheasant can also be seen in the Lloyd Botanical Garden, Darjeeling. See Lady Sarah Amherst's drawings of Government House, Calcutta, reproduced in Losty, *Calcutta*.

108. Shteir, *Cultivating Women*, 192–93; Matthew, "South-Indian Botanical Collectors."

109. Allen, *Glimpse*, 11, 27.

110. Beatrix Stanley's watercolors are in the collection of her grandson, Sir Andrew Buchanan, Hodsock Priory, Nottinghamshire, UK.

111. On North see her autobiographical works, *Recollections of a Happy Life* and *Some Further Recollections of a Happy Life*, abridged in *Vision of Eden*. See also Middleton, *Victorian Lady Travellers*, chap. 2.

112. Desmond, *European Discovery*, 106–7.

113. Bowring, *Eastern Experiences*, 385; www.horticulture.kar.nic.in/lalbagh.htm; Lear, *Indian Journal*, 176–77, 15 Aug. 1774; Desmond, *European Discovery*, 106–7.

114. For a beautifully illustrated survey of botanical gardens, see Hyams and MacQuilty, *Great Botanical Gardens*.

115. Colquhoun, *Thing in Disguise*, 26.

116. Quoted in Gorer, *Growth of Gardens*, 191.

117. Noltie, *Dapuri Drawings*, 19 and passim.

118. Robert Hay, Permanent Under-Secretary at the Colonial Office, quoted in Desmond, *Kew*, 123.

119. Drayton, 24, fig. 7, and chap. 2 passim. Satpal Sangwan has given this enterprise the appropriate label "plant colonialism"; cited in Kumar, 37.

120. Mabey, 50, 52; Endersby, 135.

121. Noltie, *Robert Wight and the Illustration of Indian Botany*, 13–14; Mabey, 141, 179–80.

122. A. Amherst, *History of Gardening in England*, 288–89.

123. Desmond, *Kew*, 344.

124. Grove, 453–54 and chap. 8 passim. See also Noltie, *Dapuri Drawings*, 28ff., about the work of Alexander Gibson as forester for the Bombay Presidency.

125. Hooker, 2:279–80.

CHAPTER 5. GARDENS OF MEMORY

1. On the history of Lucknow, see especially the works of Llewellyn-Jones: *A Fatal Friendship*; *Engaging Scoundrels*; and "Lucknow, City of Dreams," as well as two beautifully illustrated books edited by Llewellyn-Jones: *Lucknow: City of Illusion* and *Lucknow: Then and Now*. See also Sharar, *Lucknow: The Last Phase of an Oriental Culture*, and Oldenburg, *Making of Colonial Lucknow*, both reprinted in *Lucknow Omnibus* as is Llewellyn-Jones's *Fatal Friendship*.

2. Tennyson, "The Defence of Lucknow."

3. Llewellyn-Jones, *Engaging Scoundrels*, 125; Russell, *Prince of Wales's Tour*, 350ff.; Morris, *Pax Britannica*, 415. There is an enormous literature on the Uprising of 1857, but it is well summarized in the introduction to Llewellyn-Jones's *Great Uprising*.

4. Cuthell, *My Garden*, 74.

5. Eden, *Up the Country*, 294; Huggins, *Sketches in India*, 79–80.

6. Taylor, *Visit to India*, 110.

7. Llewellyn-Jones, *Fatal Friendship*, 108–9; Oldenburg, 23; Pouchepadass, "Lucknow Besieged," 96–98.

8. Llewellyn-Jones, "Lucknow, City of Dreams," passim, and Llewellyn-Jones, *Fatal Friendship*, 140ff.; David, "La Martinière," 222; Rawdon-Hastings, *Private Journal of the Marquess of Hastings*, 1:196; E. Roberts, *Scenes and Characteristics of Hindostan*, 1:198; Russell, *Diary*, 1:251.

9. Llewellyn-Jones, *Fatal Friendship*, 153–54, 212; Llewellyn-Jones, "Lucknow, City of Dreams," 63; Das, "'Country Houses' of Lucknow," 180ff.; Rawdon-Hastings, 1:201; Cuthell, 165.

10. Llewellyn-Jones, "Lucknow, City of Dream**s**," 49, 60–63, and passim; Eden, 62. Lord Valentia was probably the first to invoke the Arabian Nights apropos of Lucknow; *Voyages and Travels*, 1:132.

11. Llewellyn-Jones, *Engaging Scoundrels*, 24–25, 163; Cuthell, 54; Das, 173ff.; E. C. Archer, *Tours in Upper India*, 1:23.

12. Quoted in Llewellyn-Jones, *Engaging Scoundrels*, 21.

13. Ibid., 21–25; *Fatal Friendship*, 210–12; Gordon, "Royal Palaces," 33, 40; Rawdon-Hastings**,** 1:197; Russell, *Diary*, 1:338.

14. Llewellyn-Jones, *Engaging Scoundrels*, 1, 21–22.

15. Oldenburg**,** 9; Llewellyn-Jones, *Fatal Friendship*, ix; *Murray's Handbook*, 449; Sharar, 29.

16. Russell, *Diary*, 1:287–88, 337, 345; Pal and Dehejia, *From Merchants to Emperors*, 80–81.

17. Russell, *Diary*, 1:356; Oldenburg, chap. 2 passim; Llewellyn-Jones, *Lucknow: City of Illusion*, 19; Llewellyn-Jones, *Great Uprising*, 172; Gordon, 30–87.

18. Russell, *Prince of Wales's Tour*, 355; *Murray's Handbook*, map, 449.

19. Oldenburg, 56, 137, 244–45; J. G. Farrell, "Indian Diary," in *Hill Station*, 205.

20. Dufferin, *Our Viceregal Life*, 2:59; Oldenburg, 56–57.

21. Cuthell, 25–26, 86, 122, 164

22. Gordon, fig. 36; Alkazi, "Husainabad Complex," figs. 80, 81; Cuthell, 203–4.

23. *Murray's Handbook*, 457.

24. Cuthell, 86–87, 184; Gordon Cumming, *In the Himalayas*, 115; Llewellyn-Jones, *Engaging Scoundrels*, 152–53; Llewellyn-Jones, *City of Illusion*, 198; and Llewellyn-Jones, *Great Uprising*, 117.

25. Dufferin, 1:269–70, 2:59; Lear, *Indian Journal*, 41–42; Cuthell, 184.

26. Chelkowski, "Monumental Grief," 101ff.

27. Ward, *Our Bones Are Scattered*, 550–53; Llewellyn-Jones, *Great Uprising*, 157–58, 184–85.

28. Gordon Cumming, 100–101, 517–19; Lear, 43; Yalland, *Boxwallahs*, 2ff.; Llewellyn-Jones, *Great Uprising*, 180, 184–86. See also www.indianholiday.com/tourist-attractions/uttar-pradesh/kanpur.

29. The quote is from Llewellyn-Jones, *Fatal Friendship*, 238.

CHAPTER 6. THE TAJ AND THE RAJ

1. Curzon, letter to his wife, quoted in Gilmour, *Curzon*, 321. The most thorough study of Curzon's restorations in India is Linstrum, "Sacred Past." Linstrum devotes only two short paragraphs to the Taj gardens, however.

2. 1 Jan. 1888, quoted in Ronaldshay, *Life of Lord Curzon*, 1:64, 128.

3. Curzon Notebooks, 3:53, 62–63, Curzon Papers (hereafter CP), Mss Eur F111/104.

4. Quoted in Gilmour, 69.

5. ASI, *Annual Progress, North-Western Provinces and Oudh*, 2.

6. Ancient Monuments Bill, 1904, CP, Mss Eur F111/487, repr. in Raleigh, *Lord Curzon in India*, 198–99.

7. MacDonnell to Curzon, 29 July 1900, CP, Mss Eur F111/620.

8. Ancient Monuments Bill, 1904, repr. in Raleigh, 198.

9. See Metcalf, "Past and Present."

10. 7 April 1900, CP. Mss Eur 111/621.

11. Hogarth, "George Nathaniel Curzon," 514.

12. Dec. 1899, CP, Mss Eur F111/620 (emphasis added).

13. 29 July 1900, CP, Mss Eur F111/620, with enclosed sketch; 18 Aug. 1900, CP, Mss Eur F111/620.

14. 29 Aug. 1900, CP, Mss Eur F111/620.

15. 18 April 1904, CP, Mss Eur F111/620.

16. Quoted in Wescoat and Wolschke-Bulmahn, "Sources, Places, Representations and Prospects," 20.

17. Twining, *Travels in India*, 191.

18. Parkes, *Begums, Thugs and White Mughals*, 190, 191.

19. Lear, *Indian Journal*, 78.

20. Pal et al., *Romance of the Taj Mahal*, 199; M. Archer, *Early Views of India*, pl. 4 and fig. 28.

21. Daniell and Daniell, *Views of the Taje Mahal,* 4.
22. North, *Vision of Eden,* 127.
23. CP, BL 430/5(23).
24. Cf. Metcalf, *Imperial Vision.* 47.
25. E. Arnold, *India Revisited,* 211.
26. There is an excellent body of literature on Mughal gardens. See, in addition to Villiers-Stuart and Wescoat and Wolschke-Bulmahn: Koch, *Complete Taj Mahal*; Crowe et al., *Gardens of Mughal India*; Wescoat, "Picturing an Early Mughal Garden"; and Koch, "Mughal Waterfront Garden."
27. Bernier, *Travels in the Mogul Empire,* 295–96.
28. P. Mundy, *Travels,* 2:214–15.
29. Crowe et al, 20.
30. Khan, *Zain Khan's Tabaqat-i-Baburi,* 159.
31. Jahangir, *Jahangirnama,* 24.
32. Fazl, *Akbarnama,* 81, 83–87.
33. Manrique, *Travels,* 2:163.
34. See Thackston, "Mughal Gardens in Persian Poetry," 242–43.
35. Leoshko, "Mausoleum for an Empress," 58.
36. *Murray's Handbook,* 270.
37. Leoshko, 56.
38. Parkes, 190.
39. Hunt, *Afterlife of Gardens,* 40–41.
40. Havell, "Indian Gardens," 214.
41. Eraly, *Mughal Throne,* 30.
42. Badaoni, quoted in Welch, "Gardens That Babur Did Not Like," 60.
43. Gascoigne, *Great Moghuls,* 43.
44. Babur, *Baburnama,* 359.
45. Wescoat, "Gardens of Invention," 106; T. Lentz, "Memory and Ideology," 57.
46. Wescoat, "Gardens of Invention," 108.
47. See Ruggles, "Humayun's Tomb and Garden," 178.
48. Koch, "Hierarchical Principles of Shah-Jahani Painting," 16.
49. Koch, "Mughal Palace Gardens," 212.
50. Crowe et al., 44–45, 73.
51. I am very grateful for ideas about the Taj and Mughal kingship to conversations with Ajay Sinha and to his unpublished manuscript, "Taj Mahal and Mughal Kingship."
52. Jellicoe, "Mughal Garden," 122.
53. Quoted in Begley, "Myth of the Taj Mahal," 13.
54. These inscriptions have led Wayne Begley to read the Taj complex as a symbolic depiction of the Day of Judgment, with the tomb as the heavenly Throne of God; ibid., 7–37. Begley's interpretation has not been universally accepted, however; see, e.g., Necipoğlu's review "The Taj Mahal." Sinha also has reservations, suggesting that Begley's reading may be somewhat anachronistic, imposing a more threatening and apocalyptic nineteenth-century interpretation on the Taj's Qur'anic inscriptions; "Myth of the Taj Mahal," 8–10, and personal communication, May 25, 2005.
55. The legend that Shah Jahan intended to construct a tomb for himself of black marble across the river from the Taj Mahal has generally been discounted; see, e.g., Moynihan, "Reflections of Paradise," 19. Necipoğlu, on the other hand, argues that this may well have been

Shah Jahan's intent but it was thwarted by Aurangzeb's usurpation of power and imprisonment of his father for the last seven years of his life; "The Taj Mahal," 343.

56. Moynihan, 31. Moynihan reproduces the Daniells' aquatint in color, 32.

57. Ibid., 32.

58. Ibid., 32-38; Fritz and Michell, "Archaeology of the Garden," 79.

59. Arberry, *Koran*. This is apparently the translation quoted in Moynihan, 39, but with line breaks differing from Arberry's text.

60. Chirol, *Fifty Years*, 230.

61. Curzon to Brodrick, 17 Dec. 1903, CP, Mss Eur F111/620, 137; Spear, "Bentinck and the Taj," 184. Ironically, Bentinck was soon charged with trying to dismember and sell off the marble building materials of the Taj; ibid. and Koch, "Lost Colonnade."

62. On the budget see Ancient Monuments Bill, 1904, repr. in Raleigh, 199; Dilks, *Curzon in India*, 246.

63. Ancient Monuments Bill, 1904, repr. in Raleigh, 198.

64. Ibid., repr. Raleigh, 196.

65. 7 Feb. 1900, Speech to the Asiatic Society of Bengal, CP, Mss Eur 112/487, repr. in Raleigh, 188–89.

66. See, e.g., Rousselet, *L'Inde des Rajahs*; Rousselet visited the Taj in 1866. Commenting on the misfortunes that had befallen Agra at the hands of the Jats and Mahrattas and repeating the canard about Lord Bentinck wanting to sell off the building materials, he declared, "Today, the Queen's government better understands its duty; all the damage has been repaired, the monument has been cleaned and restored, and the gardens, enriched with rare plants, are maintained as in the old days of Shah Jahan" (317; my translation). Cf. T. Bacon, *Orientalist*, 129; Emerson, "On the Taj Mahal," 202; Robert Ogden Tyler quoted in Carroll, *Taj Mahal*, 146; Fergusson, *History of Indian and Eastern Architecture*, 3:595; Gurner, "Lord Hastings and the Monuments of Agra," 148; Orlich, *Travels in India*, 2:48.

67. 23 April 1902, CP, Mss Eur F111/620, 136; emphasis added.

68. Baker, *Architecture and Personalities*, 80.

69. Curzon Notebooks, 3:53, CP.

70. Rawdon-Hastings, *Private Journal of the Marquess of Hastings*, 2:10; cf. Metcalf, "Past and Present," 23; and Metcalf, *Imperial Vision*, 16ff.

71. Russell, *Diary*, 284; cf. the photographer Samuel Bourne's similar experience in 1863: see Pal and Dehejia, *From Merchants to Emperors*, 198.

72. A decade before Curzon, British officials argued about how much the Taj gardens should be pruned of their excess vegetation. Ultimately the argument prevailed that the view of the tomb should gradually unfold itself to the viewer; otherwise "there is nothing left to the imagination"; see Desmond, *European Discovery*, 262. If anything, the present-day lawns are more manicured than they were in Curzon's time. There have, however, been plans to restore the gardens to something more like their original design, that is, with more flowers and denser and more varied plantings of trees, although the staff have expressed fears that if fruit trees are replanted, they may be taken over as hiding places by local children and lovers; see Edensor, *Tourists at the Taj*, 190.

73. Colquhoun, *Thing in Disguise*, 33; Thacker, *History of Gardens*, 230–33.

74. See the National Trust guidebook *Kedleston Hall*, and www.peakdistrictinformation.com/visits/kedleston.php.

75. A. E. P. Griessen, Remarks.

76. J. Malcolm to Viceroy, 18 Jan. 1902, 128–29, CP, Mss Eur 111/621. In the same letter Malcolm recommended taking on a Dutch gardener.

77. Hogarth, 517.

78. E. Roberts et al., *Hindostan*; Sahni, *Guide to the Buddhist Ruins of Sarnath*; Byrom, "India," 270; www.sacred-destinations.com/india/sarnath.htm; Beames, *Memoirs of a Bengal Civilian*, 127.

79. On Khajuraho see esp. Deva, *Khajuraho*; Griffin, *Famous Monuments of Central India*; B. R. Seth, *Khajuraho in Pictures*; Zannas, *Khajuraho; Text and Photos*. There is also a useful website: http://reference.indianetzone.com/1/history.htm.

80. Sleeman, *Rambles and Recollections*, 2:32; Kisch, *Young Victorian*, 184; Russell, *Prince of Wales's Tour*, 393–94; Parkes, 192–94; Eden, *Up the Country*, 362–63.

81. Villiers-Stuart, 84–85.

82. Ibid., x, 66.

83. Dalrymple, *City of Djinns*, 222.

84. Colquhoun, 59.

85. "Orders Passed by the Viceroy on his Visit to Agra on 15th & 16th December 1903," 141–42, CP, Mss Eur F111/621.

86. Fritz and Michell, 79

87. Linstrum, 1.

88. Quoted in H. Nicolson, *Curzon*, 14.

89. Curzon, *British Government in India*, 1:177, 201. Curzon describes the project at length in this work. See also Metcalf, *Imperial Vision*, 202–10; Hardinge, *Old Diplomacy*, 244; Edwardes, *High Noon of Empire*, 127.

90. Curzon, 1:201.

91. Hodgson, "Memoir on the Illahee Guz," 56.

CHAPTER 7. IMPERIAL DELHI

1. Parkes, *Begums, Thugs and White Mughals*, 322–23.

2. The quotation is from Spear, *Delhi: A Historical Sketch*, 1.

3. Spear, *Delhi: Its Monuments and History*, 123–24; Spear, *Delhi: A Historical Sketch*, 16–18.

4. Lal, "Flora and Fauna of Delhi," 97.

5. Spear and Spear, *India Remembered*, 6.

6. Quoted in K. Singh, *Delhi*, 15

7. Arab source and Mutahar quoted ibid., 21–22; Elliot and Dowson, *History of India*, 3:345–46.

8. Battuta, *Travels*, 3:622, 739, The practice of strewing fresh flowers on Muslim graves morning and evening was still common in Arcot in 1800; see Shields, *Birds of Passage*, 111.

9. Babur, *Baburnama*, 327, 335, 353, 364.

10. Ruggles, *Islamic Gardens and Landscapes*, 110–11; Welch, "Gardens That Babur Did Not Like," 73, 83, 92. Welch's claim that the Mughals drew on the sophisticated hydraulic engineering of the Delhi sultans for their own gardens seems less convincing, since Babur implies that the use of waterwheels to create running water was a novelty in the gardens he and his nobles laid out in Agra: Welch, 83; Babur, 364. Questionable, too, is his claim that the Mughals also inherited from the Delhi sultans "an ancient ritual attitude toward water acquired from pre-Islamic India that had points of contact with the Muslim requirement for ablution before prayer" (83).

11. Moynihan, "But What a Pleasure," 117–18.

12. Crowe et al., *Gardens of Mughal India*, 44.

13. Koch, *Complete Taj Mahal*, 29–30.

14. Ibid., 22, 28, 30–31

15. A poetic self-description—the Mughals were inclined toward poetic expression—quoted in Schimmel, *Empire of the Great Mughals*, 30.

16. Mughal (and non-Mughal) rulers relied heavily on astrologers, but Humayun carried the practice to extremes.

17. One text does describe a rather fantastical plan Humayun created for a floating water palace consisting of four barges that would symbolize paradise, accompanied by other barges planted with fruit trees and flowering plants; see Leoshko, "Mausoleum for an Empress," 73.

18. Bernier, *Travels in the Mogul Empire*, 285; Spear, *Delhi: A Historical Sketch*, 24–26.

19. Gupta, "Indomitable City," 34.

20. Spear, *Delhi: A Historical Sketch*, 27.

21. Ehlers and Krafft, *Shahjahanabad/Old Delhi*, 17. The authors include a large reconstruction of a map of Shahjahanabad in the India Office dating to c. 1850.

22. Mukherji, "Changing Perception of Space," 46.

23. Bernier, 242–43.

24. Mukherji, *Red Fort*, 26.

25. Ibid., 100; Koch, *Complete Taj Mahal*, 137.

26. Koch, "Mughal Waterfront Garden," 144. The quotation is from Kanbo, poet and self-appointed historian of Shah Jahan's reign.

27. Bernier, 267. As a physician, Bernier sometimes was called upon to treat women of the imperial household, but in those cases he had to cover his face and head with a Kashmir shawl and be guided by a palace eunuch.

28. Hearn, *Seven Cities of Delhi*, 160.

29. Mukherji, "Changing Perception of Space," 59.

30. Villiers-Stuart, *Gardens of the Great Mughals*, 119.

31. For descriptions of these gardens as they were originally designed see Mukherji, *Red Fort*, passim; Koch, "Mughal Palace Gardens"; Blake, "Khanah Bagh," 177–80; Villiers-Stuart, 118–22.

32. Blake, "Khanah Bagh," 177. Quotation from an early source, in Lehrman, *Earthly Paradise*, 157.

33. Blake, "Khanah Bagh," 178. The total cost of the entire palace complex was 6 million rupees, with 600,000 going for construction of the Hayat Baksh; see Blake, *Shahjahanabad*, 43.

34. Lehrman, 157; Dalrymple, *Last Mughal*, 34.

35. Muhammad Waris, quoted in Koch, "Mughal Palace Gardens," 227.

36. Ibid., 224–28.

37. The lines are from the fourteenth-century poet Amir Khusrau, probably describing the capital of his day. The same inscription is found also in Jahangir's Shalimar Garden in Kashmir; see Blake, *Shahjahanabad*, 44n79. The designation was not unique, therefore, to Shah Jahan's creation.

38. On Versailles, see esp. Thompson, *Sun King's Garden*; Thacker, *History of Gardens*, 152ff.

39. Koch, *Complete Taj Mahal*, 24.

40. Blake, "Khanah Bagh," 186; Ehlers and Krafft, 19.

41. By the time of the last Mughal emperor, Bahadur Shah Zafar, the *zenana* seems to have become eminently porous, with wives and concubines slipping in and out for frequent trysts:

"Whatever his other qualities, running the domestic arrangements of the Red Fort was clearly not one of Zafar's talents, at least in his old age." Dalrymple, *Last Mughal*, 45.

42. Bernier, 283. See also Crowe et al., 146–47.

43. Bernier accompanied the emperor so that he was an eyewitness to the mind-boggling retinue (358–59). In 1739 the Persian invader Nadir Shah camped here on the eve of his massacre of the citizens of Delhi and seizure of the Peacock Throne; see Crowe et al., 147.

44. Blake, "*Khanah Bagh,*" passim.

45. Bernier, 246–47.

46. Spear, *Delhi: Its Monuments and History*, 29. Spear compares this to Christina Rosetti's lines, "Be the green grass above me with flowers and dewdrops wet. / And if thou wilt, remember, and if thou wilt, forget."

47. Quoted in Dalrymple, *City of Djinns*, 96–97.

48. Mirza Mohammed Rafi Sauda (1713–81), quoted in K. Singh, *Delhi*, 30.

49. On Bahadur Shah's love of gardens, see Dalrymple, *Last Mughal*, 34, 97, 276. The emperor wrote poetry under the name of Zafar.

50. Heber, *Narrative of a Journey*, 2:302–4; cf. Lady Amherst, Journal, 23 Feb. 1827.

51. Eden, *Up the Country*, 97.

52. Taylor, *Visit to India*, 80–81.

53. Sylvia Shorto, "Public Lives, Private Places: British Houses in Delhi, 1803–57" (Ph. D. diss., New York University, 2004), 110–12.

54. Heber, 2:286.

55. Shorto, 117–20.

56. E. Roberts, *Scenes and Characteristics of Hindostan*, 2:155.

57. Edwardes, *Glorious Sahibs*, 112.

58. Dalrymple, *Last Mughal*, 49–50, 167n, 234. As it turned out, Octherlony died in Meerut and was buried there. The tomb was destroyed during the fighting in 1857.

59. Shorto, 183.

60. Steel, *On the Face of the Waters*, 147–49.

61. Morris, *Stones of Empire*, 39.

62. Kaye, *Golden Calm*, 146–48. Spear comments: "If Ochterlony was the Babur and Charles [Metcalfe] the Akbar of British Delhi, Thomas Metcalfe was its Shah Jahan"; *Twilight of the Mughuls*, 157. K. Singh, *Delhi*, 13–14. Shorto comments that it was quite common to put tombs to other uses in the nineteenth century (and even today), and was not regarded as sacrilegious (190, 195). Cf. E. Roberts, 1:199; Steel, *Garden of Fidelity*, 220; North, *Vision of Eden*, 130.

63. Russell, *Diary*, 140; Shorto, 154.

64. E. Roberts, 2:148–49. According to Roberts, the begum eventually incurred the wrath of the British by failing to show them the deference they considered their due. The begum's palace in Delhi now houses the State Bank of India; see Gupta, *Delhi Between Two Empires*, 193.

65. Spear, *Twilight of the Mughuls*, 195; Gupta, *Delhi Between Two Empires*, 15–16. The Hindu attraction to the Shi'ite rituals of Mohurram is all the more surprising in that the Mughals were Sunni.

66. Gupta, "Indomitable City," 39–40. Metcalfe himself left a handwritten history of imperial Delhi, profusely illustrated by local artists. It is reproduced in facsimile by Kaye, *Golden Calm*, along with Emily Metcalfe's journal. For other views of Delhi by local artists, see J. Losty, "Delhi Palace in 1846."

67. The one exception was the curious and ambitious creation of Trevelyanganj as a model suburb for Delhi's middling classes of clerks and merchants—as opposed to the ancient families with their huge mansions and fine gardens—by a reforming British official, Charles Trevelyan. In 1830 Trevelyan acquired about three hundred acres of wasteland outside the Lahore Gate, laid out a road, and neatly mapped lots for houses and shops. His suburb survived for a long time before being swallowed up in later extensions of the city. See Prior, Brennan, and Haines, "Bad Language," 106–7; Trevelyan, *Golden Oriole,* 137–38; Gupta, "Indomitable City," 40; A. D. King, *Colonial Urban Development,* 202 (where the suburb is referred to as "Trevelyanpore," later as "Deputyganj"). The suburb is no longer remembered as Trevelyanganj (or any of the other names, for that matter); according to the website *Manorama Online,* "the name has just worn out." See www.the-week.com, 8 Aug. 2004.

68. Kaye, *Golden Calm,* 216. His queen was less fatalistic, as well as vehemently hostile to the British. There was much speculation that she may have been responsible for poisoning Thomas Metcalfe in 1853.

69. Dalrymple's splendid account of the uprising in *The Last Mughal* supersedes earlier histories in its use of newly uncovered indigenous sources.

70. Gupta, "Indomitable City," 42

71. Quoted in Gupta, *Delhi Between Two Empires,* 30

72. Mukherji, *Red Fort,* 152, 229.

73. North, 140.

74. ASI, *Annual Report, 1903–4,* 21–22.

75. Dalrymple, *City of Djinns.*

76. Kaye, *Golden Calm,* 207–8.

77. Blake, *Shahjahanabad,* 172; Mukherji, "Changing Perception of Space," 63. Later much of this area would be turned into parking.

78. Spear, *Delhi: Its Monuments and History,* 10n3. The much reduced gardens are now known as Gandhi Park: see Mukherji, *Red Fort,* 202; Hearn, 19.

79. Dalrymple, *Last Mughal,* provides a good overview of the destruction of Delhi following the uprising. See also Fanshawe, *Delhi, Past and Present,* 58; Peck, *Delhi,* 247; Spear, *Delhi: Its Monuments and History,* 16n1.

80. Villiers-Stuart, 103.

81. Ehlers and Krafft, 22; Hearn, 302–3.

82. Villiers-Stuart, 113.

83. Ibid., 114–17.

84. To Curzon's horror the gardens were no sooner restored than they were leased out to an Indian farmer who planted the lawns with turnips and whose cows broke down the water channels; see Gilmour, *Curzon,* 321. A century later the Aga Khan Trust for Culture took charge of a re-restoration of the garden; see Celia W. Dugger, "A Mughal Splendor Regained," *New York Times,* 29 Sept. 2002.

85. Fergusson, *History of Indian and Eastern Architecture,* 1:312.

86. ASI, *Annual Report, 1903–4,* 21; ASI, *Annual Report, 1909–10,* 1; Mukherji, *Red Fort,* 225.

87. Mukherji, *Red Fort,* 228.

88. Ibid., 223–25. Mukherji quotes Gordon Sanderson, *ASI Annual Report, 1911–12.*

89. Villiers-Stuart, 121.

90. Allen, *Glimpse,* 125.

91. Quoted in Metcalf, *Ideologies of the Raj,* 62.

92. In a letter to her friend Lady Canning, the queen had written, "If it was not for the heat and the *insects* how much I should like to see India"; quoted in Allen, 21.

93. Cohn, "Representing Authority," 197–98. Rao was one of the most distinguished Indian statesmen of the century, a former *diwan* of Gwalior and familiar of viceroys. On the durbar, see also Lutyens, *Lyttons in India,* chap. 8.

94. Cohn, passim.

95. Quoted in Allen, *Kipling Sahib,* 89.

96. Prinsep, *Imperial India,* 20; Fowler, *Below the Peacock Fan,* 197–98; Lutyens, 79.

97. Cohn, 199; Allen, *Kipling Sahib,* 90.

98. Metcalf, *Ideologies of the Raj,* 78–79.

99. Ibid., 197.

100. Allen, "Imperial Image," 237; James, *Raj,* 317; Wheeler, *History of the Delhi Coronation Durbar,* chap. 5.

101. Mason, *Guardians,* 199.

102. Ibid., 199–200.

103. Menpes, *Durbar,* 25.

104. CP, Mss Eur F111/274, including a clipping from the *Pioneer,* 25 July 1902.

105. Allen, "Imperial Image," 234–35. The viceroy's party alone, which had come out from England, landed in Bombay with a combined total of forty-seven tons of clothes for the Durbar festivities; see Hobbes, *Imperial India,* 8.

106. Wheeler, 50.

107. Ibid., 50–51, 57.

108. CP, Mss Eur F111/274.

109. Fowler, *Below the Peacock Fan,* 284.

110. The descriptions of the Indian camps are taken from Wheeler's wonderfully detailed chap. 4.

111. Ibid.

112. Curzon, *British Government in India,* 2:28–29; Hobbes, 49.

113. Diary of Mrs. Macpherson, quoted in Mason, 201. See also Wheeler, 170ff.; Fowler, 290ff. The peacock dress is on display in Kedleston Hall, Derbyshire, the Curzon family seat. Old India hand that she was, the novelist Flora Annie Steel thought it appalling to imagine "mankind handing ices to women kind" in Shah Jahan's gem of a building and wondered about Curzon's lapse of taste; see *Garden of Fidelity,* 220.

114. Fowler, 212, 244.

115. Wheeler, 135. The Indian leaders in attendance represented some 230 million souls, one-fifth of the world's population at the time; see Hobbes, 18–19.

116. Menpes, 56. And yet Menpes himself makes the curious comment that the Durbar "seemed no show for the Saxon"—Europeans seemed out of place, drab beetles, awkward, and "a blot in an otherwise harmonious whole" (34, 37). Curzon had wanted to erect a monument to the Durbar on the riverfront—a "Memorial to commemorate a commemoration"—but this was vetoed by the lieutenant governor, who pointed out that the site was prone to flooding; see Gupta, *Delhi Between Two Empires,* 167.

117. Hardinge, *Old Diplomacy,* 28–30.

118. Ibid., 42.

119. Hardinge, *Indian Years,* 24.

120. Ibid., 23–24; Mukherji, *Red Fort,* 227–28; ASI, *Annual Report, 1909–10.*

121. Hardinge, *Indian Years,* 56–57.

122. Villiers-Stuart, 121.

123. *Illustrated London News,* 23 Dec. 1911, 1073, quoted in Pelizzari, "From Stone to Paper," 38.

CHAPTER 8. NEW DELHI

1. P. Singh, *Of Dreams and Demons,* 6–7; Ridley, *Architect and His Wife,* 380.

2. Quoted in Frykenberg, "Coronation Durbar of 1911," 238.

3. Quoted in Chaudhuri, *Autobiography of an Unknown Indian,* 280.

4. Quoted in Lewis and Lewis, *Delhi's Historic Villages,* 144n4.

5. Hardinge, *Indian Years* 38; Dutta, *Calcutta* 129; Curzon, *British Government in India,* 1:70.

6. Irving, *Indian Summer,* 119ff.; Ridley, *Architect and His Wife,* 269–70.

7. Tavernier, *Travels in India,* 1:79.

8. Smith, "'A Grand Work of Noble Conception,'" passim.

9. The most thorough studies of the planning and politics of New Delhi are Irving, *Indian Summer,* and Volwahsen, *Imperial Delhi,* but see also Ridley, *Architect and His Wife;* A. D. King, *Colonial Urban Development;* Metcalf, *Imperial Vision;* and Metcalf, "Architecture and Empire."

10. Irving, 79–80. Hardly the first to notice the abundance of Delhi's ruins, Lutyens compared them to motorcars in London.

11. Volwahsen, 195. It is larger than the palace at Versailles: see Davies, *Splendours of the Raj,* 227.

12. Hussey, *Life of Sir Edwin Lutyens,* 247.

13. Moorhouse, *India Britannica,* 234.

14. Percy and Ridley, *Letters of Edwin Lutyens to His Wife,* 250 (3 June 1912), 280 (16 Feb. 1913), 281 (17 Feb. 1916).

15. Ridley, "Edwin Lutyens," 79–81.

16. Percy and Ridley, 280.

17. Hussey, 272.

18. Villiers-Stuart, *Gardens of the Great Mughals,* esp. 277ff.; Villiers-Stuart, "Indian Paradise Garden," 804; Wescoat and Wolschke-Bulmahn, "Sources, Places, Representations and Prospects," 17; Irving, 217–18.

19. Lively, *A House Unlocked,* 79. Lively's grandmother bought a Lutyens-style house in 1923, built some fifteen years earlier, and set about creating a large garden in the manner of Jekyll to complement it; ibid., 6.

20. Jane Brown, *Gardens of a Golden Afternoon,* 13–14, 35, 187. On a trip to South Africa where he had been commissioned to build an art gallery with Herbert Baker, Lutyens was startled to find himself referred to in the Johannesburg *Star* as an "unrivalled" landscape gardener; ibid., 153.

21. Ibid., 96.

22. Ridley, *Architect and His Wife,* 147.

23. Jane Brown, 50, 104; Stamp and Goulancourt, *English House,* 29.

24. For the best summary of the machinations by which Lutyens was appointed to the Delhi Planning Commission and then chief architect, see Ridley, *Architect and His Wife,* chap. 11. Irving gives an almost day-by-day account; chaps. 3–5.

25. Ridley, *Architect and His Wife,* 213, 215. In the end, the dome blended St. Paul's with the Buddhist motifs from Sarnath and Bodhgaya, while the Palladian portico was scaled down to more Islamic proportions; ibid., 239–40.

26. Percy and Ridley, 342 (21 Feb. 1917).

27. Edwin Lutyens to Emily Lutyens, 25 Feb. 1917, RIBA.
28. Jane Brown, 172, 202n26.
29. George, "Roadside Planting," 84; Bowe, "'Genius of an Artist.'"
30. Percy and Ridley, 412–13 (17 Jan. 1929).
31. Edwin Lutyens to Emily Lutyens, 24 Jan. 1929, RIBA; Irving, 141.
32. Percy and Ridley, 416 (31 Jan. 1929).
33. Quoted in Volwahsen, 114.
34. For descriptions of the gardens, see esp. Irving, 214ff.; Hussey, 502–4; Jane Brown, 15–52, 172; Byron, "New Delhi, IV"; Volwahsen, 124–29; and www.presidentofIndia.nic.in/mughalGarden.html.
35. For the drawing see Irving, fig. 18.
36. Byron, "New Delhi, IV," 812.
37. Hussey, 503.
38. Byron, "New Delhi," pl. VIII.
39. Byron, "New Delhi, IV," 810.
40. Irving, 223.
41. See "Mughal Garden," www.presidentofIndia.nic.in/mughalGarden.html.
42. Stanley, "Gardening in India."
43. Ibid.; H. Y. S. Prasad, *Rashtrapati Bhavan*, 81–82.
44. Hussey, 504.
45. Halifax, *Fullness of Days*, 142–43.
46. Note by N. Gupta and L. Sykes to Spear, *Delhi: Its Monuments and History*, 97n6.
47. G. Jekyll, *Wall and Water Gardens*, 135, 160, and passim; Jane Brown, 127–29.
48. Hussey, 254.
49. Irving, 218, among others, describes the disks as lotus leaves.
50. D. Lentz, "Botanical Symbolism," 52; Koch, *Complete Taj Mahal*, 177.
51. Mukherji, *Red Fort*, 58, 121 148.
52. Fowler, *Below the Peacock Fan*, 260.
53. For an illustration of the lotus flower in the Durbar Hall see Volwahsen, fig. 103. The 2,300-year-old Ashokan Bull capital standing outside the Durbar Hall, which rests on an inverted lotus, was not part of Lutyens's scheme. It was installed after an exhibition of Indian art in London in 1947–48; see H. Y. S. Prasad, 51, 58.
54. Ridley, "Edwin Lutyens," 80.
55. On the association of *Victoria regia* with Queen Victoria see Campbell-Culver, *Origin of Plants*, 330.
56. The official website designates this part of the garden complex as the Purdha Garden, but the term does not seem to have been used commonly in the literature; see www.presidentofIndia.nic.in/mughalGarden.html.
57. Jane Brown, passim. Ridley, however, argues that Lutyens Indianized his pergola in the Long Garden by building it entirely of red sandstone, like Akbar's stone beams at Fatehpur Sikri, fashioned "like wood in tension"; "Edwin Lutyens," 80.
58. Jane Brown, 151.
59. Lutyens, *Edwin Lutyens*, 269.
60. Irving, 226–28. Cf. Kaye, *Sun in the Morning*, 95.
61. Edwin Lutyens to Emily Lutyens, 22 Oct. 1938, 11 Nov. 1938, 18 Nov. 1938, RIBA; Ridley, *Architect and His Wife*, 402–3; Bence-Jones, *Viceroys*, 272, 280. Panter-Downes, *Ooty Preserved*, 43. As far as I know, the drawing remains unreproduced.

62. Stark, *Dust in the Lion's Paw,* 231.

63. Jane Brown, 97–98, 152; Volwahsen, 38–39; William Dalrymple, "The Rubble of the Raj," *Guardian,* 13 Nov. 2004.

64. Wilhide, *Sir Edwin Lutyens,* 40.

65. Lutyens, 147–48; Hussey, 320. After a day when the temperature was 117 degrees in the shade, he had also suggested Uzipore as an appropriate name for the capital; see I. Butler, *Viceroy's Wife,* 160. Edward Lear was also an inspired punster: "Making Delhineations of the Dehlicate architecture as is all impressed on my mind as inDehlibly as the Dehliterious quality of the water in that city." Quoted in Dehejia, *Impossible Picturesqueness,* 32.

66. Quoted in Volwahsen, 212. "Blaze/riot of colour" seems to have been the cliché of choice.

67. Irving, 109–10; Bence-Jones, 215; I. Butler, 28, 52, 62; Dalrymple, *City of Djinns,* 77. Lady Reading had anticipated Lady Willingdon by decorating the interior with mauves and grays. The hastily built and hastily abandoned capital of Dacca, East Bengal, also provided a trial run for New Delhi, but Lutyens does not seem to have been aware of it. See Nilsson, *New Capitals,* 101.

68. Gupta, *Delhi Between Two Empires,* 178–79.

69. Volwahsen, 233–34, 259; Irving, 264ff. Lutyens and Baker had supervisory control over all the princes' palaces, and Lutyens personally designed the lavish Hyderabad House.

70. Irving, 77–78; Davies, 225.

71. Volwahsen, 239.

72. Hardinge, *Indian Years,* 71–72; Baker, *Architecture and Personalities,* 71.

73. There was an epidemic of "Willingdonitis" in the 1930s, with a spate of places named for father, mother, and son. Some of them survived beyond India's independence,. In the 1950s the Lodi Garden was relandscaped by a Japanese team, but a decade later an American architect prepared a master plan for the park. Spear, *Delhi: Its Monuments and History,* 43nn2 and 4.

74. Patrick Geddes, consulted on a number of urban planning projects in India, strenuously argued for greater integration of the new and the old, but his ideas found little sympathy with Lutyens and his fellow planners. See Geddes, *Patrick Geddes in India,* passim.

75. Irving, 85, 51.

76. Byron, "New Delhi," 11.

77. Quoted in Parkes, *Begums, Thugs and White Mughals,* 46. Cf. Madhur Jaffrey's recollections that planting trees was the leitmotif of her childhood history classes: "Indian emperors planted a lot of trees." *Climbing the Mango Trees,* 205.

78. Roe, *Embassy,* 492; Tavernier, *Travels in India,* 1:78; Bernier, 284. More recently, Lord Wellesley had planted trees along the road laid out between Calcutta and the garden retreat of Barrackpore: "Mango, banyan, india-rubber, peepul—like white poplars, teak—with enormous leaves, laurel of several sorts, mimosas, tamarinds, etc." Lady Charlotte Canning, Journal Letter, 19 March 1856, in Hare, *Story of Two Noble Lives,* 2:60.

79. George, 85. George also offers a wonderful picture of Lutyens's modus operandi during his cold-weather visits to Delhi. He held "open house" in his offices, urging everyone to stay for tiffin (lunch), from lieutenant-governors to engineers and plumbers, "friends or foes"—a very civilized way to sort out the myriad disagreements that arose (81–82).

80. Krishen, *Trees of Delhi,* 32. Krishen provides an excellent schematic diagram showing the plantings on different avenues (34–35).

81. Krishen identifies these species as *Syzigium cumini* and *Syzigium nervosum* rather than George's *Eugenia jambolina* (89; fig. 3, 83).

82. Quotations from George, 82–83. Several sources claim that faster-growing trees were planted along with slower-growing ones to provide shade in the interim, although George does not mention this. See, e.g., Volwahsen, 212; Irving, 251.

83. George, 86.

84. Singh and Varma, *Millennium Book on New Delhi,* 47.

85. Ibid., 103.

86. Christopher Hawkins to Larry Hawkins, 28 Aug. 1937. I am grateful to Arthur Hawkins for this material.

87. See Volwahsen, fig. 179.

88. Emma Wilson, quoted in Barr, *Dust in the Balance,* 158.

89. George, 87.

90. Hussey, 571.

91. Jane Brown, 108, 111.

92. Ibid., 120–26.

93. Hussey, 509–11.

94. Mukherji, *Red Fort,* 50–51, 56, 110, 241.

95. Hussey, 551.

96. There were attempts to introduce contemporary ideas of urban planning in Bombay during the middle decades of the nineteenth century; see Dossal, *Imperial Designs.*

97. In many respects, Bangalore would have been an excellent choice as capital of British India, but it does not seem to have been considered.

98. Crowe et al., 132–33.

99. Stronach, "Parterres and Stone Watercourses," 6; Mukherji, *Red Fort,* 68–70, 121.

100. Gupta, "Indomitable City," 30–31; Gupta, *Delhi Between Two Empires,* 2; Bernier, 241; Mukherji, *Red Fort,* 92; S. Prasad, "Tale of Two Cities," passim; Fonseca, "Walled City of Old Delhi," 111.

101. S. Prasad, 187ff.

102. Volwahsen, 51, quoting Sten Nillson; H. V. Lanchester, preface to Geddes, *Patrick Geddes in India,* 32.

103. P. Singh, *Of Dreams and Demons,* 10–11, 85 (quoting Blake). In fact, Shah Jahan *did* design it, much as it changed over the centuries.

104. Hussey, 368.

105. Pevsner, quoted in Jane Brown, 157; Byron, "New Delhi," 28.

106. Ridley, "Edwin Lutyens," 75, 79–81. At the time, Byron also emphasized Lutyens's masterful synthesis of themes from both the European and Indian pasts; "New Delhi," 30 and passim.

107. Quoted in P. Singh, *Of Dreams and Demons,* 85.

CHAPTER 9. THE LEGACY

1. Orlich, *Travels in India,* 2:71–72; Barr, *Dust in the Balance,* 38; Desmond, *Victorian India,* pl. 21; Lord Irwin's letters to his father, the Second Viscount Halifax, Apr. 1926–Apr. 1931, MssEur C152/27, India Office Library and Records. Willow Pattern tea sets can be found illustrated on eBay.

2. Bromfield, *The Rains Came,* 115. Bromfield's novel was inspired by his visit to India in 1932.

3. Uglow, *Little History of British Gardening,* 282–83; Metcalf, *Imperial Vision,* 127ff., 133; E. Arnold, *India Revisited,* 94; Morris, *Pax Britannica,* 274, which notes that the palace gardens

of the Maharajah of Jaipur inspired Kipling's comment, "The Maharajah gave the order and Yakub Sahib [Swinton] made the garden."

4. Bowe, "Indian Gardening Tradition."

5. Ismail, *My Public Life,* 53, 82ff.; Srinivas, *Landscapes of Urban Memory,* 53; http://en.wikipedia.org/wiki/Krishnaraja_Sagara.

6. Ismail, 48, 82–83; www.mysoresamachar.com/brind_fount.htm.

7. Hancock, *Politics of Heritage,* 99.

8. I have relied primarily on the following sources to reconstruct the recent history of the Taj and other Agra monuments: Jessica Barry and Rahul Bedi, "Outrage at Plan to Ring Taj with Cafes and Malls," *Daily Telegraph,* 8 July 2001; Tripathi, "Saving the Taj Mahal"; Kushal S. Yadav, "Taj Corridor Project Compromises Heritage," India Environment Portal, 30 July 2003, www.indiaenvironmentportal.org.in/node/34633; Sean Farrell, "The Taj Mahal: Pollution and Tourism," TED Case Studies, No. 668, 2002, www.american.edu/TED/taj.htm; Harkness and Sinha, "Taj Heritage Corridor," quotations on 67, 68; ASLA Online, www.asla.org/meetings/awards/awds02/tajmahal.html; www.tajmahalagra.com/a-world-heritage-site.html; A. G. Krishna Menon, "Book Review: Still Another View of the Taj Corridor Project, Oct. 2003," www.architexturez.net/+/subject-listing/000170.shtml. There are also many newspaper accounts online. I have not been able to consult either Tata's *Taj Mahal, Agra, Site Management Plan* or the two-volume publication of the University of Illinois Project.

9. Brij Khandelwal, "Another Taj Project Runs into Trouble," *SME Times,* 3 Aug. 2009, http://smetimes.tradeindia.com; Dean Nelson, "Taj Mahal facelift branded 'insensitive,'" *Daily Telegraph,* 3 Aug. 2009. Oversized golf carts were introduced to ferry tourists around the Taj in June 2009; see "Tourists to View Taj Mahal in Environment-Friendly Golf Carts," www.thaindian.com/newsportal.

10. See, for example, the following articles in the *Hindustan Times:* "Dust, Vanishing Greenery Threaten Taj," 19 Apr. 2010; "Rs. 22 Crore Spent, Yet Taj Pollution Up," 1 July 2010; "Air, Water Pollution Rising Near Taj Mahal," 10 July 2010. Available at www.hindustantimes.com.

11. See the entries for Raj Ghat and Sydney Percy-Lancaster on Wikipedia.

12. Hancock, chap. 3 passim.

13. Agniva Banerjee, "Let's Ban Tennyson," *Times of India,* 30 Sept. 2007.

14. See websites devoted to Nana Rao Park Kanpur.

15. For the recent history of Humayun's Tomb and other monuments, see the forthcoming new edition of Charles Lewis and Karoki Lewis, *Delhi's Historic Villages.*

16. H. Y. S. Prasad, *Rashtrapati Bhavan,* 101.

17. Dalrymple, *City of Djinns,* 72.

18. Sykes, "Afterword—Fifty Years On," 145.

19. Dalrymple, *City of Djinns,* 23, and Dalrymple, "The Rubble of the Raj," *Guardian,* 13 Nov. 2004; "New Delhi Newsletter," www.lutyenstrust.org.uk/newsletters/newdelhi2003.htm. Tree planting since independence has also not been very successful. Lal notes that of over five million saplings planted, only some 5 percent survived: Lal, "Flora and Fauna of Delhi," 96, 99–100. Patwant Singh labels today's Delhi a "wasteland: *Of Dreams and Demons,* 75.

20. Spear, "Delhi—The 'Stop-Go' Capital," 323; Dalrymple, *City of Djinns,* 221; Volwahsen, *Imperial Delhi,* 217; Tully, "Travails of a Metropolis," 175; Luce, *In Spite of the Gods,* 212. The addition of fleets of newer, less polluting buses and the extension of the Metro to more of the city and its suburbs offers some relief.

21. "MCD Sows to Reap a Lush 2010," *Times of India,* New Delhi, 17 Mar. 2008.

22. http://2010commonwealthgamesindia.blogspot.com; "Poor Lose Homes as Delhi Cleans Up," *New York Times*, 1 Jan. 2007.

23. Patwant Singh, 197–98; cf. George "Roadside Planting," 87; Lal, 96, 99–100; Tully, 175. For a rosier view of the Buddha Jayanti Park on the Ridge, see K. Singh, *Delhi,* 50.

24. On the recent history of Kashmir, see esp. Tunzelmann, *Indian Summer,* chap. 17; and Peer, *Curfewed Night.* Quotation from Peer, 124.

25. Peer, 110–11. On the Mughal gardens of Kashmir, see Villiers-Stuart, *Gardens of the Great Mughals,* and Crowe et al., *Gardens of Mughal India.*

26. Christine Ottery, "Kashmir Fears Forests Will Disappear Through 'Timber Smuggling,'" *Guardian,* 14 July 2010; Panter-Downes, *Ooty Preserved,* 72–73, 107; Crossette, *Great Hill Stations,* 110ff.

27. Ismail, 48–49; Trevelyan, *Golden Oriole,* 341.

28. See http://en.wikipedia.org/wiki/File:Jorasanko_Thakur_Bari.jpg for an illustration of the inner garden.

29. Rahul Bedi, "Opening Meet Finds India's Only Hunt in the Pink," *Daily Telegraph,* 19 July 2004.

30. Panter-Downes, 124. Ruskin Bond observes that when the British departed from India in 1947, they left their ghosts behind: foreword to Chaudry, *Ghost Stories.*

31. See the official website, www.horticulture.kar.nic.in/lalbagh.htm. On the political implications of garden gnomes, see the review of Shirley Williams, *Climbing the Bookshelves, Times Literary Supplement,* 23 Oct. 2009, 34.

32. Jayapal, *Bangalore,* 186–88.

33. Mishra, *Romantics,* 73; www.nal.res.in/pages/nalcampus.htm. Cf. a video featuring the Infosys campus in Banglore, www.youtube.com/watch?v=osFCN4iU-hI, uploaded on 15 July 2007.

34. Swaminarayan Akshardham Guide, www.akshardham.com. The website reprints an article from the *Economic Times,* 23 Feb. 2007, commenting that the temple "borrows in equal measure from the spiritual as well as from Las Vegas and Walt Disney."

35. Judith Brown, *Nehru,* 104–5, 143, 151, 153, 191. Cf. V. Seth, *A Suitable Boy,* 1072.

36. Murphy, *On a Shoestring,* 191.

37. C. P. Sujaya, personal communications, 24 Feb. and 30 Mar. 2004, 26 Aug. and 1 Sept. 2009. I am very grateful to Mrs. Sujaya for sharing her experiences.

38. V. Seth, 1405 and passim.

CONCLUSION

1. Hyams and MacQuilty, *Great Botanical Gardens,* 229; Sharwood-Smith, *Diary of a Colonial Wife,* chap. 16.

2. Baker, *Architecture and Personalities,* 16; Lamb, *Africa House*; Lively, *Oleander, Jacaranda* 28, 31; Raafat, *Maadi,* 23, 33ff.

3. Bennett, "A Nigerian Garden"; Ngugi wa Thiong'o, *A Grain of Wheat,* 36; Gavaghan, *Of Lions and Dung Beetles,* 243.

4. Orlich, *Travels in India,* 2:230; Morris, *Pax Britannica,* 204–5; A. Coats, *Quest for Plants,* 193.

5. Duncan, *Simple Adventures,* 166; Bella Woolf, *From Groves of Palm,* 63.

6. Mortimer, *Clinging to the Wreckage,* 153.

7. Jaffrey, *Climbing the Mango Trees,* 42–43. As with Dwarkanath Tagore's family in

nineteenth-century Calcutta, the women in Jaffrey's household led a somewhat more traditional life than the men.

8. J. Marshall, epigraph to Cannadine, *Ornamentalism*; Hunt, "Imitation," 205; Tidrick, *Empire and the English Character*, 135; Ruggles, *Islamic Gardens and Landscapes*, 132ff.

9. Cf. Fraenkel, *No Fixed Abode*, 125–26, referring to Lusaka in 1939. See also McMaster, "Colonial District Town," 341–42; Awam Ampka, personal communication. The quotation is from Kipling's "The Glory of the Garden," in *Complete Verse*, 735.

10. *Richard II*, 3.4.48–52, quoted in Uglow, *Little History of British Gardening*, 82.

11. Fazl, *Akbarnama*, quoted in Crowe et al., 46.

12. Fazl, *Akbarnama*, quoted in Richards, "Historiography of Mughal Gardens," 261.

13. Kipling, "The Glory of the Garden."

14. Sharp, *Good-bye India*, 6–7, 221; Edwardes, *High Noon of Empire*, 41. Cf. Eden, *Up the Country*, 138.

15. Campbell-Culver, *Origin of Plants*, 435; Euan Dunn, review of Jeremy Mynott, *Birdscapes: Birds in Our Imagination and Experience*, Times Literary Supplement, 11 Sept. 2009, 23; Hyams, *English Garden*, 9–10.

16. Quoted in Hadfield, *Gardening in Britain*, 198; Steel, *Garden of Fidelity*, 192.

17. Thomas, *Man and the Natural World*, 239–41. The hot bath at the end of the day was a staple of British colonial life. One of the more extreme examples concerned the viceregal train that carried the newly arrived Lord Irwin and his wife from Bombay to New Delhi in 1926. Each had a suite complete with bathroom, with giant boilers for hot water being kept on the simmer at local stations, "where the Viceroy's arrival was timed to a minute by a schedule kept with military precision"; see Birkenhead, *Halifax*, 175.

18. Letter to Lady Douglas, 9 Aug. 1799, in Shields, *Birds of Passage*, 92; Quest-Ritson, *English Garden Abroad*, 78. Quest-Ritson notes that in the hundreds of letters written by Elizabeth Barrett-Browning during her life in Italy, she only mentions meeting one Italian socially.

19. The quotation is from Jane Brown, *Pursuit of Paradise*, 10–11.

20. See, e.g., Lear, *Flora Nonsensica*; Sellar and Yeatman, *Garden Rubbish*; and the drawings of Osbert Lancaster accompanying Scott-James, *Pleasure Garden*.

21. Hutchins, *Illusion of Permanence*, chap. 5.

22. Gorer, *Growth of Gardens*, 194; J. Kincaid, *My Garden*, 8; F. Bacon, *Of Gardens*, n.p.; Harrison, *Gardens*, 41, 146, and passim.

23. Macaulay, "Lord Macaulay's Minute, 2nd February 1835," 102.

24. Quoted in Dalrymple, introduction to Parkes, *Begums, Thugs and White Mughals*, Parks xiii.

25. Villiers-Stuart, *Gardens of the Great Mughals*, 278–79; and Villiers-Stuart, "Indian Paradise Garden," 804.

26. Tidrick, 1.

BIBLIOGRAPHY

UNPUBLISHED SOURCES

Lady Sarah Amherst. Journal. 3 vols. Archives, Amherst College, Amherst, Massachusetts.
Emily Bayley. Memorial volume for Charlotte Canning. Mss Eur D661, India Office Library and Records (now India Office Select Materials in the Asia, Pacific and Africa Collections of the British Library, London).
Curzon Papers. India Office Library and Records.
John N. Hawkins. Letters. Arthur Hawkins, Mineola, N.Y.
Lord Irwin. Letters to his father, the Second Viscount Halifax, April 1926–April 1931. MssEur C152/27, India Office Library and Records.
William Jones Collection, Royal Asiatic Society, London.
Edwin Lutyens, letters to his wife. RIBA, Victoria and Albert Museum, London.
Ajay Sinha, "Taj Mahal and Mughal Kingship," unpublished manuscript.
Stanley Collection of photographs and botanical watercolors. Sir Andrew Buchanan, Hodsock Farm, Nottinghamshire, UK.

PUBLISHED SOURCES

Ali, Daud. *Courtly Culture and Political Life in Early Medieval India*. Cambridge: Cambridge University Press, 2004.
Alkazi, E. "The Husainabad Complex and Nuances of Urban Design." In Llewellyn-Jones, *Lucknow: City of Illusion*, 135–66.
Allen, Charles. *A Glimpse of the Burning Plain: Leaves from the Indian Journals of Charlotte Canning*. London: M. Joseph, 1986.
———. "Imperial Image: The Grand Durbars of 1903 and 1911." In Dehejia, *India Through the Lens*, 231–48.

———. *Kipling Sahib: India and the Making of Rudyard Kipling*. London: Little, Brown, 2007.

———. *Plain Tales from the Raj*. New York: St. Martin's, 1976.

Amherst, Alicia. *A History of Gardening in England*. London: Quaritch, 1895.

Arberry, A. J. *Asiatic Jones: The Life and Influence of Sir William Jones*. London: Longmans Green, 1946.

———. *The Koran Interpreted: A Translation by A. J. Arberry*. London: Allen & Unwin, 1955.

Archaeological Survey of India (ASI). *Annual Progress, North-Western Provinces and Oudh*. Calcutta: Government Printing Office, 1900.

———. *Annual Report, 1903–4*. Calcutta: Archaeological Survey of India, 1906.

———. *Annual Report, 1909–10*. Calcutta: Archaeological Survey of India, 1914.

Archer, Maj. Edward Caulfield. *Tours in Upper India, and in Parts of the Himalaya Mountains....* 2 vols. London: Richard Bentley, 1833.

Archer, Mildred. *British Drawings in the India Office Library*. 2 vols. London: HMSO, 1969.

———. *Company Drawings in the India Office Library*. London: HMSO, 1972.

———. *Company Paintings: Indian Paintings of the British Period*. London: Victoria and Albert Museum, 1992.

———. *Early Views of India: The Picturesque Journeys of Thomas and William Daniell, 1786–1794: The Complete Aquatints*. New York: Thames & Hudson, 1980.

———. "India and Natural History: The Role of the East India Company, 1785–1858." *History Today* 11 (1959): 736–43

Archer, Mildred, and Ronald Lightbown. *India Observed: India as Seen by British Artists, 1760–1860*. London: Victoria and Albert Museum, 1982.

Arnold, David. *Colonizing the Body: State Medicine and Epidemic Disease in Nineteenth-Century India*. Berkeley: University of California Press, 1993.

———. *The Tropics and the Traveling Gaze: India, Landscape, and Science, 1800–1856*. Seattle: University of Washington Press, 2006.

Arnold, Sir Edwin. *India Revisited*. Boston: Roberts Bros., 1886.

Arthur, Rev. William. *A Mission to Mysore: With Scenes and Facts Illustrative of India, Its People, and Its Religion*. London: Partridge & Oakey, 1847.

Axelby, Richard. "Calcutta Botanic Garden and the Colonial Re-ordering of the Indian Environment." *Archives of Natural History* 35, no. 1 (2008): 150–68.

Babur, Zahiruddin Muhammad. *The Baburnama: Memoirs of Babur, Prince and Emperor*. Translated and edited by Wheeler M. Thackston. Washington, D.C.: Freer and Sackler Galleries / New York: Oxford University Press, 1996.

Bacon, Francis. *Of Gardens*. 1625. Northampton, Mass.: Gehenna Press, 1959.

Bacon, Thomas. *The Orientalist*. London: T. Arnold, 1842.

Baikie, Dr. Robert. *Observations on the Neilgherries, etc*. Calcutta: Baptist Mission Press, 1834.

Baker, Sir Herbert. *Architecture and Personalities*. London: Country Life, 1944.

Barr, Pat. *The Dust in the Balance: British Women in India, 1905–1945*. London: Hamish Hamilton, 1989.

———. *The Memsahibs: The Women of Victorian India*. London: Secker and Warburg, 1976.

Barr, Pat, and Ray Desmond. *Simla: A Hill Station in British India*. London: Scolar Press, 1978.

Battuta, Ibn. *The Travels of Ibn Battuta, A.D. 1325–1354*. Vol. 3. Translated and edited by H. A. R. Gibb. Cambridge: Cambridge University Press for the Hakluyt Society, 1971.

Beames, John. *Memoirs of a Bengal Civilian*. Introduction by Philip Mason. Columbia, Mo.: South Asian Books, 1984.

Begley, W. E. "The Garden of the Taj Mahal: A Case Study of Mughal Architectural Planning." In Wescoat and Wolschke-Bulmahn, *Mughal Gardens*, 213–32.

———. "The Myth of the Taj Mahal and a New Theory of Its Symbolic Meaning." *Art Bulletin* 61, no. 1 (1979): 7–37.

Begley, W. E., and Z. A. Desai, eds. *Taj Mahal: The Illumined Tomb: An Anthology of Seventeenth-Century Mughal and European Documentary Sources*. Cambridge, Mass.: Aga Khan Program for Islamic Architecture, 1989.

Bence-Jones, Mark. *Palaces of the Raj: Magnificence and Misery of the Lord Sahibs*. London: George Allen & Unwin, 1973.

———. *The Viceroys of India*. New York: St. Martin's, 1982.

Bennett, Muriel. "A Nigerian Garden." *Overseas Pensioner* 85 (April 2003): 34–36.

Bernier, François. *Travels in the Mogul Empire, A.D. 1656–1668*. Translated and edited by Archibald Constable and Vincent A. Smith. London: Humphrey Milford, 1916.

Bhasin, Raja. *Simla: The Summer Capital of British India*. New Delhi: Penguin, 1992.

———. *Viceregal Lodge and the Indian Institute of Advanced Study, Shimla*. Shimla: Indian Institute of Advanced Study, 1995.

Bhatt, Vikram. *Resorts of the Raj: Hill Stations of India*. Ahmedabad: Mapin, 1998.

Birkenhead, Lord. *Halifax: The Life of Lord Halifax*. Boston: Houghton Mifflin, 1966.

Blake, Stephen P. "The *Khanah Bagh* in Mughal India: House Gardens in the Palaces and Mansions of the Great Men of Shahjahanabad." In Wescoat and Wolschke-Bulmahn, *Mughal Gardens*, 171–89.

———. *Shahjahanabad: The Sovereign City in Mughal India, 1639–1739*. Cambridge: Cambridge University Press, 1991.

Bond, Ruskin, and Ganesh Saili. *Mussoorie and Landour: Days of Wine and Roses*. New Delhi: Lustre Press, 1992.

Booth, Martin. *Opium: A History*. New York: St. Martin's, 1998.

Bowe, Patrick. "'The Genius of an Artist': William Mustoe and the Planting of the City of New Delhi and Its Gardens." *Garden History* 37, no. 1 (Summer 2009): 68–79.

———. "The Indian Gardening Tradition and the Sajjan Niwas Bagh, Udaipur." *Garden History* 27, no. 2 (Winter 1999): 189–205.

Bowring, Lewin B. *Eastern Experiences*. London: Henry S. King, 1871.

Brockway, Lucile. *Science and Colonial Expansion: The Role of the British Royal Botanic Gardens*. New York: Academic Press, 1979.

Bromfield, Louis. *The Rains Came: A Novel of Modern India*. New York: Harper, 1937.

Brown, Hilton. *The Sahibs: The Life and Ways of the British in India, as Recorded by Themselves*. London: Hodge, 1948.

Brown, Jane. *Gardens of a Golden Afternoon: The Story of a Partnership, Edwin Lutyens and Gertrude Jekyll*. New York: Van Nostrand Reinhold, 1982.

———. *The Pursuit of Paradise: A Social History of Gardens and Gardening*. London: HarperCollins, 1999.

Brown, Judith M. "India." In *The Twentieth Century*, edited by Judith M. Brown and William. Roger Louis, vol. 4 of *The Oxford History of the British Empire*, 421–46. Oxford: Oxford University Press, 1999.

———. *Nehru: A Political Life*. New Haven: Yale University Press, 2003.

Buchanan, Francis. *A Journey from Madras Through the Countries of Mysore, Canara and Malabar*. 3 vols. 1807. New Delhi: Asian Educational Services, 1988.

Buck, Edward. *Simla Past and Present*. 1904. Delhi: Summit, 1979.

Burton, Sir Richard Francis. *Goa and the Blue Mountains; or, Six Months of Sick Leave.* 1851. Edited by Dane Kennedy. Berkeley: University of California Press, 1991.

Butler, A. S. G., with the collaboration of George Steward and Christopher Hussey. *The Architecture of Sir Edwin Lutyens.* 3 vols. London: Country Life, 1950.

Butler, Iris. *The Viceroy's Wife: Letters of Alice, Countess of Reading, from India, 1921–25.* London: Hodder & Stoughton, 1969.

Byrom, J. "India." In *The Oxford Companion to Gardens*, edited by Patrick Goode, Geoffrey Jellicoe, Susan Jellicoe, and Michael Lancaster, 270–71. Oxford: Oxford University Press, 1986.

Byron, Robert. "New Delhi." *Architectural Review* 69, no. 11 (Jan. 1931): 1–30.

———. "New Delhi, IV.—The Setting of the Viceroy's House." *Country Life* 69 (27 June 1931): 808–15.

Campbell, Maj. Walter. *The Old Forest Ranger; or, Wild Sports of India.* London: Routledge, 1869.

Campbell-Culver, Maggie. *The Origin of Plants.* London: Eden Project Books, 2004.

Cannadine, David. *Ornamentalism: How the British Saw Their Empire.* New York: Oxford University Press, 2001.

Cannon, Garland, ed. *Letters of Sir William Jones.* 2 vols. Oxford: Clarendon Press, 1970.

———. *The Life and Mind of Oriental Jones: Sir William Jones, the Father of Modern Linguistics.* Cambridge: Cambridge University Press, 1990.

———. *Oriental Jones.* Bombay: Asia Publishing House, 1964.

Carlton, Charles, and Caroline Carlton. *The Significance of Gardening in British India.* Lewiston, N.Y.: Edwin Mellen, 2004.

Carroll, David. *The Taj Mahal.* New York: Newsweek, 1972.

Chaucer, Geoffrey. *The Canterbury Tales.* In *Chaucer's Poetry: An Anthology for the Modern Reader*, edited by E. T. Donaldson. 2nd ed. New York: Ronald Press, 1975.

Chaudhuri, Nirad C. *The Autobiography of an Unknown Indian.* 1951. New York: New York Review of Books, 2001.

Chaudhury, Pradip, and Abhijit Mukhopadhyay. *Calcutta: People and Empire: Gleanings from Old Journals.* Calcutta: India Book Exchange, 1975.

Chaudry, Minakshi. *Ghost Stories of Shimla Hills.* Introduction by Ruskin Bond. New Delhi: Rupa & Co., 2005.

Chelkowski, Peter. "Monumental Grief: The Bara Imambara." In Llewellyn-Jones, *Lucknow: City of Illusion*, 101–34.

Chirol, Valentine. *Fifty Years in a Changing World.* London: Cape, 1927.

Coats, Alice M. *Flowers and Their Histories.* 2nd ed. New York: McGraw-Hill, 1971.

———.*The Quest for Plants: A History of the Horticultural Explorers.* London: Studio Vista, 1969.

Coats, Peter. *Flowers in History.* New York: Viking, 1970.

Cohn, Bernard S. "Representing Authority in Victorian India." In *The Invention of Tradition*, edited by Eric Hobsbawm and Terence Ranger, 165–210. New York: Cambridge University Press, 1983.

Colley, Linda. *The Ordeal of Elizabeth Marsh: A Woman in World History.* New York: Pantheon, 2007.

Collingham, Lizzie. *Curry: A Tale of Cooks and Conquerors.* Oxford: Oxford University Press, 2006.

Colquhoun, Kate. *A Thing in Disguise: The Visionary Life of Joseph Paxton.* London: Fourth Estate, 2003.

Cotton, Sir Evan. *Calcutta, Old and New: A Historical and Descriptive Handbook to the City.* 1909. Edited by N. R. Ray. Calcutta: General Printers, 1980.

Crossette, Barbara. *The Great Hill Stations of Asia.* Boulder, Colo.: Westview, 1998.

Crowe, Sylvia, Sheila Haywood, Susan Jellicoe, and Gordon Patterson. *The Gardens of Mughal India.* London: Thames & Hudson, 1972.

Curzon, Lord. *British Government in India: The Story of the Viceroys and Government Houses.* 2 vols. London: Cassell, 1925.

Cuthell, Edith. *My Garden in the City of Gardens.* London: John Lane, 1905.

Dalrymple, William. *City of Djinns: A Year in Delhi.* London: HarperCollins, 1993.

———. *The Last Mughal: The Fall of a Dynasty: Delhi, 1857.* New York: Knopf, 2007.

———. *White Mughals: Love and Betrayal in Eighteenth-Century India.* New York: Viking, 2002.

Daniell, Thomas, and William Daniell. *Views of the Taje Mahal at the City of Agra, Taken in 1789.* London: T. Bensley, 1801.

Darwin, Erasmus. *The Botanic Garden.* London: J. Johnson, 1791.

Das, Neeta. "The 'Country Houses' of Lucknow." In Llewellyn-Jones, *Lucknow: City of Illusion*, 167–92.

David, Nina. "La Martinière: An Enlightened Vision." In Llewellyn-Jones, *Lucknow: City of Illusion*, 221–47.

Davies, Philip. *Splendours of the Raj: British Architecture in India, 1660–1947.* London: John Murray, 1985.

Dehejia, Vidya, ed. *Impossible Picturesqueness: Edward Lear's Indian Watercolours, 1873–1875.* New York: Columbia University Press, 1989.

———. *India Through the Lens: Photography, 1840–1911.* Washington, D.C.: Freer Gallery and Arthur M. Sackler Gallery, 2000.

Desmond, Ray. *The European Discovery of the Indian Flora.* Oxford: Oxford University Press, 1992.

———. *Kew: The History of the Royal Botanic Gardens.* London: Harvill Press, 1995.

———. *Victorian India in Focus: A Selection of Early Photographs from the Collection of the India Office Library and Records.* London: H.M.S.O., 1982.

Deva, Krishna. *Khajuraho.* New Delhi: Archaeological Survey of India, 2002.

Dilks, David. *Curzon in India.* London: Hart-Davis, 1969.

Diver, Maud. *The Englishwoman in India.* Edinburgh: W. Blackwood & Sons, 1909.

Dossal, Miriam. *Imperial Designs and Indian Realities: The Planning of Bombay City, 1845–1875.* Delhi: Oxford University Press, 1991.

Drayton, Richard. *Nature's Government: Science, Imperial Britain, and the "Improvement" of the World.* New Haven: Yale University Press, 2000.

Dufferin, Lady Harriot. *Our Vicegeral Life in India.* 2 vols. London: John Murray, 1889.

Duncan, Sara [Mrs. Everard Cotes]. *On the Other Side of the Latch.* London: Methuen, 1901.

———. *The Simple Adventures of a Memsahib.* New York: D. Appleton, 1893.

Dutta, Krishna. *Calcutta: A Cultural and Literary History.* Oxford: Signal Books, 2003.

Dye, Joseph M., III. "Artists for the Emperor." In Pal et al., *Romance of the Taj Mahal*, 88–127.

Dyson, Ketaki Kushari. *A Various Universe: A Study of the Journals and Memoirs of British Men and Women in the Indian Subcontinent, 1765–1856.* 1978. New Delhi: Oxford University Press, 2002.

Eden, Emily. *Letters from India.* 2 vols. London: Richard Bentley & Sons, 1872.

———. *Up the Country: Letters Written to Her Sister from the Upper Provinces of India.* 1867. London: Oxford University Press, 1932.

Edensor, Tim. *Tourists at the Taj: Performance and Meaning at a Symbolic Site.* London: Routledge, 1998.

Edwardes, Michael. *Bound to Exile: The Victorians in India.* New York: Praeger, 1970.

———. *The Glorious Sahibs: The Romantic as Empire Builder, 1799–1838.* New York: Taplinger, 1969.

———. *High Noon of Empire: India Under Curzon.* London: Eyre & Spottiswoode, 1965.

———. *Warren Hastings: King of the Nabobs.* London: Hart-Davis, MacGibbon, 1976.

Ehlers, Eckart, and Thomas Krafft, eds. *Shahjahanabad/Old Delhi: Tradition and Colonial Change*, 2nd ed. New Delhi: Manohar, 2003.

Elliot, H. M., and J. Dowson. *The History of India, as Told by Its Own Historians.* 8 vols. 1871. New York: AMS, 1966.

Elliott, Brent. *Victorian Gardens.* Portland, Ore.: Timber Press, 1986.

Elwood, Anne. *Narrative of a Journey Overland from England, by the Continent of Europe, Egypt, and the Red Sea, to India, . . . 1825, 26, 27, & 28.* 2 vols. London: H. Colburn & R. Bentley, 1830.

Emerson, William. "On the Taj Mahal at Agra." *Transactions of the Royal Institute of British Architects*, 1st ser., 20 (1869–70): 195–203.

Endersby, Jim. *Imperial Nature: Joseph Dalton Hooker and the Practices of Victorian Science.* Chicago: University of Chicago Press, 2008.

Eraly, Abraham. *The Mughal Throne: The Saga of India's Great Emperors.* London: Weidenfeld and Nicolson, 2003.

Fanshawe, H. C. *Delhi, Past and Present.* London: John Murray, 1902.

Farrell, J. G. *The Hill Station.* London: Weidenfeld & Nicholson, 1981.

Fay, Mrs. Eliza. *Original Letters from India (1779–1815).* New York: Harcourt, Brace, 1925.

Fazl, Abu-l. *The Akbarnama of Abu-l-Fazl.* Translated by H. Beveridge. New Delhi: Atlantic, 1989.

Fenton, Elizabeth Sinclair. *The Journal of Mrs. Fenton: A Narrative of Her Life in India. . . .* Edited by Sir Henry Lawrence. London: Edward Arnold, 1901.

Fergusson, James. *History of Indian and Eastern Architecture.* 3 vols. London: John Murray, 1876.

Firminger, T. A. C. *A Manual of Gardening for Bengal and Upper India.* 4th ed. Calcutta: Thacker, Spink, 1890.

Fisher, Michael Herbert, ed. *Visions of Mughal India: An Anthology of European Travel Writing.* London: I. B. Tauris, 2007.

Fonseca, Rory. "The Walled City of Old Delhi." In *Shelter and Society*, edited by Paul Oliver, 103–15. New York: Praeger, 1969.

Forbes, James. *Oriental Memoirs. A Narrative of Seventeen Years Residence in India.* 2 vols. 2nd ed. London: Richard Bentley, 1834.

Forrest, Denys. *Tiger of Mysore: The Life and Death of Tipu Sultan.* London: Chatto & Windus, 1970.

Fowler, Marian. *Below the Peacock Fan: First Ladies of the Raj.* New York: Viking, 1987.

Fraenkel, Peter. *No Fixed Abode: A Jewish Odyssey to Africa.* London: I. B. Tauris, 2005.

Fritz, John M., and George Michell. "Archaeology of the Garden." In Moynihan, *The Moonlight Garden*, 79–93.

Frykenberg, R. E. "The Coronation Durbar of 1911: Some Implications." In Frykenberg, *Delhi Through the Ages*, 225–46.

Frykenberg, R. E., ed. *Delhi Through the Ages.* New Delhi: Oxford University Press, 1986.

Gascoigne, Bamber. *The Great Moghuls.* London: Cape, 1971.

Gavaghan, Terence. *Of Lions and Dung Beetles*. Ilfracombe, UK: Arthur H. Stockwell, 1999.
Geddes, Patrick. *Patrick Geddes in India*. Edited by Jacqueline Tyrwhitt. Preface by H. V. Lanchester. London: L. Humphries, 1947.
Geldhill, David. *The Names of Plants*. Cambridge: Cambridge University Press, 2002.
George, Walter. "The Roadside Planting of Lutyens' New Delhi." *Urban and Rural Planning Thought* 1 (1958): 78–90.
Ghosh, Durba. *Sex and the Family in Colonial India: The Making of an Empire*. Cambridge: Cambridge University Press, 2006.
Gibbes, Phebe. *Hartly House, Calcutta*. 1789. New Delhi: Oxford University Press, 2007.
Gilmour, David. *Curzon: Imperial Statesman*. London: John Murray, 1994.
———. *The Ruling Caste: Imperial Lives in the Victorian Raj*. New York: Farrar, Straus & Giroux, 2005.
Gleig, G. R. *The Life of Major-General Sir Thomas Munro*. 2 vols. London: Henry Colburn & Richard Bentley, 1831.
———. *Memoirs of the Life of the Right Hon. Warren Hastings*. 3 vols. London: R. Bentley, 1841.
Godden, Jon, and Rumer Godden. *Two Under the Indian Sun*. 1966. New York: Beech Tree Books, 1987.
Goody, Jack. *The Culture of Flowers*. Cambridge: Cambridge University Press, 1993.
Goradia, Nayana. *Lord Curzon: Last of the British Moguls*. New York: Oxford University Press, 1993.
Gordon, Sophie. "The Royal Palaces." In Llewellyn-Jones, *Lucknow: City of Illusion*, 30–87.
Gordon Cumming, Constance F. *In the Himalayas and on the Indian Plains*. London: Chatto & Windus, 1884.
Gorer, Richard. *The Growth of Gardens*. London: Faber & Faber, 1978.
Graff, Violette, ed. *Lucknow: Memories of a City*. Delhi: Oxford University Press, 1997.
Graham, Maria. *Journal of a Residence in India: Illustrated by Engravings*. Edinburgh: George Ramsay, 1812.
Griessen, A. E. P. Remarks on a talk given by Mrs. Patrick Villiers-Stuart, 17 July 1931. *Journal of the Royal Society of Arts* 79, no. 4104 (1931): 807.
Griffin, Henry Lepel. *Famous Monuments of Central India*. With photographs by Raja Deen Dayal. London: Autotype, 1886.
Griffiths, Percival. *The History of the Indian Tea Industry*. London: Weidenfeld and Nicolson, 1967.
Grindal, E. W. *Everyday Gardening in India*. Bombay: D. B. Taraporevala, 1942.
Grove, Richard. *Green Imperialism: Colonial Expansion, Tropical Island Edens, and the Origins of Environmentalism, 1600–1860*. New York: Cambridge University Press, 1995.
Grover, Satish. *Islamic Architecture in India*. New Delhi: Galgotia, 1996.
Gupta, Narayani. *Delhi Between Two Empires, 1803–1931*. 1983. New Delhi: Oxford University Press, 2002.
———. "The Indomitable City." In Ehlers and Krafft, *Shahjahanabad/Old Delhi*, 29–44.
Gurner, C. W. "Lord Hastings and the Monuments of Agra." *Bengal, Past and Present* 27 (1924): 148–53.
Hadfield, Miles. *Gardening in Britain*. London: Hutchinson, 1960.
Halifax, Earl of [Lord Irwin]. *Fullness of Days*. New York: Dodd, Mead, 1957.
Hancock, Mary E. *The Politics of Heritage from Madras to Chennai*. Bloomington: Indiana University Press, 2008.

Hardinge, Lord Charles [Baron of Penshurst]. *My Indian Years, 1910–1916*. London: John Murray, 1947.

———. *Old Diplomacy*. London: John Murray, 1947.

Hare, Augustus J. C. *The Story of Two Noble Lives: Being Memorials of Charlotte, Countess Canning, and Louisa, Marchioness of Waterford*. 3 vols. London: George Allen, 1893.

Harkness, Terence, and Amita Sinha. "Taj Heritage Corridor: Intersections Between History and Culture on the Yamuna Riverfront." *Places* 16, no. 2 (2004): 62–69.

Harler, Agnes Wrey. *The Garden in the Plains*. 1901. 4th ed. Oxford: Oxford University Press, 1962.

Harrison, Robert Pogue. *Gardens: An Essay on the Human Condition*. Chicago: University of Chicago Press, 2008.

Harrop, F. Beresford. *Thacker's New Guide to Simla*. Simla: Thacker, Spink, 1925.

Hasan, M. Fazlul. *Bangalore Through the Centuries*. Bangalore: Historical Publications, 1970.

Havell, Ernest B. "Indian Gardens." *House and Garden*, Nov. 1904, 213–20, 268–74.

Head, Raymond. *Catalogue of Paintings, Drawings, Engravings and Busts: The Collection of the Royal Asiatic Society, London*. London: Royal Asiatic Society, 1991.

———. "Divine Flower Power Recorded." *Country Life* 176 (1984): 703–5.

Hearn, G. *Seven Cities of Delhi*. London: W. Thacker, 1906.

Heber, Bishop Reginald. *Narrative of a Journey Through the Upper Provinces of India: From Calcutta to Bombay, 1824–1825*. 3 vols. 2nd ed. London: John Murray, 1828.

Hickey, William. *Memoirs of William Hickey*. Edited by Peter Quennell. London: Routledge & Kegan Paul, 1975.

Hobbes, John Oliver [Pearl Craigie]. *Imperial India: Letters from the East*. London: T. Fisher Unwin, 1903.

Hodges, Arthur. *Lord Kitchener*. London: T. Butterworth, 1936.

Hodges, William. *Travels in India During the Years 1780, 1781, 1782, and 1783*. London: J. Edwards, 1793.

Hodgson, Col. J. A. "Memoir on the Illahee Guz, or Imperial Land Measure of Hindostan." *Journal of the Royal Asiatic Society* 7 (1843): 42–63.

Hogarth, D. G. "George Nathaniel Curzon, Marquess Curzon of Kedleston, 1859–1925." *Proceedings of the British Academy* 11 (1925): 502–24.

Hooker, Sir Joseph Dalton. *Himalayan Journals*. 1854. London: Ward, Lock, 1905.

Huggins, William. *Sketches in India, Treating on Subjects Connected with the Government and Military Establishments. . . .* London: John Letts, Jnr, 1824.

Hunt, John Dixon. *The Afterlife of Gardens*. Philadelphia: University of Pennsylvania Press, 2004.

———. "Imitation, Representation, and the Study of Garden Art." In *The Art of Interpreting*, edited by Susan C. Scott, 198–215. University Park: Pennsylvania State University Press, 1995.

Husain, Ali Akbar. *Scent in the Islamic Garden: A Study of Deccani Urdu Literary Sources*. Karachi: Oxford University Press, 2000.

Hussey, Christopher. *The Life of Sir Edwin Lutyens*. London: Country Life, 1950.

Hutchins, Francis G. *The Illusion of Permanence: British Imperialism in India*. Princeton: Princeton University Press, 1967.

Hyams, Edward. *The English Garden*. New York: Abrams, 1964.

Hyams, Edward, and William MacQuilty. *Great Botanical Gardens of the World*. London: Thomas Nelson, 1969.

Irving, Robert Grant. *Indian Summer: Lutyens, Baker, and Imperial Delhi.* New Haven: Yale University Press, 1981.
Ismail, Sir Mirza. *My Public Life: Recollections and Reflections.* London: George Allen & Unwin, 1954.
Jaffrey, Madhur. *Climbing the Mango Trees: A Memoir of a Childhood in India.* New York: Knopf, 2005.
Jahangir. *The Jahangirnama: Memoirs of Jahangir, Emperor of India.* Translated and edited by Wheeler M. Thackston. Washington, D.C.: Freer Gallery of Art, 1999.
James, Lawrence. *Raj: The Making and Unmaking of British India.* London: Little, Brown, 1997.
Jasanoff, Maya. *Edge of Empire: Conquest and Collecting in the East, 1750–1850.* New York: Knopf, 2005.
Jayapal, Maya. *Bangalore: The Story of a City.* Chennai: EastWest Books, 1997.
Jekyll, Francis. *Gertrude Jekyll: A Memoir.* Northampton, Mass.: Bookshop Round Table, 1934.
Jekyll, Gertrude. *Wall and Water Gardens.* London: Newnes / Country Life, 1901.
Jellicoe, Susan. "The Mughal Garden." In *The Islamic Garden,* edited by Elizabeth B. MacDougall and Richard Ettinghausen, 109–29. Washington, D.C.: Dumbarton Oaks, 1976.
Jones, Lady Anna Maria, ed. *The Works of Sir William Jones.* 6 vols. London: G. G. & J. Robinson, 1799.
Judd, Denis. *The Lion and the Tiger: The Rise and Fall of the British Raj, 1600–1947.* New York: Oxford University Press, 2004.
Kanwar, Pamela. *Imperial Simla: The Political Culture of the Raj.* Delhi: Oxford University Press, 1990.
Kaye, M. M., ed. *The Golden Calm: An English Lady's Life in Moghul Delhi.* New York: Viking Press, 1980.
———. *The Sun in the Morning: My Early Years in India and England.* New York: St. Martin's, 1990.
Keay, John. *The Honourable Company.* New York: Macmillan, 1994.
———. *India Discovered: The Achievement of the British Raj.* Leicester: Windward, 1981.
———. *India: A History.* New York: Grove Press, 2000.
———. *When Men and Mountains Meet: The Explorers of the Western Himalayas, 1820–75.* London: John Murray, 1977.
Kennedy, Dane. *The Magic Mountains: Hill Stations and the British Raj.* Berkeley: University of California Press, 1996.
Kenny, Judith T. "Climate, Race, and Imperial Authority: The Symbolic Landscape of the British Hill Station in India." *Annals of the Association of American Geographers* 85 (1995): 694–714.
Kesevan, Mukul. *Looking Through Glass.* New York: Farrar, Straus & Giroux, 1995.
Khan, Zain. *Zain Khan's Tabaqat-i-Baburi.* Translated by S. Hasan Askari. New Delhi: Idarah-i-Adabiyat-I Delli, 1982.
Khanna, Krishen. "I Went Back." In Sidhwa, *City of Sin and Splendour,* 105–12.
Kincaid, Dennis. *British Social Life in India, 1608–1937.* London: Routledge, 1939.
Kincaid, Jamaica. *My Garden.* New York: Farrar, Straus and Giroux, 1999.
King, Anthony D. *The Bungalow: The Production of a Global Culture.* London: Routledge & Kegan Paul, 1984.
———. *Colonial Urban Development: Culture, Social Power, and Environment.* London: Routledge & Kegan Paul, 1976.

King, E. Augusta. *The Diary of a Civilian's Wife in India, 1877–1882*. 2 vols. London: R. Bentley, 1884.

Kipling, John Lockwood. *Beast and Man in India: A Popular Sketch of Indian Animals in Their Relations with the People*. London: Macmillan, 1891.

Kipling, Rudyard. *City of the Dreadful Night*. New York: P. F. Collier, n.d.

———. *Complete Verse: Definitive Edition*. New York: Doubleday Anchor, 1940.

———. *Kim*. 1901. London: Penguin, 1987.

———. *Wee Willie Winkie, City of the Dreadful Night, American Notes*. London: Edinburgh Society, 1909.

Kisch, Hermann Michael. *A Young Victorian in India: Letters of H. M. Kisch of the Indian Civil Service*, edited by Ethel A. Waley Cohen. London: Jonathan Cape, 1957.

Kling, Blair. *Partner in Empire: Dwarkanath Tagore and the Age of Enterprise in Eastern India*. Berkeley: University of California Press, 1976.

Knighton, William. *Elihu Jan's Story; or, The Private Life of an Eastern Queen*. London: Longman Green, 1865.

Koch, Ebba. *The Complete Taj Mahal and the Riverfront Gardens of Agra*. New York: Thames & Hudson, 2006.

———. "The Hierarchical Principles of Shah-Jahani Painting." In *Mughal Art and Imperial Ideology*, 130–62.

———. "The Influence of the Jesuit Missions on Symbolic Representations of the Mughal Emperors." In *Mughal Art and Imperial Ideology*, 1–11.

———. "Jahangir and the Angels: Recently Discovered Wall Paintings Under European Influence in the Fort of Lahore." In *Mughal Art and Imperial Ideology*, 12–37.

———. "The Lost Colonnade of Shah Jahan's Bath in the Red Fort of Agra." In *Mughal Art and Imperial Ideology*, 255–88.

———. *Mughal Art and Imperial Ideology,: Collected Studies*. New Delhi: Oxford University Press, 2001.

———. "Mughal Palace Gardens from Babur to Shah Jahan (1526–1648)." In *Mughal Art and Imperial Ideology*, 203–28. Originally published in *Muqarnas* 14 (1997): 203–8.

———. "The Mughal Waterfront Garden." In *Gardens in the Time of the Great Muslim Empires: Theory and Design*, edited by Attilio Petruccioli, 140–60. Leiden: Brill, 1996. Repr. in *Mughal Art and Imperial Ideology*, 183–202.

Krishen, Pradip. *Trees of Delhi: A Field Guide*. Delhi: Dorling Kindersley India, 2007.

Kumar, Deepak. *Science and the Raj, 1857–1905*. 2nd ed. New Delhi: Oxford University Press, 2006.

Lal, Ranjit. "The Flora and Fauna of Delhi." In Singh and Varma, *Millennium Book on New Delhi*, 94–117.

Lamb, Christina. *The Africa House: The True Story of an English Gentleman and His African Dream*. New York: HarperCollins, 2004.

[Lang, C.]. "Chota Mem." *The English Bride in India: Being Hints on Indian Housekeeping*. London: Higginbotham, 1909.

Lang, John. *Wanderings in India, and Other Sketches of Life in Hindostan*. London: Routledge, Warne & Routledge, 1859.

Lawrence, Lady. *Indian Embers*. 1949. Palo Alto: Trackless Sands Press, 1991.

Lawson, Sir Charles. *Memories of Madras*. London: Swan Sonnenschein, 1905.

———. *The Private Life of Warren Hastings, First Governor-General of India*. London: Swan Sonnenschein, 1895.

Lear, Edward. *Flora Nonsensica*. Cambridge: Harvard College Library, 1963.

———. *Indian Journal: Watercolours and Extracts from the Diary of Edward Lear*. Edited by Ray Murphy. London: Jarrolds, 1953.

Lehrman, Jonas. *Earthly Paradise: Garden Courtyards in Islam*. Berkeley: University of California Press, 1980.

Lentz, David L. "Botanical Symbolism and Function at the Mahtab Bagh." In Moynihan, *The Moonlight Garden*, 42–55.

Lentz, Thomas W. "Memory and Ideology in the Timurid Garden." In Wescoat and Wolschke-Bulmahn, *Mughal Gardens*, 31–58.

Leoshko, Janice. "Mausoleum for an Empress." In Pal et al., *Romance of the Taj Mahal*, 53–87.

Lewandowski, Susan. *Migration and Ethnicity in Urban India: Kerala Migrants in the City of Madras, 1870–1970*. New Delhi: Manohar, 1980.

Lewis, Charles, and Karoki Lewis. *Delhi's Historic Villages: A Photographic Evocation*. New Delhi: Ravi Dayal, 1997. New edition forthcoming: Penguin India, 2011

Linstrum, Derek. "The Sacred Past: Lord Curzon and the Indian Monuments." *South Asian Studies* 11 (1995): 1–17.

Lively, Penelope. *A House Unlocked*. New York: Grove Press, 2001.

———. *Oleander, Jacaranda: A Childhood Perceived*. New York: HarperCollins, 1994.

Llewellyn-Jones, Rosie. *Engaging Scoundrels: True Tales of Old Lucknow*. New Delhi: Oxford University Press, 2000.

———. *A Fatal Friendship: The Nawabs, the British, and the City of Lucknow*. New Delhi: Oxford University Press, 1985. Repr. in *The Lucknow Omnibus*. New Delhi: Oxford University Press 2001.

———. *The Great Uprising in India, 1857–58*. Woodbridge, Suffolk: Boydell Press, 2007.

———. "Lucknow, City of Dreams." In Graff, *Lucknow: Memories of a City*, 49–66.

Llewellyn-Jones, Rosie, ed. *Lucknow: City of Illusion*. New York: Alkazi Collection of Photography / Munich: Prestel, 2006.

———. *Lucknow: Then and Now*. Mumbai: Marg, 2003.

Lloyd, Sir William. *Narrative of a Journey from Caunpoor to the Boorendo Pass*. London: J. Madden, 1840.

Losty, J. P. *Calcutta, City of Palaces: A Survey of the City in the Days of the East India Company, 1690–1858*. London: British Library, 1990.

———. "The Delhi Palace in 1846: A Panoramic View by Mazhar 'Ali Khan." In *Arts of Mughal India: Studies in Honour of Robert Skelton*, edited by Rosemary Crill, Susan Stronge, and Andrew Topsfield, 286–302. London: Victoria and Albert Museum / Ahmedabad: Mapin, 2004.

Love, H. D. *Vestiges of Old Madras, 1640–1800, Traced from the East India Company Records....* 4 vols. 1913. New York: AMS, 1968.

Luce, Edward. *In Spite of the Gods: The Strange Rise of Modern India*. New York: Doubleday, 2007.

Lutgendorf, Philip. "All in the (Raghu) Family: A Video Epic in Cultural Context." In *Media and the Transformation of Religion in South Asia*, edited by L. A. Babb and S. S. Wadley, 217–53. Philadelphia: University of Pennsylvania Press, 1995.

Lutyens, Mary. *Edwin Lutyens*. 1980. London: Black Swan, 1991.

———. *The Lyttons in India: An Account of Lord Lytton's Viceroyalty, 1876–1880*. London: John Murray, 1979.

M. D. L. T. [Maistre de la Tour], M. *The History of Hyder Shah . . . and of His Son, Tippoo Sultan.* 1855. Delhi: Cosmo, 1976.

Mabey, Richard. *The Flowers of Kew: 350 Years of Flower Paintings from the Royal Botanic Gardens.* New York: Atheneum, 1989.

Macaulay, "Thomas Lord Macaulay's Minute, 2nd February 1835." In W. Nassau Lees, *Indian Musalmans . . . With an Appendix Containing Lord Macaulay's Minute.* London: Williams & Norgate, 1871.

Macfarlane, Alan, and Iris Macfarlane. *Green Gold: The Empire of Tea.* London: Ebury, 2003.

Macfarlane, Iris. *Daughters of the Empire: A Memoir of Life and Times in the British Raj.* New Delhi: Oxford University Press, 2006.

Macmillan, Margaret. *Women of the Raj.* New York: Thames & Hudson, 1988.

Maitland, Julia. *Letters from Madras During the Years 1836–1839, by a Lady.* London: John Murray, 1846.

Malhotra, Vijay Kumar. *Lotus: Eternal Cultural Symbol.* Delhi: Clarion, 1999.

Manrique, Fr. *Travels of Fray Manrique, 1629–1643.* 2 vols. Translated by C. E. Quard and H. Hosten. Oxford: Hakluyt Society, 1927.

Mason, Philip. *The Guardians.* Vol. 2 of *The Men Who Ruled India.* New York: St. Martin's, 1954.

Matthew, Fr. K. M. "Little-Known South-Indian Botanical Collectors, Collections, Records and Plant Portraits." *Huntia* 10, no. 2 (1999): 125–37.

McCracken, Donal P. *Gardens of Empire: Botanical Institutions of the Victorian British Empire.* London: Leicester University Press, 1997.

McMaster, D. J. "The Colonial District Town in Uganda." In *Urbanisation and Its Problems: Essays in Honour of E. W. Gilbert,* edited by R. P. Beckinsale and J. M. Houston, 330–51. Oxford: Blackwell, 1968.

Mehta, Ved. "A House Divided. In Sidhwa, *City of Sin and Splendour,* 113–22.

Menpes, Mortimer. *Durbar.* London: A. & C. Black, 1903.

Metcalf, Thomas R. "Architecture and Empire: Sir Herbert Baker and the Building of New Delhi." In Frykenberg, *Delhi Through the Ages,* 247–56.

———. *Ideologies of the Raj.* New York: Cambridge University Press, 1994.

———. *An Imperial Vision: Indian Architecture and Britain's Raj.* Berkeley: University of California Press, 1989.

———. "Past and Present: Towards an Aesthetic of Colonialism." In Tillotson, *Paradigms of Indian Architecture,* 12–25.

Michaud, Joseph. *History of Mysore Under Hyder Ali and Tippoo Sultan.* 1801. Translated by V. K. Raman Menon. New Delhi: Asian Educational Services, 1985.

Middleton, Dorothy. *Victorian Lady Travellers.* New York: E. P. Dutton, 1965.

Milton, John. *Paradise Lost.* 1671. New York: Collier, 1962.

Mishra, Pankaj. *The Romantics.* New York: Random House, 2000.

Mitchell, Nora. *The Indian Hill Station: Kodaikanal.* Research Paper no. 141. Chicago: University of Chicago, Department of Geography, 1972.

Molony, J. Chartres. "An Indian Hill Station." *Blackwood's Magazine* 247:1495 (May 1940): 625–39.

Moore, Thomas. *Lalla Rookh: An Oriental Romance.* New York: Leavitt & Allen Bros., 1817.

Moorhouse, Geoffrey. *Calcutta.* New York: Harcourt Brace Jovanovich, 1972.

———. *India Britannica.* New York: Harper & Row, 1983.

Morris, James [Jan]. *Farewell the Trumpets: An Imperial Retreat.* New York: Harcourt Brace Jovanovich, 1978.

———. "Hill Stations." In *The Age of Kipling: The Man, His Work, and His World*, edited by John Gross, 51–56. New York: Simon & Schuster, 1972.

———. *Pax Britannica: The Climax of an Empire*. New York: Harcourt, Brace & World, 1968.

———. *Stones of Empire: The Buildings of the Raj*. New York: Oxford University Press, 1983.

Mortimer, John. *Clinging to the Wreckage: A Part of Life*. New Haven: Ticknor & Fields, 1982.

Moynihan, Elizabeth B. "But What a Pleasure to Have Known Babur." In Wescoat and Wolschke-Bulmahn, *Mughal Gardens*, 91–126.

———. "Reflections of Paradise." In *The Moonlight Garden*, 15–41.

Moynihan, Elizabeth B., ed. *The Moonlight Garden*. Washington, D.C.: Smithsonian Institution / Seattle: University of Washington Press, 2000.

Mukherjee, S. N. *Sir William Jones: A Study in Eighteenth-Century British Attitudes to India*. Cambridge: Cambridge University Press, 1968.

Mukherji, Anisha Shekhar. "The Changing Perception of Space, History of the Red Fort, Shajahanabad." In Ehlers and Krafft, *Shahjahanabad/Old Delhi*, 45–70.

———. *The Red Fort of Shahjahanabad*. New Delhi: Oxford University Press, 2003.

Mundy, Capt. G. C. *Pen and Pencil Sketches, Being the Journal of a Tour in India*. 2 vols. London: John Murray, 1832.

Mundy, Peter. *The Travels of Peter Mundy in Europe and Asia, 1608–67*. 2 vols. Edited by Sir Richard Carnac Temple. Oxford: Hakluyt Society, 1905–19.

Murphy, Dervla. *On a Shoestring to Coorg: An Experience of South India*. London: Murray, 1976.

Murray's Handbook for Travellers in India, Burma and Ceylon, 13th ed. London: John Murray, 1929.

Naipaul, V. S. *An Area of Darkness*. Harmondsworth: Penguin, 1964.

Nair, Janaki. *The Promise of the Metropolis: Bangalore's Twentieth Century*. New Delhi: Oxford University Press, 2005.

Nair, P. T., ed. *Calcutta in the Eighteenth Century: Impressions of Travellers*. Calcutta: Firma KLM, 1984.

National Trust. *Kedleston Hall*. London: National Trust, 1999.

Necipoğlu, Gülru. "The Taj Mahal: Review of W. E. Begley and Z. A. Desai, *Taj Mahal: The Illumined Tomb*." *Journal of the Society of Architectural Historians* 51, no. 3 (1992): 341–44.

Neild, Susan M. "Colonial Urbanism: The Development of Madras City in the Eighteenth and Nineteenth Centuries." *Modern Asian Studies* 13, no. 2 (1979): 217–46.

Ngugi wa Thiong'o. *A Grain of Wheat*. London: Heinemann, 1986.

Nicolson, Harold. *Curzon: The Last Phase, 1919–1925: A Study in Post-War Diplomacy*. New York: Houghton Mifflin, 1939.

Nicolson, Marjorie Hope. *Mountain Gloom and Mountain Glory: The Development of the Aesthetics of the Infinite*. Ithaca: Cornell University Press, 1959.

Nilsson, Sten. *European Architecture in India, 1750–1850*. Translated by Agnes George and Eleonore Zettersten. London: Faber & Faber, 1968.

———. *The New Capitals of India, Pakistan, and Bangladesh*. Translated by Elisabeth Andréasson. Lund: Studentlitteratur, 1973.

Noltie, Henry J. *The Dapuri Drawings: Alexander Gibson and the Bombay Botanical Gardens*. Woodbridge, UK: Antique Collectors' Club, 2002.

———. *Robert Wight and the Botanical Drawings of Rungiah & Govindoo*. 3 vols. Edinburgh: Royal Botanic Garden Edinburgh, 2007.

———. *Robert Wight and the Illustration of Indian Botany.* Hooker Lecture, special issue no. 6. London: Linnean Society, 2005.

North, Marianne. *Recollections of a Happy Life.* 2 vols. London: Macmillan, 1892.

———. *Some Further Recollections of a Happy Life.* London: Macmillan, 1893.

———. *A Vision of Eden.* New York: Holt, Rinehart & Winston, 1980.

Nugent, Lady Maria. *A Journal from the Year 1811 till the year 1815. . . .* 2 vols. London: n.p., 1839.

Oldenburg, Veena Talwar. *The Making of Colonial Lucknow, 1856–1877.* Princeton: Princeton University Press, 1984.

Orlich, Leopold von. *Travels in India.* 2 vols. London: Longman, Brown, Green & Longmans, 1845.

Pal, Pratapaditya, and Vidya Dehejia. *From Merchants to Emperors: British Artists and India, 1757–1930.* Ithaca: Cornell University Press, 1986.

Pal, Pratapaditya, Janice Leoshko, Joseph M. Dye III, and Stephen Markel, eds. *Romance of the Taj Mahal.* Los Angeles: Los Angeles County Museum / London: Thames & Hudson, 1989.

Panter-Downes, Mollie. *Ooty Preserved: A Victorian Hill Station.* London: Hamish Hamilton, 1967.

Parks [Parkes], Fanny. *Begums, Thugs and White Mughals: The Journals of Fanny Parkes.* Selected and introduced by William Dalrymple. London: Sickle Moon Books, 2002.

———. *Wanderings of a Pilgrim in Search of the Picturesque.* 1850. 2 vols. Karachi: Oxford University Press, 1975.

Peck, Lucy. *Delhi: A Thousand Years of Building.* New Delhi: Roli Books, 2005.

Peer, Basharat. *Curfewed Night: One Kashmiri Journalist's Frontline Account of Life, Love, and War in His Homeland.* New York: Scribner, 2010.

Pelizzari, Maria Antonella. "From Stone to Paper." In *Traces of India: Photography, Architecture, and the Politics of Representation, 1850–1900,* edited by Pelizzari, 20–57. New Haven: Yale Center for British Art, 2003.

Percy, Clayre, and Jane Ridley, eds. *The Letters of Edwin Lutyens to His Wife, Lady Emily.* London: Collins, 1985.

Percy-Lancaster, S. *Gardening in India: An Amateur in the Indian Garden.* 2nd ed. Calcutta: author, 1935.

Pogson, Fred. *Indian Gardening: A Manual of Flowers, Fruits and Vegetables. . . .* Calcutta: Wyman, 1872.

Pope, Alexander. "Epistle IV, to Richard Boyle, Earl of Burlington." *The Poems of Alexander Pope,* ed. F. W. Bateson, vol. 3, part 2. London: Methuen, 1951, 130–51.

Postans, Mrs. [Marianne Young]. *Western India, in 1838.* 2 vols. London: Sannders & Otley, 1839.

Pott, Janet. *Old Bungalows in Bangalore, South India.* London: Pott, 1977.

Pouchepadass, Jacques. "Lucknow Besieged (1857): Feminine Records of the Event and the Victorian Mind on India." In Graff, *Lucknow: Memories of a City,* 91–113.

Prasad, H. Y. Sharada. *Rashtrapati Bhavan: The Story of the President's House.* New Delhi: Ministry of Information, 1992.

Prasad, Sunand. "A Tale of Two Cities: House and Town in India Today." In Tillotson, *Paradigms of Indian Architecture,* 176–99. London: Curzon Press, 1998.

Price, Sir Frederick. *Ootacamund: A History.* 1908. Chennai: Rupa, 2002.

Prinsep, Val. *Imperial India: An Artist's Journal.* London: Chapman & Hall, 1879.

Prior, Katherine, Lance Brennan, and Robin Haines. "Bad Language: The Role of English, Persian and Other Esoteric Tongues in the Dismissal of Sir Edwarde Colebrooke as Resident of Delhi in 1929." *Modern Asian Studies* 35 (2001): 75–112.

Pubby, Vipin. *Simla Then and Now: Summer Capital of the Raj.* New Delhi: Indus, 1988.

Quest-Ritson, Charles. *The English Garden Abroad.* London: Viking, 1992.

Quraeshi, Samina. *Lahore: The City Within.* Singapore: Concept Media, 1988.

Raafat, Samir. *Maadi, 1904–1962: Society and History in a Cairo Suburb.* Cairo: Palm Press, 1995.

Raleigh, Thomas, ed. *Lord Curzon in India, Being a Selection from His Speeches as Viceroy and Governor-General of India.* London: Macmillan, 1906.

Randhawa, G. S., K. L. Chadha, and Daljit Singh, eds. *Famous Gardens of India.* New Delhi: Malhotra, 1971.

Rawdon-Hastings, Francis. *The Private Journal of the Marquess of Hastings.* Edited by the Marchioness of Bute. 2 vols. London: Saunders & Otley, 1858.

Richards, John F. "The Historiography of Mughal Gardens." In Wescoat and Wolschke-Bulmahn, *Mughal Gardens,* 259–66.

Ridley, Jane. *The Architect and His Wife: A Life of Edwin Lutyens.* London: Chatto & Windus, 2001.

———. "Edwin Lutyens, New Delhi, and the Architecture of Imperialism." *Journal of Imperial and Commonwealth History* 26 (1998): 67–83.

Roberts, Emma. *Scenes and Characteristics of Hindostan, with Sketches of Anglo-Indian Society.* 2 vols. Philadelphia: Carey, Lea & Blanchard, 1836.

Roberts, Emma, Robert Elliot, and George Francis White. *Hindostan: Its Landscapes, Palaces, Tombs. . . .* 2 vols. London: Fisher, Son, 1845.

Roberts, Judith. "English Gardens in India." *Garden History* 26, no. 2 (Winter 1998): 115–35.

Robinson, William. *The English Flower Garden.* 6th ed. London: John Murray, 1898.

Roche, George. *Childhood in India.* Ed. Richard Terrell. London: Radcliffe Press, 1994.

Roe, Sir Thomas. *The Embassy of Sir Thomas Roe to India, 1615–19.* Edited by Sir William Foster. London: Oxford University Press, 1926.

Ronaldshay, The Earl of. *The Life of Lord Curzon, Being the Authorized Biography of George Nathaniel, Marquess Curzon of Kedleston.* 2 vols. London: E. Benn, 1928.

Rousselet, Louis. *L'Inde des Rajahs.* Paris: Hachette, 1875.

Ruggles, D. Fairchild. "Humayun's Tomb and Garden." In *Gardens in the Time of the Great Muslim Empires: Theory and Design,* edited by Attilio Petruccioli, 173–86. Leiden: Brill, 1996.

———. *Islamic Gardens and Landscapes.* Philadelphia: University of Pennsylvania Press, 2008.

Russell, William Howard. H. *My Diary in India, in the Year 1858–9.* 2 vols. London: Routledge, Warne & Routledge, 1860.

———. *The Prince of Wales's Tour.* London: Sampson Low, Marston, Searle & Rivington, 1877.

Sahni, Daya Ram. *Guide to the Buddhist Ruins of Sarnath.* 1917. Simla: Government Central Press, 1923.

Sassoon, Siegfried. *Siegfried's Journey, 1916–20.* New York: Viking, 1945.

Saunders, Gill. *Picturing Plants: An Analytical History of Botanical Illustration.* Berkeley: University of California Press in association with the Victoria and Albert Museum, 1995.

Schiebinger, Londa, and Claudia Swan, eds. *Colonial Botany: Science, Commerce, and Politics in the Early Modern World.* Philadelphia: University of Pennsylvania Press, 2005.

Schimmel, Annemarie. *The Empire of the Great Mughals: History, Art and Culture.* 2000. Translated by Corinne Attwood; edited by Burzine K. Waghmar. London: Reaktion Books, 2004.

Scott, Paul. *Staying On*. New York: Avon, 1979.

———. *The Towers of Silence*. New York: Avon, 1971.

Scott-James, Anne, and Osbert Lancaster. *The Pleasure Garden: An Illustrated History of British Gardening*. Ipswich, Mass.: Gambit, 1977.

Sellar, W. C., and R. J. Yeatman. *Garden Rubbish and Other Country Bumps*. New York: Farrar & Rinehart, 1936.

Seth, B. R. *Khajuraho in Pictures*. Delhi: Asia Press, 1970.

Seth, Vikram. *A Suitable Boy*. New York: HarperCollins, 1993.

Sharar, Abdul Halim. *Lucknow: The Last Phase of an Oriental Culture*. Translated and edited by E. S. Harcourt. In *The Lucknow Omnibus*. New Delhi: Oxford University Press, 2001.

Sharp, Henry. *Good-bye India*. Oxford: Oxford University Press, 1946.

Sharwood-Smith, Joan. *Diary of a Colonial Wife: An African Experience*. London: Radcliffe Press, 1992.

Shields, Nancy K. *Birds of Passage: Henrietta Clive's Travels in South India, 1798–1801*. London: Eland, 2009.

Shore, John [Baron Teignmouth]. *Memoirs of the Life, Writings, and Correspondence of Sir William Jones*. 1804. Philadelphia: Classic Press, 1805.

Shteir, A. B. *Cultivating Women, Cultivating Science: Flora's Daughters and Botany in England, 1760–1860*. Baltimore: Johns Hopkins University Press, 1996.

Sidhwa, Bapsi, ed. *City of Sin and Splendour: Writings on Lahore*. New Delhi: Penguin Books India, 2005.

Singh, B. P., and Pavan K. Varma, eds. *The Millennium Book on New Delhi*. New Delhi: Oxford University Press, 2001.

Singh, Khushwant. *Delhi: A Portrait*. Photographs by Raghu Rai. Delhi: Delhi Tourism Corp. / New York: Oxford University Press, 1983.

Singh, Patwant. *Of Dreams and Demons: An Indian Memoir*. New York: Kodansha International, 1995.

Sinha, Amita. *Landscapes in India: Forms and Meanings*. Boulder: University Press of Colorado, 2006.

Skinner, Capt. Thomas. *Excursions in India; Including a Walk over the Himalaya Mountains. . . .* 2 vols. London, Henry Colburn & Richard Bentley, 1832.

Sleeman, Lt. Col. William Henry. *A Journey Through the Kingdom of Oude, in 1849–1850*. 2 vols. London: R. Bentley, 1858.

———. *Rambles and Recollections of an Indian Official*. 2 vols. London: J. Hatchard & Son, 1844.

Smith, Tori. "'A Grand Work of Noble Conception': The Victoria Memorial and Imperial London." In *Imperial Cities*, edited by Felix Driver and David Gilbert, 21–39. Manchester: Manchester University Press, 1999.

Spear, Percival. "Bentinck and the Taj." *Journal of the Royal Asiatic Society of Great Britain and Ireland*, October 1949: 180–87.

———. *Delhi: A Historical Sketch*. 1937. New Delhi: Oxford University Press, 2002.

———. *Delhi: Its Monuments and History*. 3rd ed. Updated and annotated by Narayan Gupta and Laura Sykes. New Delhi: Oxford University Press, 1994.

———. "Delhi—The 'Stop-Go' Capital." In Frykenberg, *Delhi Through the Ages*, 309–25.

———. *The Nabobs: A Study of the Social Life of the English in Eighteenth-Century India*. 1932. Oxford: Oxford University Press, 1963.

———. *Twilight of the Mughuls: Studies in Late Mughul Delhi*. 1951. Repr. in *The Delhi Omnibus*. New Delhi: Oxford University Press, 2002.

Spear, Percival, and Margaret Spear. *India Remembered*. Delhi: Orient Longman, 1981.
Speede, G. T. *The New Indian Gardener and Guide to the Successful Culture of the Kitchen and Fruit Garden in India*. 2 vols. Calcutta, W. Thacker, 1848.
Srinivas, Smriti. *Landscapes of Urban Memory: The Sacred and the Civic in India's High-Tech City*. Minneapolis: University of Minnesota Press, 2001.
Stamp, Gavin, and André Goulancourt. *The English House, 1860–1914: The Flowering of English Domestic Architecture*. Chicago: University of Chicago Press, 1986.
Stanley, Lady Beatrix. "Gardening in India." *The Gardeners' Chronicle*, 23 May 1931, 392.
Stark, Freya. *Dust in the Lion's Paw*. New York: Harcourt, Brace & World, 1962.
Steel, Flora Annie. *The Garden of Fidelity*. London: Macmillan, 1929.
———. *On the Face of the Waters: A Tale of the Mutiny*. New York: Macmillan, 1897.
Steel, Flora Annie, and Mrs. Grace Gardiner. *Complete Indian Housekeeper and Cook*. New ed. London: Heinemann, 1898.
Steevens, G. W. *In India*. New York: Dodd, Mead, 1899.
Stewart, Rory. *The Places in Between*. Orlando: Harcourt, 2004.
Stronach, David. "Parterres and Stone Watercourses at Pasargadae: Notes on the Achaemenid Contribution to Garden Design." *Journal of Garden History* 14, no. 1 (1994): 3–12.
Stronge, Susan. *Painting for the Mughal Emperor: The Art of the Book, 1560–1660*. London: Victoria and Albert Publications, 2002.
Surtees, Virginia. *Charlotte Canning: Lady-in-Waiting to Queen Victoria and Wife of the First Viceroy of India, 1817–1861*. London: John Murray, 1975.
Sykes, Laura. "Afterword—Fifty Years On." In Spear, *Delhi: Its Monuments and History*, 110–45.
Sykes, Laura, ed. *Calcutta Through British Eyes, 1690–1990*. Madras: Oxford University Press, 1992.
Tagore, Rabindranath. 1911. *My Reminiscences*. New York: Macmillan, 1917.
Tavernier, Jean-Baptiste. *Travels in India by Jean-Baptiste Tavernier*. 2 vols. Edited by William Crooke. Oxford: Oxford University Press, 1925.
Taylor, Bayard. *A Visit to India, China, and Japan, in the Year 1853*. 1855. New York: Putnam, 1877.
Temple-Wright, Mrs. R. *Flowers and Gardens in India: A Manual for Beginners*. 4th ed. Calcutta: Thacker, Spink, 1898.
Tennyson, Alfred, Lord. "The Defence of Lucknow." *Ballads and Other Poems*. London: C. Kegan Paul, 1880.
Thacker, Christopher. *The History of Gardens*. Berkeley: University of California Press, 1979.
Thackston, Wheeler M. "Mughal Gardens in Persian Poetry." In Wescoat and Wolschke-Bulmahn, *Mughal Gardens*, 233–58.
Thomas, Keith. *Man and the Natural World: A History of the Modern Sensibility*. New York: Pantheon, 1983.
Thompson, Ian. *The Sun King's Garden: Louis XIV, André Le Nôtre, and the Creation of the Gardens of Versailles*. New York: Bloomsbury, 2006.
Tidrick, Kathryn. *Empire and the English Character: The Illusion of Authority*. London: I. B. Tauris, 1990.
Tillotson, G. H. R., ed. *Paradigms of Indian Architecture*. New Delhi: Oxford University Press, 1998.
Tindall, Gillian. *City of Gold: The Biography of Bombay*. London: Temple Smith, 1982.

Tobin, Beth Fowkes. "The English Garden Conversation Piece in India." In *The Global Eighteenth Century*, edited by Felicity Nussbaum, 165–81. Baltimore: Johns Hopkins University Press, 2003.

Tod, Capt. James. *Annals and Antiquities of Rajasthan*. 2 vols. Calcutta: L. M. Auddy, 1896.

Trevelyan, G. O. *The Competition Wallah*, 2nd ed. London: Macmillan, 1866.

Trevelyan, Raleigh. *The Golden Oriole: A 200-Year History of an English Family in India*. London: Secker & Warburg, 1987.

Tripathi, Purnima S. "Saving the Taj Mahal." *Frontline* 20, no. 15 (19 July–1 Aug. 2003), 1–6.

Tully, Mark. "The Travails of a Metropolis." In Singh and Varma, *The Millennium Book on New Delhi*, 164–85.

Tulsidas. *The Rámáyana of Tulsi Dás*. Translated by F. S. Growse. 6th ed. Allahabad: Ram Narain Lal, 1922.

Tunzelmann, Alex von. *Indian Summer: The Secret History of the End of the Empire*. New York: Henry Holt, 2007.

Twining, Thomas. *Travels in India a Hundred Years Ago*. Edited by H. G. Twining. London: Osgood, McIlvaine, 1893.

Tytler, Harriet. *An Englishwoman in India: The Memoirs of Harriet Tytler, 1828–1858*. Edited by Anthony Satin. London: Oxford University Press, 1986.

Uglow, Jenny. *A Little History of British Gardening*. New York: North Point Press, 2004.

Valentia, Viscount George. *Voyages and Travels*. 4 vols. 1809. London: C. & J. Rivington, 1811.

Veblen, Thorstein. *The Theory of the Leisure Class*. 1899. New York: Augustus M. Kelley, 1975.

Villiers-Stuart, Constance. *Gardens of the Great Mughals*. 1913. New Delhi: Cosmo, 1983.

———. (Mrs. Patrick Villiers-Stuart). "Horticultural Club Lecture on Indian Garden Craft." *Gardeners' Chronicle*, 16 May 1914, 337–39.

———. "The Indian Paradise Garden." *Journal of the Royal Society of Arts* 79 (17 July 1931): 793–808.

Volwahsen, Andreas. *Imperial Delhi: The British Capital of the Indian Empire*. Munich: Prestel, 2002.

Waddell, L. A. *Among the Himalayas*. Philadelphia: J. B. Lippincott, 1900.

Ward, Andrew. *Our Bones Are Scattered: The Cawnpore Massacre and the Indian Mutiny*. New York: Henry Holt, 1996.

Welch, Anthony. "Gardens That Babur Did Not Like." In Wescoat and Wolschke-Bulmahn, *Mughal Gardens*, 59–93.

Wescoat, James L. "Gardens of Invention and Exile: The Precarious Context of Mughal Garden Design During the Reign of Humayun (1530–1556)." *Journal of Garden History* 10, no. 2 (1990): 106–16.

———. "Picturing an Early Mughal Garden." *Asian Art* 2, no. 4 (1989): 59–79.

Wescoat, James L., and Joachim Wolschke-Bulmahn, eds. *Mughal Gardens*. Washington, D.C.: Dumbarton Oaks, 1996.

———. "Sources, Places, Representations and Prospects: The Mughal Garden." In *Mughal Gardens*, 5–30.

Westlake, Graeme D. *An Introduction to the Hill Stations of India*. New Delhi: Indus, 1993.

Wheeler, Stephen. *History of the Delhi Coronation Durbar*. London: John Murray, 1904.

Wilhide, Elizabeth. *Sir Edwin Lutyens: Designing in the English Tradition*. New York: Abrams, 2000.

Williamson, Thomas. *East India Vade Mecum*. 2 vols. London: Black, Parry & Kingsbury, 1810.

Williamson, Tom. *Polite Landscapes: Gardens and Society in Eighteenth-Century England*. Baltimore: Johns Hopkins University Press, 1995.

Wilson, Lady Anne. *Letters from India*. 1911. London: Century, 1984.

Woodrow, G. M. *Hints on Gardening in India*. 4th ed. Bombay: Education Society Press, 1888.

Woolf, Bella Sidney. *From Groves of Palm*. Cambridge, UK: Heffer, 1925.

Wright, Gillian. *The Hill Stations of India*. Lincolnwood, Ill.: Passport Books, 1991.

Wulf, Andrea, and Emma Gieben-Gamal. *This Other Eden: Seven Great Gardens and Three Hundred Years of English History*. London: Little, Brown, 2005.

Yalland, Zoë. *Boxwallahs: The British in Cawnpore, 1857–1901*. Wilby, UK: M. Russell, 1994.

Zannas, Eliky. *Khajuraho: Text and Photos*. The Hague: Mouton, 1960.

INDEX

Aden, 305
Africa, xi, 260, 303–5 (fig. 56)
Agra, 47, 78, 197, 201, 216, 217, 220, 259, 261; Fort, 213, 241, 274, 290, 291; Mughal capital, 231–32; riverfront gardens, 231, 235; tomb of I'timad-ud-Daulah, 220, 231, 290
Akbar, 20, 102, 166–67, 208, 216, 219, 295, 308; Fatehpur Sikri, 185, 216, 232, 258, 280, 346n57; tomb, 220
Akshardam Temple, 299–300
Amherst, Lady Sarah, 40, 55, 77, 85, 87, 88, 103, 104, 148–49; *Amherstia nobilis,* 149–51, 174, 178; botanical study, 174; golden pheasant, 174, 335n107
Amherst, Lady Sarah Elizabeth (daughter), 77–78, 174
Amherst, Lord, 105
Arabian Nights, 29, 186, 189
Archaeological Survey of India (ASI), 199, 201–2, 222, 229, 243, 244–48, 254, 291, 293, 299
Archer, Maj. Edward, 100, 186
Ashoka, 133, 229; Bull, 346n53
Assam, 41, 47–48, 100, 162, 176, 314; tea-growing in, 157–58

Auckland, Lord, 46, 68, 70, 88, 105–6, 113, 312–13
Augusta, Princess, 14, 143
Aurangzeb, 20, 106, 207, 213, 226, 238, 239
Awadh (Oudh), 181, 183, 184, 187, 196; annexation, 187–88; king's exile in Calcutta, 71. *See also* Lucknow

Babur, 260; *Baburnama,* 167; dislike of Hindustan, 8, 19, 60, 210, 230–31; Garden of Fidelity, 210, Pl. 18; love of gardens, 7, 19, 102, 129, 208, 210, 211, 231, 235, 255, 258, 280
Bacon, Francis, 304, 312
Bahadur Shah (Zafar), 240, 243–44, 341n41
Baikie, Dr., 121–22, 124
Baker, Sir Herbert, 217, 260, 270, 274, 283
Bangalore, xii, 4, 122, 130–36, 280, 294, 298, 301, 348n97; bungalows, 131–32 (fig. 25), 135; Lal Bagh, xii, 133–34, 136 (fig. 26), 139–41, 176, 298, Pl. 27; Residency, 133
Banks, Sir Joseph, 143–44, 149, 157, 162, 178, 179
banyan trees, 29, 59, 91, 95, 174, 285, Pl. 8, 12

Baroda, 273, 285 (fig. 53)
Barrackpore, 31, 62, 83–96 passim (fig. 22), 175, 297, Pl. 5, 7, 8; menagerie, 84, 86, 161–62; 1857 Mutiny, 92, 182, 244
Benares (Varanasi), 4, 52, 60, 156, 167, 221, 299
Bengal, 20, 21, 46–47, 51, 68, 87, 96, 149, 153, 181, 259, 297; Bay of, 24, 63, 114
Bentinck, Lord, 86, 216–17, 339n61, 66; Lady, 78
Bernier, François, 98, 106, 163, 201, 202, 207, 209, 219, 223, 233, 235, 238, 247, 281
Bombay (Mumbai), 2, 15, 20, 21, 24, 28, 33–36, 51, 60, 97, 100, 122, 184, 280, 348n96; Elphinstone Circle and Gardens, 50, 59 (fig. 16); Malabar Hill, 30; Parel, 89–90, Pl. 6; summer bungalows, 98–99; Victoria Gardens, 50, Pl. 2; Victoria Terminus, 131; University, 299, Pl. 32
botanical gardens, 141–43, 303, 307: Darjeeling, 153 (fig. 27); Mauritius (Pamplemousses), 143; Saharanpur, 146, 152; St. Vincent, 143, 171, 303. *See also* Calcutta Botanic Garden; Dapuri; Kew
botanical illustration, 164, 166–69, 172–76
boxwallahs, 22, 101, 119
Brighton Pavilion, 7, 56, 196
Brindavan Gardens (Krishnaraja Sagara), 287, 288, Pl. 26
Brown, Capability, xi, 31, 33, 67, 85, 164, 219
Buchanan, Francis, 130, 161
Buddha, Buddhism, 5, 12, 149, 172, 220, 284; *Buddhacarita*, 6
Burton, Richard, 121, 122, 126

Calcutta (Kolkata), 15, 20–21, 24, 28, 34, 35, 37, 48, 55, ch. 2 passim, 97, 104, 115, 119, 122, 158, 160, 167, 170, 184, 242, 258–59, 280, 306; Alipur, 65, 66, 83; Belvedere, 65, 67, 81, 268; Botanic Garden, 87, 93, 146–52, 161, 168, 174, 187, 325n47; Chowringhee, 65, 66, 72; Eden Gardens, 50, 74; flower market, Pl. 1; Garden Reach, 65–68, 71–72, 83, 170, 314; Government House, 64, 73–81 (figs. 18–20), 88, 96, 241, Pl. 4; *maidan*, 65, 73–75, 77, Pl. 3; Marble Palace, 71; St. Paul's Cathedral, 73; South Park St. Cemetery, 67, 147, 172; Tollygunge Club, 297, Pl. 30; Victoria Memorial, 224–26 (fig. 44)
Canning, Lady Charlotte, 26, 29–30, 55, ch. 2 passim, 107, 119, 151, 312, Pl. 7; botanical illustration, 175, Pl. 8; design for Cawnpore sculpture, 194; durbars, 194, 248; grave, 94–95, 297, 327n121, Pl. 29; Highcliffe, 90; Lady Canning's Seat, 93, 125, 298; visit to the Nilgiris, 124–25
Canning, Lord, 77, 88, 92, 94–95, 151, 194, 244, 297
Carey, William, 55, 87
Cawnpore (Kanpur), 40, 194–96 (fig. 35), 314; *Angel of the Resurrection*, 194, 292
Ceylon, 153–54, 158, 169, 314
Chandi Chowk (Delhi), 233, 237, 238, 245, 246, 260, 272, 277, 281, 283
Charnock, Job, 63, 76
Chatsworth. *See* Duke of Devonshire
Cheltenham, 123, 128, 134
chunam, 29, 36, 185
Churchill, Winston, 40, 132
cinchona, 145, 153–54, 179
Clive, Edward, 30–32, 161
Clive, Lady Henrietta, 13, 24, 30, 130–31, 140, 310, 332n3, 335n101
Clive, Robert, 21, 70
Coonor, 99, 124, 125, 298
Crystal Palace, xii, 176; in Lal Bagh, 176, Pl. 15
Cubbon, Sir Mark, 133, 136
Curzon: Lord, 75, 81–83, 88, 92, 95–96, 114, 116, 288, 297; dislike of Simla, 118–19; durbar of 1902–3, 250–53, 272, 294; restoration of Taj Mahal, ch. 6 passim, 290, 314; opposition to New Delhi, 258, 259
Curzon, Lady Mary, 94, 95, 109, 252–53, 269, 344n113
Cuthell, Edith, 43, 48, 50, 53, 58, 182, 190–93 passim

Dacca, 52; cotton, 146
Dalhousie, Lord, 74, 108, 122, 179–80; Dalhousie Square (Calcutta), 75
Dalrymple, William, 7, 35, 128, 223, 245, 293
Daniell, Thomas and William, 56, 64, 203–4 (fig. 39), 218, Pl. 19
Dapuri, 177 (fig. 31)
Dara Shikoh, 237, 241; *Album,* 167, Pl. 13
Darjeeling, 60, 93–94, 99, 106, 107, 119, 120; botanical garden, 153 (fig. 27), 163; tea, 158
Deegah, 48–49
deforestation: Delhi Ridge, 278, 296; Himalayas, 179–80; Kashmir, 296; Nilgiri Hills, 126, 296–97
Dehra Dun, 119, 300
Delhi, 15, 37, 60, 83, 96, 98, 128, 152, 167; decline in eighteenth and nineteenth centuries, 184, 188, 227–28 (fig. 45), 239–41; durbars, 248–56 (fig. 48, 49); pre-Mughal rulers, 228–30; Shahjahanabad, 232–39, 258 (fig. 46); under British control, 239–56; 1857 and its aftermath, 243–47, 260. *See also* Red Fort
Devonshire, Duke of, 68, 124, 162, 165, 178, 219
Dietrich, Marlene, 154
Dilkusha (Lucknow), 185–86, 188, 191; Dil Kusha ("Metcalfe's Folly," Delhi), 242
Dufferin, Lady, 2, 32, 35, 42, 44, 49, 76, 103, 104, 109, 113–16, 120, 190, 192
Dufferin, Lord, 75, 113–16
Duncan, Sara, 110–11, 129, 306
durbars, 42, 80, 293, 304; 1877, 248–49; 1902–3, 248–53 (fig. 48), 272; 1911, 253–56, 257

East India Company (British), 4, 20–21, 26, 31, 35, 37, 63, 66, 83, 97, 99, 100, 101, 123, 142, 147, 149, 161, 185, 207, 285; directors, 30, 76, 146; support of botanical research, 169; trade in tea and opium, 155–58
Eden: Emily, 23, 46, 60–61, 68, 70, 78–79, 84, 88, 105, 107, 108, 111–13, 127–28, 134–35, 186, 222, 240, 312; Eden Gardens, 50, 74; fragility of imperialism, 128, 182
Edward VII, 133, 253; Emperor of India, 249–50. *See also* Prince of Wales
Elizabeth I, Queen, 20, 22
Elphinstone, Montstuart, 37, 89–90
Emerson, William, 225–26

Fay, Eliza, 29, 65, 67
Fenton, Elizabeth, 59, 67
Firoz Shah Tughlak, 229–30, 295
Fitzpatrick, James Achilles, 32–34, 139–40
Forbes, James, 4, 9, 13, 23, 36, 50, 53–55, 312
Fortune, Robert, 160

Gandhi, Mahatma, 2, 127
Ganges, 61, 63, 64, 89, 94, 119, 156, 195; fish, 161
Garden of Eden, 12, 13, 71, 142, 148, 149
Gardner, William Linnaeus, 36–37, 242, 313
garlands, 2–4 (fig. 1)
George III, King, 143, 144
George V, King, 254–59, 263, 273, 293
George, Walter, 275–77, 293
ghosts, 196, 298, 350n30
Gibson, John, 165
Goddens, 47, 53; Jon and Rumer, 51
Govindoo, 169
Graham, Maria, 25, 35, 36, 57, 77, 83, 168, 310
Griffith, William, 150–51, 162

Haidar Ali, xii, 21, 28, 130, 136, 139; Lal Bagh, 139, 141
Hamilton, Capt. Alexander, 24, 65, 66
Hampstead Garden Suburb, 257, 263
Hampton Court, 141, 272
Hardinge, Lady, 258, 262–64
Hardinge, Lord, 75, 119, 253–55, 258, 261, 268, 274
Hastings, Lord (Earl of Moira), 77, 218; Lady Flora, 87

Hastings, Warren, 21, 56, 65–66, 157, 185; Belvedere, 65, 67, 81; Daylesford, 55, 81; Hastings House, 81–83; Lady (Marian Imhoff), 81–82; naturalist, 161, 163; Zoffany painting of, 82 (fig. 21)
Hayat Baksh. *See* Red Fort
Heber, Bishop Reginald, 8, 30, 40, 67, 68, 70, 73, 76, 89, 148, 240
Himalayas, xii, 55, 93–94, 99, 101–20 passim, 152, 153, 195, 303, 314; plant hunting in, 162–65 (fig. 29), 174, 179, 180
Hinduism, 6, 12; caste and food taboos, 35, 81, 326n87; deities, 5, 56, 101–2, 127, 134, 187, 221, 228; festivals, 243; gardens, 4–5, 15, 219, 278
Hodges, William, 56, 203–4 (fig. 38)
Hodgson, Col. J. A., 200–201 (fig. 37), 226
Hooker, Sir Joseph Dalton, xii, 68, 100, 107, 150, 162; botanizing in the Himalayas, 163–65 (fig. 29), 168, 169, 179, 180; director of Kew, 145–46, 151, 154
Hooker, Sir Wiliam, 145–46, 150, 151, 165
Hughli River, 63, 65, 96, 146
Humayun, 211; Tomb, 211–12 (fig. 42), 213, 220, 246, 268, 274, 293, 343n84; water palace, 341n17
Hyde Park, 67, 68, 74, 245, 250
Hyderabad, 140, 252, 273; Residency, 32–34 (fig. 9)

Impey, Sir Elijah, and Lady Impey, 174
Indraprastha, 228, 259
Irwin, Lord, 32, 264, 268, 285, 351n17; Lady, 264, 271
Islam, 7, 35; Islamic gardens, 7; Mohurram, 243, 342n65; social relations with Muslims, 32, 35, 243. *See also* Mughal gardens
Ismail, Sir Mirza, 287–88

Jahanara, 237–39; garden renamed Queen's Gardens, 246
Jahangir, 20, 102, 129, 167, 208, 231, 280, 311
Jains, 6, 12

Jekyll, Gertrude, 13, 42, 219, 262–64, 269, 270, 278, 279, 304, 314
Jones, Anna Maria, 170–74 (fig. 30), 175
Jones, Sir William, 55, 65, 169–72, 175, 312; Royal Asiatick Society, 170

Kamasutra, 6
Kashmir, 8, 102–3, 162, 167, 223, 295–96, 308; gardens: 103, 211, 262, 267, 288, 296; Pl. 9
Kedleston Hall, 75, 219, Pl. 20
Kew, Royal Botanic Gardens, xi, 7, 30, 89, 91, 141–45 passim, 149, 151, 153–54, 174, 177, 178, 312; botanical exploration, 162, 168, 178–80; Rhododendron Dell, xi, 164
Khajuraho, 220, 221, Pl. 21
Kingdon-Ward, Frank, 306
Kipling, J. L., 45 (fig. 14), 329n65
Kipling, Rudyard, xii, 23, 34–35, 61, 72–73, 226, 348n3; *City of the Dreadful Night,* 66; "Glory of the Garden," 308–9; *Kim,* 99; opium production, 156–57
Kirkpatrick, James Achilles, 32–33, 36
Kitchener, General, 118, 329n84
Kodaikanal, 101, 127, 174
Koenig, Johann Gerhard, 161, 171, 172
Kyd, Col. Robert, 146–47, 149

Lahore, 50, 66, 106, 152, 232, 274; Shalimar Garden, 268
Lalla Rookh (Thomas Moore), 55, 102–3, 186, 295
Landour, 99, 100, 103, 109, 119
Landsowne, Lord and Lady, 116
lawns, 14, 37, 38 (fig. 10), 49–52, 112, 113, 116, 119, 185, 219, 285, 296, 299, 300, 302, 304, 307, 309; Delhi durbars, 250–56 passim; *doob* grass, 192, 268, 298; mowers, 51 (fig. 15); New Delhi, 257, 267, 268, 274, 277–78, 293, 298; Red Fort, 247; Taj Mahal, 203, 206, 223, 290, 292, 293
Lear, Edward, 40, 47, 59–60, 68, 105, 108, 119, 125, 313, 347n65; Bangalore, 131, 132, 141, 176, 195; *Flora Nonsensica,* 169; Taj Mahal, 203, 205, 217

Lindley, John, 145–46
Lively, Penelope, xi, 304
lotus, 1, 5–7, 174, 214, 249, 269–70, 300, 319n7, 346n53
Loudon, J. C., 176, 177
Lucknow, 2, 10, 15, 43, 48, 50, 57, 152, 167, ch. 5 passim, 268, 314; Botanical Garden, 191; Qaisar Bagh, 185, 187, 191, 193 (fig. 33); Residency, 182–84 (fig. 32), 188, 192–93 (fig. 34), 292
Lutyens, Edwin, 260–84 passim, 314; on the Taj Mahal, 261, 262, 268; visit to Red Fort, 268–69
Lutyens, Emily, 265
Lytton, Lord, 76, 106, 113, 121, 263; 1877 durbar, 248–49, 250; Lady Lytton, 80

Macaulay, Thomas Babington, 121, 124, 312
Madras (Chennai), 15, 20, 21, 47, 57–58, 97, 122, 123, 132, 147, 168, 242, 280, 288; Chepauk Palace, 31; Choultry Plain, 26, 27; early history, 24–32, 34–35, 37, 184; Fort St. George, 24 (fig. 4), 27 (fig. 5), 30; garden houses, 26–29 (fig. 6); Government Houses, 30–33 (fig. 7, 8), 36, 124, 297; MGR Memorial Arch, 292; St. Thomas Mount, 26; Triplicane, 30
Mahabaleshwar, 100
Mahabharata, 6, 228
Mahtab Bagh (moonlight garden), 9; Agra, 5, 215–16, 290, 291; Delhi, 235, 236, 244–45, 255–56
maidans, 50, 65; Calcutta, 73–75, 77, Pl. 3
Maitland, Julia, 56–58, 132
malis, 40–42 (fig. 12), 45, 47, 81, 219, 265, 295, 301–2
manuals, garden, 42–46 (fig. 13), 49–50, 53
Martin, Claude, 185, 187
Mary, Queen, 255, 271
Mashobra, 117–18 (fig. 24)
Mayo, Lord, 75; Lady, 80
medicinal plants, 12, 142, 152–53 (fig. 27), Ayurvedic medicine, 12, 160; physic gardens, 141

Metcalfe, Charles, 36, 107, 241, 243, 342n62
Metcalfe, Emily, 242, 245
Metcalfe, Thomas, 241–43, 343n68, Pl. 22
Minto, Lord, 84; Lady, 116
Moonlight Garden. *See* Mahtab Bagh
Mount Kailash, 101, 127
Moynihan, Elizabeth, 215
Mughals, 14, 20, 76, 184, 227–29, 256, 257, 258; botanical illustration, 166–67; gardens, 7–10, 12, 14–15, 19, 24, 33, 37, 49, 56, 70, 139, 187, 197, 206–16, 278–80, 306, 308, 311, 340n10; Kashmir, 102–3, 128; penchant for opium, 156. *See also individual rulers*
Mumtaz Mahal, 209, 212, 213, 232, 286
Mundy, Peter, 207–9
Munro, Sir Thomas, 32, 121, 125, 161, 297; Lady Munro, 32, 36
Mussoorie, 99, 101, 103, 119–20, 127, 153
Mustoe, William Robertson, 264–65, 293–95, 314
Mysore, 122, 127, 130, 133, 140, 161, 287

Naini Tal, 99, 116
Napier, Col. Robert, 189
nautches 9, 190
Nehru, Jawaharlal, 224, 291, 300–301, 312
New Delhi, 47, 190, 217, 226, 243, ch. 8 passim (fig. 52), 292–93, 306, 314; Commonwealth Games, 294, 299; Connaught Place, 273, 274, 277, 282; Government House (Viceroy's House, later Rashtrapati Bhavan), 261, 264, 271, 279–80, 283–84, 293, 294; Imperial Hotel, 298, Pl. 31; Jaipur Column, 269; King's Way (Processional Way, later Raj Path), 257, 261, 273, 274, 276–77, 283, 284, 288 (fig. 55), 293 Pl. 24; Lodi Garden, 274, 347n73; Mughal Garden, 264–72 (fig. 50, 51), 293, 313, Pl. 23; Purana Qila, 259–61; Talkatora Gardens, 246, 275; War Memorial, 273
Nilgiri Hills, 49, 92–93, 99–100, 121–26, 296, 314; invasion of Australian trees, 126; tea, 158, Pl. 1. *See also* Ootacamund

North Marianne, 169, 175, 205, 218, 244; gallery at Kew, 176; Pl. 17
Nur Jahan, 167, 311

Ochterlony, David, 36, 75, 241, 242, 342n62
Ootacamund, 99, 121–27 passim, 175, 180, 296–97, 298; Botanical Garden, 124, 175, 297; cinchona, 153–54; Government House, 124, 125, 297; Hunt Club, 297–98
opium, 156, 314; factory at Ghazipur, 156–57; War, 1838–42, 157
Orlich, Baron von, 47, 187, 285, 305

Paradise, in Qur'an, 10, 12, 207, 213, 215–16, 223, 283; in Milton, 148
parks, 58, 286–91, 307
Parks [Parkes], Fanny, 10, 37, 52, 54–56, 60, 98–101, 103–5, 120, 134, 186, 227; Taj Mahal, 203, 209, 222
Parsees, 35, 68, 127
Paxton, Joseph, 68, 124, 287
peepal tree (*bo*), 5, 54, 61, 270, 276, 347n78
Pelsaert, Francisco, 231
photography in India, 88, 191, 205, 213
picturesque, the, 60–61, 85, 90, 131, 218, 313
potted plants, 38–39 (fig. 11), 53, 131 (fig. 25), 132, 133, 242, 278, Pl. 31
Prince of Wales: visit to India, 2, 176, 182, 189, 222, 250. *See also* Edward VII
Prinsep, Val, 249, 328n15

railroads, 72–73, 104, 106, 126, 134, 135, 180, 245
Raj Ghat, 291, Pl. 28
Rajputs, 8, 229, 252, 306, 312; Amber Fort, 8 (fig. 2)
Ramayana, 2, 6
Ranelagh, 155, 187
Reading, Lady, 28, 116, 117, 119, 272–73
Red Fort (Delhi), 233–38 (fig. 47), 241, 260, 268, 279–80; Diwan-i-Am, 247–48, 253, 254; Diwan-i-Khas, 237, 247, 253, 254; Hayat Baksh, 235–38, 244, 247, 254–55 (fig. 49), 269; Moti Masjid, 245, 269; post-1857, 244–48, 258, 293; Rang Mahal, 5, 247, 270. *See also* Delhi; New Delhi
rhododendrons, xi, 107–8, 110, 163–64, 176
Ridge (Delhi), 228, 250–51, 259, 262, 278, 295, 296
Roberts, Emma, 29, 36, 40, 46, 48–49, 54, 69, 80, 185, 241; Barrackpore, 85–87, 89
Robinson, William, 42, 43, 219
Roe, Sir Thomas, 275
Roshanara Garden, 239, 240, 246, 294
Roxburgh, William, 147, 167–68
Royal Botanic Garden Edinburgh, 169
Royal Horticultural Society, 162
Royle, John Forbes, 152
Rungiah, 169
Ruskin, John, 93, 135
Russell, Patrick, 170, 172
Russell, William Howard, 185, 187–90 passim, 218, 222

Sakuntala, 170, 171
Samru, Begum, 243, 342n64
Sarnath, 220–21, 261, 345n25
scent, importance of, 7, 9, 13, 56–57, 203, 207–9, 302
Scindia, Maharaja of Gwalior, 252
Scots in India, 160–61, 168, 169, 304
Serampore, 87, 147
Shah Jahan, 50, 78, 224, 226, 255, 260, 283; creation of Shajahanabad, 223, 226, 232–39 (fig. 46), 280–81; "flower-mania," 167, 211; Peacock Throne, 233, 239; Taj Mahal, 197, 198, 206, 209, 211, 213, 215, 216, 223
Shalimar Garden, 133; Delhi, 238, 241, 245; Lahore, 238, 268; Kashmir, 211, 238; Sibpor, 146, 147
Sikkim, 162, 163, 179
Simla (Shimla), 83, 96, 99, 103, 104–20 passim, 122, 127, 258, 295, 298; Barnes Court, 112, 118; Peterhof, 113, 114, 116; picture-postcard England, 128–29; Viceregal Lodge, 111–16 (fig. 23), 295

Singh, Patwant, 257, 283, 295
Sleeman, William, 201; Mrs. Sleeman, 222
Spear, Percival, 65, 81, 229
Srirangapatnam. *See* Tipu Sultan
Stanley, Lady Beatrix, 32, 47, 53, 175, 268
Steel, Flora Annie, 45–46, 52, 53, 57, 310, 344n113
Sujaya, C. P., 301–2, 312
Sullivan, John, 121–23, 125
Surat, 9, 20, 24, 64

Tagore, Dwarkanath, 35, 70; Jorasanko, 70, 297
Tagore, Rabindranath, 5, 70–72 (fig. 17), 297
Taj Mahal, 5, 195, ch. 6 passim (figs. 37–43), 268; floral decoration, 213–15 (fig. 43), Pl. 16, 17, 19; Lutyens's disdain for, 261–62; proposed changes, 290–91; Taj Ganj, 199 (fig. 36), 209–10, 213
Tavernier, Jean-Baptiste, 219, 233, 275
tea, 145, 146, 159 (fig. 28), 179, 314; drinking in England, 154–55; drinking in India, 159–60, 326n87; and opium, 157
Tennyson, Alfred Lord, 182, 184, 292
terai, 94, 119
Theosophy, 112, 265
Timur (Tamerlane), 19, 76, 229, 231
Tipu Sultan, 130–31, 136, 139–40; defeat at Srirangapatnam, 21, 30, 76, 77, 130, 140, 161; embassy to Louis XVI, 140; Lal Bagh, 139–40; mechanical tiger, 321n7
Trevelyan, Charles, 31, 297, 343n67

Uprising of 1857, 62, 88, 92, 136, 175, 182–84, 188, 194, 196, 199, 243–47, 260, 292. *See also* Cawnpore; Delhi; Lucknow

Valentia, Lord, 29, 52, 76, 147–48, 150
Vauxhall, 104, 155, 187, 196
Vedas, 12, 171
Versailles, 237, 238, 285
Victoria, Queen, 63, 88–89, 94, 95, 124, 143, 175, 224, 245, 249, 302; Empress of India, 248; statues of, 133, 226, 260, 297; Victoria Memorial Hall, 224–26 (fig. 44), 259, 285 (fig. 54), 297; *Victoria amazonica* (*Victoria regia*), 74, 151, 178, 269–70
Villiers-Stuart, Constance, 9, 44, 222, 245, 246, 255–56, 262, 268, 313

Wallich, Nathaniel, 87, 88, 147, 150, 164, 165, 174
Wardian case, 164–65
Wellesley, Lord Richard, 31, 64, 75–76, 83, 85–87, 259; naturalist, 161
Western Ghats, 100; tea, 158, 159 (fig. 28), 168, 314
Wight, Robert, 123, 168–69, 179
Willingdon, Lady, 271, 280, 347n73; Park, 274
Wren, Christopher, 261–62, 272

Yamuna River, 54, 119, 120, 210, 228, 235, 260, 294, 299

Zayn al-Din, 172, 174
zenana (purdah) gardens, 10, 11 (fig. 3), 12, 33, 37, 194, 235, 244, 265, 270, 296

ACKNOWLEDGMENTS

I WOULD NEVER have thought of extending my researches to India without the prompting of my friend Nancy Frieden, to whom I shall always be profoundly grateful for enlarging my world to this exciting subcontinent, as well as for most helpful comments on several of the chapters. Indira Viswanathan Peterson has been a much-valued source of information and support. Thanks also to Alan and Martha Armstrong, Robert Batchelor, Sir Andrew Buchanan, Ray Desmond, Olivia Fraser, Rosemary Herbert, Rob Irving, Andy Lass, Alex de Montrichard, Sophie Moochhala, Henry Noltie, Dede Ruggles, June Siegel, Ajay Sinha, Frances Soubry, C. P. Sujaya, Antonia Woods, and the resourceful staffs of the Mount Holyoke College Library and the Asia, Pacific and Africa Collections of the British Library. As always, Don O'Shea, Dean of the Faculty of Mount Holyoke College, has been generous of spirit and purse. James Gehrt provided high-quality scans of many of the illustrations. My students in Colonial Worlds in the fall of 2009 served as guinea pigs, reading most of an earlier draft of the book and providing lively commentary.

I would also like to thank fellow travelers on trips to India in addition to Nancy: Jeanne Armor, David Taylor, David London, Cathy Herbert, Eric Tilles, Genie Robbins, Tim Herbert, and Mara Lytle; thanks, too, to TransIndus for all the arrangements, and especially Shafi Khan for his resourcefulness and good company in Kashmir. Chapters 2 and 6 in this book were previously published in slightly different form in *Studies in the History of Gardens and Designed Landscapes*. I am indebted to the editor, John Dixon Hunt, for his early encouragement, and to the staff of Penn Press who have been a pleasure to work with.

My husband, Bob Herbert, has been my most astute reader and most enthusiastic supporter, ready to venture wherever I next propose. The late David Apter was a much loved and unfailingly generous mentor; David's own insatiable curiosity embraced the entire world. Ellie Weld, dear friend for more than sixty years, gracious host for innumerable visits to England and shipmate on the voyage of discovery to India, shares my fascination with the subcontinent. To her and to David Apter I gratefully dedicate this book.